Resou

Learn to Program

with C++

Learn to Program

with C++

John Smiley

McGraw-Hill/Osborne

New York   Chicago   San Francisco   Lisbon   London   Madrid   Mexico City
Milan   New Delhi   San Juan   Seoul   Singapore   Sydney   Toronto

The McGraw·Hill Companies

McGraw-Hill/Osborne
2600 Tenth Street
Berkeley, California 94710
U.S.A.

To arrange bulk purchase discounts for sales promotions, premiums, or fund-raisers, please contact **McGraw-Hill**/Osborne at the above address. For information on translations or book distributors outside the U.S.A., please see the International Contact Information page immediately following the index of this book.

Learn to Program with C++

1234567890 FGR FGR 0198765432

ISBN 0-07-222535-1

Publisher Brandon A. Nordin	**Indexer** Karin Arrigoni
Vice President & Associate Publisher Scott Rogers	**Proofreader** Pat Mannion, Pamela Woolf
Editorial Director Wendy Rinaldi	**Computer Designers** Carie Abrew, George Toma Charbak
Project Editor Patty Mon	**Illustrators** Michael Mueller, Lyssa Wald
Technical Editor Zach Martin	**Series Design** Kelly Stanton-Scott
Copy Editor Bart Reed	**Cover Series Design** Pattie Lee

This book was composed with Corel VENTURA™ Publisher.

This book is dedicated to my wife, Linda.

About the Author

John Smiley, a Microsoft Certified Professional (MCP) and Microsoft Certified Solutions Developer (MCSD) in Visual Basic, has been programming and teaching for more than 20 years. He is the President of John Smiley and Associates, a computer consulting firm serving clients both large and small in the Philadelphia metropolitan area. John is an adjunct professor of Computer Science at Penn State University, Philadelphia University, and Holy Family College, and also teaches in a variety of Internet venues, including SmartPlanet and ElementK.

On the writing front, John is the author of the immensely popular *Learn to Program with Visual Basic 6*, along with *Learn to Program with Visual Basic Examples, Learn to Program Databases with Visual Basic 6, Learn to Program Objects with Visual Basic 6, Learn to Program with Java, Learn with Program with Visual Basic .NET*, and *Learn to Program with C#*. He has also done technical editing on a number of Visual Basic titles for Wrox and Que, in addition to being a popular guest on TechTV's *ScreenSavers* program.

Feel free to visit John's website at **www.johnsmiley.com** or contact him via e-mail at **johnsmiley@johnsmiley.com**. He religiously answers all his e-mails, although not necessarily instantaneously!

Contents at a Glance

Contents

Acknowledgments

I want to thank first and foremost my wife, Linda, for her love and support.

This is the eighth book I've written, and the process is no easier on the family of the author than the first book—there are still pleas for quiet, which is almost impossible with three children. My thanks also go to my three wonderful children, Tom, Kevin, and Melissa. Each one contributed in a way to this book. Tom and Kevin, as budding programmers, provided me with ideas for questions that beginning C++ programmers might need answered. Melissa, who at the time I wrote my first book spent time on my lap asking me to read *Snow White* to her, is now a 6-year-old who once again frequently kept me company while writing this book.

Many thanks go to the great people at StudioB for their faith in the continuing viability of my books. Special thanks go to David Rogelberg and David Talbott for their assistance in finding a new "home" for my books, and for their belief in the uniqueness of the way in which I teach beginners to program.

At McGraw Hill/Osborne, I want to give special thanks to Wendy Rinaldi, who also shares the vision and belief that books written in my style can help beginners learn like no others. Your enthusiasm and support, Wendy, have meant much to me. Many thanks also go to Tim Madrid and Patty Mon for their tireless efforts in working out the details of the *Learn to Program* series for Osborne, and in keeping everything on schedule. Many thanks to my Technical Editor Zach Martin, who did a great job testing and verifying all the code in the book, and making suggestions for improvements along the way.

Books aren't produced in a vacuum. Behind the scenes there are reviewers, technical editors, artists, layout specialists, copy editors, indexers, and a group of marketing experts, all working toward the goal of making the book a success. My thanks to all of you.

I also want to thank the many readers of my first seven books who took the time to write to me about the books. I truly appreciate hearing from you, and I want you to know that I read and respond to each e-mail I receive.

Thanks to the many members of my C++ study group, who worked with the manuscript for this book, evaluating it, testing the code, and making suggestions for improvements, especially Catherine Cramer, Jim Combs, Linda Mason, Shaom Wang, Catherine Kinslow, Wayne Green, Thelma Chenault, Lon Anderson, Joe Churchman, Efren Aguilar, Mark Spalding, David Smith, Martin Perez, and Bruce Neiger. Special thanks to Bruce Neiger for his meticulous reading of the manuscript, and for his many suggestions.

I want to thank all the members of my family for their belief in and support of me over the years, in particular my mother, who continues to say several hundred novenas for the success of my books, and who has probably said just as many for this one I'm sure. Special thanks to Bob and Pat for giving my books priority placement in bookstore windows whenever they can!

Finally, I want to acknowledge my father, who although not physically here to see this book, is surely flipping through the pages of it now. It's been over 25 years since I last saw you—and your role in the writing of this and my others books can never be understated. You and mother have been a great inspiration and role model for me. As I've said before, I know that the God who made us all will someday permit us to be together again.

Introduction

Why I Wrote the Book

A few years ago I had the occasion to talk to a very successful author whose beginner-level book I was using to teach introductory programming at my university. He asked me how I was making out using his book in my class, and I told him that the students in my class with no prior programming experience were having a hard time with it. He told me that didn't surprise him—and furthermore, he didn't offer any apologies for or seem upset by it. This was my first inkling that in the world of computer books, many books claim to be aimed at the beginner market, but often it's a lukewarm effort. Most beginner-level books are aimed at the reader or learner who already has some programming experience under their belts.

I encountered a similar attitude in a faculty meeting some years back when one of my fellow instructors seemed to derive great delight in having one-third of her class drop the course. It was as if the large number of withdrawals somehow proved that the course she was teaching was extremely difficult. When I replied that, as a teacher, I felt like a failure if even one student dropped the course because he or she couldn't keep up, I felt like a maverick.

Shortly thereafter I decided to take matters into my own hands, producing a manuscript for Visual Basic that I knew would never lose anyone. I boldly proclaimed that, using my book, I could teach anyone to program in Visual Basic, and so far that's been the case. I also developed an unusual delivery for my book—presenting the book as a simulated classroom, complete with a professor willing to teach and 18 students eager to learn. Some of them ask smart questions, some of them ask questions you might consider "dumb"—but amazingly, just about every question you would ask yourself during the course of reading the book is anticipated and answered for you.

As a reader once wrote me, so many technical books talk down to the reader—my books make it "OK" and even fun to be a real beginner learning to program.

Who the Book Is For

This book presumes you have absolutely no programming experience. If that's you, and you want to learn how to write a computer program using what can be a very difficult language to learn, C++, then this book is definitely for you.

If you have some programming experience and want to learn how to program in C++, this book is also for you. Experienced programmers tell me that my thorough, methodical method of teaching works for them as well.

XV

Either way, as one of my readers wrote me, my books make it OK *not* to understand something the first time you read it. My patient method of teaching ensures that you will learn the material eventually.

Organization/Conventions Used in the Book

Each chapter of this book follows a session in my fictitious classroom. Read along and learn the material with the rest of the students. Most chapters have examples that I present to the students. Feel free to follow along and code them yourself. Each chapter also provides practice exercises for you to complete, most of which lead to the completion of a class "project"—in this case, the Grades Calculation Project.

Chapter

1

Where Do I Begin?

Where do I begin? is a question I am frequently asked by my students, and this seems like a good question to tackle right at the beginning of this book. In this first chapter, we'll look at the development process of an actual working program through the eyes and ears of my university programming class, and you will also be introduced to our "class project." By the end of the book, we'll have taken a real-life application from the concept all the way to the finished product!

NOTE

Occasionally, my students get disillusioned when they hear that we won't be diving straight in and coding our application. However, when I remind them that programming is much the same as writing a report (in other words, it is a two-stage process of planning and then producing), they tend to settle down.

Where Do I Begin?

As part of answering the question Where do I begin?, this chapter looks at the Systems Development Life Cycle (SDLC), which is a methodology that ensures systems are developed in a systemic, logical, step-by-step approach. We'll be looking at the SDLC in quite a bit of detail because the majority of this book will be spent developing a real-world application. In this chapter, we'll meet with a prospective client and conduct a preliminary interview with him. From that interview (and a subsequent one), we'll develop a *Requirements Statement*, which provides details as to what the program should do. This Requirements Statement will form the basis of the application we will develop throughout the rest of the book.

NOTE

From this point on, you will follow me as I lead a group of my university students in an actual class on C++. If I do my job right, you will be a part of the class, learning along with the other students as we complete a multiweek course about programming in C++.

Many books on computer programming have the reader, perhaps as early as the first chapter, code a program which "cutely" displays a message box that says "Hello World." Then the author will point to the fact that within the first few minutes of reading their book, the reader has already written a working program. I'm not so naive as to believe that writing such a program makes you a programmer. Therefore, we'll opt for a slower approach. Simple programs, although great for the ego, are not the programs found in the real world. Real-world programs are written to meet someone's needs. These needs are frequently complex and difficult to verbalize. In this book, you and I will embark on a journey together that will see us complete the prototyping stage of a real-world project. I believe that this is the best way to learn programming.

In my university classes, I don't usually introduce the class project until several weeks into the semester. When I finally do, I give the students in my class a Requirements Statement. I never tell my students exactly *how* the application should look or how to program it. I tell them only what is required. In other words, I complete the hard part for them: gathering the user requirements.

Programming the Easy Way

When I first began to teach programming, some of my students would tell me that they just didn't know where to start when they began to work on their programming assignments. They would start to program the application, then stop. Some of them would find themselves rewriting their code and redesigning their application several times. Then they would change it again. Face to face, I could usually clear things up for them by giving them a gentle nudge or hint in the right direction. However, their work showed a definite lack of direction. What was the problem? They lacked a plan.

As soon as I realized this, I began to teach them more than just programming. I began to teach them the Systems Development Life Cycle (SDLC), the methodology I mentioned earlier. You see, people need blueprints or maps. They need something tangible, usually in writing, before they can begin a project. Just about all my students agree that having a blueprint of some kind makes the development process much easier.

Sometimes I meet former students of mine at the university and ask them how their other programming classes are coming along. Occasionally, they tell me that they're working on a great *real-world* assignment of some kind, but they just don't know where to begin. At that point, I remind them of what I told them in class—that they should begin with the design of the user interface, observe the behavior of the interface, and then add code to fill in the gaps. That's not the problem, they tell me. The problem is that they don't know how to gather the user requirements for the system. They don't really know what the system should do.

Often the real problem is that the client isn't prepared to give the programmers a detailed enough Requirements Statement. In class, the professor distributes a well-defined Requirements Statement, but in the real world, programmers need to develop this themselves. Unfortunately, they may not know how to sit down with the prospective user of their system to determine what is required to satisfy the user's needs.

That skill—to listen to the user and determine their needs—is something that I now teach to some extent in all my computer classes, whether they are programming courses, courses on systems analysis and design, or courses on database management.

Planning a Program Is Like Planning a House

A friend of mine is a general contractor and homebuilder. His job is similar to that of a programmer or system designer. He recently built an addition to a customer's house. He wouldn't think of beginning that work without first meeting with the owners of the house to determine their needs. He couldn't possibly presume to know what the owners want or need. The builder's role, in meeting with the owners, is largely to listen and then to advise.

My friend the homebuilder tells me that certain homeowners may want a design that is architecturally unsound—either because their ideas and design are unsafe and would violate accepted building code regulations or because they would violate local zoning regulations for their neighborhood. In some cases, he tells me, owners ask for features that he is certain they will later regret—and probably hold him responsible for. His role as an advisor demands that he inform the homeowners of these problems.

As soon as my friend believes that he understands what the owners want, he prepares a set of blueprints to be reviewed by the homeowners. Frequently the owners, after seeing their own vision on paper, will decide to change something, such as the location of a window or the size of a closet. The *concrete* characteristics of the blueprints make it easier to arrive at an agreement between the builder and owners. The same can be said of a concrete plan for the writing of a program or the development of a system.

The big advantage of developing a plan on paper is that, while the project is still on paper, it's relatively painless to change it. Once the house has been assembled and bolted together, it becomes much more of a problem to change something.

The same is true of a computer program. Although it's not physically nailed or bolted together, once a programmer has started to write a program, changing it becomes very labor intensive. It's much easier to change the design of a system prior to writing the first line of code.

In the world of software development, you would be surprised how many programmers begin work on an application without really having listened to the user. I know some programmers who get a call from a user, take some quick notes over the phone, and deliver an application without ever having met them! It could be that the user's requirements sound similar to something the programmer wrote last year, so the developer feels that will be good enough for the new client.

Other developers go a step further and may actually meet with the client to discuss the user's needs. Nevertheless, sometimes the developer may not be a good listener, or just as likely, the user may communicate their needs poorly. The result may be that the user receives a program that doesn't come close to doing what they wanted it to do.

In this course, we'll develop a prototype for a real-world application called the Grade Calculation Project, *and then take it through to the complete product.* As we progress through the course together, we will work through one possible solution, but I want you to know that in C++

programming, the number of solutions are almost infinite. As I tell my students all the time, there are many ways to paint a picture. One of the things I love about teaching C++ is that I have never received the same solution to a project twice. Everyone brings their own unique qualities to the project.

I want you to feel free to take the Grade Calculation Project and make your solution different from mine. In fact, I encourage it. However, you should stick close to the Requirements Statement we are going to develop in this chapter.

We Receive a Call from Our "Client"

During my fall semester Visual Basic class, I was lucky enough to be contacted by a client, Joe Bullina, owner of the Bullina China Shop, who needed a fairly high-tech computer program written to produce price quotations for the customers in his shop, and I used the development of his program as the class project for my Visual Basic course.

C++, by its very nature, is much more difficult to learn than Visual Basic, and although I knew I could ask the students in my C++ class to write the same program in C++, I also knew that incorporating every feature—particularly the Windows user interface—found in the Visual Basic version of the China Shop program would be difficult to squeeze into a one-semester C++ course. Furthermore, I also knew that many of those same Visual Basic students would be present in the C++ class, and most likely they would be in the mood for a fresh challenge, not a rehash of the China Shop program.

So I was glad when, one Monday morning, about a week before meeting with my C++ class for the first time, I received a phone call from Frank Olley, a fellow professor at the university and dean of the English department. Frank and I knew each other well—in fact, at one time he had been a teacher of mine. Frank was wondering if I could write a program that he could use to calculate student grades.

I asked Frank if he had considered using a spreadsheet program such as Excel to do the calculations—it seemed like a fine application for his requirements.

He told me he had considered Excel, but he ultimately wanted the program to be able to prompt the user for the correct grade "pieces" necessary to calculate the student's final grade—something he didn't know how to do in Excel.

Frank and I agreed to meet on Tuesday afternoon in his office.

We Meet with Our Client

I arrived at Frank Olley's office around 2 P.M. on a sunny Tuesday afternoon. Going into the Liberal Arts building, a large brick building, brought back pleasant memories of my college years. I hadn't been in the Liberal Arts building since I graduated some years back—the Computer Science building was now my haunt.

I found Frank's office and was greeted by his secretary.

"Hi, I'm John Smiley, I'm here to meet Frank Olley."

"Just a minute Mr. Smiley. Mr. Olley is expecting you."

A few moments later, Frank came out of his office.

"Sorry to keep you waiting, John," Frank said, warmly extending his hand. "I was on the phone with Robin Aronstram and David Burton. I believe you know who they are."

Indeed I did. Robin Aronstram is the chairman of the Mathematics department, and David Burton is the chairman of the Science department.

"I hope you don't mind if Robin and David attend our meeting," Frank continued, "I think they may want to piggyback some requirements of their own on top of mine."

"Piggyback?" I asked.

"That's right, John," Frank replied. "I saw them both in the faculty dining room today at lunch, and I mentioned to them that you were coming over to discuss writing a program to calculate student grades. They were wondering if you could include their requirements in the program also."

"I don't see why not," I said. Just then, Robin and David arrived. During the course of the next 20 minutes or so, the three of them laid out for me their unique requirements. There was a commonality in that each one required a program that could calculate the final grade for a student in their own department—English, Math, or Science. On the other hand, each had their own requirements.

 NOTE

This project, though "real world," has been simplified a bit for learning purposes. Most notably, it will not have a Windows interface but will take the form of a C++ console application.

"The English department," Frank Olley explained, "calculates the final grade for a student taking an English course as 25 percent of their midterm grade, 25 percent of their final examination grade, 30 percent for a semester-long research paper, and—because we expect our students to be able to speak in public and make oral presentations—20 percent for a half-hour-long class presentation."

"The Science department is similar," David chimed in, "except that we don't require a class presentation. We calculate the grade for a student taking a science course as 40 percent of their midterm grade, 40 percent of their final examination grade, and 20 percent for a semester-long research paper."

Robin then explained that for a student taking a math course, only a midterm and final examination grade entered into the equation. "Each counts 50 percent toward their final grade," she said.

"Those requirements don't seem terribly complicated," I assured them. "Do you have any details in mind as to what you want the program to look like?"

"Not really," Frank said. "I guess we were really hoping that you could take care of those details. Don't get us wrong. We know what we want the program to do—that is, calculate a student's grade. Beyond that, our biggest requirement is that the program be simple to use."

"Can you think of anything else?" I asked.

"Eventually, we'd like to have the program be accessible from the Web," David added. He hesitated for a moment and then added hopefully, "What do you think? The program doesn't sound too difficult, does it?"

Famous last words, I thought to myself. "No David, it doesn't," I said, "I could probably write this program in an hour or so...."

Robin noticed that my voice had trailed off.

"What's wrong?" she asked.

"Nothing's wrong," I said, "I was just thinking."

I explained to Frank, Robin, and David that on Saturday I would be meeting with my Introduction to Programming with C++ spring semester class for the first time. I then went on to explain to them that in my fall semester Visual Basic course, the class and I had developed a real-world application for a client in West Chester.

"Perhaps," I said, "this time around, I could have them work on your requirements as their class project."

Frank looked excited and nervous at the same time. "How would that work?" he asked.

"Well," I said, "each semester I give my C++ programming students a project to work on. C++ is a bit more complicated than Visual Basic, so although I was tempted to have them work on the same project as my fall semester Visual Basic students, I really thought that might be too much for a first C++ class. However, your project sounds ideal, and I think it will excite them. It's better than anything I could ever dream up, because it's real with a real client—you—expecting real results. And your requirements, though they seem simple enough from a user point of view, have a few quirks that will make it pretty challenging from a C++ programming perspective."

I looked at the group for a reaction. I saw a look of unease on David's face.

"I can take these requirements," I continued, "distribute them to my students on Saturday, and over the course of the semester, they can write the program for you. By the end of the semester, you'll have your program, and they'll have some real experience under their belts. Unless of course, you're in a huge hurry."

"No," Frank said. "As long as they finish the program by the end of the spring semester, we can use the program to calculate the grades in each of our departments. Of course, I'm guessing that the program your students write won't be as sophisticated as one that you would write. After all, your students are just beginners."

"To some degree that's true, Frank," I said. "Most notably, the program we produce for you won't have a Windows user interface. It will be something that in the C++ world we call a console application."

"Like an old DOS program?" Robin chimed in.

"That's right, Robin," I said. "Developing a Windows user interface in an introductory C++ program is really way beyond the scope of the class, but bearing in mind that you eventually want this program to be available on the Web, and that's something we can easily do in the JavaScript class I'll be teaching this summer."

"So we'll start out with a C++ console application to calculate the spring semester grades," Frank said, "and then have a Web version available for the fall semester?"

"That shouldn't be a problem, Frank," I said. "And I'll be working with them every step of the way. You can expect a top-notch program, and I have no doubt that we can finish the first version on time for you to use in May."

I must have said the magic words; at this, Frank smiled, extended his hand and said, "That sounds like a deal to me."

"There's just one more thing, Frank," I said sheepishly.

"What's that, John?" he asked.

"Would it be possible to pay my students something for the development of the program?" I asked. "It doesn't have to be much, but paying them will permit them to legitimately cite this experience as paid professional experience."

"I'm sure there's something in the English department budget to pay them," Frank said smiling. "How about the Math and Science departments?"

"That shouldn't be a problem," Robin said. "You mentioned that your fall semester Visual Basic class wrote a program for a local business. How much did you charge him?"

"He paid us $450," I said. "I was able to give each one of my students $25."

"Sounds like a bargain to me," David said. "I'm sure each of our departments will be able to kick in $150 for your students work—sounds like a great idea to me."

As I prepared to leave, I warned the group that what we had done this afternoon merely represented the first step—the tip of the iceberg, so to speak—in a six-step process known as the Systems Development Life Cycle (SDLC). The first phase, the Preliminary Investigation, had begun and ended with our initial interview. Five phases of the SDLC remained.

As I walked to the door, Frank and I mutually agreed that I would deliver to him, in a week or so, a Requirements Statement drawn from the notes taken at today's meeting. I warned the group that when they read the Requirements Statement, the possibility existed that they would find some things that I had misinterpreted, and perhaps some things that they would be sure they had mentioned wouldn't appear at all. I told them that the Requirements Statement would act as a starting point for their project. Until I received a confirmation from them confirming the requirements, neither my student team nor I would proceed with the development of the program.

As I walked out the door of Frank's office, we all exchanged warm good-byes. Frank, David, and Robin are all genuinely likable people, and I hoped this experience would be a rewarding one for them and the students in my class. I left Frank, Robin, and David discussing an upcoming freshman social, and I headed off to teach a late-afternoon class at the university.

The Systems Development Life Cycle (SDLC)

During my walk to my class, I gave a lot of thought to Frank's program. The more I thought about it, the more I believed that having my students write the program was a great idea, and I was sure they would think so too. Working on a real-world application would be a great practical assignment for them. Even more so than something I made up, this project would give each of them a chance to become deeply involved in the various aspects of the SDLC. For instance:

- Someone in the class would need to work on the user requirements.
- Someone else would be involved in a detailed analysis of the grading program.
- Everyone would be involved in coding the program.
- Some students would work on installing the software.
- Some students would be involved in training and implementation.

Four days later, on Saturday morning, I met my Introduction to Programming with C++ class for the first time. For the last few semesters, my university has been using both Visual Basic and C++ as the introductory programming languages. Probably nothing is as easy as Visual Basic to learn, and probably nothing is as flexible and platform independent as C++.

As is my custom during my first class, I took roll and asked each of the students to write a brief biography on a sheet of paper. Doing this gives me a chance to get to know them without pressuring them to open up to a room full of strangers, although many of them will become good friends during the course of the class.

I only called out their first names, because I like to personalize the class as much as possible. Usually, I have some duplicated first names, but this semester, that wasn't a problem.

"Valerie, Peter, Linda, Steve, Katherine Rose."

"If you don't mind, just call me Rose," she said.

"Rhonda, Joe, John."

"Jack, if you don't mind."

"Barbara, Kathy, Dave, Ward, Blaine, Kate, Mary, Chuck, Lou, Bob."

That makes 18 students.

After giving them 15 minutes to write, I collected their biographies and began to read them. A few had some programming experience using languages that were a bit dated. A number were looking to get into the exciting world of computer programming, either because they had an opportunity at work or believed one would open up shortly. A couple of them were people looking to get into the workforce after years away from it. One of the students, Chuck, was just 15, a local high school student. Another student, Lou, was permanently disabled although he didn't look it, and he wrote that his disability would probably end up restricting him to a wheelchair.

My classroom is about 40 feet by 20 feet, and there are three rows of tables containing PCs. Each student has their own PC, and at the front of the room I have my own, cabled to a projector that enables me to display the contents of my video display.

My first lecture usually involves bringing the class up to a common level so that they feel comfortable with both the terminology and methodology of using a PC-based environment. This time, however, instead of waiting a few weeks before introducing the class project, I could hardly wait to tell them. In the first few minutes of class, I introduced the students to the Grade Calculation Project. Just about everyone in the class seemed genuinely excited at the prospect of developing a real-world application. They were even more excited after I offered to split the profits with them. For most of the class, this was their first programming course—and at its conclusion, they would all be paid as professionals, with a legitimate project to add to their resumes.

"You mean this course isn't going to be the usual 'read the textbook and code the examples' course?" Ward asked.

"Exactly," I said. "We'll be developing a real-world application and getting paid for it!"

"How will we know what to do?" Rose asked nervously.

I explained that in today's class, we'd actually develop a Requirements Statement.

"A Requirements Statement," I said, "is just an agreement between the contractor (in this case, us) and the customer (in this case, Frank, Robin, and David) that specifies in detail exactly what work will be performed, when it will be completed, and how much it will cost."

I continued by explaining that at this point, all we had were my notes from my initial interview with them. For the most part, this was just a quick sketch of the program. Although we might very well have produced a quick sketch of the user interface in the following hour or so, the students still did not know how to write a single line of code in C++. There was still much to learn! Furthermore, although we could probably pretty easily come up with a sketch of what the program would look like, we still needed to concern ourselves with the processing rules (for example, the grade components) that Frank, Robin, and David had given to me during our meeting.

TIP

Processing rules are also known as either business rules or work rules.

"Can you give us an example of a business rule?" Peter asked.

"Sure, Peter," I answered. "A good example would be a Web-based ticket-purchasing site, where customers are typically restricted from ordering large quantities of tickets. The web site might have a business rule that prohibits the same customer from purchasing more than four tickets to the same event."

"That very thing happened to me just last week," Valerie said. "I tried to purchase an entire row of tickets to the upcoming Elton John concert, but the web site restricted me to just four."

I pointed out that I had agreed to drop off the Requirements Statement to Frank Olley sometime before we met for class next Saturday. I told my class that there was the possibility that the Requirements Statement would have some mistakes in it, and even some missing items. Frank might very well see something on the Requirements Statement that will cause him to think of something else he wants to the program to do. I cautioned the class not to be too hasty at this point in the project. There was still a lot of planning left to do!

"Such hastiness," I said, "is exactly why the Systems Development Life Cycle was developed."

TIP
The SDLC was developed because many systems projects were developed that did not satisfy user requirements and because the projects that did satisfy user requirements went over budget or over time.

I saw some puzzled looks. I explained that the Systems Development Life Cycle (SDLC) is a methodology that ensures that systems are developed using a logical, step-by-step approach. There are six steps, known as *phases*, in the Systems Development Life Cycle:

NOTE
Different companies may have different versions of the SDLC. The point is that just about everyone who does program development can benefit from one form or other of a structured development process such as this one.

- The Preliminary Investigation phase
- The Analysis phase
- The Design phase
- The Development phase
- The Implementation phase
- The Audit and Maintenance phase

I continued by explaining that out of each phase of the SDLC, a tangible product, or *deliverable*, is produced. This deliverable may consist of a Requirements Statement, or it may be a letter informing the customer that the project cannot be completed within their time and financial constraints. An important component of the SDLC is that at each phase in the SDLC, a conscious decision is made to either continue development of the project or drop it. In the past, projects developed without the guidance of the SDLC were continued well after common sense dictated that it made no sense to proceed further.

"Many people say that the SDLC is just common sense," I said. "Let's examine the elements of the SDLC now. You can judge for yourself."

Phase 1: The Preliminary Investigation

I told my class about my meeting with Frank, Robin, and David, which essentially constituted the Preliminary Investigation phase of the SDLC.

"This first phase of the SDLC," I said, "may begin with a phone call from a customer, a memorandum from a vice president to the director of systems development, or a letter from a customer to discuss a perceived problem or deficiency or a requirement for something new in an existing system. In the case of the Grade Calculation Project, it was a desire on the part of Frank Olley to develop a program to calculate the grades of English students in his department—of course, you already know how it's quickly grown beyond that to include the Math and Science departments."

I continued by explaining that the purpose of the Preliminary Investigation phase is not to develop a system but to verify that a problem or deficiency really exists, or to determine whether a brand-new requirement makes sense to pursue.

The duration of the preliminary investigation is typically very short—usually not more than a day or two for a big project—and in the instance of the Grade Calculation Project, it was about an hour.

The end result, or deliverable, from the Preliminary Investigation phase is either a willingness to proceed further or the decision to call it quits. What influences the decision to abandon a potential project at this point? There are three factors, typically called *constraints*, that result in a go or no-go decision:

- **Technical** The project can't be completed with the technology currently in existence. This constraint is typified by Leonardo da Vinci's inability to build a helicopter even though he is credited with having designed one in the sixteenth century. Technological constraints made the construction of the helicopter impossible.

- **Time** The project can be completed, but not in time to satisfy the user's requirements. This is a frequent reason for the abandonment of the project after the Preliminary Investigation phase.

■ **Budgetary** The project can be completed on time to satisfy the user's requirements, but the cost is prohibitive.

"In the case of the Grade Calculation Project," I told my students, "Frank and I never came close to dropping the project. This is a project that all of us really want to pursue. And paying us something to do the programming is just icing on the cake!"

Needless to say, the students and I formally decided to take on the project and proceed with the second phase of the SDLC.

Phase 2: Analysis

The second phase of the SDLC, the Analysis phase, is sometimes called the Data Gathering phase.

I told my students that in this phase we study the problem, deficiency, or new requirement in detail. Depending on the size of the project being undertaken, this phase could be as short as the Preliminary Investigation phase, or it could take months.

I explained that what this meant for my class was potentially another trip to the Liberal Arts building to meet with Frank, Robin, and David to gather more detailed requirements or seek clarification of information gathered during the preliminary investigation.

I warned my students that as developers, we are inclined to believe that we know everything we need to know about the project from our preliminary investigation. However, you would be surprised to find out how much additional information we can glean if we spend just a little more time with the user.

You might be inclined to skip portions of what the SDLC calls for, but it forces you to follow a standardized methodology for developing programs and systems. As you'll see shortly, skipping parts of the SDLC can be a big mistake, whereas adhering to it ensures that you give the project the greatest chance for success.

I told the class that although some developers would make the case that we have gathered enough information in Phase 1 of the SDLC to begin programming, the SDLC dictates that Phase 2 be completed before the actual writing of the program begins.

"The biggest mistake we could make at this point would be to begin coding the program. Why is that? As we'll see shortly, we need to gather more information about the business from the 'owners'—in this case Frank, Robin, and David. There are still some questions that have to be asked."

In discussing the SDLC with the class, I discovered that one of my students, Linda, had some systems-analysis experience. Linda offered to contact Frank Olley to set up an appointment to spend part of the day with the person who currently calculates the grades for the English department. This meeting would fulfill the data-gathering component of the Analysis phase. In the short time I had spent with Linda, I sensed she had a great communicative ability, so I felt very comfortable having Linda tackle the Analysis phase of the SDLC.

Typically, our first class meeting is abbreviated, and because we were basically frozen in time until we could complete Phase 2 of the SDLC, I dismissed the class for the day. Prior to Linda's meeting with Frank Olley, I sent him the following e-mail.

Hi Frank,

I want to thank you for taking the time to meet with me last Tuesday afternoon. As I discussed with you at that time, it is my desire to work with you in developing a program that can calculate student grades for the English, Math, and Science departments.

The program will be developed as part of my Introduction to Programming with C++ computer class at the university. As such, your costs will be $450, payable upon final delivery of the program. In return, you agree to allow me to use your contract to provide my students with a valuable learning experience in developing a real-world application.

Sometime during the coming week, one of my students, Linda Schwartzer, will be contacting you to arrange to spend some time meeting with the person or persons who currently calculate grades in the English department. Although you may not see the necessity of this additional meeting, it will satisfy the next phase of the Systems Development Life Cycle I discussed with you at our meeting. Adhering strictly to the SDLC will result in the best possible program we can develop for you.

I'd like to take this opportunity to highlight the major points we discussed last week. We will develop a PC-based program, for you, with an eye toward Web-enabling it in my summer JavaScript course. Here are the major functions that the developed program will perform:

1. This program will provide the user with a console application C++ interface for calculating a student's grade.
2. The user will be requested to designate the type of student—English, Math, or Science—for which they wish to calculate a grade.

3. If the user indicates they wish to calculate the grade for an English student, the program will prompt them for a midterm examination grade, a final examination grade, a research paper grade, and a presentation grade. The final grade will be calculated as 25 percent of the midterm examination grade, 25 percent of the final examination grade, 30 percent of the research paper grade, and 20 percent of the presentation grade.

4. If the user indicates they wish to calculate the grade for a science student, the program will prompt them for a midterm examination grade, a final examination grade, and a research paper grade. The final grade will be calculated as 40 percent of the midterm examination grade, 40 percent of the final examination grade, and 20 percent of the research paper grade.

5. If the user indicates they wish to calculate the grade for a math student, the program will prompt them for a midterm examination grade and a final examination grade. The final grade will be calculated as 50 percent of the midterm examination grade and 50 percent of the final examination grade.

6. Once calculated, the final grade will then be displayed.

I think I've covered everything that we discussed last Tuesday. If I have missed anything, please let Linda know when she arrives in your office.

Regards,
John Smiley

This e-mail, in essence, will become the Requirements Statement that we will formally develop shortly. The next day I received the e-mail on the following page from Frank Olley.

Complicate the program? Sure, a bit. I was sure Linda would more than likely find other surprises as well. This new requirement was about par for the course. I checked my notes, and Frank was correct—he never mentioned it. Of course, a good developer can anticipate requirements such as these. I just missed it.

Linda called me on Monday morning to tell me that she had arranged to meet with Frank Olley on Thursday morning. That Thursday evening, Linda called to tell me that her observations of the English, Math, and Science departments current operations had gone well. Contrary to what I expected, she saw nothing in her observations of their day-to-day operation that contradicted the notes I took during my preliminary investigation.

Dear John,

I reviewed your e-mail, and everything looks fine.

One thing we forgot to mention last Tuesday is that the numeric grades need to be converted to letter grades for report card purposes. Complicating matters is that the letter grade equivalents of all the departments are different. Here is a table explaining the breakdown.

Grade	English Department	Math Department	Science Department
A	93 or greater	90 or greater	90 or greater
B	85 to 93	83 to 90	80 to 90
C	78 to 85	76 to 83	70 to 80
D	70 to 78	65 to 76	60 to 70
F	Less than 70	Less than 65	Less than 60

Regards,
Frank Olley

Linda reported that nothing out of the usual occurred and that it was obvious, from her observations, that the program would pay for itself in no time. All three departments had work study students performing the calculations manually—and making lots of mistakes.

That Saturday, I again met with our class. After ensuring that I hadn't lost anyone in the intervening week (yes, everyone came back), we began to discuss the third phase of the SDLC—the Design phase.

Phase 3: Design

"Phase 3 of the SDLC is the Design phase," I said.

I explained that design in the SDLC encompasses many different elements. Here is a list of the different components that are "designed" in this phase:

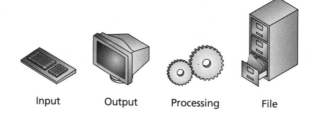

Input   Output   Processing   File

"Typically," I said, "too little time is spent on the Design phase. Programmers love to start programming." I continued by saying that you can hardly blame them; writing a program is exciting, and everyone wants to jump in and start writing code right away. Unfortunately, jumping immediately into coding is a huge mistake.

"After all," I said, "you wouldn't start building a house without a blueprint, would you? You simply cannot and should not start programming without a good solid design."

I pointed out that critics of the SDLC agree that it can take months to complete a house, and making a mistake in the building of a house can be devastating; writing a C++ program, on the other hand, can be accomplished in a matter of hours, if not minutes. If there's a mistake, it can be corrected quickly.

Even though at this point the class knew very little about C++, they were already familiar with computer applications of one kind or another—either Microsoft Windows, Macintosh, Linux, or Web-based programs (a knowledge of one of these is a requirement for the course). Designing and developing the look of an application program is really independent of the tool that you'll use to program it.

I should point out here that my role in the Design phase was to act as a guide for my students. Frank Olley told us what he wanted the program to do. Like any client, he described his program requirements in functional terms that he understood. My students were already familiar with computer applications, but at this point in our course, they were not C++ experts and their programming knowledge was not sufficient for them to know how to translate Frank Olley's requirements into C++ programming terms. Ultimately, it was my job to help them translate those requirements into C++ terms.

Critics of the SDLC further argue that time constraints and deadlines can make taking the "extra" time necessary to properly complete the Design phase a luxury that many programmers can't afford.

"I answer that criticism in this way," I said to the class, citing a familiar phrase that you have probably heard before. "It seems there is never time to do something right the first time, but there's always time to do it over."

The exceptional (and foolish) programmer can begin coding without a good design. Programmers who do so may find themselves going back to modify pieces of code they've already written as they move through the project. They may discover a technique halfway through the project that they wish they had incorporated in the beginning, and then go back and change code. Worse yet, they may find themselves with a program that runs but doesn't really work, with the result that they must go back and start virtually from the beginning.

"With a good design," I said, "the likelihood of this nightmare happening will be reduced dramatically. The end result is a program that will behave in the way it was intended and, generally, a shorter overall program-development time."

Armed with our notes from the preliminary investigation, Linda's notes from the detailed analysis, and Frank Olley's e-mails, my students and I began the Design phase of the SDLC in earnest. By the end of the Design phase, we hoped to have a formal Requirements Statement for the program and perhaps even a rough sketch of what the user interface will look like.

I reminded everyone that the Requirements Statement would form the basis of our agreement with Frank, Robin, and David. For some developers, the Requirements Statement becomes the formal contract to which both they and the customer agree and sign.

Linda began the Design phase by giving the class a summary of the three or four hours she spent in the English, Math, and Science departments. Linda said that she felt comfortable in stating that nothing she had observed that day contradicted the view expressed in my notes and in my e-mail to Frank Olley.

Not everyone in the class had had the benefit of seeing my notes or the e-mail, so I distributed to the class copies of my notes, my e-mail to Frank Olley, and his reply e-mail to me. I gave everyone a few minutes to review and digest the material.

We began to discuss the program requirements. I could see there was some hesitation as to where to begin, so I began the process with a question. "Let's begin by making a statement as to what we are trying to accomplish here," I said.

"We need to write a program to display the calculated final grade for a student in either the English, Math, or Science department," Dave said.

"Excellent," I said. Dave had hit the nail squarely on the head. The primary purpose of the program was to calculate a student's grade. To be sure, there would be more to the program than that, but from Frank Olley's point of view, all he needed the program to do was to display a student's grade.

"To clarify," Kate said, "we should probably state the student's letter grade as opposed to the student's numeric grade."

"Good clarification, Kate," I said. "Frank did add that in his e-mail, didn't he?"

Frequently, new programmers are unable to come to grips with where they should begin in the Design phase. I suggested to my class that most programs are designed by first determining the output of the program. The reasoning behind starting with the output is that if you know what the output of the program should be, you can pretty easily determine the input needed to produce that output. Once you know both the output from and the input to the program, you can then determine what processing or calculations need to be performed to convert that input to output.

Output Design

I told my students that we were fortunate in that the class's first project was one where the output requirements could be stated so simply: a grade calculation.

"Where will the grade calculation go?" I asked.

"To a printer?" Jack suggested.

"On the computer screen," Rose countered.

"I agree with Rose," I said. "Probably to the computer screen."

Some of the students seemed perplexed by my answer. "Probably?" Dave asked.

I explained that Frank Olley and I had never formally agreed where the grade calculation would be displayed. The issue had never really come up.

"Let's be sure," I said, "to explicitly specify a display of the grade calculation in the Requirements Statement. Speaking of which, would anyone care to volunteer to begin to write up the specifications for it?" Dave volunteered to begin writing our Requirements Statement, so he opened Microsoft Word and started typing away.

Rhonda made a suggestion for the color and font size for the program's grades display, but Peter said that it was probably a bit premature to be talking about colors and font sizes at this point in our design. I agreed, pointing out that in this class, we would be creating a C++ console application.

"Do you mean a DOS program?" Peter asked.

"That's one way of looking at it, Peter," I answered. "For this introductory-level C++ class, writing a Microsoft Windows program is definitely beyond its scope. We need to concentrate on learning good fundamental, object-oriented programming techniques. There are advanced courses here at the University that can teach you how to develop a program that has a Microsoft Windows user interface; however, in this class, you'll learn to write a C++ console application, which will resemble an old-time DOS program."

"Will there be any other output from the program?" Rhonda asked, after several moments went by.

"I'd like to suggest that we display the date and time on the computer screen," Valerie suggested.

"Good idea," Mary said.

However, Linda disagreed, arguing that the display of the date and time was unnecessary considering the fact that the PCs at the university were all running Windows and displayed the current time on the Windows taskbar anyway.

"We could display the current date and time," I said, "but I'm inclined to agree with Linda— all the PCs at the university that will run our program are Microsoft Windows–based PCs and are capable of displaying a date and time on their own. And although it's true that the beauty of the C++ programs you will learn how to write in this class is that they can run on virtually any operating system—and also within a web page—I can't think of any environment in which the user can't be aware of the current date and time if they so desire."

The majority of the class agreed.

"Getting back to the display of the grade," Peter said. "Do you think it would be a good idea to display the calculated numeric grade as well as the letter grade?"

"Yes, I think that's a great idea," Kathy agreed.

Taking a moment to consider, I said, "I agree also. So we now have two output requirements: a grade calculation that displays both the calculated numeric grade for the student and the corresponding letter grade. I can't think of anything else from an output point of view, can you?"

"What about the individual components that make up the grade?" Rhonda asked. "Should we display those?"

"Great idea, Rhonda," I said.

"But won't the user be inputting those values?" Blaine responded. "Is it really necessary to repeat them."

"I think it's a good idea to display the values that the user has input," I said. "That way, the user can be sure what component pieces make up the final grade that is being displayed."

I waited to see whether there were any questions, but there were none.

"I think we now have enough information to proceed to our next step," I said. "What's that? Anyone?"

Barbara suggested that because we seemed to have the output requirements identified—the component grade pieces that the user has entered, along with a calculated final grade—we should move on to a discussion of processing.

"As I explained earlier, it will be easier for us if we discuss input into the program prior to discussing processing," I said. "It's just about impossible to determine processing requirements if we don't know our input requirements."

Input Design

"So does anyone have any suggestions as to what input requirements we need?" I asked the class.

Dave quickly rattled off several input requirements: a midterm grade, a final examination grade, a research paper grade, and a presentation grade.

"Excellent," I said. "Of course, those requirements will vary depending on the type of student whose grade is being calculated."

"Is that another piece of input?" Mary suggested. "The type of student whose grade is being calculated?"

"Excellent observation, Mary," I said. "Only for an English student will all four grades be required. A science student's final grade is comprised of three component pieces—midterm, final examination, and research paper—and a math student's final grade is comprised of only two pieces—the midterm and final examination grades.

"Anything else?" I asked.

"How will the input be entered into the program?" Kathy asked. "How will the user of the program let the program know what type of student they are entering?"

Designating the Type of Student

Several students suggested that the user of the program could designate the type of student by entering the type using the computer's keyboard.

"My motto is to have the user do as little typing as possible," I said. "If we ask the user of the program to use the keyboard to enter the type of student into the program, we're going to have to insist that each user of the program type it consistently—that's something we can't count on. For instance, one user may type 'Math,' another may type 'Mathematics,' and still a third may type 'Calculus.'"

"I see what you mean," Rhonda said. "But what's our alternative?"

I could see that some of the students were perplexed about the alternatives to entering the type of student via the PCs keyboard.

"Can we prompt the user to enter a number instead?" Kathy asked.

"What do you mean, Kathy?" Rhonda asked.

"Well," Kathy said, "instead of asking the user to type 'English,' 'Math,' or 'Science,' why not have them type the number 1 for English, the number 2 for Math, and the number 3 for Science? There's only one way to type the numbers 1, 2, and 3—that should cut down on user input error."

"Excellent, Kathy," I said. "That's certainly one way—and probably the best way—to handle this dilemma."

Designating the Component Grades

"OK," Ward said. "Now that we have come up with a way for the user to identify the student type, what happens next?"

"I'd like to suggest," Dave said, "that depending on the value the user enters—1, 2 or 3—that the program then prompt the user for the appropriate component grades—midterm examination, final examination, research paper, and presentation."

"What do you mean by appropriate component grades, Dave?" Rhonda asked.

"Well," Dave replied, "if the user tells the program that they wish to calculate the grade for an English student, then the program needs to prompt for all four component pieces—midterm examination, final examination, research paper, and presentation. If the user tells the program that they wish to calculate the grade for a math student, then the program needs to prompt for just two component pieces—midterm examination and final examination. Finally, if the user tells the program that they wish to calculate the grade for a science student, then the program needs to prompt for three component pieces—midterm examination, final examination, and presentation."

"Excellent, Dave," I said.

"This sounds like it's all going to be a lot of fun," Rhonda said. "I just wish I could envision what the interface will look like. Do we have to wait until we write the program to see what the interface will actually look like?"

"Good question, Rhonda," I said. "No, we don't have to wait that long. There's no rule that says we can't sketch the user interface using pencil and paper well before that."

"How can we have an interface if we aren't designing our program as a Windows program?" Kate asked.

"I see your point, Kate," I answered, "but even though our program won't have a Windows look and feel, we still need to make some design decisions about how the program will interface with the user of our program. Without a good interface—whether it be Windows or not—a program is doomed to failure."

The First Interface Design As it turned out, during the course of our discussions, Barbara had been sketching a preliminary interface design. Upon hearing my remarks about sketching the interface, she offered to show the class what she had sketched so far, and I displayed it on the classroom projector.

```
Enter student type (1=English, 2=Math, 3=Science): 1

Enter the Midterm Grade: 100
Enter the Final Examination Grade: 100
Enter the Research Grade: 100
Enter the Presentation Grade: 100

Final Numeric Grade is: 100
Final Letter Grade is: A
```

"That looks great, Barbara," Rhonda said. "Seeing the interface design on paper really makes this easier for me to envision."

"I agree, Rhonda," I said. "And you'll find that having a blueprint like this will make programming the interface much easier later on."

I then asked Barbara if she would mind explaining the interface design to the rest of the class.

"It's kind of basic," she said, "but based on our previous discussion, I figured the first thing we would want to do is to ask the user the type of grade they wished to calculate. I did that by displaying a message asking them to enter 1 for an English student, 2 for a math student, and 3 for a science student. In the sketch, I've presumed they've selected 1 for an English student, and after they've typed the number 1, the program then prompts them to enter the component grade pieces for an English student. I hope this is OK."

"It's really great, Barbara," I said, "exactly what I had in mind. Does anyone have any suggestions? Don't be shy now—this sort of collaborative effort is the way things are frequently done in the real world."

"I have a suggestion, but I don't want to appear to be picky," Blaine said.

"Go ahead, Blaine," Barbara answered. "I realize this is a bit rough."

"I was going to suggest that there's no title or identifying caption for the program," he answered. "Someone walking by the PC wouldn't know what the user was working on. I guess the interface, while perfectly functional, just seems a bit 'unfriendly' to me."

"Blaine's right," Barbara answered. "I didn't include any such element in the sketch. Should I be that detailed here?"

"It can't hurt," I said. "It's one less thing to forget when it comes time to actually write our code."

"I can fix that," Barbara said, and in a minute, version 2 of the interface design was displayed for everyone to see—this one having a user-friendly message, thanking the user for using the program.

```
Enter student type (1=English, 2=Math, 3=Science): 1

Enter the Midterm Grade: 100
Enter the Final Examination Grade: 100
Enter the Research Grade: 100
Enter the Presentation Grade: 100

Final Numeric Grade is: 100
Final Letter Grade is: A

Thanks for using the Grades Calculation program!
```

"Anything else?" I asked.

"I'd like to suggest," Dave said, "that we repeat the grades that the user has entered, and that we right justify both the grades and the calculated answer."

"I'm not sure what you mean, Dave," Barbara said. "Why don't you take over here?" She then handed Dave her sketchpad.

"I'm not much of an artist," Dave said, but in a minute or two he had modified Barbara's sketch to look like this.

```
Enter student type (1=English, 2=Math, 3=Science): 1

Enter the Midterm Grade: 100
Enter the Final Examination Grade: 100
Enter the Research Grade: 100
Enter the Presentation Grade: 100

**** ENGLISH STUDENT ****

Midterm Grade:            100
Final Examination Grade:  100
Research Grade:           100
Presentation Grade:       100

Final Numeric Grade is:   100
Final Letter Grade is:    A

Thanks for using the Grades Calculation program!
```

"Oh, I see," Rhonda said, "Dave's changes have 'neatened up' the interface quite a bit."

"This is starting to shape up quite nicely," Steve said.

That seemed to be the majority opinion of the class. I waited to see if there were any other suggestions.

"I have a question." Chuck said. "Is the program going to end after the user calculates just one grade? Shouldn't we ask the user if they have any more grades to calculate?"

"Chuck's right," Barbara said, "I never thought of that!"

"That's a great point, Chuck," I said, "I'd like to suggest that the first thing we do is ask the user if they have a grade to calculate. If they answer 'No,' we immediately thank them for using the program, and end it. If they answer 'Yes,' then we ask them the type of student they wish to calculate. After prompting them for the appropriate data, we display the final grade, and then ask them if they have another grade to calculate. If they answer 'Yes,' then once again we prompt them to tell us the type of student they wish to calculate...."

"And we repeat the process all over again," Ward chimed in. "Sounds like a perfect application for a loop?"

"A what?" Rhonda asked.

"A loop is a programming structure," I said smiling, "and it's something that you'll learn about a few weeks from now. Until then, please don't worry about it."

I noticed that Barbara had finished making my suggested changes to her sketch, and I took it from her and displayed it on the classroom projector.

```
Do you want to calculate a grade? YES

Enter student type (1=English, 2=Math, 3=Science): 1

Enter the Midterm Grade: 100
Enter the Final Examination Grade: 100
Enter the Research Grade: 100
Enter the Presentation Grade: 100

**** ENGLISH STUDENT ****

Midterm Grade:              100
Final Examination Grade:    100
Research Grade:             100
Presentation Grade:         100

Final Numeric Grade is:     100
Final Letter Grade is:      A

Do you have another grade to calculate? NO

Thanks for using the Grades Calculation program!
```

"That really is beginning to shape up," Ward said. "Did we forget anything?"

"I can't think of anything," I said. "But the great thing about doing the design on paper first is that if you do forget anything, it's a matter of making some changes to a sheet of paper, not to your program code."

I waited to see if there were any questions, but there were none.

The Requirements Statement   We had been working pretty intensely and, in my opinion, making some excellent progress, so I suggested that we take a break. Before adjourning, I asked Dave, the student who was developing the Requirements Statement, to let us see what he had developed so far. I made copies of his work. After the break, I handed these out to the rest of the class for discussion. On the following page is the copy of the Requirements Statement I gave to everyone.

REQUIREMENTS STATEMENT
Grades Calculation Program
General Description

The program will consist of an interface in which the user will be asked if they have a grade to calculate.

- If the answer is No, the program will thank them and immediately end.
- If the answer is Yes, the program will prompt them for the type of student for which they wish to calculate a grade. Depending on the answer, the user will then be prompted to enter the appropriate component grades (see Business Rules below).

After displaying both a calculated numeric and letter grade, the program will ask the user if they have another grade to calculate.

- If the answer is Yes, once again the program will prompt the user for a student type and the appropriate grade component pieces.
- If the answer is No, the program will thank them and immediately end.

Output from the System

The student's final numeric grade and letter grade will be displayed. In addition, the program will indicate the type of student for which it has displayed a grade, and repeat (or echo back) the values it used to calculate the grade.

Input to the System

The user will specify the type of student whose grade is to be calculated by entering 1 for an English student, 2 for a math student, or 3 for a science student.

- If an English student, the midterm, final examination, research paper, and class presentation grades will be prompted for and entered by the user.
- If a math student, the midterm and final examination grades will be prompted for and entered by the user.
- If a science student, the midterm, final examination, and research paper grades will be prompted for and entered by the user.

Business Rules

An English student's grade is calculated as 25 percent of the midterm grade, 25 percent of the final examination grade, 30 percent of the research paper grade, and 20 percent of the class presentation grade.

A math student's grade is calculated as 50 percent of the midterm grade and 50 percent of the final examination grade.

A science student's grade is calculated as 40 percent of the midterm grade, 40 percent of the final examination grade, and 20 percent of the research paper grade.

Each department has unique letter grade equivalents for the student's calculated final numeric average. Here is a table of the letter grade equivalents:

Grade	English Department	Math Department	Science Department
A	93 or greater	90 or greater	90 or greater
B	85 to 93	83 to 90	80 to 90
C	78 to 85	76 to 83	70 to 80
D	70 to 78	65 to 76	60 to 70
F	Less than 70	Less than 65	Less than 60

I explained to the class that the Requirements Statement can easily form the basis of a contract between the customer and the developer of the program. The Requirements Statement should list all the major details of the program. You should take care not to paint yourself into any unnecessary programming corners by including any window dressing. These can just get you into trouble later. For instance, notice here that we didn't specify the exact text of how we would thank the user for using our program, and we didn't mention the welcome message the program would display (although we did include these details on our sketch). Suppose, for instance, we later decided against displaying a welcome message—theoretically, deviating from the Requirements Statement could be construed as a violation of contractual terms.

I asked for comments on the Requirements Statement, and everyone seemed to think that it was just fine. Everyone agreed that the project was coming along quite nicely, but as they say, the proof is in the pudding. It's only the customer's opinion that counts, and we'd have to see how Frank, Robin, and David felt about it. With no more comments or suggestions on the user interface or the Requirements Statement, we set about completing the Design phase of the SDLC by looking at processing.

Processing Design

"Processing is the conversion of inputs to outputs, the conversion of data to information," I said. "At this point in the Design phase of the SDLC, we should now have identified all the output from the program—a calculation of the student's grade—and all the input necessary to produce that output—the component pieces of the grade."

I explained that a good novel will typically have several subplots; a C++ program is no exception. It contains several processing "subplots" as well.

We have the main plot (the calculation of the student's grade), but we also have several subplots:

- Determining the type of student whose grade is being entered
- Selectively displaying the appropriate prompts for component grades based on the student type selected
- Ensuring that valid data is entered as a response to the prompts
- Making the appropriate calculation
- Displaying the calculated grade

It's important to note that in processing design, we don't actually write the program. That's done later. In processing design, we specify the processes that need to be performed to convert input into output.

Looking at Processing in Detail
"Let's look at a simple example that isn't part of the Grade Calculation Project and that most of you are probably familiar with," I said. "The calculation of your paycheck."

I continued by saying that if you want to calculate your net pay, you need to perform several steps. Here are the steps or functions necessary to calculate your net pay:

1. Calculate gross pay.
2. Calculate tax deductions.
3. Calculate net pay.

 NOTE
Programming is done in the next phase of the SDLC, the Development phase. Specifying how processing is to occur is not as important in this phase as specifying what is to occur. This sequence identifies the "what" of processing, not the "how." The how is a part of the Development phase.

These functions can be broken down even further. For instance, the calculation of your gross pay will vary depending on whether you are a salaried employee or an hourly employee. If you are an hourly employee, your gross pay is equal to your hourly pay rate multiplied by the number of hours worked in the pay period. The specification of these functions is exactly what the designer must detail in the Processing Design phase of the SDLC.

When it comes to processing design, documenting the processing rules is crucial because translating processing rules into a narrative form can sometimes result in confusion or misinterpretation. Over the years, systems designers have used various tools to aid them in documenting the design of their systems.

Some designers have used tools called *flowcharts*. Flowcharts use symbols to graphically document the system's processing rules. Here are the net pay processing rules we discussed earlier depicted by a flowchart. (My apologies to any accountants reading this; these calculations have been simplified for illustration purposes.)

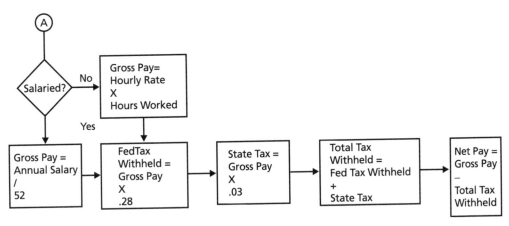

Other designers favor pseudocode. *Pseudocode* is an English-like language that describes in nongraphical form how a program should execute. Here are the same net pay processing rules depicted using pseudocode:

Assumption: Pay is calculated on a weekly basis (52 pay periods per year).

Assumption: Salaried employee pay is annual salary divided by 52.

Assumption: Hourly employee pay is hourly rate multiplied by hours worked.

1. If employee is salaried, go to step 4.
2. If employee is hourly, calculate gross pay equal to hourly wage rate multiplied by hours worked in pay period.
3. Go to step 5.
4. Employee is salaried, so calculate gross pay equal to annual salary divided by 52.
5. Calculate federal tax withheld equal to gross pay multiplied by 0.28.
6. Calculate state tax withheld equal to gross pay multiplied by 0.03.

7. Calculate total tax withheld equal to federal tax withheld plus state tax withheld.

8. Calculate net pay equal to gross pay less total tax withheld.

 NOTE

Both of these techniques found favor in the era of the procedural program. A procedural program is one that executes from top to bottom, virtually without interruption. A procedural program ordains to the user exactly how they will interact with your program. For instance, in the Grade Calculation Project, the user will select a type of student and then enter values for component grade pieces, such as the midterm or final examination grade. I frequently find students who have strong programming backgrounds writing procedural programs. Procedural programming (using languages such as Basic, Fortran, and COBOL) is like taking a ride on a tour bus, where all the destination stops are predetermined and preordered.

Windows programs are event-driven programs. Event-driven programs (using languages such as Visual Basic, Java, and C++) don't force the user to behave in a certain way; rather, the program reacts to the user. An event-driven program presents users with a visual interface that permits them to interact with the program. This is more like someone choosing the rides at a carnival. Once entry has been gained, the rides they go on and the order in which they ride them are entirely up to the patrons. An event-driven program must be able to work and respond to any eventuality.

"In my classes," I said, "I don't require the use of either flowcharting or pseudocode. All that I ask from you is that you give careful thought to the processing that is necessary to solve the problem before beginning to code in C++."

I could see some happy faces, and I continued by saying that, invariably, this means working out a solution on a piece of paper prior to coding it. Some students are more visually oriented than others and prefer to design their solution in graphical terms. Others are less visual, and their solutions look very much like the pseudocode you saw earlier. The point is, without some written plan, the programming process can go awry.

I cited an example. Several years ago, I was teaching a class on another language called COBOL, and I gave my students the following programming problem:

Write a program to calculate the net wage of a laborer who works 40 hours at a pay rate of $5 per hour. Income tax at the rate of 20 percent of the gross pay will be deducted. What is the net pay?

The correct answer is $160. Forty hours multiplied by $5 per hour results in a gross pay of $200. The income tax deduction is 20 percent of $200, which is $40. $200 less the $40 income tax deduction results in a net pay of $160.

A number of students calculated the net pay as $240. Instead of deducting the income tax deduction of $40 from the gross pay, they *added* it instead. When I questioned the methodology behind their incorrect answer, most of them told me they thought the problem had been so simple that they hadn't bothered to work out the solution on a piece of paper ahead of time. They just started coding. Had they taken the time to work out the solution on paper first, they would have known what the answer was and wouldn't have submitted a program to me that calculated the results incorrectly.

"This is what I'm suggesting to you," I said to the C++ class. "Take the time to work out the solution on paper. You'll be happy that you did."

Back to the Grade Calculation Program   We continued by discussing processing design. I reminded my students that, in general, design is an iterative process. It's rare that the designer or programmer hits the nail perfectly on the head the first time. It's very possible that after going through the processing design, you will discover you are missing some crucial piece of input necessary to produce a piece of output. In that case, you would need to look at your input processing again. For instance, with the Grade Calculation Program, we could have forgotten to ask the user to specify the type of student whose grade they wished to calculate—such an omission would have catastrophic consequences.

As a starting point in our processing discussion, we agreed to begin with our primary goal: *to calculate a student's grade.* We had already determined that in order to calculate a grade, we needed to know the type of student and, once we knew that, the individual grade components that made up the final grade.

We started with a hypothetical user entering a hypothetical student's information.

"Can anyone tell me," I asked, "what the final grade for an English student would be if they scored an 88 on their midterm examination, a 90 on their final examination, an 85 on their research paper, and a 75 on their class presentation? Plus, can you tell me how you arrive at the result?"

"If I were solving this problem using pencil and paper," Ward said, "I would take the score for the student's midterm grade, 88, and multiply it by .25, giving me a result of 22, which I would then set aside. I would then take the score for the final examination, 90, and multiply it by .25, giving me a result of 22.5, which I would then set aside. I would then take the score for the student's research paper, 85, and multiply it by .3, giving me a result of 25.5, which I would then set aside. I would then take the score for the class presentation, 75, and multiply it by .2, giving me a result of 15, which I would then set aside. Finally, I would take the four set-aside results— 22, 22.5, 25.5, and 15—and add them together to arrive at a sum of 85—which, if we refer to the Requirements Statement, equates to the letter grade B for an English student."

"That's excellent, Ward," I said.

"I think we've got a problem here," Chuck said. "I went through the same process Ward just did, but I come up with a letter grade of C."

Sure enough, we did have a problem. In looking over the Requirements Statement, it indicated that for an English student, the numeric grade of 85 equated to both the letter B and the letter C.

"How did that happen?" Kate asked.

"Those are the numbers that Frank Olley supplied in his e-mail," I said. "Unfortunately, I missed catching this. Right now, we have a little problem, but I happen to know that Frank is in his office today. Let's hope he can give us a quick solution to the problem."

I pulled out my cell phone (ah, the wonders of modern life!) and gave Frank a quick call. I explained that in his e-mail to me outlining the numeric grade-letter equivalents, he had used the phrase "78 to 85" to describe the letter grade of C for an English student and the phrase "85 to 93" to describe the letter grade of B. What happens if the student scores a final numeric grade of 85 right on the nose?

I had to explain the problem once more for Frank and then he apologized and explained that a numeric grade of 85 was the starting point for a B. Anything less than 85 was a C. I asked him if the same applied to the other categories, because we also had overlapping there. He said that it did. Based on our discussion, the class and I reworked that table from the Requirements Statement to look like this:

Grade	English	Math	Science
A	Greater than or equal to 93	Greater than or equal to 90	Greater than or equal to 90
B	Less than 93 AND greater than or equal to 85	Less than 90 AND greater than or equal to 83	Less than 90 AND greater than or equal to 80
C	Less than 85 AND greater than or equal to 78	Less than 83 AND greater than or equal to 76	Less than 80 AND greater than or equal to 70
D	Less than 78 AND greater than or equal to 70	Less than 76 AND greater than or equal to 65	Less than 70 AND greater than or equal to 60
F	Less than 70	Less than 65	Less than 60

"That's better," I said, admiring my work.

"Maybe for you," Rhonda responded, "but this reminds me of Algebra, and I think the table is a lot more difficult to read this way. Do we really have to express the rules for the letter grade computations this way? Those less-than and greater-than symbols always confused me."

"In the long run, we'll be better off," I said. "The way we've phrased the rules for forming the letter grades isn't much different from the C++ code we'll write. Plus, these are expressed in certain terms, unlike the previous version of the table, which had the overlapping values."

"Have we missed anything with the grade calculation?" I asked. "Suppose," I added, "the user selects a student type of English and enters values for a midterm, a final examination, and a research paper but fails to enter a value for the class presentation—what should the program do?"

"How can that happen?" Kate asked. "I mean, doesn't the user have to respond to the prompts that are displayed?"

"That's true Kate," I said, "but it's possible for the user to simply press the ENTER key, thereby not providing a value for that particular grade component."

Everyone agreed that we needed to display some sort of error message if we didn't have all the ingredients necessary to arrive at a valid grade calculation—either because the user simply pressed the ENTER key or because they entered an invalid value (a value less than 0 or greater than 100). An error message is another form of output.

Now it seemed as though we were gaining momentum. As I mentioned earlier, during the course of processing design, we may uncover holes in the input or output design, such as the overlapping grade. That had been the case here. Although it's certain that we would have eventually noticed these holes when we were coding the program, fixing these flaws while we were still in the design phase of the SDLC is much easier and cheaper than fixing them in the midst of programming the application.

In large projects particularly, portions of a project may be given to different programmers or even different teams of programmers for coding. It could be some time before flaws in the design are uncovered—in some cases weeks or even months. The longer it takes to discover these flaws, the more likely it is that some coding will have to be scrapped and redone. A well thought-out Design phase can eliminate many problems down the line.

We'd plugged the hole in the grade calculation processing—now it remained to be seen if there were any other processing design issues.

"What about ending the program?" Steve asked. "Do we need to write code for that?"

I explained that we would need to write a few lines of C++ code to end the program, but that there was no need to formally state that in the Requirements Statement. After a few moments of silence, it seemed that we were finished with the Design phase of the SDLC. On the following page is the final Requirements Statement that the class approved.

REQUIREMENTS STATEMENT
Grades Calculation Program
General Description

The program will consist of an interface in which the user will be asked if they have a grade to calculate.

- If the answer is No, the program will thank them and immediately end.
- If the answer is Yes, the program will prompt them for the type of student for which they wish to calculate a grade. Depending on the answer, the user will then be prompted to enter the appropriate component grades (see Business Rules below).

After displaying both a calculated numeric and letter grade, the program will ask the user if they have another grade to calculate.

- If the answer is Yes, once again the program will prompt the user for a student type and the appropriate grade component pieces.
- If the answer is No, the program will thank them and immediately end.

Output from the System

The student's final numeric grade and letter grade will be displayed. In addition, the program will indicate the type of student for which it has displayed a grade and repeat (or echo back) the values it used to calculate the grade.

Input to the System

The user will specify the type of student whose grade is to be calculated by entering 1 for an English student, 2 for a math student, or 3 for a science student.

- If an English student, the midterm, final examination, research paper, and class presentation grades will be prompted for and entered by the user.
- If a math student, the midterm and final examination grades will be prompted for and entered by the user.
- If a science student, the midterm, final examination, and research paper grades will be prompted for and entered by the user.

Business Rules

An English student's grade is calculated as 25 percent of the midterm grade, 25 percent of the final examination grade, 30 percent of the research paper grade, and 20 percent of the class presentation grade.

A math student's grade is calculated as 50 percent of the midterm grade and 50 percent of the final examination grade.

A science student's grade is calculated as 40 percent of the midterm grade, 40 percent of the final examination grade, and 20 percent of the research paper grade.

Each department has unique letter grade equivalents for the student's calculated final numeric average. Here is a table of the letter grade equivalents:

Grade	English Department	Math Department	Science Department
A	Greater than or equal to 93	Greater than or equal to 90	Greater than or equal to 90
B	Less than 93 AND greater than or equal to 85	Less than 90 AND greater than or equal to 83	Less than 90 AND greater than or equal to 80
C	Less than 85 AND greater than or equal to 78	Less than 83 AND greater than or equal to 76	Less than 80 AND greater than or equal to 70
D	Less than 78 AND greater than or equal to 70	Less than 76 AND greater than or equal to 65	Less than 70 AND greater than or equal to 60
F	Less than 70	Less than 65	Less than 60

I polled the class to see if everyone agreed with the Requirements Statement and then revealed that we were done with the Design phase of the SDLC. I once again reminded everyone that the Design phase of the SDLC tends to be an iterative process and that we might find ourselves back here at some point. We then moved on to a discussion of the fourth phase of the SDLC: the Development phase.

Phase 4: Development

I told my class that we wouldn't spend a great deal of time discussing the Development phase here because the rest of the course would be spent in developing the Grade Calculation Project, in which they would play an active role!

"The Development phase," I said, "is in many ways the most exciting time of the SDLC. During this phase, computer hardware is purchased, if necessary, and the software is developed. Yes, that means we actually start coding the program during the Development phase. And in this class, we'll be using C++ as our development tool."

I explained that during the Development phase, we'd constantly examine and reexamine the Requirements Statement to ensure that we were following it to the letter, and I encouraged all of them to do the same on their own. I explained that any deviations (and there may be a surprise or two down the road) would have to be approved either by the project leader (me) or by our clients (Frank, Robin, and David).

Everyone in the class seemed anxious to begin, but they promised me they would remain patient while I discussed the final two phases of the SDLC.

Phase 5: Implementation

The Implementation phase is the phase in the SDLC in which the project reaches fruition. I explained to my students that after the Development phase of the SDLC is complete, we begin to actually implement the system. In a typical project, what this means is that any hardware that has been purchased will be delivered and installed in the client's location.

"In the instance of our clients," I said, "they already have the equipment. So instead, during the Implementation phase, the C++ program that we write will be loaded to their PCs."

Not surprisingly, everyone in the class agreed that they wanted to be there for that exciting day.

Barbara raised the issue of program testing. During the Implementation phase, both hardware and software are tested. We agreed that students in the class would perform most of the testing of the program because we agreed that it would be unreasonable and unfair to expect our clients to test the software that we had developed in a live situation. Naturally, our goal was that when the software is installed in the English, Math, and Science departments, the program should be bug (problem) free.

On the other hand, I cautioned them, almost invariably the user will uncover problems that the developer was unable to generate. We would discuss handling these types of problems in more detail in our class on error handling.

"I've heard the term 'debugging' used among the programmers at work," Valerie said. "Is that something we'll be doing?"

"Most definitely, Valerie," I said. "Debugging is a process in which we run the program, thoroughly test it, and systematically eliminate all the errors that we can uncover. We'll be doing this prior to delivering the program to Frank, Robin, and David."

I then explained that during the Implementation phase, we would also be training the users of the program—most likely work study students in the English, Math, and Science departments, but perhaps Frank, Robin, and David as well. Again, everyone in the class wanted to participate in user training. Linda noted that she thought that there needed to be two levels of training performed—one level for Frank, Robin, and David, and a more detailed level of training for the person or persons actually working with the program.

Several students thought that it would be a good idea to have a student observing the users of the program during its first week of operation to assist users in the operation of the system and to ease any computer anxiety that the users might be suffering. I thought this was a great idea and also pointed out these observations would provide valuable feedback on the operation of the program from the most important people in the loop—the end users.

In fact, the mention of the word "feedback" led quite naturally into a discussion of the final phase of the SDLC—the Audit (sometimes called *Feedback*) and Maintenance phase.

Phase 6: Audit and Maintenance

Phase 6 of the SDLC is the Audit and Maintenance phase. In this phase, someone (usually the client but sometimes a third party, such as an auditor) studies the implemented system to ensure that it actually fulfills the details of the Requirements Statement. The bottom line is that the system should have solved the problem or deficiency or satisfied the desire that was identified in Phase 1 of the SDLC—the preliminary investigation.

More than a few programs and systems have been fully developed that, for one reason or another, simply never met the original requirements. The maintenance portion of this phase deals with any changes that need to be made to the system.

Changes are sometimes the result of the system not completely fulfilling its original requirements, but they could also be the result of customer satisfaction. Sometimes the customer is so happy with what they have got that they want more. Changes can also be forced upon the system because of governmental regulations, such as changing tax laws, while at other times changes come about due to alterations in the business rules of the customer.

As I mentioned in the previous section, we intended to have one or more members of the C++ class in the English, Math, and Science departments during the first week of system operation. That opportunity for the user to provide direct feedback to a member of the development team would more than satisfy the Audit portion of Phase 6.

In the future, we hoped that Frank, Robin, and David would be so happy with the program that we had written for them that they would think of even more challenging requirements to request of the class.

Where to from Here?

It had been a long and productive session for everyone. I told my students that in our next meeting we would start to discuss how a computer works, and we would actually begin to work with C++.

Ward asked me how the progression of the project would work—that is, would we finish the project during our last class meeting or would we be working on it a little bit each week? I said that I thought it was important that we develop the program incrementally. Each week we met, we would attempt to finish some portion of the project. Developing the project in steps like this would hold everyone's interest and give us a chance to catch any problems well before the last week of class.

Summary

The aim of this chapter was to tackle the question Where do I begin? You saw that the design of an application is best done systematically with a definite plan of action. That way, you know that everything has been taken into account.

A good place to begin is with a Requirements Statement, which is a list of what the program has to be able to do. Usually, you get the information for this from whoever is asking you to write the program. It's a good idea to keep in continuous contact with this person so that any changes they want can be tackled before it becomes too much of a problem.

A good systematic approach is embodied in the Systems Development Life Cycle (SDLC), which consists of six phases:

- **The Preliminary Investigation phase**   Involves considering the technical, time, and budgetary constraints and deciding on the viability of continuing development of the application

- **The Analysis phase**   Involves gathering the information needed to continue

- **The Design phase**   Involves creating a blueprint of the program's appearance and program structure without actually starting any programming

- **The Development phase**   Involves creating the application, including all interface and code

- **The Implementation phase**   Involves using and testing the program

- **The Audit and Maintenance phase**   Involves making refinements to the product to eliminate any problems or to cover new needs that have developed

Using the SDLC method can make any problems you encounter in your design more obvious, making it easier for you to tackle them at a more favorable point in your design, rather than changing existing code.

2

Getting Comfortable with C++

In this chapter, we follow my computer class as the students take their first look at the C++ environment. The purpose of this chapter is to give you an overview of how to create a C++ program using Windows Notepad, how to compile it, and how to run it.

Sit Down and Get Cozy with C++

I began our second class by getting straight to the point.

"In today's class," I said, "we're going to concentrate on writing our first C++ program. Let's do that now."

I then started Windows Notepad.

"Are you going to write this program using Notepad?" Ward asked. "Doesn't C++ have an Integrated Development Environment—an IDE—like Visual Basic?"

"That's a loaded question," I said. "C++ is a language for which many compilers have been developed. Some of these compilers can be downloaded for free from the Internet, and some are commercial products that you can purchase here at the University bookstore. There are two major commercial compilers available—one from Microsoft, and one from Borland. In this class, we'll be using the Borland compiler, but the code we write can also be compiled and run successfully by the Microsoft compiler because both compilers are written to adhere to the ANSI C++ standard."

"What's ANSI?" Rhonda asked. "Is that the coding scheme for bits and bytes?"

"No, Rhonda," I said. "You're thinking of ASCII. ANSI stands for the American National Standards Institute. This institute, among other things, provides oversight for various programming languages that have been developed. ANSI publishes standards for the C++ language, and if a compiler is developed that adheres to these standards, ANSI provides its 'stamp of approval.' Both Borland and Microsoft have produced ANSI standard C++ compilers."

"Why are we using the Borland product then?" Peter asked. "In our other classes, we used Microsoft products."

"We're using Borland's C++ compiler in this course," I explained, "because Borland has made a version of its compiler available as a free download. Therefore, you won't have to incur any cost to use the Borland C++ compiler."

NOTE

You can download the free Borland compiler from http://www.borland.com/ bcppbuilder/freecompiler/cppc55steps.html. For instructions on installing it, check out the C++ web page on Professor Smiley's web site at http:// www.johnsmiley.com/c++/c++.htm.

"The free Borland C++ compiler will be perfectly fine to enable us to produce the console applications we'll be creating in this class. Both the Microsoft and Borland commercial C++ compilers permit you to write code in an Integrated Development Environment, such as the Windows environment, but most C++ students learn by writing their code using an editor such as Windows Notepad and using a command prompt for the Windows Run button to compile and run their programs."

> **NOTE**
> *The programs we write during this course will also run using the batch compiler (lc.exe) provided with Microsoft's Visual C++ package.*

"Are you talking about the MS-DOS prompt," Rhonda said with a worried look on her face. "I know next to nothing about DOS."

"Don't worry, Rhonda," I said. "Once you have the C++ compiler installed, compiling and executing your programs isn't difficult. I'll be showing you how to do that today—and you'll have some exercises of your own to complete later on in the class for reinforcement."

I waited to see if I was about to lose any of my students. No one got up in a panic to leave the classroom (you think I'm kidding, but I've seen it happen!), and so I began again.

Writing Our First C++ Program

"Creating a C++ program is a three-step process," I said.

1. Create the source file with a filename extension of .cpp.

2. Use the C++ compiler to create an executable file with a filename extension of .exe.

3. Run the program.

Create the Source File with a Filename Extension of .cpp

"First, we use a text editor—Notepad is easiest in the Microsoft Windows environment—to create what is known as a *source file*. The source file is just an ordinary text file containing C++ code. We then save the C++ source file to the hard drive of our PC, giving it virtually any name of our choice. However, the name of a C++ source file should end with a period, followed by the letters *cpp*. This is called its filename extension. For instance, shortly we'll create a C++ source file whose name is ILoveCPlusPlus.cpp…"

TIP
It's recommended that a C++ source file end with the extension .cpp, but it is NOT required.

"...where the period followed by the letters *cpp* is the filename extension."

I paused to see if I had lost anyone. "Once we use a text editor to create a source file," I continued, "we then use a C++ compiler to convert or 'compile' that source file into what is called an *executable file*."

NOTE
A C++ compiler that runs on a Windows platform will generate an executable whose filename extension ends in .exe. A C++ compiler that runs on a Unix or Linux system creates an executable file, but it need not end in an extension of .exe.

"Is a C++ executable file just like the kind of executable file we created last semester in our Visual Basic class?" Dave asked.

"That's right, Dave," I said. "But remember, a Visual Basic program can run only on a PC that is running Windows. C++ compilers have been written for just about every operating system in existence. C++ code is very transportable, which means code written for the Borland compiler in this class can easily be compiled to run on a Unix or Linux system."

Again I paused to see if there were any questions before continuing. "Using Notepad to write our first C++ program is a snap," I said. "Let's write a C++ program that will display the message, 'I love C++!'"

I then entered the following code into Notepad.

```
/*
   This program displays "I love C++" to the Standard
Output
*/

#include <iostream>

int main ()
{
  std::cout << "I Love C++";
  return 0;
}
```

"Before I discuss this code," I said, "let's save this file first by selecting File | Save As from Notepad's menu bar, which will then display this window."

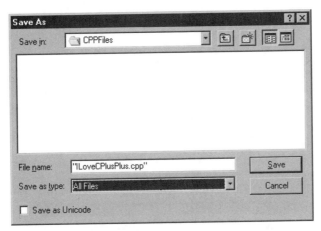

"I like to save all my files in a folder called CPPFiles," I said, "which is why I'm specifying 'CPPFiles' in the 'Save in:' drop-down list box. Notice how I have sandwiched the name of my C++ source file within quotation marks, ensuring that the filename extension ends in cpp. I also need to specify 'All Files' in the 'Save as type' drop-down list box. After clicking the Save button, you should notice that Notepad reflects the new filename."

```
/*
  This program displays "I love C++" to the Standard
Output
*/

#include <iostream>

int main ()
{
  std::cout << "I Love C++";
  return 0;
}
```

"Now that we have a good C++ source file," I said, "our second step is to compile this source file into an executable file. To do that, we need to bring up an operating system command prompt. The command prompt can appear in a number of different places. For instance, it can be a shortcut on the Desktop or it can appear in the Control Panel. If you can't find it, you can just click the Windows Start | Run button, enter **COMMAND.COM** or **CMD**..."

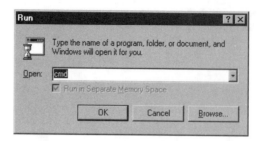

"...and then click the OK button. This will launch the Command Prompt application, and when the application launches, it should look like this."

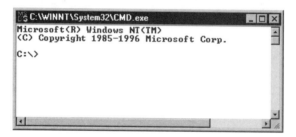

"The prompt shows you the current directory, which is usually 'Windows' for Windows 95/98 or 'WINNT' for Windows NT. To compile our source code file, we need to change the current directory to the folder where our C++ source code file is located. To do that, we enter

```
CD C:\CPPFILES
```

at the command prompt and press ENTER. The prompt will now change to this."

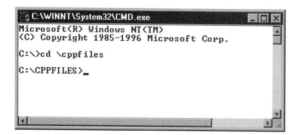

"At this point, we can confirm the location of our C++ source file by entering

```
DIR
```

at the command prompt and pressing ENTER."

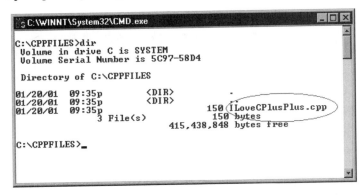

Compile the C++ Source File into an Executable File

"Now we can compile our source file into an executable file," I said, "which is a file that we can then execute to see the results of our program. To do that, we enter

```
bcc32 ILoveCPlusPlus.cpp
```

at the command prompt and then press ENTER."

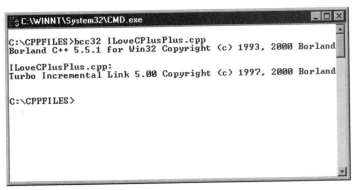

"What happened?" Linda asked. "Are those error messages?"

"We're OK," I answered. "These are normal compiler messages. Generating an executable file from a C++ source file, behind the scenes, is really a two-step process—compilation and then linking. First, the compiler does its work, and that's what the first message is telling us. Then something called a *linker* does its work—and that's what the second message is telling us. Any problems with the C++ source file would manifest themselves in the form of explicit error messages here. We can confirm that our C++ source file has been compiled into an executable file by executing the DIR statement we executed earlier."

```
C:\WINNT\System32\CMD.exe                                        _ □ ×

C:\CPPFILES>dir
 Volume in drive C is SYSTEM
 Volume Serial Number is 5C97-58D4

 Directory of C:\CPPFILES

01/20/01  09:39p      <DIR>          .
01/20/01  09:39p      <DIR>          ..
01/20/01  09:35p                    150 ILoveCPlusPlus.cpp
01/20/01  09:39p                112,640 ILoveCPlusPlus.exe
01/20/01  09:39p                  4,082 ILoveCPlusPlus.obj
01/20/01  09:39p                393,216 ILoveCPlusPlus.tds
               6 File(s)          510,088 bytes
                              414,632,448 bytes free

C:\CPPFILES>_
```

"Notice that our source file has been compiled into an executable file—one ending with the extension .exe."

"What does a linker do?" Blaine asked.

"We'll look at the code in a bit more detail in a moment or two, Blaine," I answered, "but you'll see that writing programs in C++ is frequently a matter of using code that someone else has already written. This code is found in Standard C++ libraries, and the function of a linker is to examine your code for references to those libraries and ensure that your executable file can access those libraries at runtime—in other words, when we run our program."

"What are those other files," Kathy asked, "the ones ending in .obj and .tds"?

"The .tds file is something called a debugging file," I said, "which is a file that can be used to help you discover logic errors in your program. All compilers provide a way to debug your program, but the .tds file is unique to the Borland compiler we're using here in the classroom, and we won't be discussing it here in the class."

"What about the .obj file?" Mary asked.

"The .obj file," I continued, "is an intermediate file produced by the compiler and is the direct result of the compiler's actions on our C++ source file. Do you remember the two messages we receive when we compile a C++ source file? One is from the compiler, and one from the linker. The compiler produces the .obj file, and the linker reads it, adds some additional instructions to it, and then produces the final executable file."

"So there's no way to directly execute the .obj file?" Dave asked.

"Exactly, Dave," I said. "There's no way to execute an .obj file. The linker must first read the .obj file, add some instructions to it, and create an .exe file—that's the file we ultimately execute."

Common Compiler Errors "I've been following along with you," Rhonda said, "but when I tried to compile my source file, I didn't have much luck. I received an error message—

something about not being able to find my file. Does my source file need to be named with the extension .cpp?"

Oops—Could Not Find File   "No, that's not required," I said. "The compiler we're using here in class—and every C++ compiler I've used for that matter—does not require that your C++ source file end in the extension .cpp. Let me check this out for you."

I took a quick walk to Rhonda's workstation. The error was simple enough to fix. She had typed the name of her source file incorrectly. Instead of typing ILoveCPlusPlus, she had typed ILoveCPlusCPlus. The error message indicated that the compiler simply couldn't find the file.

"Wow, thanks. I bet I would have stared at that all morning and not have figured out what was wrong," Rhonda admitted.

"We'll take a look at C++ syntax and language errors as we go through the class," I said, "but compiler errors—when the compiler simply refuses to work as it did here—are pretty rare. The error you just triggered, Rhonda, by trying to compile a source file that doesn't exist, is probably the most common type of compiler error you'll encounter."

Oops—Can't Find the Compiler   "The second most common error is when the operating system can't find the C++ compiler—and that's really a setup issue. In that case, you'll receive this error message when you attempt to compile your source file."

I then intentionally caused the error message that would be displayed if Windows cannot find the C++ compiler.

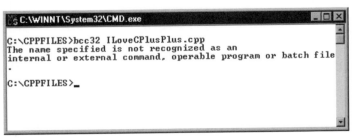

"If you receive this error message, it means the 'path' to your C++ compiler is not properly registered on your computer. This is an installation issue, and you'll need to review the instructions for the setup and installation of your C++ compiler."

NOTE

The Borland C++ compiler that we are using in this class requires that you manually update the PATH environmental setting of the Windows operating system and that you create two configuration files. Instructions for doing so can be found at my web site (http://www.johnsmiley.com/c++/c++.htm).

Run the C++ Program

"Now that we have a C++ executable file—that's the .exe file," I said, "we can now run the program simply by executing this statement at the command prompt."

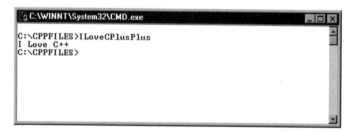

"That worked!" I heard Rhonda say excitedly.

"Why didn't we code '.exe' at the end of the filename?" Kate asked.

"It's not necessary," I answered, "although we could have done it that way. Also, although we went to some trouble to name our program using mixed case—that is, a mixture of upper- and lowercase letters to make the name more readable—we could type the name of the executable like this and the program would still run."

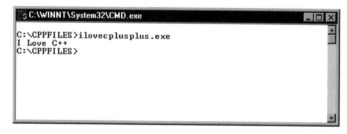

"Is it the compiler that's executing our program now?" Peter asked.

"No, it's the operating system," I said. "In this class, we're compiling our source code into a Windows executable file. It's actually Windows that is running the program when we type its name at the command prompt."

"Are you going to explain this code?" Rose asked.

"You bet, " I answered.

I suggested that because we had been working for a while, it would be a great time to take a break.

Elements of a C++ Program

Fifteen minutes later, I debated with myself as to whether I should begin my discussion of the code with a full-fledged entry into object-oriented programming or whether I should simply explain what the code was doing and then relate it to object-oriented programming—something that can be confusing to beginner students but is something that C++ excels at. Finally, I decided to begin with a simple discussion of the code, so I displayed it on the classroom projector.

```
/*
  This program displays "I Love C++" to the Standard Output
*/

#include <iostream>

int main()
{
   std::cout << "I Love C++";
   return 0;
}
```

Program Comments

"These first three lines of code," I said, "are program comments. Program comments are explanatory statements that you can include in the C++ code that you write. All programming languages allow for some form of comments. The trick is how to tell C++ that the statement you are entering is a comment and not a C++ command. In C++, there are two ways to specify that the code that follows is a comment."

"Is that what the asterisks indicate?" Mary asked. "They remind me of the comments from C."

"That's right, Mary," I said. "These three lines of code do look like comments in the C language."

```
/*
  This program displays "I Love C++!" to the standard output.
*/
```

"This type of comment," I said, "is used whenever your comment spans more than one line, and it's sometimes called a *block comment*. There's also this form of comment in which you tell the compiler to ignore everything that follows the double slash until the end of the line."

```
//  This program displays "I Love C++!" to the standard output.
//  This program written by John Smiley
```

"In this case, the compiler ignores everything from the double forward slashes to the end of the line."

"Can a comment only appear on a line by itself," Dave asked, "or can it follow a C++ statement?"

"You can place a comment after a C++ statement," I answered. "Just follow the C++ statement with the double forward slash characters, like this."

```
std::cout << "I Love C++";        //Displays an output message
```

"Is there a standard format for comments?" Rose asked. "Should they always appear at the top of the code, or can they appear anywhere?"

"I wouldn't say there's a real standard," I answered. "Some programmers include a comment at the 'top' of their code, indicating the author of the program, the date the program was written, and anything else they—or someone reading it later—might find useful. Some programmers never comment their code. Myself, I use comments whenever I write code that I needed to look up in a help file or a reference manual. I figure that if I needed to look it up, then a comment explaining the code will be helpful the next time I or someone else views the code. Some programmers really make their comments elaborate by using asterisks to draw something that is known as a 'flower box' in their code, like this."

```
/*****************************************************************
 * Programmer: John Smiley
 * Date Written: May 1, 2001
 * This program displays "I love C++!" to the standard output.
 *****************************************************************/
```

"I know you said earlier that we would be doing exercises of our own for practice," Kathy said. "Will we be coding comments in the exercises that we do?"

"I've already noticed," I said, "that some of you are not the fastest typists in the world, so our exercises will not explicitly include comments. I'll leave the comments up to you to insert as you complete the exercises."

"Getting back to the intricacies of a comment," Rhonda said, "are you saying that the first three lines of code in our C++ program really don't mean anything? Does C++ just ignore them?"

"Exactly right," I answered. "As far as C++ is concerned, those first three lines of code are meaningless. When the C++ compiler evaluates these lines of code, it doesn't translate them into the executable file. As a result, when we run our executable file, these lines of code are effectively ignored."

No one had any other questions about comments.

The Include Statement

"Let's take a look at the next line of code," I said. "It may be the most important line of code in a C++ program."

```
#include <iostream>
```

"What are we including?" Mary asked. "I presume that's what the word 'include' indicates?"

"You're right, Mary," I said. "Do you remember a little while ago when I indicated that much of what we do in C++ involves executing code that is included in other libraries? That's what is going on here—we're telling the compiler to include the code in the file iostream, just as if we had typed it in ourselves."

"How does the compiler know where to find this file?" Steve asked.

"Files like this," I answered, "called *include files*, are found in a special directory that is established when you install your compiler. Therefore, the C++ compiler knows where to find them. By the way, these include files are also known as *header files*."

"Are there other files that can be included besides iostream?" Valerie asked. "And what would happen if we didn't include it here? What kind of code is in there?"

"Good question, Valerie," I replied. "There are easily over 1,000 include files containing nearly a million lines of code that have been installed on our PCs here in the classroom, each one providing the programs we write with a different piece of functionality that otherwise we would have to write ourselves. As to the particulars of iostream—the letters *io* in iostream refer to input-output, which is a computer term that describes how data is input into our programs and how we get information out of them. If we fail to include the iostream file in our program, we wouldn't be able to display the words 'I Love C++' on our computer monitors. Let me show you."

I then deleted the line of code in my source file referencing iostream and recompiled the program. The following was displayed on the classroom projector.

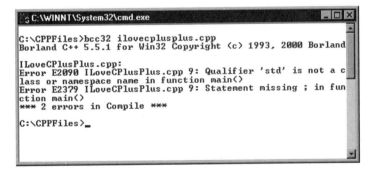

"What's that mean?" Rhonda asked. "It seems to be saying there's a problem with the word 'std.'"

"The problem," I said, "is that std is something called a namespace—and it's included in the file iostream. Because I deleted the reference to iostream, the C++ compiler doesn't know what std, and more importantly, the statement cout, means—and that line of code is how we display our message to the computer's monitor."

"Will you be talking more about namespaces?" Dave asked. "My C++ buddies at work have mentioned that word more than once."

"Yes, we'll be discussing namespaces in just a few more minutes," I replied, "but first I want to discuss the **main**() function."

The main() Function   "I should mention," I continued, "that the program we'll be producing for Frank Olley and the others will actually consist of more than one C++ file. In fact, we'll probably have close to ten files in the final program. One of these files—and one file only—will look similar to the C++ source file we just produced here to display the phrase 'I Love C++' on the computer monitor, in that it will contain a line of code containing the word *main*. In C++ terms, this is the header for the **main()** function, and at least one C++ file in the collection of files making up a program must contain a **main()** function."

"So you're saying that you can have more than one file in a program?" Joe asked.

"That's right, Joe," I said. "In complex C++ programs, you can have thousands. The point is that one of those files—the one we execute from the command prompt—must contain a function called **main()**."

"What about the other files?" Dave asked. "What will they contain?"

"Those files will contain class definitions," I said. "Something you'll be learning about in future classes. Files containing nothing but class definitions are not required to contain a **main()** function."

"What exactly is a function?" Lou asked.

"In programming terms," I said, "a function is a line or lines of code that performs a single task. As you'll learn later on in the course, it's possible—in fact, desirable—to write functions of our own. The **main()** function is a little different. C++ demands that the executable file we execute from the command prompt—what I call the *startup file*—contain a **main()** function. We have no choice but to code one in the startup file. Let's take a closer look at the header for the **main()** function now."

```
int main()
```

"What's 'int'?" Linda asked.

I hesitated as I debated the merits of taking this single line of code apart. I had done so in previous C++ courses I had taught, and the discussion dragged and dragged, so I decided against it. After the fact, my students told me that in the beginning of a C++ class, it's best to keep things moving, and dissecting this single line of code frequently involved many minutes of discussion.

"int refers to something called the *return value* of the **main()** function," I said. "Later on in the course, you'll learn that each function we write must do something called 'return a value,' which is similar to a friend calling you on the telephone to tell you they've arrived safely from a long journey. In this case, we're telling C++ that when the **main()** function wraps up, it will return a value in the form of an integer, which is a whole number."

I looked around for signs of confusion before adding, "If this doesn't make perfect sense to you, don't worry a great deal about it—we'll be examining functions in more detail later on in the course. For now, take my word for it that this line of code is one you must have in each C++ program you write."

"Those lines of code between the curly brackets of the **main()** function," Kate pointed out. "Are they the actual program?"

"That's right, Kate. Everything between the left curly bracket and the right curly bracket here represents the instructions in the **main()** function," I said. "There are two lines of code in this **main()** function. This first line of code, when executed, results in the phrase 'I Love C++' being displayed in the console window. Take note that C++ statements must end in a semicolon, as this one does."

```
std::cout << "I Love C++";
```

"What is 'cout'?" Peter asked.

"cout is actually something called a C++ object," I answered, "and it enables us to direct output to the computer's monitor—or in technical terms, the *standard output*."

"What do the two less-than symbols indicate," Linda asked.

"The two less-than symbols comprise an output-redirection symbol," I said. "When C++ sees them, it knows to direct whatever is on the other side of them—in this case the characters within the quotation marks—to the computer's monitor."

I waited a moment before continuing. "Look at the next line. Do you remember what I said earlier about the return value of the **main()** function?"

"I do," Lou said. "You said that because of the word *int* in the **main()** function header, the **main()** function must return an integer value."

"That's excellent, Lou," I said. "And that's exactly what this line of code is doing—returning an integer value of 0. Notice again that we end the line with a semicolon."

```
return 0;
```

"C++ statements must be terminated with a semicolon."

 NOTE
All C++ statements must end with a semicolon (;).

"Finally, the last line of code completes our work."

```
}
```

"Notice that we have one right curly bracket to mark the end of the **main()** function."

I paused before continuing.

"Ordinarily," I continued, "there would be more than just two C++ statements in the **main()** function. The **main()** function is a section of code where the major instructions of a C++ program are placed. Quite frequently, within the **main()** function, we instantiate objects from classes that have been compiled in other source files."

"Objects?" Joe asked. "Like the cout object we coded here."

"The cout object is one already defined for us and is available as part of the C++ environment," I said. "Later on in the course, you'll learn that we can define objects of our own. We'll define these objects in something called a *class* and then create 'instances' of our objects from the class, much like cookies are created from a cookie cutter. For instance, in our Grade Calculation Project, we'll define a Student class and then create an instance of a Student object from that class."

NOTE
When you instantiate a class, you create an instance of its object.

I could see some puzzled faces, and so I drew this illustration on the class projector.

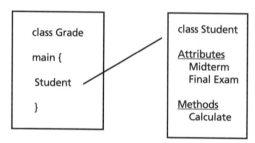

"Most likely," I said, "we'll create a Student class and compile it into a special file called an *hpp file*. An hpp file is similar to the C++ file we just created, except that it contains only a class definition without a **main()** function. We'll then create a C++ file—perhaps we'll call it Grade—and within the **main()** function of that file, instantiate a Student object from the Student class."

"So if I understand you correctly," Dave said, "we'll be working with more than one file."

"That's right, Dave," I said. "In C++, just about everything is a class and an object. They form the building blocks of our programs. It's not unusual for a C++ program to work with dozens of classes and objects—that's fundamental to the language. In a workplace environment, you might have a team of several programmers, each creating classes that form pieces of the larger puzzle. Although everyone in this course will create all the classes and objects for the Grade Calculation Project, because C++ is object oriented, we could assign the creation of the classes that will make up our project to different teams of students, who could each work fairly independently to arrive at the solution to their piece of the puzzle."

"I think I understand," Rhonda said, "but I do have a question. Will all the objects with which we'll work in our C++ program be objects that we create on our own?"

"Not all of them, Rhonda," I answered. "C++ has a bunch of already built classes from which we can instantiate objects. We've already seen one—the cout object. That's one of the reasons the C++ language is so powerful. Suppose tonight, when you open your front door at home, your doorknob were to break. Imagine the dilemma you would face if you couldn't just drive down to your local hardware store and pick up a replacement doorknob. Many of the parts in a home are made from readily available components that can be used to customize a home. The same is true of C++. C++ classes and objects are like the 'objects' you see in a home. Using them is just a matter of knowing what they are, where to find them, and how to install them and work with their attributes and methods."

"There's a new term," Ward said. "What's a method?"

"A method is a function that is contained within a class," I said. "That's the only difference."

NOTE

A method is a function defined within a class.

"Is there a list of these already-built C++ objects anywhere?" Blaine asked.

"There are hundreds of these already-built C++ objects," I said. "The compiler you are using will undoubtedly have some documentation included with it—although the free version we're using here in class, even though it has a help file, doesn't provide a lot of guidance on these objects. But you don't need to concern yourself with that too much in this class. I'll be pointing out and giving you directions on the objects you'll need to use."

"Can we get back to the code you wrote?" Linda asked. "You didn't mention what the word *std*, appearing in front of cout, means."

"Good question, Linda," I answered. "std refers to something known as the Standard namespace, which is contained in the iostream library. Namespaces are subdivisions in libraries and are created to handle potential conflicts with objects and functions within them having identical names. In order to refer to the cout object here in our code, we need to preface the object name with the namespace in which it is contained within the iostream library. There is an alternative to doing this—we can include a namespace directive or declaration in our code instead, like this."

I then displayed this code on the classroom projector.

```
/*
  This program displays "I love C++" to the Standard Output
*/

#include <iostream>

int main ()
{
  using namespace std;

  cout << "I Love C++";
  return 0;
}
```

"The line of code

```
using namespace std;
```

contained in the **main()** function is called a *namespace declaration.* It allows us to refer to the cout object without prefacing the name of the std namespace."

```
cout << "I Love C++";
```

"C++ experts will tell you, however, that the namespace directive

```
using namespace std::cout;
```

is even better in that it restricts the scope of the namespace included in our program. This line of code allows us to use cout without having to include 'std' in front of it, but doesn't do the same for any other objects in that namespace—in programming terms, you want to include in your program only as much additional information as necessary."

"You used two new terms—declaration and directive. Did you make a mistake?" Linda asked.

"Good observation, Linda," I said. "When you use the using statement with an entire namespace, that's called a 'using directive.' When you restrict the namespace the way we just did here with cout, that's called a 'using declaration.' It's a fine distinction, but you may come upon it in the C++ documentation."

"How important is indentation?" Ward asked. "And you mentioned that C++ is case sensitive—I guess my question is, How case sensitive is it?"

"C++ is very case sensitive," I replied. "You need to be very careful about the spelling of object names in C++. For instance, the line of code

```
std::cout << "I Love C++";
```

is not the same as this line."

```
std::Cout << "I Love C++";
```

"Spelling 'cout' as 'Cout' will cause C++ not to be able to find its definition in the std library," I said, "thus resulting in a compiler error."

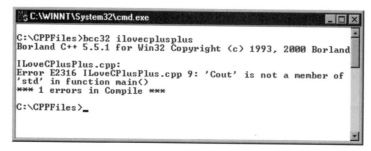

"In the same way, spelling 'std' as 'Std' will result in the same error. I tell my students that if they receive a compiler error indicating that an object is not a member of something, or that an object is not a class or namespace, check the spelling of those object names immediately—they must match exactly the way they are specified in the C++ help files. Later on, when we learn more about functions, you'll find that C++ is equally 'picky' about the spelling of those names also."

"What about indentation?" Ward asked. "I noticed that some of the code is indented?"

"Indentation and blank lines in code are ignored by the C++ compiler," I said. "For instance, I know it's a far-fetched example, but we could have written this entire program as a single line of code."

"How important is indentation?" Blaine asked.

"Indentation is important for readability," I said. "That is, you want other programmers to be able to read your code as easily as possible, and indenting the way we did here can make it easier for someone who understands the language to more easily pick out where a class definition begins and ends, and the functions within a class."

"What is white space?" Kate asked. "Some of the C++ programmers in work refer to this from time to time."

"White space refers to space between C++ statements, and blank lines in the code," I answered. "You can use white space, as you can with indentation, to make your code more readable. For instance, the code

```
std::cout << "I Love C++";
```

using white space could look like this and still function in the same way."

```
std::cout <<    "I Love C++";   return 0;
```

"The thing to remember is that you don't want to go to one extreme or another with this. Although it's possible to write a C++ program on a single line, it would be very difficult to read it. And although you can insert lots of white space in your program, most programmers like the condensed nature of their program code, so you won't see a lot of blank lines and spaces in their code."

"Will we be learning about inheritance, encapsulation, polymorphism, and some of those other object-oriented terms I've heard about?" Bob asked.

"We will," I said, "but not in today's class. We'll save those for a few weeks down the line."

"Is there a continuation character in C++ like there is in Visual Basic?" Rose asked. "In Visual Basic, if we want to split up a long line of code into two pieces, we use an underscore. Does C++ have something similar?"

"Because of the 'white space' nature of C++ code," I answered, "if you want to split up a single line of code into two or more lines, just hit the ENTER key—C++ doesn't care. For instance, the line of code

```
std::cout << "I Love C++";
```

can be broken up into two lines of code, like this."

```
std::cout <<
    "I Love C++";
```

"The only place you can't 'split' the line is within the middle of a quoted string—the code between the quotation marks that is displayed on the console. For instance, this code would result in a syntax error."

```
std::cout << "I
  Love C++";
```

I waited to see if there were any other questions, but no one seemed to have any more.

"What I'd like to do now," I said, "is to give you a chance to write, compile, and run a C++ program of your own—with my assistance. As we'll do during the remainder of the course, I have a series of exercises for you to complete that will lead you through the process."

I then distributed this exercise for the class to complete.

| Exercise 2-1 | **Coding Your first C++ Program—Grades.cpp** |

In this exercise, you'll write your first C++ program, which will form the basis of our class project.

1. Create a folder on your hard drive called \CPPFiles\Grades. This will be the "home" of our class project, the Grades Calculation Project.

2. Using the editor of your choice (if you are using Windows, use Notepad), enter the following code (be *extremely* careful of the capitalization):

```
//Grades.cpp
#include <iostream>

int main ()
{
  using namespace std;

  cout << "It's not much, but it's a start!";
  return 0;
}
```

3. Save your source file as Grades.cpp in the \CPPFiles\Grades folder (select File | Save As from Notepad's menu bar). Be sure to save your source file with the filename extension "cpp".

Discussion Aside from some people in the class who didn't seem very familiar with Notepad, this exercise went pretty smoothly. In just a few moments, everyone in the class had completed coding their first C++ program—the Grades program. This source file, although very simplistic, would eventually form the basis of the program we would give to Frank, Robin, and Dave.

"Is this the program we'll be using to calculate grades for the English, Math, and Science departments?" Mary asked. "It looks like all this does is display a message to the console."

"That's right, Mary," I said. "Have you heard the expression that the journey of a thousand miles begins with the first step? This is the first step—the creation of the Grades class. From there, everything else will be built. And even though displaying this message isn't part of the user requirements, I want the program to do 'something' when you compile and run it—just to prove to you that there is some activity going on in there."

There were no questions about the actual coding of the class. It was almost identical to the example we had been working on. So, I distributed this exercise for the class to complete.

Exercise 2-2 ## Compiling Grades.cpp

In this exercise you'll compile the C++ source file you created in Exercise 2-1, Grades.cpp, into an executable file called Grades.exe.

1. Bring up the MS-DOS command prompt. You can do this in a number of ways—one easy way is to select Start | Run and enter **cmd** in the Open text box.

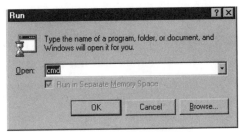

2. At the command prompt, change to the directory (folder) containing your Grades.cpp source file by entering

   `CD C:\CPPFILES\GRADES`

   and pressing the ENTER key (pressing the ENTER key is necessary for all of the command-prompt steps).

   NOTE
   If you saved your source file to another drive, substitute that drive letter for C.

3. Confirm the existence and location of your C++ source file by entering

DIR

at the command prompt and pressing ENTER. You should see an entry for Grades.cpp, similar to the following illustration.

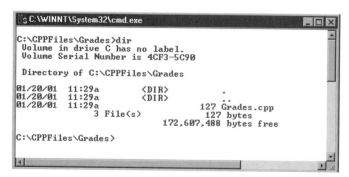

If you don't see your source file, something went wrong in Exercise 2-1, and you will need to verify your work there before proceeding.

4. Compile your Grades.cpp file by entering

bcc32 Grades.cpp

at the command prompt and pressing ENTER. You should see two informational messages—one from the compiler and one from the linker. The absence of any error messages will indicate that your source file has been compiled into an executable file.

5. Confirm the existence of your C++ executable file by entering

DIR

at the command prompt and pressing ENTER. You should see an entry for Grades.exe, as in the following illustration.

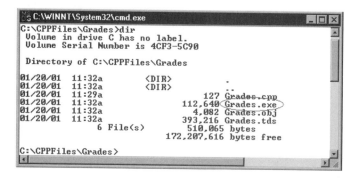

Discussion As smoothly and easily as the first exercise had seemed to have gone, this one was the opposite—over half of the students in the class had problems of one form or other compiling their first C++ program. The typical errors were the ones I had warned everyone about just a few minutes earlier, but warning students about problems is different from having them experience them on their own—experience is the great teacher—and so I gave everyone a lot of time to try to complete this exercise on their own.

"I just can't get this thing to compile," Rhonda complained. "This exercise seemed simple enough—I can't believe I'm having so much trouble with it. The compiler keeps telling me I haven't coded cout, but it's there."

I took a quick walk to Rhonda's workstation. In her Command Prompt window was the following message.

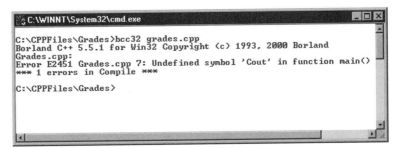

```
C:\WINNT\System32\cmd.exe

C:\CPPFiles\Grades>bcc32 grades.cpp
Borland C++ 5.5.1 for Win32 Copyright (c) 1993, 2000 Borland
Grades.cpp:
Error E2451 Grades.cpp 7: Undefined symbol 'cout' in function main()
*** 1 errors in Compile ***

C:\CPPFiles\Grades>_
```

"That one's easy, Rhonda," I said. "Although most beginners wouldn't notice this, you're referencing cout, but you forgot to tell C++ where to find it. You haven't coded the using namespace statement. Either that, or you need to explicitly tell C++ where to find the cout object by changing the line of code

```
cout << "It's not much, but it's a start!";
```

to this."

```
std::cout << "It's not much, but it's a start!";
```

Sure enough, as soon as Rhonda coded the using namespace statement, her C++ source file was successfully compiled into an executable file, and a big smile appeared on her face.

Next was Ward. This is the error message his PC was displaying.

```
C:\WINNT\System32\cmd.exe

C:\CPPFiles\Grades>bcc32 grades.cpp
Borland C++ 5.5.1 for Win32 Copyright (c) 1993, 2000 Borland
Grades.cpp:
Error E2451 Grades.cpp 7: Undefined symbol 'Cout' in function main()
*** 1 errors in Compile ***

C:\CPPFiles\Grades>
```

Dave, who had successfully compiled his source file already, knew immediately what the problem was.

"I see the problem," Dave said.

"Well, don't just stand there, Dave," Ward said smiling, "what is it?"

"You spelled 'cout' with a capital C," Dave said. "The C++ cout object is spelled in all lowercase letters—same thing happened to me."

"I think," Ward added "that's because we're used to objects in some of the other languages we've used—such as Java—beginning with an uppercase letter."

Dave was right, and I took this opportunity to call out to the rest of the class that attention to case sensitivity would be crucial during the class. Ward brought up Notepad, made the change to his source file, and then compiled it. He, too, was shortly happy, as his program compiled successfully.

On the way back to my PC at the front of the classroom, I passed Kate's PC and saw her staring at this error message.

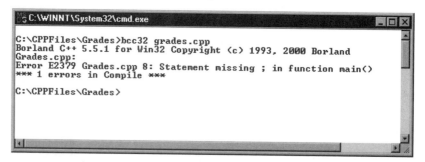

"Need help?" I asked her.

"I've been trying to correct this for the last ten minutes," she said. "This isn't nearly as easy as Visual Basic, is it?"

"C++ requires a lot more attention to detail," I said, "Actually, this is a fairly common error. Remember, in C++, statements need to end with a semicolon. This error message indicates that somewhere in your program you didn't end a statement with one."

Kate smiled, then found the line of code missing the semicolon, added it, and recompiled her program successfully. Everyone else in the class who had been having problems managed to fix them on their own, and for the most part, they were either the errors I noted here or variations thereof.

I did spot something in Steve's source file that had not prevented the program from compiling but that might cause a problem down the road. At this point, everyone had a compiled executable file, and they were anxiously looking forward to running their program. I then distributed this exercise for them to complete.

Exercise 2-3   ### Executing (Running) Grades.exe

In this exercise you'll run the program you created in Exercise 2-2, Grades.exe.

1. Bring up the MS-DOS Command Prompt application.

2. At the command prompt, change to the directory (folder) containing your Grades.cpp source file.

3. Run your program by entering

   `Grades`

   at the command prompt, and pressing ENTER. You should see the following displayed in your Command Prompt window.

Discussion   As dejected as some members of the class had been while completing the previous exercise, this one produced just the opposite effect—just about everyone's program ran on their first attempt. The only one who had a problem was Peter, who apparently had missed a compiler error message and believed he had a compiled file that he could execute. His problem was relatively easy to fix. Like Kate, he had missed a semicolon, and after correcting this mistake and compiling his program, it worked fine.

"I know we haven't done all that much," Rhonda said, "but I feel pretty good about what we've done so far. My programming friends all told me how difficult C++ was—but so far, so good."

"C++ can be difficult," I said, "but as you know, here at the university we have a reputation for doing a pretty good job with beginners. One step at a time, I always say, and the next logical step in next week's class will be to give you a C++ code overview to show you what the language can do."

It had been a very productive class—everyone now had the beginnings of the Grades Calculation Program in place. It had also been a pretty long class, and as I glanced up at the clock on the wall, I realized our class was over. I then dismissed class for the day.

Summary

In this chapter you were exposed to the "nitty-gritty" of the C++ environment. You saw that writing a program in C++ is pretty basic. You use an editor to create a C++ source file, compile the program from a command prompt using the C++ compiler, and then run the program from that same command prompt by typing in the name of the executable file.

In the next chapter, you'll learn about computer data—and how your C++ program works with it.

I n a computer program, data is extremely important. As you learned in Chapter 1, data is input into a computer program to be processed into meaningful output. In this chapter, we'll discuss the concept of data in a computer program. You'll learn about program variables, constants, the different types of C++ data types, and the many operations that can be performed on that data.

Computer Data

"Data can be a very complex topic," I said to the class at our third meeting, "but it's an extremely important one. Failure to understand data can lead to problems with your programs down the line. What you learn today may seem very theoretical to you, but it will be vital for your future programming career. Even if you don't see an immediate application for it, look at the information you receive today as something that you can tuck into your programming back pocket for future use."

Variables

"In the C++ programs that we write," I said, "the data with which we work will come from three places: the user, in the form of selections that they make, either via a console program or selections from objects in a window; external sources, such as disk files or databases; and sometimes internal sources in the form of variables."

"Variables?" Rhonda asked.

I explained that variables are placeholders in the computer's memory where we can temporarily store information. Values—numbers and characters, for example—are stored in variables while the program is running. As the name implies, the values of the variables can change at any time.

"I'm a little confused as to why we would create a variable in the first place," Barbara said. "Isn't all the data that we need—especially in the program we're writing in this class—entered by the user? Why do we need to store anything temporarily?"

"That's a good question, Barbara," I said. "And to a great degree, you're right. Most of the data that computer programs need is entered by the user, or it comes from a disk file or database. However, there may be times when your program will need to create and use a variable to store the answer to a question that you have asked of the user or the result of a calculation, or, as you'll see a little later on in today's class, to keep track of a counter, which is a variable that counts something."

"You said that variables enable us to store information temporarily," Kate said. "I assume that means until our program ends. A variable can't last beyond the running of a program, can it?"

"For the most part that's true, Kate," I said. "In most other programming languages, variables are born when the program in which they appear starts to execute and die when that program ends. But C++ is a little different. C++ has a special type of variable called a *static* variable, which you'll see a little later on in the course when you learn how to create classes. Today, we'll be concentrating our learning efforts on the *local* variable, which is a variable declared in a function.

There are three other types of variables that you can create in C++: global variables, which are variables declared outside of a function; class variables, technically called *member variables*, which are variables declared in a C++ class; and static variables, as I just mentioned."

Our First Variable: The Local Variable

I asked everyone to consider a hypothetical program that I hoped would illustrate the need for variables in a program.

"Let's write a C++ program," I said, "to take two numbers and display their sum in the console. Later on in the course (next week, in fact), you'll learn that there are ways for the user to communicate with our running program, but for now, the best we can do is to declare two numeric variables, assign values to them, and then display their sum in the console. I should warn you that most of what you will see in this program you haven't learned yet, but you will today."

I then displayed this program on the classroom projector:

```cpp
//Example3_1.cpp
#include <iostream>

int main()
{
   using namespace std;
   int number1;
   int number2;
   number1 = 12;
   number2 = 23;

   cout << (number1 + number2);
   return 0;
}
```

I saved the program as Example3_1.cpp, compiled it, and ran it for the class. The following screen was displayed on the classroom projector:

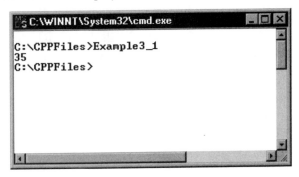

"Let me explain what's going on here," I said. "The first thing we did was to tell C++ that we would be using the iostream library in our program."

```
#include <iostream>
```

"After that comes the first line of the **main()** function. Every C++ program that runs directly from the command prompt *must* have a function named **main()**."

```
int main()
```

"What exactly do you mean by that?" Kate asked. "Are you implying there are some C++ programs that won't be executed directly from the command prompt?"

"That's right, Kate," I answered. "As you'll see later on in the course, some C++ code we'll write will be *classes*, which are not required to contain a **main()** function. Classes can't be run directly from the command prompt. Last week we created our first piece of the class project puzzle, the Grades.cpp file, which we compiled into the Grades.exe file. As you saw last week, the Grades executable file is executed from the command prompt. As the course progresses, and you begin to learn more about the object-oriented nature of C++, we'll create C++ class files called Student, EnglishStudent, MathStudent, and ScienceStudent. The Grades executable file will instantiate objects from these classes but won't actually have the code for the classes included in it."

 NOTE
It is possible to include the code for classes in your C++ executable file. However, in the real world of programming, code for classes is kept in separate files. This makes changing or updating the behavior of the class much easier.

"In other words," Dave said, "the code in the classes won't be executed directly from the command prompt."

"Exactly, Dave," I said. "A C++ application may consist of many files, but only one of them, the C++ file containing the **main()** function, will be executed directly from the command prompt. Others, such as the class files I cited here, will have objects instantiated from their classes from within the executable file."

I waited to see if anyone had any other questions before continuing.

"The next line of code we saw last week," I said. "It's the line of code that tells the compiler that we'll be using the std namespace in our program. Using the namespace statement means we won't need to preface our C++ statement with the word *std*."

```
using namespace std;
```

Declaring a Variable

"This next line of code," I said, "declares an integer type variable called *number1*. We'll be discussing exactly what an integer is in just a few moments. In C++, we need to notify the compiler that we intend to use some of our computer's memory to hold data—and that's what it means to declare a variable."

```
int number1;
```

"In a similar way, this next line of code declares an integer type variable called *number2*."

```
int number2;
```

Assigning a Value to a Variable

"Now that we've informed C++ that we wish to have two integer variables in our program called *number1* and *number2*, these next two lines of code assign values to those variables."

```
number1 = 12;
number2 = 23;
```

"Because both of these variables are declared within a function—the **main**() function—they are called *local* variables. That means that the variables and the values they contain can only be seen or accessed by code within the **main**() function. In fact, this next line of code is doing exactly that—accessing the values of the variables *number1* and *number2*, adding them together, and displaying the result in the console using the cout object you learned about last week."

```
    cout << (number1 + number2);
    return 0;
}
```

"What's going on with those parentheses?" Rhonda asked. "Last week when we used the cout object, we had 'I love C++!' inside quotation marks. This is different. And why didn't the words *number1* and *number2* appear in the console?"

"In this case, Rhonda," I answered, "we are telling C++ to take the *value* of the variables *number1* and *number2*, add them together, and then display them in the console. The parentheses tell C++ to perform the addition prior to displaying the values in the console."

"That makes sense," Blaine said. "Although I must confess, I'm still not totally clear on this concept of a variable."

NOTE

In C++, variable names must start with either a letter or an underscore and may not contain spaces.

"I like to compare a variable," I said, "to a post office box. When you rent a post office box, you are assigned a box number. When mail for your box arrives, the postal clerk places your mail in your box according to the number you've been assigned. If you need to retrieve your mail, you can use your key to access it because you know the number of your box. Variables in C++ are very similar. When you declare a variable, you use the syntax

```
int number1;
```

which tells C++ that you wish to declare an integer type variable with the name *number1*. This is similar to going to the post office and renting a box. The great thing about C++ (and other programming languages as well) is that you can give the variable an easy-to-remember name that you can recognize later. You don't need to work with a hard-to-remember post office box number. Thereafter, whenever you need to interact with the variable, you use its easy-to-remember name, as we did when we assigned a value to *number1* using the C++ assignment statement."

```
number1 = 12;
```

"We also did this when we used the variables with the cout object."

```
cout << (number1 + number2);
```

"Do you need to assign a value to a variable after you've declared it?" Chuck asked. "In other words, do you have to initialize it? I presume you have to declare a variable before you use it."

NOTE

Assigning an initial value to a variable is called initialization.

"Excellent question," I said. "You're right, Chuck. You must first declare a variable before you can use it, and although it's good practice to initialize the values of your variables, the C++ compiler doesn't force you to do so."

NOTE

The Borland C++ compiler won't complain at all if you don't initialize your variables. The Microsoft C++ compiler will display a warning message but still compiles your program.

"What would happen if we didn't initialize the variables *number1* and *number2*?" Mary asked. "Would the number 0 be displayed? Are each of the variables considered to have a value of zero?"

"Some languages are like that," I replied, "but C++ is different. Let me show you."

I then modified our program to look like this:

```
//Example3_2.cpp
#include <iostream>

int main()
{
   using namespace std;
   int number1;
   int number2;

   cout << (number1 + number2);
   return 0;
}
```

"Notice how I've removed the two lines of code that initialize the values of our variables," I said. I then saved the program as Example3_2.cpp, compiled it, and ran it for the class. The following screen was displayed on the classroom projector:

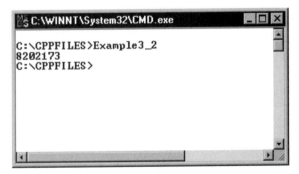

"What happened?" Ward asked. "Shouldn't the answer be zero?"

"You're assuming Ward," I said, "that the value of an uninitialized variable in C++ is zero. In reality, in the C++ world, the value of an uninitialized variable, as we see here, can be anything."

NOTE

Depending on the compiler you are using, you may not see the results you see in this screenshot.

"So the lesson to be learned here," Blaine said, "is never to forget to initialize your variables."

"That's right, Blaine," I said. "Some languages do initialize the value of variables for you, but C++ doesn't. You need to do that for yourself. Having to be responsible for details like this is very common in C++. As your experience in C++ grows, you'll find that the language gives you much more control than other programming languages. On the other hand, it also expects you to take much more responsibility for the 'little things' that other programming languages do for you."

Declaration and Assignment Combined

"I think some languages permit you to combine the declaration and assignment of a value to a variable," Dave said. "Can you do that in C++?"

"Yes, you can combine them, Dave." I answered. "Here's Example3_1 using that technique." I entered and displayed this program on the classroom projector:

```
//Example3_3.cpp
#include <iostream>

int main()
{
    using namespace std;
    int number1 = 12;
    int number2 = 23;

    cout << (number1 + number2);
    return 0;
}
```

"Programmers," I said, "frequently look for ways to streamline their code. This is one way to do it."

```
int number1 = 12;
```

"One more thing I'd like to show you," I said, "is how to make our output in the console a little more user friendly." I displayed this code on the classroom projector:

```
//Example3_4.cpp
#include <iostream>

int main()
{
    using namespace std;

    int number1 = 12;
    int number2 = 23 ;
```

```
    cout << "The answer is \n";
    cout << (number1 + number2);
    return 0;
}
```

I then saved the program as Example3_4.cpp, compiled it, and ran it for the class. The following screen was displayed on the classroom projector:

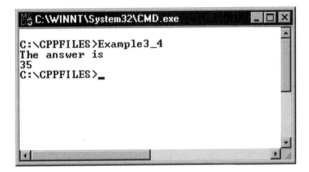

"I'm pretty confused with this," Rhonda said. "What's going on?"

"In this case," I said, "we're using the cout object to display both a message—'The answer is'—and the value of a variable to the console."

"I'm okay with that," Kate said. "I presume that the text contained within the quotation marks is displayed on the console. Is that right?"

"Exactly, Kate," I said. "Text that appears within quotation marks is called a *string literal,* and as the name implies, it's displayed literally on the console."

"What's the purpose of the backslash and the letter *n* ?" Barbara asked.

"That combination of characters is called a newline character," I said, "it's the text representation for hitting the ENTER key in your program—it tells C++ to insert a new line after the word *is.* The result is that the number 35 is printed on a line by itself."

"I was wondering how that happened," Ward said. "So far, you're right. It seems that C++ doesn't do anything without you explicitly telling it to. I was wondering how we managed to get the number 35 on a new line."

"So without the 'backlash n,' the newline character," Rhonda said, "the number 35 would appear on the same line with the text?"

"That's right, Rhonda," I said. "Let me show you."

I then displayed this code on the classroom projector:

```
//Example3_5.cpp
#include <iostream>
```

```
int main()
{
   using namespace std;

   int number1 = 12;
   int number2 = 23 ;

   cout << "The answer is ";
   cout << (number1 + number2);
   return 0;
}
```

I then saved the program as Example3_5.cpp, compiled it, and ran it for the class. The following screen was displayed on the classroom projector:

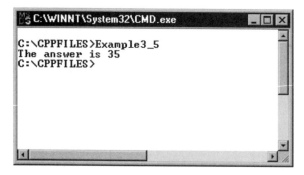

"Notice," I said, "that the number 35—the result of the addition of the values of the variables *number1* and *number2*—is displayed on the same line as the phrase 'The answer is.' That's the difference not including the newline character makes."

"I've been following along with you and doing pretty well so far," Rhonda said, "but when I compile and run my version of the program, I don't have a space between the word *is* and number 35. Can you tell me what I did wrong?"

"Did you include a space after the word *is* in your string literal?" I asked. "I bet you put your ending quotation mark right after the word *is*. My version looks like this."

```
cout << "The answer is ";
```

"I bet yours looks like this."

```
cout << "The answer is";
```

"You're absolutely right," Rhonda said. "I guess I thought C++ might insert that space automatically."

"As Blaine pointed out a little while ago," I replied, "C++ doesn't do anything you don't tell it to do. If you want text to appear on a new line in the console, you need to use the newline character. If you want a space to appear between a word and the value of your variable, you need to include a space somewhere."

"Could we combine the code that writes to the console onto one line?" Rose asked.

"Sure thing, Rose," I said, as I displayed this code on the classroom projector.

```cpp
//Example3_6.cpp
#include <iostream>

int main()
{
    using namespace std;

    int number1 = 12;
    int number2 = 23 ;

    cout << "The answer is " << (number1 + number2);
    return 0;
}
```

"Do you see how we used the redirection symbol here?" I asked. "The line of code

```cpp
cout << "The answer is " << (number1 + number2);
```

takes the place of the previous version, which required two lines of code to do the same thing."

"Which version is better?" Kate asked.

"C++ programmers tend to think that less is best," I said. "However, from my perspective as a teacher, I prefer that my students write code that they will understand a week from now—which version that is, is entirely up to you."

"Is it possible to declare more than one variable on the same line of code?" Steve asked.

"Yes, you can, Steve," I said. "In fact, you can declare and initialize more than one variable on the same line of code, provided they are all the same data type, like this."

```cpp
int number1 = 12, number2 = 23;
```

"What are the rules for naming a variable?" Jack asked.

"Variables can begin with any letter of the alphabet or with an underscore," I said, "but may not begin with a number, although a name can contain a number. Variable names can be of any length. But remember this: Variables with long names make coding more difficult, because invariably you'll need to refer to the variable again somewhere in your code. Make your variable names short but meaningful. You should also avoid single-character variable names such as *x*, unless it's what programmers sometimes refer to as a *throwaway variable*—that is, a variable that is used locally only within a function and has no meaning outside of it."

I waited to see if there were any other questions before proceeding.

"You mentioned that there are three other types of variables that we can declare in C++," Barbara said. "Will you be showing us those today?"

"We'll be examining the global variable in a minute," I said. "We'll look at the other two—class variables and static variables—when we start to get deeper into creating our own classes and objects."

A Quick Look at the Global Variable

"The global variable," I continued, "as the name implies, is a variable that can be seen 'globally.' In the case of a C++ program, that means the variable is declared outside of any function, and because of that, the variable can be accessed—updated and retrieved—from any function in the program. In order to demonstrate a global variable, I'll need to create a program with two functions—one called **main()**, the other **smiley()**—and show you why global variables are important."

I then displayed this code on the classroom projector:

```
//Example3_7.cpp
#include <iostream>

void smiley();          //function prototype
int main()
{
   using namespace std;
   smiley();
   cout << "The value of number within main is " << number;
   return 0;
}

void smiley()
{
   using namespace std;

   int number = 44;
   cout <<"smiley has executed and \n";
   cout <<"the value of number is " << number << "\n";
}
```

"There are a couple of new things I've introduced here," I said. "The first is, when you create a function other than **main()** in your program, you need to do something called 'create a function prototype.' This lets the compiler know that the function **smiley**() will appear later on in our code. We'll discuss this in more detail later on in the course, but here is the function prototype for the function **smiley**()."

```
void smiley();           //function prototype
```

"Again, we'll discuss creating our own functions—and function prototypes—later on in the course. Here's the code for the **smiley**() function itself."

```
void smiley()
{
   using namespace std;

   int number = 44;
   cout <<"smiley has executed and \n";
   cout <<"the value of number is " << number << "\n";
}
```

"Notice that we've declared a local variable called *number* and assigned it a value of 44. No problem there—the problem comes in the **main**() function when we try to refer to the variable declared in **smiley**()."

```
int main()
{
   using namespace std;
   smiley();
   cout << "The answer is " << number;
   return 0;
}
```

"If we compile this program, the C++ compiler will give us an error message."
I did exactly that, and the following error message was displayed on the classroom projector:

```
C:\WINNT\System32\cmd.exe                                    _ □ X

C:\CPPFILES>bcc32 Example3_7.cpp
Borland C++ 5.5.1 for Win32 Copyright (c) 1993, 2000 Borland

Example3_7.cpp:
Error E2451 Example3_7.cpp 9: Undefined symbol 'number' in f
unction main()
*** 1 errors in Compile ***

C:\CPPFILES>
```

"What's the problem?" Blaine asked. "It looks like you're executing the **smiley()** function, which then assigns a value to *number*. Why can't we refer to the value of the *number* variable declared in **smiley()** within the **main()** function?"

"You're right, Blaine," I said. "We are executing the **smiley()** function. However, in C++, variables declared in a function are local to that function, which means the variable and its value cannot be accessed from outside the function."

"So what are we to do?" Kate asked. "I can foresee needing to see the value of a variable in another function."

"If you need to 'share' variables across functions like this," I replied, "you can use a global variable, which is a variable declared outside of a function. Global variables, and their values, can be accessed from all the functions in your program. Look at this code."

I then displayed the following code on the classroom projector:

```cpp
//Example3_8.cpp
#include <iostream>

int number;

void smiley();          //function prototype
int main()
{
   using namespace std;
   smiley();
   cout << "The value of number within main is " << number;
   return 0;
}

void smiley()
{
   using namespace std;

   number = 44;
   cout <<"smiley has executed and \n";
   cout <<"the value of number is " << number << "\n";
}
```

I then saved the program as Example3_8.cpp, compiled it, and ran it for the class. The following screen was displayed on the classroom projector:

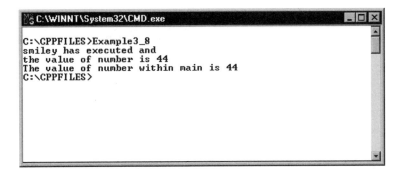

"As you can see," I said, "we received no error messages when we compiled the program. Also, when we ran our program, both the **main()** function and the **smiley()** function were able to access the same variable—that's the beauty of a global variable."

"So *number* is a global variable because it appears above the **main()** function?" Rhonda asked.

"That's right, Rhonda," I said. "In C++, global variables are declared outside of any function, and they must be located 'above' the **main()** function if you want to use them in the main function. That's generally true, by the way. In C++ you have to alert the compiler to what's coming before you use it."

"Is that sort of the reason why you had to include that function prototype?" Kate asked.

"Pretty much," I replied, "but don't worry, I'll still show that to you later, as promised."

Variable Scope and Lifetime

"I think I understand what a variable is and what it's used for," Rhonda said. "But what do the programmers I work with mean when they talk about variable scope and lifetime?"

"Scope and lifetime?" Chuck asked, adding emphasis to Rhonda's question.

"Scope," I said, "refers to what parts of your C++ program can see the variable you've declared. As we just saw here, a variable declared in the **smiley()** function has local 'scope'—it can't be 'seen' from within the **main()** function. Global variables, on the other hand, can be 'seen' by code in any function. As I've mentioned, some C++ programs that we write will consist of a program containing a **main()** function, which then creates or instantiates objects from special C++ files called *classes*. Classes can also contain variables—these technically are called *data members*. In the case of a class, scope also describes whether a class variable—a data member—declared in Class1 can be seen from the **main()** function that creates an object from it, or whether a data member declared in Class2 can be seen from Class1. Unlike the behavior of a local variable, which is always 'local,' and unlike the behavior of a global variable, which is always 'global,' variables declared in a class (data members) can be declared so that they can either be seen or not be seen outside the class, depending upon whether they are declared with the Private or Public keyword."

> **NOTE**
> *Confused? Don't be too concerned at this point. We'll be discussing classes later on in the book, and I guarantee you'll be comfortable with the notions of Private and Public at that point.*

"Sounds confusing," Peter said. "All this talk of classes—what exactly are they, and when will we learn about them?"

"Classes are what make C++ object oriented," I said. "You'll learn about classes during the last half of the course."

"I'm a little confused," Rhonda said. "Is local scope a good thing or a bad thing?"

"The rule of thumb," I said, "is to give your variable as narrow a scope as possible. Provided your variable's value does not need to be accessible to code in other functions, local scope is a good thing. On the other hand, if you need to have the value of that variable accessible from another function in your program, then that's..."

"...a bad thing!" Rhonda answered, finishing my sentence, and obviously understanding what I was getting at. "Okay, I think I'm beginning to understand. Declaring variables requires a bit more thought than I believed."

"If you wanted to make the value of that variable visible to other functions in your class," Steve said, "that's when you would declare it outside of your functions, above the **main**() function."

"What about lifetime?" Lou asked.

"Lifetime refers to how long a variable, once declared, lives," I said. "Again, as was the case with scope, this will depend on the type of variable that you declare. Local variables exist for as long as the function is executing. As soon as the function ends, the variable—and its value—goes away. Global variables exist for as long as the program itself is running. And variables declared inside of a class exist for as long as the object, created from the class, exists. And static variables are the most interesting of all: These variables exist as long as *any* object created from their template or blueprint exists. You'll learn more about these in a future class."

"Can I ask a question that I'm not entirely sure is on-topic?" Barbara asked. "You keep talking about objects—and I know I'll become more comfortable with these as time goes by—but where exactly do these objects exist?"

"Objects exist in the computer's memory," I said. "I know the name sounds intimidating, but you'll see, when we start creating objects of our own, that objects actually consist of data and functions (instructions) that are designed to operate on that data. When objects are created from a class, they are set up in the computer's memory, much like a variable, with space made available for their data and for their functions. As long as a program maintains a reference to an object— that is, the program is using the object in some way by executing its code or referring to its data—the computer's operating system maintains a reference to it. When no programs are referring to the object any longer (it's possible for more than one program to refer to the same object), the operating system decides the object is no longer being referenced and uses the space it occupied in memory for something else. Does that help?"

 NOTE

A reference is a pointer to an object in the computer's memory.

"That's a little better," Barbara answered, "but, like a lot of things, your answer has generated more questions in my mind. But I'll hold off on those for a while."

I didn't dissuade her. C++ is highly object oriented, and when it comes to objects, everyone (beginners and experienced programmers alike) need some time to acquire a comfort level. My experience teaching C++ indicated that time and practice would eventually give my students this comfort level.

Constants

"So far," I said, "we've spent most of this class looking at variables, which are placeholders in memory, given an easy-to-remember name. Variables contain values that can change. Now it's time to take a look at constants."

"Constants?" Linda asked. "That sounds like they should be the opposite of variables."

"You're absolutely right, Linda," I said. "Still, a constant is similar to a variable in that it is a placeholder in the computer's memory that's given an easy-to-remember name and holds a value. Unlike a variable, however, once you assign a value to a constant, its value can never be changed."

"How are constants declared?" Peter asked.

"You declare a constant in a manner similar to a variable," I answered. "In C++, you use the keyword const to designate a constant, like this."

I entered the following code and displayed it on the classroom projector:

```
//Example3_9.cpp
#include <iostream>

int main()
{
    using namespace std;

    int number1 = 12;
    const int BOOSTER = 100;

    cout << "The answer is " << (number1 + BOOSTER);
    return 0;
}
```

I then saved the program as Example3_9.cpp, compiled it, and ran it for the class. The following screen was displayed on the classroom projector:

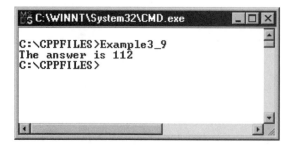

"It's this line of code that tells C++ that BOOSTER is a constant," I said.

```
const int BOOSTER = 100;
```

"In many languages" I continued, "constants are named using all capital letters, and that's my preference with C++. Once we've declared and initialized the constant, we can use it in our code in the same way we would a variable. In this case, we take the value of the constant BOOSTER, add it to the value of the variable *number1*, and display the result in the console."

"What's the purpose of a constant?" Steve asked. "That is, when should you use one?"

I thought for a moment. "One good rule of thumb is this: Whenever you find yourself declaring a variable and assigning it a value that never changes, it should probably be a constant. Also, if you use numeric literals in your code—a numeric literal is just a number—consider using a constant instead. It can save you some headaches down the road."

"I was going to ask," Kate said, "why you didn't simply take the number 100 and add it to the value of the variable *number1* instead? Is it more efficient to use a constant?"

"Using a constant makes your program more readable and easier to modify," I answered.

"Can you give us an example to illustrate why a constant is more readable?" Linda asked.

"Sure thing, Linda," I replied. "Let's say you are writing a program to calculate payroll. Let's assume that there's a state income tax rate equal to 1 percent of an employee's gross pay. Somewhere in your program, you are going to need to multiply the gross pay amount by 0.01, and in C++, that would look something like

```
GrossPayAmount * .01
```

where *GrossPayAmount* is a variable in which you've stored the employee's gross pay. Now, further suppose you perform this same calculation in several different places in your program, each time multiplying the value of the *GrossPayAmount* variable pay by the number 0.01. Now let me ask this question: What happens to your program if the state income tax rate changes from 1 percent to 2 percent?"

"Obviously," Dave said, "we would have to change the number we've been using from 0.01 to 0.02."

"That's right, Dave," I agreed, "and because we have that number hard-coded in several places in our program, we would need to go through each and every line of code in our program looking for the value 0.01 and then change it to 0.02."

"How can a constant help here?" Steve asked.

"Instead of using the number 0.01 in our calculations a number of times," I answered, "we could instead declare a constant called STATETAXRATE, assign it the value of 0.01, and then use the constant in all our calculations instead, like this."

```
GrossPayAmount * STATETAXRATE
```

"I see now," Rhonda said. "So if the state tax rate changes, because we used the name of the constant, not the number 0.01 in our calculation, we only need to change the declaration statement for the constant to reflect the new value."

"That's perfect, Rhonda, " I said.

"Couldn't we just use a search-and replace feature in our editor?" Blaine asked. "Even Notepad gives us search-and-replace."

"You might, Blaine," I responded, "but I would be a bit nervous. The code might have a couple of '0.01' terms that I didn't want to replace, and Notepad wouldn't know the difference."

"Can we see that constant declaration?" Barbara asked. I displayed the declaration on the classroom projector:

```
const float STATETAXRATE = .01;
```

"As I mentioned before," I said, "by convention, constants are named using all capital letters. This makes it pretty easy to identify constants in your code."

"I see what you mean," Dave said, "about a constant being very similar to a variable. In fact, they don't seem very different at all. I guess the primary difference is that a constant, once assigned a value, can never be changed."

"What's a float?" Kate asked.

"Good question, Kate," I said. "A float is a data type capable of storing a number with a fractional part—unlike an int, which can only store whole numbers."

"Wow, I had no idea working with data could be so complicated," Peter said.

"For the most part," I said, "it's not usually a problem. But the choice of a variable's data type— and the data you place in it—is something to be mindful of, and we'll be discussing that shortly."

"I have a question," Rhonda said. "In your example of the state tax rate, couldn't you have declared a variable, assigned it a value, and then used that variable in all your calculations?"

"You've raised an interesting point," I said. "In fact, that's what a lot of programmers do. However, if you declare a variable, assign it a value, and find that the value of the variable never changes, it really should have been a constant instead. Using a constant can have enormous benefits in our program, because the value of a constant cannot be changed once it has been declared. This can prevent disastrous results in a program where a programmer accidentally changes the value of a variable that really should have been declared a constant in the first place. The bottom line is this: If you declare a variable, assign it a value, and there is no reason for the value of that variable to ever change, what you have then is a constant, and you should declare it as such."

I realized that we had been working pretty intensely for some time and, because there were no more questions, I suggested that we take a break.

C++ Data Types

Resuming after a 15-minute break, I said, "Let's take a closer look at the available data types in C++. An understanding of the C++ data types and their characteristics is essential. We saw earlier that in order to declare a variable or a constant, we need to designate its data type. In our simple examples this morning, we used int for an integer data type. Now it's time to learn what the others are."

"How many data types are there in C++?" Rose asked.

"There are 11 data types," I said, "that are known as *fundamental data types* and are declared using special keywords such as int and float. In addition to the 11 fundamental data types, as I've mentioned, C++ also allows you to work with objects."

"What type of objects?" Rhonda asked.

"Objects," I said, "such as the cout object we've used to output in the console and also objects that we'll create from classes that we build. In order to work with objects of our own, we first need to declare a variable of that object's class name. For instance, as we progress in working with our class project, we'll eventually create a class called Student. You'll see that in order to create an instance of a Student object, we will first need to declare a variable of type Student. We'll discuss how to do that in just a few weeks."

I could see some confusion on my students' faces, but they seemed to trust me enough to wait for a fuller explanation until then.

"The choice of a data type for your variable," I said, "can be crucial to the proper operation of your program. Each C++ data type has unique memory requirements, along with capabilities and operations that you can perform on them. Declaring a data type that is not appropriate for the data you wish to store in it is a common beginner's error and can result in a range of problems— from your program not compiling at all, to it compiling and running but giving incorrect results."

I then displayed this list of the 11 C++ fundamental data types on the classroom projector:

Data Type	Storage Size	Value Range
short	16 bits	-32,768 to 32,767
unsigned short	16 bits	0 to 65,535
int	32 bits	-2,147,483,648 to 2,147,483,647
unsigned int	32 bits	0 to 4,294,967,295
long	32 bits	-2,147,483,648 to 2,147,483,647
unsigned long	32 bits	0 to 4,294,967,295
float	32 bits	1.2×10^{-38} to 3.4×10^{38}
double	64 bits	2.2×10^{-308} to 1.8×10^{308}
char	8 bits	256 character values
wchar_t	16 bits	65,535 character values
bool	8 bits	False or True

"As you can see," I said, "each data type has specific storage requirements in the computer's memory and different range values. For the next half-hour or so we'll discuss all these data types in detail. Let's start with the data types that are used to store numbers."

Numeric Data Types

I began to discuss the C++ numeric data types—the first eight data types listed in the table. "You should declare your variable as one of the C++ numeric data types," I said, "when you know you will be using that variable to store a number that will later be used in a mathematical calculation."

"Like we did when we declared number1 and number2 variables of the int data type?" Blaine asked.

"That's right, Blaine," I said. "In C++, there are two categories of numeric data types: integers, which are whole numbers, such as 1 or 2, and floating-point numbers, which are numbers with a fractional part, such as 1.2 or 2.4. Plus, within the integer category you have a choice of a data type that supports both negative and positive numbers or positive numbers only."

"What about a telephone number or a social security number?" Ward asked. "Those both contain numbers but are usually written with dashes in them. Should we use a numeric data type to store these?"

"A String data type is a better choice for those two," I said. "Although both of the examples you cite contain numbers, neither one of them is likely to be used in a mathematical calculation, and as you pointed out, both contain hyphens, or dashes, which aren't numbers at all."

"I don't see a String data type in the list of data types you displayed," Linda said. "Did you forget to include it in your table?"

"Good question, Linda," I said. "The String data type is technically not a fundamental data type. The String data type is actually an object—but don't worry, we'll be discussing the String data type later on in today's class."

Here are some general recommendations on the numeric data types:

- Choose short, unsigned short, int, unsigned int, long, and unsigned long data types to store whole numbers (called integers) such as 23, 45, and 34470. short, int, and long allow for both positive and negative numbers. unsigned short, unsigned int, and unsigned long are 'unsigned' data types and permit positive numbers only. On the other hand, because they lack the capability to store a sign, their upper storage limits are higher.

- Choose float or double data types to store numbers with fractions such as 3.1416, 23.12, 45.22, and 357644.67. In C++, the decimal data type is the most precise data type you can select, having a precision of 28 digits. On the other hand, its storage requirements are much higher—16 bytes to store the number as opposed to 4 bytes for the float and 8 bytes for the double. The bottom line: If precision is important, select the decimal data type.

- Select a data type appropriate for the values you wish to store in the variable. If the data type has a range much larger than you will need, you will waste valuable computer memory. If the data type has a range smaller than the value you attempt to store in it, your program may bomb—or worse yet, produce erroneous results.

"What do you mean when you say the program will bomb?" Rhonda asked.

"That's a term that means the program will come to an abnormal termination," I said. "Actually, sometimes you're lucky if that's what happens; other times, your program will just produce incorrect results, and that can be worse. For instance, look at this code in which I've declared a short data type variable, and I am attempting to assign a value to it beyond the range for a short data type."

I displayed the following code:

```
//Example3_10.cpp
#include <iostream>

int main()
{
```

```
using namespace std;

short number1 = 32768;    //short upper range is 32,767

cout << "The value of number1 is " << number1;
return 0;
}
```

NOTE
When assigning a numeric value to a variable, don't include commas in the number. For example, 5,028 should be coded as 5028.

I then reminded everyone that the upper range for a short data type is 32,767. I then saved the program as Example3_10.cpp, compiled it, and ran it for the class. The following screen was displayed on the classroom projector:

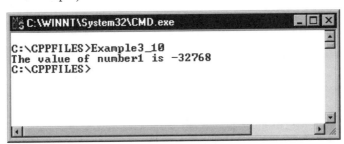

"What happened?" Rhonda asked. "I thought we assigned a value of positive 32,768 to the variable—a negative number is being displayed."

"What you're seeing," I said, "is the result of assigning a value to a variable that exceeds the range of its data type. Unlike some other programming languages, which will warn you that you're about to do so, C++ allows you to assign an inappropriate value to a variable—the results can be disastrous. In this case, when we exceeded the upper limit of the short data type by just one number, instead of giving us a positive 32,768, C++ actually 'wrapped around' to the lowest value possible, a negative 32,768. If we had tried to assign a value of positive 32,769, C++ would have assigned a value of negative 32,767. This is called an out-of-bounds, or out-of-range error. As I have said, you take responsibility for what happens in your C++ program, and that certainly includes selecting the appropriate data types for your variables, and ensuring that you don't assign inappropriate values to them."

NOTE
You may want to experiment on your own, assigning values beyond the range for a short data type and observing the incorrect values that result.

"I've seen the same thing in C," Dave said. "I guess this points out the need to be super careful when you declare the type of a variable."

"Absolutely, Dave," I said. "C++ is a very powerful language, but in this regard, it can be unforgiving."

short

"So what kind of variables are candidates to be short data types?" Bob asked.

"The short data type can hold only whole numbers; it can't be used to store a number with a fractional part. The size of the number that you can store in a short data type is not very large—from –32,768 to 32,767. Only use the short data type if you are certain that the number you will store in it is within that range; otherwise, you will get the incorrect results that you saw here."

"Can you give us a real-world example for an short data type?" Kate asked.

"How about the number of students on this campus?" I suggested. "The university itself would exceed the storage capacity for a short data type, but I know for a fact that the upper limit of 32,767 is more than enough for our campus."

unsigned short

"unsigned short is the unsigned version of the short data type," I said.

"Unsigned?" Blaine asked.

"Unsigned means that the data type is incapable of storing a negative number," I answered. "As a result of that, it's storage capacity is just about twice that of the short data type: 0 to 65,535."

"Am I correct in saying that unsigned short would be the best data type to store the number of students on our campus?" Linda asked. "I don't think we can have a negative number of students. Doing so would also allow us to store a value greater than 32,767, provided it didn't exceed 65,535. Is that right?"

"I couldn't have said it better myself, Linda," I answered. "unsigned short is a better choice."

int and long

"Next up is the int data type," I said, "which stands for integer. int is a larger version of the short data type. Like all the numeric data types we've discussed so far, the int data type can store only whole numbers. Its storage range is pretty large: –2,147,483,648 to 2,147,483,647."

"Something that confused me when I saw your chart a minute ago," Dave said, "is that it appears that the range for an int is the same as it is for a long—same with the unsigned int and unsigned long. Is that a typo in your chart?"

"Good observation, Dave," I said. "The designers of C++ wrote the standards for the language in such a way that C++ compilers must ensure that the int data type is larger than the short. However, there is no requirement that a long data type be larger than the int, only that it be equal to or greater. In the original C++ compilers, an int data type was implemented using 16 bits of memory, and its storage range was correspondingly smaller. However, most modern C++ compilers implement the int using 32 bits of memory—the same as for a long. As a result, typically you will see this peculiarity. The int has the same value range as a long—same with the unsigned int and the unsigned long."

"So which one should we choose if we need to store a larger number?" Kate asked. "int or long? You say there's no difference?"

"That's right, Kate," I replied, "with the compiler we're using here in class, there is no difference, so it's your choice. But my preference is to use the long. If for some reason you wind up compiling your source code on an older compiler, choosing long can prevent you from having the same kind of erroneous behavior we saw in Example3_10."

"What happens if you try to store a number with a fractional part in a variable declared as an int?" Dave asked.

"Good question, Dave," I said. "Let's see."

I displayed the following code on the classroom projector:

```cpp
//Example3_11.cpp
#include <iostream>

int main()
{
    using namespace std;

    short number1 = 12.75;    //short may contain only whole numbers

    cout << "The value of number1 is " << number1;
    return 0;
}
```

I then saved the program as Example3_11.cpp, compiled it, and ran it for the class. The following screen was displayed on the classroom projector:

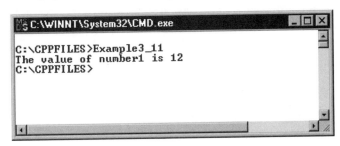

"C++ truncated the decimal portion of the number," I said. "Notice that C++ didn't round the value of 12.75 before assigning it to the variable *number1*. Instead, it actually 'chopped' the decimal portion off the number."

"I see what you mean by C++ being unforgiving," Ward said. "It did that without so much as a warning message."

"That's right, Ward," I answered. "Even more reason to be very careful in your choice of data type—it must match exactly the type of data that will ultimately be assigned to it."

unsigned int and unsigned long

"If the pattern holds true," Dave said, "then I presume that the unsigned int data type is the unsigned version of the int data type, which means it cannot hold negative numbers and it therefore has a larger range than the int?"

"Exactly, Dave," I said. "unsigned int can be used to store larger whole numbers than the int—but only positive numbers."

"Would it hurt to declare all our numeric variables as an int?" Linda asked.

"Declaring a variable larger than it needs to be is a waste of storage," I said. "As you can see from our table, the int data type requires 32 bits (or 4 bytes) of storage. That may not seem like a big deal, but if you know that the range of values you'll be storing in a variable requires only a short data type, which consumes only 16 bits (or 2 bytes) of storage, you should declare the variable as a short. This type of attention to detail can make your program run faster, reduce its runtime memory requirements, and will be something that a prospective employer will be looking for when examining any sample code you write or bring to a job interview."

"Can you give us some examples of when we would want to use the various data types?" Rose asked.

"Sure thing, Rose," I said. "As I mentioned, we could use the short data type to store the number of students on this campus of the university. For that matter, we could also use the short data type to store the number of students in this class. However, because there are more than 32,767 students in total at the university, we would need to use an int data type to store that number. We could also use the int data type to store the total number of people in the United States. However, we couldn't use an int data type to store the total number of people in the world, because there are more than 2,147,483,647 of us—in fact, there are over 6 billion, which also makes the unsigned int and the unsigned long bad choices, too."

"Wow, I'm starting to get a headache just thinking about this," Rhonda said. "I had no idea this could be so complicated."

"Wait a minute," Ward said. "What can we use to store the number of people in the world? You said unsigned int and unsigned long can't store a large enough value."

"In that case," I said, "we need to use either the float or double data type."

"Shouldn't we use a data type that supports only whole numbers?" Kathy asked.

"We don't really have a choice," I replied. "If we need a data type to store very large numbers, such as the number of people in the world or even the number of stars in the sky, we have to use one of the two data types that permits the storage of numbers with fractional parts. Those data types are the only ones capable of storing a number that large."

float

"The difference between the float and double data types and the integer data types that we've examined so far is that float and double can store values that mathematicians call real numbers, which are numbers with fractional parts. You may also hear these data types referred to as floating-point data types."

"I explained that variables declared as float data types require 32 bits (or 4 bytes) of computer memory to hold them. Values for the float data type can range from 1.2×10^{-38} to 3.4×10^{38}. If you need to store a value with a fractional part in a variable, you'll need to use one of these two data types."

"What kind of number is that?" Peter asked. "What does 1.2×10^{-38} mean?"

"Unless you're fresh from a math class," I said, "you may have trouble making sense of that range, because it's expressed in a format known as *scientific* or *exponential notation*, which is a special notation used to represent very large numbers. The positive range for this number is read as '3.4 multiplied by 10 raised to the 38th power.' That's a pretty large number, and if we were to write out the upper positive limit in normal notation, it would look like this:"

```
340,000,000,000,000,000,000,000,000,000,000,000,000
```

"Notice," I continued, "that there are 38 digits that follow the leading 3—that's the significance of the exponent or power in 10^{38}. Trying to write out the upper positive limit for the double data type is a great deal more difficult, since it has 308 zeroes in it. Quite honestly, we wouldn't have room on a piece of paper to write that number—that's why larger numbers like this are best represented with exponential or scientific notation."

"I'm sold," Kate said laughing. "I guess any way you look at it, those are huge numbers. I'm not likely to think of a number that requires those values."

double

"Just as the long data type is really a bigger version of the int data type," I said, "so too the double data type is a bigger version of the float."

I explained that variables declared as double data types require 64 bits (or 8 bytes) of computer memory. Values for the double can range from 2.2×10^{-308} to 1.8×10^{308}.

"If you take the upper limit for the float data type," I said, "and add about 270 zeros to it, that will give a good idea for the upper limit of the double!"

I doubted that there was anyone in the class who could think of a value that would exceed the range for the double data type.

Finished with our discussion of numeric data types, we then moved on to the bool data type.

Nonnumeric Data Types

"We've discussed 8 of the 11 fundamental data types that C++ has to offer," I said. "We'll finish our discussion of data types by looking at the special bool data type, followed by two character type data types: the char data type and the wchar_t data type. Finally, we'll look at the special case of the String."

bool

"bool data types," I said, "can have only two possible values: True and False."

I displayed this code on the classroom projector:

```
//Example3_12.cpp
#include <iostream>

int main()
{
    using namespace std;

    bool married = true;
    bool retired = false;

    cout << "The value of married is " << married << endl;
    cout << "The value of retired is " << retired ;

    return 0;
}
```

I then saved the program as Example3_12.cpp, compiled it, and ran it for the class. The following screen was displayed on the classroom projector:

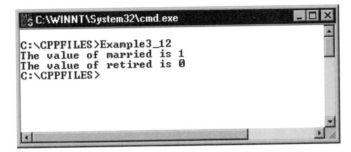

I explained that I had declared two bool variables—one called married and the other retired—and then assigned the values True and False to the respective variables.

"What we've done here," I said, "is to declare two bool variables: one to represent someone's marital status and the other to represent their retirement status. The bool variable is ideal to use when the value of the variable can only be a true/false or yes/no outcome. Notice how the assignment of True or False to a bool variable is made without enclosing it within quotation marks or apostrophes, which is something that beginning students sometime do."

"What about the output to the console?" Ward asked. "Why is it that the values 1 and 0 are output, not True and False."

'Traditionally, in both C and C++," I said, "the number 1 has been used to represent True, and 0 to represent False. In fact, the compiler actually interprets the values 'true' and false as if they were one and zero respectively. Unfortunately, when we use the cout object to display the value of our Boolean variables to the console, the numbers are displayed, not the values True and False."

"Is there anything we can do about this?" Steve wondered.

"Yes, there is," I said, "and it's something that starts to lead us to a realization as to how 'object oriented' C++ is."

"What do you mean?" Lou asked.

"Before we redirect the value of our Boolean variables to the cout object," I said, "we can first redirect them to a special C++ object called boolalpha, which will output the Boolean True and False values and then redirect those values to the cout object. Let me show you."

I then displayed this code on the classroom projector:

```
//Example3_13.cpp
#include <iostream>

int main()
{
    using namespace std;
```

```
bool married = true;
bool retired = false;

cout << "The value of married is " << boolalpha << married << endl;
cout << "The value of retired is " << boolalpha << retired ;

return 0;
}
```

I then saved the program as Example3_13.cpp, compiled it, and ran it for the class. The following screen was displayed on the classroom projector:

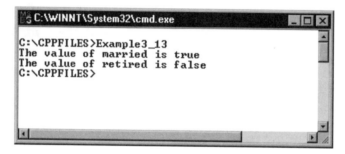

"That's better," Ward said. "Now it shows the value of the Boolean variables as either True or False."

"That's right, Ward," I said. "These two lines of code did the trick by redirecting the value of the Boolean variables to a special C++ object called boolalpha."

```
cout << "The value of married is " << boolalpha << married << endl;
cout << "The value of retired is " << boolalpha << retired ;
```

"I just noticed something," Dave said. "What's 'endl' doing at the end of that first line of code? Is that a replacement for the backslash+n we were using earlier?"

"That's excellent, Dave," I said. "I knew I couldn't sneak that one by you. endl is another kind of C++ object—by redirecting it to the cout object, in effect we are generating the same carriage return and line feed we generate by redirecting the backslash+n to the cout object. The biggest difference is that the compiler interprets the backslash+n as a character—that's why we had to enclose it in double quotes. Since endl actually refers to an object, it's handled differently."

I waited to see if there were any more questions before moving onto a discussion of the char data type.

char and wchar_t

"The char data type is used to store a single character," I continued. "The storage requirement for the char data type is 8 bits and its value range is 0 to 255."

"I thought this was a character data type," Kate said. "Why is the value range expressed in numbers?"

"We're not talking about storing numbers per se here," I said. "We're talking about storing numbers that equate to a character, such as the letter *C* or any of the characters you see on the keyboard."

"What's the wchar_t data type?" Lou asked.

"wchar_t stands for wide character," I said. "Essentially, it's the same as the char data type, used to store character data, except that it's 16 bits and its value range is 0 to 65,535."

Why do we need a data type so large to store a single character?" Ward asked. "As I recall, ASCII code is used to represent characters, and the ASCII values range from 0 to 255, just like the char data type."

"That's true, Ward," I said. "Many languages use the ASCII code to represent characters, but ASCII is an older coding scheme. Because C++ is a relatively new programming language, it is capable of using the new Unicode standard, which is capable of displaying character sets from every language and alphabet in existence—some of which have thousands of characters in their alphabet. As a result, the wchar_t data type requires an extra byte of storage, which is why its range of values is so high."

"Would an assignment to a char data type be the same as the assignment of a number?" Linda asked.

"Assigning values to a char data type is different from assigning values to a numeric or bool variable," I said. "Let me show you."

I entered the following code on the classroom projector:

```cpp
//Example3_14.cpp
#include <iostream>

int main()
{
    using namespace std;

    char character1 = 'a';

    cout << "The value of character1 is " << character1;

    return 0;
}
```

I then saved the program as Example3_14.cpp, compiled it, and ran it for the class. The following screen was displayed on the classroom projector:

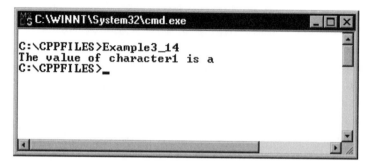

"Assignments to a char data type are done by enclosing the character within apostrophes, not quotation marks," I said.

"Can you assign more than one character to a char data type?" Mary asked.

"No, you can't, Mary," I said. "The char data type is limited to storing a single character. If you try to assign more than one character to a char data type, only the first character will be assigned to the char variable."

The String Object

"Suppose you need to store more than one character in a variable then?" Blaine asked.

"If you need to store more than one character in a variable," I said, "you'll need to declare a String data type instead. Strictly speaking, a String is not a fundamental data type. In C++, a String is an object, but a String variable is declared just like any other data type. However, the assignment of characters to a String variable is slightly different from the char data type. Let me show you."

I entered the following code:

```
//Example3_15.cpp
#include <iostream>
#include <string> // include for C++ standard string class

int main()
{
    using namespace std;

    string string1 = "John Smiley";

    cout << "The value of string1 " << string1;
```

```
    return 0;
}
```

I then saved the program as Example3_15.cpp, compiled it, and ran it for the class. The following screen was displayed on the classroom projector:

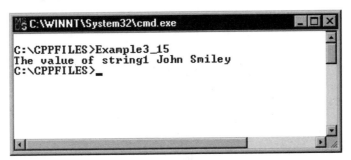

"Just a couple of things to note here," I said. "Although it's not absolutely required with the C++ compiler we're using here in the classroom, I've included a reference to the C++ 'string' library. That's the particular library that contains the code that allows us to use the string object. Some C++ compilers will complain that they can't find the string object if you don't include a reference to the library."

```
#include <string> // include for C++ standard string class
```

"Secondly, assignments to a String data type are done by enclosing the character within quotation marks, not apostrophes, as we used with the char data type."

"I just realized," Rhonda said, "that when we assign values to a numeric variable, we don't use apostrophes *or* quotation marks."

"That's right, Rhonda," I said. "Numeric literals—numbers—are not sandwiched in any way."

I then displayed this code on the classroom projector:

```
int number1 = 12;
```

"char variables are assigned using apostrophes, like this."

```
char character1 = 'a';
```

"And String variables are assigned using quotation marks, like this."

```
string string1 = "John Smiley";
```

No one had any other questions about C++ data types, and so, after a quick break, we moved onto a discussion of data operations.

Operations on Data

"Because you now all know something about C++ data types," I said, after the break, "it's time to learn how to perform operations on that data. Let's start with arithmetic operations."

Arithmetic Operations

I explained that arithmetic operations are performed on data stored in numeric variables or numeric constants.

"You can't perform arithmetic operations on any other kind of data," I said. "If you try, you'll either get a compiler error or a runtime error. Now let's look at the various arithmetic operations available in C++."

I paused a moment before continuing.

"Before I begin," I said, "it's important to note that most operations are performed on operands. Operands appear on either side of an operator, and when the statement is executed, some result is generated. You have several choices as to what to do with this result. You can choose to ignore it or discard it. You can assign it to a variable, or you can use it in an expression of some kind, as we did earlier today when we displayed the result of an addition operation in the console by using it with the cout object."

Here's a list of the C++ arithmetic operators:

Operator	Meaning	Example
+	Addition	11 + 22
–	Subtraction	22 – 11
*	Multiplication	5 * 6
/	Division	21 / 3
%	Remainder	12 percent 2

The Addition Operator

"The addition operation (+) adds two operands," I said, as I displayed this example of the addition operation on the classroom projector:

```
number3 = number1 + number2;
```

"In this example, we're taking the result of the addition of the variables *number1* and *number2* and assigning that value to the variable *number3*. Notice that I didn't say that the addition operation adds two numbers—that's not necessarily the case, as it isn't here. In C++, an expression can be a number, a variable, a constant, or any expression that results in a number. Ultimately, as long as C++ can evaluate the expression as a number, the addition operation will work."

"What do you mean when you say *evaluate?*" Kate asked.

"When C++ evaluates an expression," I replied, "it examines the expression, substituting actual values for any variables or constants that it finds."

I took a moment to emphasize that C++ performs operations on only one pair of operands at one time, which means that even a complex expression like this will be done one step at a time:

```
number4 = number1 + number2 + number3;
```

"We'll learn more about complex expressions like this later," I promised.

"What's an operand, again?" Ward asked.

"An operand is something to the left or right of the operator symbol," I said. "In the assignment statement I just showed you, number1, number2 and number3 are all operands. No matter how many operators appear in an expression, C++ performs an operation on just two operands at a time."

"That's a little surprising to me," Rhonda said. "Are you saying that no matter how fast my PC is, it still performs arithmetic the way I was taught in school, one step at a time?"

"That's right, Rhonda," I said. "One operation at a time—at the speed of light!"

I then displayed this program from Example3_6 to my students once more:

```cpp
//Example3_6.cpp
#include <iostream>

int main()
{
   using namespace std;

   int number1 = 12;
   int number2 = 23 ;

   cout << "The answer is " << (number1 + number2);
   return 0;
}
```

"Remember this one?" I asked. "Here we're taking the result of the addition operation of *number1* and *number2* and using it as an expression with the cout object. The parentheses around the addition operation ensure that it is executed first prior to it being passed to the cout object for display on the console."

"In this example," Linda said, "you first assigned values to variables and then performed the addition operation on the value of the variables. Is it possible to perform the addition on numeric literals?"

"Yes, you can," I said, as I displayed this code:

```cpp
//Example3_16.cpp
#include <iostream>

int main()
{
   using namespace std;
   cout << "The answer is " << (12 + 23);
   return 0;
}
```

I then saved the program as Example3_16.cpp, compiled it, and ran it for the class—once again, the number 35 was displayed in the console.

"What are the numeric literals that Linda was talking about?" Rhonda asked. "Are those the numbers within the parentheses?"

"Exactly, Rhonda," I replied. "Numeric literals are literally just numbers."

I waited to see if there were any other questions before moving onto the subtraction operator.

The Subtraction Operator

"As you may have guessed," I said, "the subtraction operator (–) works by subtracting one operand from another and returning a result. In actuality, it subtracts the operand on its right side from the operand on its left. Look at this example."

I showed the following code on the class projector:

```cpp
//Example3_17.cpp
#include <iostream>

int main()
{
   using namespace std;

   int number1 = 44;
   int number2 = 33;
   int result = 0;
```

```
    result = number1 - number2;

    cout << "The answer is " << result;
    return 0;
}
```

I then saved the program as Example3_17.cpp, compiled it, and ran it for the class. The following screenshot was displayed on the classroom projector:

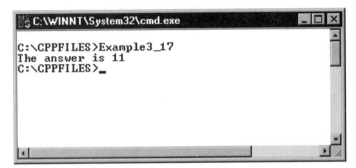

 NOTE

Depending on the compiler you are using, you may receive a warning message indicating that the variable result is assigned a value that is never used. This is because of our decision to initialize the value of the result variable—it's nothing to worry about.

"As you can see," I said, "*number2* was subtracted from *number1* and the result was then...."

"You switched things up a bit here," Ward interrupted.

"What do you mean?" I answered.

"You declared an extra variable called *result*," he answered.

"That's right," I said. "I wanted to show you how you can assign the result of the subtraction operation to another variable. I called it *result*, but we could have called it anything we want."

"What would have happened if you hadn't initialized result to 0?" Ward continued. "Would it have given us a crazy result like it did last week?"

"Not this time, Ward." I explained. "Without the initialization, the value of result probably did start out as some crazy value. However, once we assigned a value to it, the old 'crazy' value was discarded. C++ discarded our assignment to 0 in the same way. The only difference is that we took the trouble to make the assignment. As I explained last week, you should initialize your variables, but it's cases like this one, where it doesn't much matter, that can make some programmers a bit lazy."

Since there were no further questions, I then proceeded to the multiplication operator.

The Multiplication Operator

"The multiplication operator (*) multiplies two operands," I said.

"Now this is a little different from what I used in school," Mary said. "In school, we used the letter *X* to denote multiplication."

"I did as well," I said, "but the computer uses the asterisk instead—except for the operator, everything works as you would expect."

I displayed the following code on the classroom projector:

```cpp
//Example3_18.cpp
#include <iostream>

int main()
{
    using namespace std;
    int number1 = 4;
    int number2 = 3;
    int result = 0;
    result = number1 * number2;
    cout << "The answer is " << result;
    return 0;
}
```

I then saved the program as Example3_18.cpp, compiled it, and ran it for the class. The following screenshot was displayed on the classroom projector:

The Division Operator

"The division operator (/) works by dividing one operand by another and returning a result. In actuality, it divides the operand on the left side of the division operator by the operand on the right. Division can be a little tricky in C++ because you must be conscious that the result may be something other than an integer—and that has implications if you decide to assign the result to a variable that you have declared as an int. Look at this example."

```cpp
//Example3_19.cpp
#include <iostream>

int main()
{
   using namespace std;

   int number1 = 5;
   int number2 = 2;
   int result = 0;

   result = number1 / number2;

   cout << "The answer is " << result;
   return 0;
}
```

I then saved the program as Example3_19.cpp, compiled it, and ran it for the class. The following screenshot was displayed on the classroom projector:

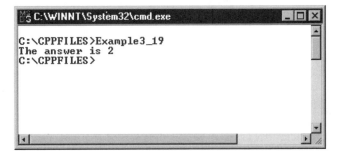

"Wait a minute," Linda said. "That answer's not correct—it should be 2.5. Looks like we got an integer result."

"That's exactly the problem I was alluding to a moment ago," I answered. "Because we assigned the result of the subtraction operation to an int variable, C++ truncated, not rounded, our result. If this program had been one of the many pieces of a critical application, such as the computer program that keeps the International Space Station aloft, we would have a serious problem."

"What can we do to fix this?" Ward asked.

"Let's change the data type for our *result* variable and see whether that helps," I answered.

I changed the code as follows:

```cpp
//Example3_20.cpp
#include <iostream>
```

```
int main()
{
    using namespace std;

    int number1 = 5;
    int number2 = 2;
    float result = 0;

    result = number1 / number2;

    cout << "The answer is " << result;
    return 0;
}
```

I then saved the program as Example3_20.cpp, compiled it, and ran it for the class. The following screenshot was displayed on the classroom projector:

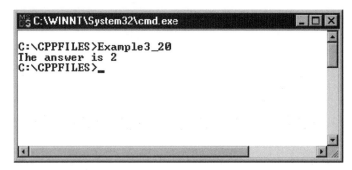

"The answer's still wrong." Rose said. "What's the problem?"

"You're right, Rose," I said. "The answer is still wrong. The problem here is that C++ has rules for dealing with divergent data types. One of these rules is that when C++ divides one integer by another, the result will always be an integer—assigning the result to a floating-point variable doesn't help. Also, remember what I told you earlier today—C++ does all of its operations one at a time. This means that it first divides the integer 5 by the integer 2—follows its rules for integer division to come up with the integer 2—and then assigns that to the floating point result."

"Should we have declared number1 and number2 as float types?" Kate asked.

"You pretty much hit the nail on the head, Kate," I said. "In order to calculate a result that is a float data type, at least one of the two operands in the division operator needs to be a float data type also. Like this."

I showed them this code:

```
//Example3_21.cpp
#include <iostream>
```

```
int main()
{
   using namespace std;

   int number1 = 5;
   float number2 = 2;
   float result = 0;

   result = number1 / number2;

   cout << "The answer is " << result;
   return 0;
}
```

I then saved the program as Example3_21.cpp, compiled it, and ran it for the class. The following screenshot was displayed on the classroom projector:

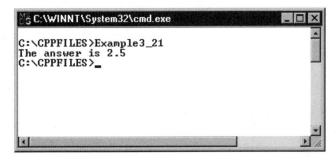

"That's better," Steve said. "But I'm a bit confused. Why did making only one of the operands a floating point type fix the problem?"

"Great question, Steve," I replied. "In our first version, the C++ compiler knew that we were dividing two integers, so it knew that we wanted to perform integer-type division on them. When we next tried to assign the result to a floating-point type, it knew that we were trying to mix data types, and that something had to be done. What it did was to promote the data type of the result of the division—2—from an integer to a floating point data type. Internally, the number 2 actually became a floating-point 2.0, which is compatible with our floating-point type variable result. Now, when we try to divide the floating point 5 by the integer 2, the compiler sees the different types earlier, and..."

"...and promotes the 2 into floating-point 2.0 before it does the division," Steve exclaimed, finishing my sentence. From the looks on other faces, I could see that everyone else followed along, too.

"That's better," Steve said. "Do we need to be this careful in C++? In Visual Basic, it seemed that a lot of this was taken care of for us."

"You're right, Steve," I replied. "In some languages, particularly Visual Basic, you hardly need to concern yourself with the data types you are dealing with when performing operations. C++ is different. If you're not careful, what your program does versus what you intend it to do may be vastly different. Most languages, particularly C and C++, expect the programmer to be aware of the types of data they are working with and to be careful when working with that data."

 NOTE
Changing both number1 and number2 to floating-point types would have worked just as well.

The Remainder Operator

I continued, "A few moments ago, Rose mentioned the remainder that we lost when we performed division with two integer operands. The remainder operation—sometimes called the *modulus operation* in other programming languages—deals with remainders. In fact, you can think of the remainder operation as the reverse: The result of the remainder operation is the remainder of a division operation. For instance, 5 divided by 2 is 2, with a remainder of 1. That's the result of a remainder operation. It's that simple, really."

"What's the symbol for the remainder operation?" Ward asked.

"It's the percent (%) sign," I said. "Let me give you an example of the remainder operation."

```cpp
//Example3_22.cpp
#include <iostream>

int main()
{
   using namespace std;

   int number1 = 5;
   int number2 = 2;
   int result = 0;

   result = number1 % number2;

   cout << "The remainder is " << result;
   return 0;
}
```

I then saved the program as Example3_22.cpp, compiled it, and ran it for the class. The following screenshot was displayed on the classroom projector:

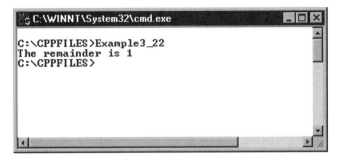

"As you can see," I said, "the remainder operation has resulted in a remainder of 1 being displayed in the console."

"I think I'm okay with the mechanics of the remainder operation," Rhonda said. "I just can't understand why you would ever want to use it. Can you give us an example?"

"The usefulness of the remainder operation," I said, "is not as obvious as some of the other arithmetic operators. One of the more useful characteristics of a remainder operation is that if the result of the remainder operation is 0, you know that the first expression is evenly divisible by the second expression. Even better, if you perform the remainder operation of *operand1* by the number 2, and the result is 0, that means that *operand1* was an even number. If the result is 1, *operand1* was odd."

I gave everyone a chance to think about this for a moment.

"So if you 'mod' a number by 2, there are only two possible results, 0 and 1?" Ward asked.

"That's right, Ward," I said. "Let me show you."

I displayed the following:

```
//Example3_23.cpp
#include <iostream>

int main()
{
    using namespace std;

    int oddnumber1 = 3;
    int evennumber1 = 4;
    int oddnumber2 = 5;
    int evennumber2 = 6;
```

```
    int result = 0;

    result = oddnumber1 % 2;
    cout << "The remainder is " << result << endl;
    result = evennumber1 % 2;
    cout << "The remainder is " << result << endl;
    result = oddnumber2 % 2;
    cout << "The remainder is " << result << endl;
    result = evennumber2 % 2;
    cout << "The remainder is " << result;

    return 0;
}
```

"What I'm doing here," I pointed out, "is declaring four variables and assigning two of them even numbers and two of them odd. Using the remainder operator, we can determine whether the number is even or odd by its result; a result of 0 from the remainder operation indicates an even number, and a result of 1 from the remainder operation indicates an odd number."

I then saved the program as Example3_23.cpp, compiled it, and ran it for the class. The following screenshot was displayed on the classroom projector:

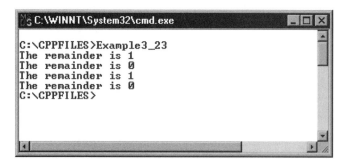

"As you can see," I said, "the result of the remainder operation is either a 0 or a 1; 0 indicates an even number, and 1 indicates an odd number."

"It can't be that easy," Ward said. "I think I had a programming assignment like this to do in a class I took several years ago, and as I recall, it was quite a bear to solve—the remainder operator. I'll need to remember that one."

"Could we have used an If statement here to make this code a bit more elegant?" Dave asked.

"We could have, Dave," I said, "except we won't be talking about the If statement until next week. Remind me about it then and we'll use the remainder operator along with an If statement."

I glanced at the clock on the wall and knew it was just about time for a break.

"We have two more operators to discuss before break," I said, "the increment operator and the decrement operator."

The Increment Operator

"One of the most common operations performed on a variable," I said, "is to increment it. That is, to add 1 to its value. In other programming language, this code would be used to do that."

I displayed the following:

```cpp
//Example3_24.cpp
#include <iostream>

int main()
{
    using namespace std;

    int number1 = 5;
    number1 = number1 + 1;
    cout << "The answer is " << number1;

    return 0;
}
```

I then saved the program as Example3_24.cpp, compiled it, and ran it for the class. The following screenshot was displayed on the classroom projector:

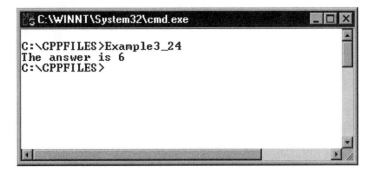

"How is that assignment statement read?" Rhonda asked. "It's confusing me a little bit."

"The expression to the right of the equal sign is performed first," I said. "Read it this way: Take the current value of the variable *number1*, which is 5, add 1 to it, giving a result of 6, and then assign that value to the variable *number1*."

"So that's how that's done," Blaine said. "But what about this increment operator you mentioned?"

"The increment operator is a shortcut function," I said. "Take a look at this."

I then modified the code to look like this:

```
//Example3_25.cpp
#include <iostream>
int main()
{
    using namespace std;
    int number1 = 5;
    number1++;
    cout << "The answer is " << number1;
    return 0;
}
```

"In C++," I said, "the increment operator is ++, which tells C++ to take the current value of the variable and add 1 to it."

I then saved the program as Example3_25.cpp, compiled it, and ran it for the class. The following screenshot was displayed on the classroom projector:

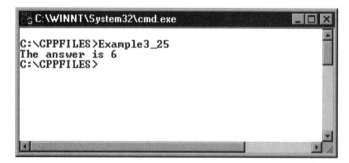

"The increment operator produces the same results," I said, "but saves us a few keystrokes—and probably results in less mistakes by programmers overall. The increment operator is often used on variables that are used to count things. You'll see this when you learn about loops in a few weeks time."

The Decrement Operator

"What about the decrement operator?" Dave asked. "Is that the opposite of the increment operator? Does it subtract 1 from the value of the variable?"

"You're psychic, Dave," I said. "That's exactly what it does. In C++, the decrement operator is --. Take a look at this code."

I displayed the following:

```
//Example3_26.cpp
#include <iostream>

int main()
{
   using namespace std;

   int number1 = 5;
   number1--;
   cout << "The answer is " << number1;

   return 0;
}
```

I then saved the program as Example3_26.cpp, compiled it, and ran it for the class. The following screenshot was displayed on the classroom projector:

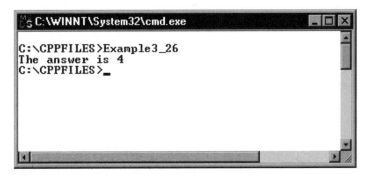

"As you can see," I said, "*number1* was initialized with a value of 5. We subtracted 1 from it using the decrement operator, giving us a result of 4. Again, this is just a shortcut to using this code."

```
number1 = number1 - 1;
```

No one seemed to have any problems with either the increment or decrement operators, so I called for a break.

Order of Operations

"I mentioned earlier," I said, as we resumed after break, "that when C++ evaluates an expression containing more than one operation, it performs each operation one at a time. The natural question then is, Which operation does C++ perform first?"

"That's right," Jack said. "If there's an expression that contains more than one operation, how does it decide which operation to execute first?"

"I would think," Rose said, "that C++ would perform the operations left to right in the expression. That's how I would do it."

"I think you're right, Rose," I said, "that most people would evaluate an expression that way, but that's not the way C++ does it. C++ follows a set of rules, known as the Order of Operations, that governs the order in which it performs these operations. Knowing the Order of Operations is crucial if you want your expressions to be evaluated the way you intend."

I then displayed this code on the classroom projector. Before running it, I asked everyone in the class to perform the calculation mentally themselves and tell me the number they thought would be displayed in the console:

```cpp
//Example3_27.cpp
#include <iostream>

int main()
{
   using namespace std;

   cout << (3 + 6 + 9 / 3);

   return 0;
}
```

I received a number of different responses. A couple of students suggested the number 12 would be displayed, a few said 6, and a number of students said that the answer would depend on exactly when the division operation was performed. Not wishing to keep them in suspense any longer, I saved the program as Example3_27.cpp, compiled it, and then executed it. The following screenshot was displayed on the classroom projector:

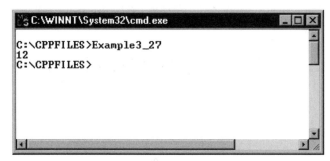

"It looks as though C++ performed the division first," Dave said.

"You're right, Dave," I said. "C++ evaluated the expression and broke it into three separate operations."

- 3 + 6
- + 9
- / 3

"Following the rules for the order of operations, C++ actually performed the third operation, division, first," I said. "The Order of Operations is determined by the following rules."

- Operations in parentheses are performed first.
- Exponentiation operations are performed next.
- Multiplication and division operations are performed next, from left to right in the expression.
- Finally, addition and subtraction operations are performed, from left to right in the expression.

"What does all that mean?" Rhonda asked.

"Here's what happens," I said. "When C++ examines an expression, it first looks to see if there are any operations within parentheses. If it finds parentheses, it performs every operation within the parentheses first. Once all the operations within parentheses are executed, C++ then looks for any operations involving exponentiation, and if it finds any, it performs those."

"Suppose there's more than one exponentiation operation?" Lou asked.

"If there's more than one exponentiation operation," I answered, "C++ performs each one in turn, from left to right.

"Next," I continued, "C++ looks for operations involving multiplication or division and performs them. If it finds more than one, it performs them from left to right.

"Finally, C++ looks for operations involving addition or subtraction and performs them. Once again, it performs each one in turn, starting at the left side of the expression and working its way to the right."

"Can you relate the Order of Operations to the code example you showed us?" Kathy asked.

"Sure," I said. "C++ first looked for parentheses in the expression. Because the entire expression appeared within parentheses, this had no impact on the evaluation of the expression. C++ then looked for an exponentiation operator, but it found none. Next, it looked for any multiplication or division operators. It found just the single division operator, which it then performed first."

"So it actually performed the operation of 9 divided by 3 first," Valerie said. "No wonder the answer didn't agree with mine."

"After the division operation," I continued, "C++ looked for any addition or subtraction operators. It found two of them and performed these operations from left to right: It added 3 plus 6 first, then added that result, 9, to 3. I can show you how this all took place, step by step. Here are the results of the intermediate operations."

I displayed this on the classroom projector:

- Step 1: 3 + 6 + 9 / 3
- Step 2: 3 + 6 + 3
- Step 3: 9 + 3
- Step 4: 12

I gave everyone a chance to take all of this in. "I hope this example shows you not only how C++ evaluates an expression containing mathematical operators, but how important it is to compose the expressions you code carefully. For instance," I said, "suppose we had intended to calculate the average of three numbers—3, 6, and 9—with this piece of code. We know that to calculate an average, we would add 3 plus 6 plus 9 and then divide by 3. However, if we were to wager our jobs on getting the answer we wanted using this C++ code, we wouldn't have one very long!"

"You're right about that," Rose said. "But how could we code the expression to correctly compute the average of 3, 6, and 9?"

"One word," Jack suggested. "Parentheses."

"That's right," I said, agreeing with Jack, as I modified the code and displayed it on the classroom projector:

```
//Example3_28.cpp
#include <iostream>

int main()
{
   using namespace std;

   cout << ((3 + 6 + 9) / 3);

   return 0;
}
```

Now when I compiled and executed the program, the following screenshot appeared on the classroom projector:

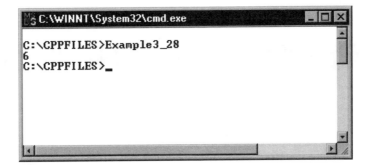

"That's better," I said. "This time, because we sandwiched the addition operations within a set of parentheses, C++ performed both addition operations prior to the division, which is exactly what we wanted to happen. Step by step, it looks like this."

I displayed the following:

- Step 1: (3 + 6 + 9) / 3
- Step 2: (9 + 9) /3
- Step 3: 18 / 3
- Step 4: 6

"Please excuse my dear Aunt Sally," I heard Linda mutter.

"What was that, Linda?" Rhonda asked. "Please excuse what?"

"Please excuse my dear Aunt Sally," Linda repeated. "I learned that in ninth grade math class as a way to remember the Order of Operations: Parentheses, Exponentiation, Multiplication, Division, Addition, Subtraction."

"I had forgotten all about that, Linda," I said. "That expression does summarize the Order of Operations perfectly."

Comparison Operators

"I was talking to a programmer friend of mine," Ward said, "and she mentioned something called *comparison operators*. Will we be covering those as well?"

"Yes, we will," I replied. "Just as arithmetic or mathematical operators perform an operation based on operands to the left and right of an operator and then return a result, comparison operators compare two expressions to the left and right of a comparison operator and return a result. In the case of a comparison operator, however, the result isn't a number; it's a value of either True or False. Here are the six comparison operators."

I displayed the following on the classroom projector:

Symbol	Explanation
==	Equal to
!=	Not equal to
<	Less than
<=	Less than or equal to
>	Greater than
>=	Greater than or equal to

"We'll only be discussing the most common comparison operator today: the equal to (==) operator," I said.

"Is that right?" Barbara asked. "Should that be two equal signs? Isn't the equal sign also used to assign a value to a variable?"

"You're right," I said. "The equal sign is used to assign a value to a variable in C++. However, two equal signs are used for the comparison operator. We haven't yet learned about If statements—we'll do that next week—but in C++, we could use this code to determine whether the value of the variable *number1* is equal to 22."

I displayed the following code:

```
//Example3_29.cpp
#include <iostream>

int main()
{
    using namespace std;

    int number1 = 22;

    if (number1 == 22) cout << "number1 is equal to 22";

    return 0;
}
```

"Notice that the assignment statement uses one equal sign," I said, pointing out the following line:

```
int number1 = 22;
```

"But within the If statement, we use the double equal sign (==) to compare the value of *number1* to the literal 22."

"So the result of the If statement expression will either be True or False, depending on the current value of *number1*?" Dave asked.

"That's exactly right, Dave," I replied. "If the current value of *number1* is 22, the result of this comparison will be True. As you'll see next week, when an If statement expression evaluates to True, the imperative statement following it—in this case, a statement to display a message in the console—is executed."

I then saved the program as Example3_29.cpp, compiled it, and ran it for the class. The following screenshot was displayed on the classroom projector:

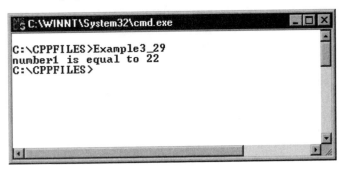

"Now let's modify the program slightly," I said, "so that you can actually see the result of the comparison operation."

I then modified it like so:

```
//Example3_30.cpp
#include <iostream>

int main()
{
    using namespace std;

    int number1 = 22;

    cout << boolalpha << (number1 == 22);

    return 0;
}
```

I saved the program as Example3_30.cpp, compiled it, and ran it for the class. The following screenshot was displayed on the classroom projector:

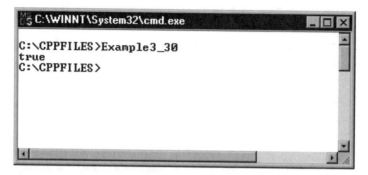

"As you can see," I said, "using the boolalpha object, we can display the result of C++'s evaluation of 'number1 = 22'—which is True."

"That's cool," Kate said. "We really did display the result of the comparison operation, didn't we?"

"Yes, we did, Kate," I replied. "Likewise, if the value of *number1* is not equal to 22, the result of the comparison operation would be False, like this."

I modified the code slightly:

```
//Example3_31.cpp
#include <iostream>

int main()
{
   using namespace std;

   int number1 = 99;

   cout << boolalpha << (number1 == 22);

   return 0;
}
```

I saved the program as Example3_31.cpp, compiled it, and ran it for the class. The following screenshot was displayed on the classroom projector:

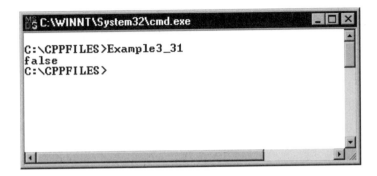

Logical Operators

"So far," I said, "we've examined arithmetic operators and comparison operators. Now it's time to look at a set of operators that sometimes cause beginner's hearts to skip a beat: logical operators."

"Are those the And, Or, and Not operators?" Blaine asked.

"That's right, Blaine," I said. "In this C++ class, we'll be discussing three logical operators: And, Or, and Not. Just like comparison operators, logical operators return a True or False value as the result of performing an operation on two operands. I must warn you that logical operations can be confusing for the beginner, primarily because of the necessity to understand the 'truth' or 'falseness' of their expressions. Let's take a look at these operators individually."

The And Operator (&&)

"An And operation," I said, "returns a True value if the expressions on both sides of the And operator evaluate to True."

"Can you give us a real-world example to make this easier to understand?" Ward asked.

"I think so, Ward," I said, as I thought a moment. "On Wednesday morning, your best friend Melissa telephones you and invites you to lunch on Friday. You'd love to go, but you have two problems that prevent you from saying yes right away. First, you and your boss have not been on the best of terms lately, and you don't want to chance taking an extra long lunch on Friday, something that invariably happens when you go to lunch with Melissa. The only way you can envision going to lunch with your friend is if your boss happens to be out of the office on Friday."

"And the second problem?" Barbara asked. "You said there were two problems."

"The second problem," I said, "is that you're short of cash and it's your turn to pick up the tab for lunch. Luckily though, Friday happens to be payday, and cash won't be a problem, provided the direct deposit of your paycheck goes through early Friday morning, something that is 50-50 at best. You decide to call your friend on Friday at 11 A.M. to let her know for sure."

I could see that some of the students were wondering what my heart-felt example had to do with the And operator. I explained that we can express our dilemma in the form of two expressions joined with the And operator in this way: "You can go to lunch with your friend Melissa if your boss is out of the office on Friday *and* if the direct deposit of your paycheck gets into your bank account by 11 A.M. on Friday morning," I said.

"In other words, both the left-hand expression, 'Boss out of office,' and the right-hand expression, 'Money in account,' must be true for the And operator to return a value of True."

```
Boss out of office AND Money in account
```

"So what happens?" Rhonda asked.

"On Friday morning," I said, "you arrive at the office. You're saddened to hear that your boss has called in to say she has the flu and won't be in at all that day."

"So the left-hand expression, 'Boss out of office,' is True," Dave said.

"That's right, Dave," I said. "We're halfway there. Our left-hand expression evaluates to True. Now we have to wait on the direct deposit. The morning drags by as lunch time gets closer and closer. For the moment though, the And operation is returning a False value, because the right-hand expression, 'Money in account,' is still returning a False value. Remember, the And operation is True only if both the left-hand expression and right-hand expressions are True. Right now, only the left-hand expression, 'Boss out of office,' is True. Unfortunately, the last time you checked your balance, you found that your direct deposit still hadn't been made to your account, and $1.38 won't buy you and your friend Melissa much of a lunch."

"I wish we could see this graphically," Peter said.

"Actually Peter," I said, "we can express this dilemma in the form of something called a *truth table*. Here it is."

I displayed the following on the classroom projector:

Expression 1	And	Expression 2	Statement
True	And	True	True
True	And	False	False
False	And	True	False
False	And	False	False

"A truth table," I said, "shows you the four possible outcomes for the And operation. As you can see, there's only one way for an And operation to return a True value, and that's if both Expression 1 (the left-hand side) and Expression 2 (the right-hand side) are True. On the other hand, there are three ways for the And operation to return a value of False."

"I don't like those odds," Kate said, laughing. "I don't think lunch looks too promising!"

"Can you rewrite the truth table in terms of the boss and the money?" Rhonda said. "I think that might help me visualize this."

I took a moment to work up this revised table and then displayed it on the classroom projector. The current situation is highlighted in bold:

Boss Out?	And	Money in Bank?	Go to Lunch?
True	And	True	True
True	**And**	**False**	**False**
False	And	True	False
False	And	False	False

"That's better," Steve said. "This is beginning to make some sense to me now."

"Let's continue on with the story," I said. "As of 10:30, with no cash in the bank, lunch is a remote possibility. Just as you're about to call Melissa and tell her no, one last check of your bank balance shows that the direct deposit has made it, which means the right-hand expression, Expression 2, is now True. Because both the left-hand and right-hand expressions evaluate to True, the entire And operation is True, and you and Melissa can now go off to lunch."

Boss Out?	And	Money in Bank?	Go to Lunch?
True	**And**	**True**	**True**
True	And	False	False
False	And	True	False
False	And	False	False

"What is the And operator in C++?" Kate asked. "Is it the word 'And'?"

"Thanks, Kate," I said. "I almost forgot—the C++ And operator is the ampersand (&&)."

"Can you give us an example of the use of the And operation in C++?" Dave asked.

I thought for a moment, then came up with this example, which I displayed on the classroom projector:

```cpp
//Example3_32.cpp
#include <iostream>
#include <string>

int main()
{
```

```
using namespace std;

string name = "Smith";
int number1 = 99;

if (name == "Smith" && number1 == 22)
   cout << "Both sides of the AND expression are True";

return 0;
}
```

"Once again," I said, "let's use an If statement to evaluate the truth or falseness of the logical expression we've coded, where we check to see whether the value of the name variable is Smith *and* the value of the number variable is 22. If the expression evaluates to True, we display an appropriate message in the console."

I saved the program as Example3_32.cpp, compiled it, and ran it for the class. The following screenshot was displayed on the classroom projector:

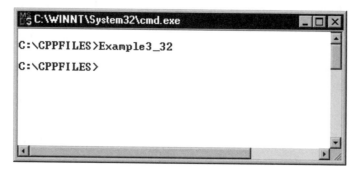

"Nothing happened," Rhonda said.

"You're right, Rhonda," I said, "in that no message was displayed. In this expression, the left-hand side of the expression is True, because *name* is equal to Smith, but the right-hand side expression is False, because the value of *number1* is 99, not 22. Therefore, the And operation returns a value of False (consult the truth table to see this for yourself)."

I then changed the code to assign the value 22 to the variable number:

```
//Example3_33.cpp
#include <iostream>
#include <string>

int main()
{
```

```
using namespace std;

string name = "Smith";
int number1 = 22;

if (name == "Smith" && number1 == 22)
    cout << "Both sides of the AND expression are True";

return 0;
}
```

I saved the program as Example3_33.cpp, compiled it, and ran it for the class. The following screenshot was displayed on the classroom projector:

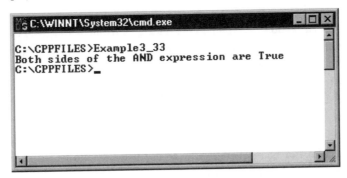

"Now the And operation returns a True value," I said, "because both the left-hand and right-hand expressions are True, and True and True equals True."

The Or Operator (||)

"I think if you're comfortable with the And operation," I said, "you won't have too much trouble with the Or operation. An Or operation, just like the And operation, evaluates expressions to the left and right of the Or operator, returning a value of True or False. The difference is the rules for determining whether the expression is True or False."

I displayed this truth table representing the Or operation on the projector:

Expression 1	Or	Expression 2	Statement
True	Or	True	True
True	Or	False	True
False	Or	True	True
False	Or	False	False

"Notice," I said, "that with the Or operation, as was the case with the And operation, we have four possibilities. In the case of the Or operator, however, three out of four results are True. In fact, with the Or operation, there is only one combination that returns a False value, and that's if both the left-hand and right-hand expressions are False."

"Can you give us another real-world example to illustrate the Or operation?" Linda asked. "Although I think it will be pretty hard for you to top that last one."

I thought for a moment. "Okay," I said, "let's try this one. It's Friday morning. While dressing for work, you receive a phone call from the host of an early morning radio show that is running a contest. He tells you that if the month of your birthday ends in *r* or the last digit of your Social Security Number is 4, you'll be the lucky winner of $10,000!"

"Sounds great to me!" Ward said.

"Let me get this straight," Rhonda said. "All you need to do to win the $10,000 is to have one of those conditions be True—is that right?"

"That's right, Rhonda," I said. "According to the rules of the contest, you'll win the $10,000 if either the left-hand expression is True (the month of your birthday ends in the letter *r*) or the right-hand expression is True (the last digit of your Social Security Number ends in 4). Unlike our lunch date dilemma, where we needed both expressions to be True to go to lunch with our friend, with an Or operation, only one side of the expression needs to be True. How do you like your odds now, Kate?"

"I love 'em," she answered. "If that call were placed to me, I'd win the prize."

Kate wasn't alone—a quick poll of the class revealed that 4 out of the 18 students would win using the Or operation. And guess what—if the contest had called for the And operation, *none* of the students in the class would have won the cash!

I then displayed this truth table to reflect the radio contest. The three outcomes where the Or operation returns a True value are highlighted in bold.

Birthday Month Ends in *r*?	Or	Last Digit of Social Security Is 4?	Win $10,000?
True	**Or**	**True**	**True**
True	**Or**	**False**	**True**
False	**Or**	**True**	**True**
False	Or	False	False

I then took the previous code example and modified it by changing the And operator to an Or operator. In C++, the Or operator is the double pipe character (||):

NOTE

The Or operator is the double pipe character (||). The pipe character appears on the same key as the backslash (\ ) on the keyboard. Beginners frequently mistake it for an exclamation point.

```cpp
//Example3_34.cpp
#include <iostream>
#include <string>

int main()
{
   using namespace std;

   string name = "Smith";
   int number1 = 99;

   if (name == "Smith" || number1 == 22)
     cout << "One or both sides of the OR expression are True";

   return 0;
}
```

I saved the program as Example3_34.cpp, compiled it, and ran it for the class. The following screenshot was displayed on the classroom projector:

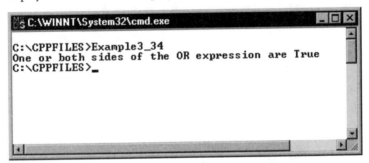

"Because one side of the expression is True—the left-hand side," I said, "True is returned from the Or operation. If we were to change the value of *name* from Smith to Smiley, both the left-hand and right-hand expressions would be false, and the Or operation would return a False value."

I did exactly that, changing the code to look like this:

```cpp
//Example3_35.cpp
#include <iostream>
#include <string>

int main()
{
   using namespace std;

   string name = "Smiley";
```

```
   int number1 = 99;

   if (name == "Smith" || number1 == 22)
      cout << "One or both sides of the OR expression are True";

   return 0;
}
```

I saved the program as Example3_35.cpp, compiled it, and ran it for the class. The following screenshot was displayed on the classroom projector:

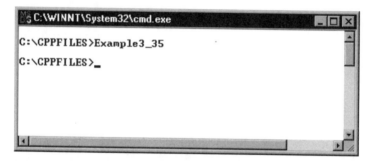

"Nothing is displayed in the console because the Or expression evaluates to False," I said. "The only way that an Or operation can return a False value is if both the left-hand and right-hand expressions evaluate to False. That's the case here—*number1*, with a value of 99, is *not* 22, and *name*, with a value of Smiley, is definitely *not* Smith."

"I just entered some code on my own and I didn't get the correct result," Kathy said.

I took a quick walk to her PC and saw that she had written the following code:

```
//Example3_36.cpp
#include <iostream>
#include <string>

int main()
{
   using namespace std;

   int number = 99;

   if (number == 22 || 88)
      cout << "One or both sides of the OR expression are True";

   return 0;
}
```

I took Kathy's code, saved it as Example3_36.cpp, and compiled and executed it on my PC. The following screenshot was displayed on the classroom projector:

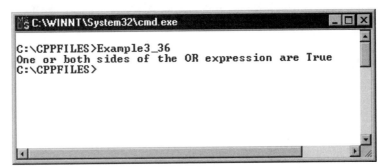

"What did I do wrong?" she asked. "The message is telling me that one or both sides of the Or expression are true, but that's not the case. The value of the variable *number* is 99—that's neither 22 nor 88."

"I know what you wanted to do," I said, "but you confused C++. Your code was very English-like, which is very tempting to do in C++, but you see, you don't really have two expressions on either side of the Or operator. Your left-hand expression is 'number == 22', and your right-hand expression is just the number 99. It's a bit complicated to describe what goes on behind the scenes, but essentially the right-hand expression was evaluated to be true, and so the entire expression was determined to be true. I know it's difficult not to fall into this trap of writing a program the way you speak—I've seen it many times."

"So how could I rewrite my code?" she asked.

I displayed the correct code on the classroom projector:

```cpp
//Example3_37.cpp
#include <iostream>
#include <string>

int main()
{
   using namespace std;

   int number = 99;

   if (number == 22 || number == 88)
     cout << "One or both sides of the OR expression are True";

   return 0;
}
```

"Wow, that was simple," Kathy said. "Why didn't I think of that?"

"You did what a lot of beginners do, Kathy," I answered. "You wrote the code the way you would ask the question in conversation. Unfortunately, as English-like as C++ may appear to be, there are still some statements that can confuse it."

The Not Operator (!)

"We have one more logical operator to discuss today," I continued, "and it's the Not operator. As opposed to the other logical operators, which operate on two operands or expressions, the Not operator is called a *unary* operator because it operates on just a single expression. By the way, the increment and decrement operators are also unary."

"What does the Not operator do?" Steve asked.

"The Not operator is used as a negation," I replied. "It evaluates an expression, takes the True or False result, and then returns the opposite value. So, if an expression evaluates to True, the Not operator returns False. If the expression evaluates to False, the Not operator returns True."

"Why in the world would you want to do something like that?" Rhonda asked.

"The Not operator can simplify some types of program code," I said, "and make it easier to read and understand. Let me show you."

I then displayed this code on the classroom projector:

```
//Example3_38.cpp
#include <iostream>
#include <string>

int main()
{
   using namespace std;

   int number = 13;

   cout << boolalpha << (number == 13);

   return 0;
}
```

"Can anyone tell me what will happen when we run this code?" I asked. Dave suggested that the word *True* would be output in the console.

"That's right," I said. "Because the value of number is 13, C++ will evaluate the expression number == 13 as True."

I then saved the program as Example3_38.cpp, compiled the program, and executed it. As Dave had predicted, the word *True* appeared in the console. I then changed this line of code from

```
cout << boolalpha << (number == 13);
```

to

```
cout << boolalpha << (!(number == 13));
```

"Now what will happen?" I asked. Dave answered that he thought the word *False* would appear in the console.

"Can you tell us why?" I replied.

"Because," he said, "the expression (number == 13) will evaluate to True. Executing the Not operator on a True value gives us a False value."

"Excellent, Dave," I said. "Bill Gates himself couldn't have stated it better." I then compiled the program with the change and executed it. Dave was right; the word False was output in the console.

"Without the Not operator, determining whether a variable's value wasn't a particular value would require some very hard-to-read-and-understand code, like this."

```
cout << boolalpha << (number < 13 || number > 13);
```

"Is that all there is to the Not operator, then?" Barbara asked.

"Basically, yes," I said. I paused before suggesting that we end the class by completing an exercise.

"In this exercise," I said, "you'll have a chance to continue working with the class project—the Grade Calculation Project—which you created last week. We don't have a lot of changes to make to it, but we will enhance it with some variable and constant declarations."

NOTE

You may notice that I use both terms Grade Calculation Project and Grade Calculation Program throughout the book. As you'll see, initially the class project consists of just a single file called Grades.cpp—and so the term program seems to be a good fit. However, as we enhance the class project, we'll create more and more files for it, and so it will no longer be just a single C++ program. At that time, Grades Calculation Project will be a better description.

I then distributed this exercise for the class to complete.

Exercise 3-1 **Add Variables and Constants to the Grade Calculation Program**

In this exercise, you'll find and load up the Grades.cpp program you wrote last week and then modify it to include variable and constant declarations. For the sake of demonstration, you'll calculate the grade for an English student who has received a midterm grade of 70, a final examination grade of 80, a research grade of 90, and a presentation grade of 100 for the four individual component pieces.

1. Using the editor of your choice (most likely Notepad), locate and load up the Grades.cpp source file you created last week. (It should be in the \CPPFiles\Grades folder.)

2. Modify the code so that it looks like this:

```cpp
//Grades.cpp
#include <iostream>

int main ()
{
  using namespace std;

  const float MIDTERM_PERCENTAGE = .25;
  const float FINALEXAM_PERCENTAGE = .25;
  const float RESEARCH_PERCENTAGE = .30;
  const float PRESENTATION_PERCENTAGE = .20;
  int midterm = 70;
  int finalExamGrade = 80;
  int research = 90;
  int presentation = 100;
  float finalNumericGrade = 0;

  finalNumericGrade =
    (midterm * MIDTERM_PERCENTAGE) +
    (finalExamGrade * FINALEXAM_PERCENTAGE) +
    (research * RESEARCH_PERCENTAGE) +
    (presentation * PRESENTATION_PERCENTAGE);

  cout << "Midterm grade is    : " << midterm << endl;
  cout << "Final Exam grade is : " << finalExamGrade << endl;
  cout << "Research grade is   : " << research << endl;
```

```
cout << "Presentation grade is: " << presentation <<
    endl << endl;
cout << "The final grade is: " << finalNumericGrade;

return 0;
}
```

3. Save your source file as Grades.cs in the \CPPFiles\Grades folder (select File | Save As from Notepad's menu bar). Be sure to save your source file with the filename extension .cpp.

4. Compile your source file into an executable file (if you have forgotten how to compile your C++ source file into an executable file, consult Exercise 2-2 from last week).

5. Execute your program (if you have forgotten how to execute your C++ program, consult Exercise 2-3 from last week). You should see output similar to this screenshot:

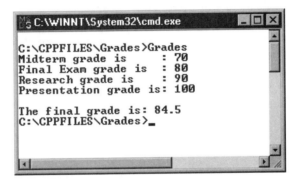

Discussion C++ is a sensitive language, and as such I didn't expect everything to go smoothly with this exercise. All in all, the exercise went well, although some students, particularly those who didn't follow the exercise precisely, had a number of problems. For instance, it took Rhonda four or five compilations of her source file before she wound up with a compiled executable file. In fact, the first time she compiled her source file, she just went right ahead and executed her executable file. Because she still had the old executable file from the previous week, when she executed her program, it produced the results from the previous week. Ultimately, most of her problems stemmed from not spelling her variable names the same way she declared them.

"I admit," Rhonda said, smiling, "I should have paid more attention to the syntax of the variable names. I guess I'm just not used to the case sensitivity of C++."

Ward entirely missed the fact that the constants were declared as float data types, instead declaring them as int. This caused C++ to truncate the assigned value of the constants to zero, and when he executed his program, the final grade result was zero.

A number of students just forgot to end statements with a semicolon, something you need to do in C++.

After about ten minutes, all the students had finally compiled their programs, and it was time to discuss what they had done.

"As you are beginning to realize by now," I said, "each program that writes to the console must have this include statement."

```
#include <iostream>
```

"In addition, each program that is executed from the command-line prompt *must* have a **main()** function."

```
int main ()
```

"As you've also learned, including the using namespace statement for the std library eliminates the need for us to preface our C++ statements with the keyword std."

```
using namespace std;
```

"C++ convention suggests that constant names be capitalized, and if there is more than one word in the constant name, they should be separated by an underscore. That's why we named the constants like this."

```
const float MIDTERM_PERCENTAGE = .25;
const float FINALEXAM_PERCENTAGE = .25;
const float RESEARCH_PERCENTAGE = .30;
const float PRESENTATION_PERCENTAGE = .20;
```

"Notice that C++ constants must be initialized," I said. "I should tell you that as our project evolves, much of the code you see in this class will be moved to one or more support C++ classes. In fact, this code will be placed in a class called EnglishStudent, but more on that in a few weeks."

"I was a little confused," Blaine said, "about your variable-naming conventions. I think I would have begun the variable names with a capital letter."

"By convention," I said, "variable names begin with a lowercase letter. If a variable name consists of more than one word, as some of ours do, the words are joined together and each word after the first begins with an uppercase letter. That's why we named the variables like this."

```
int midterm = 70;
int finalExamGrade = 80;
int research = 90;
int presentation = 100;
float finalNumericGrade = 0;
```

I had thought that this next section of code would give the class problems, but it hadn't, although Mary did have a question:

```
finalNumericGrade =
    (midterm * MIDTERM_PERCENTAGE) +
    (finalExamGrade * FINALEXAM_PERCENTAGE) +
    (research * RESEARCH_PERCENTAGE) +
    (presentation * PRESENTATION_PERCENTAGE);
```

"I understand what you were doing in this next section of code," she said. "You're multiplying the component grade pieces by the applicable constant values, but why didn't each line of code end with a semicolon?"

"Because those five lines of code are really just a single C++ statement," I answered. "Because a C++ statement can span more than one line—in this case, five—we only needed the semicolon at the very end."

"Did we really need those parentheses?" Dave asked. "Based on the Order of Operations, wouldn't the multiplication operations have been performed before the additions?"

"That's right, Dave," I said. "We could have written the code like this, and the answer would still be correct."

```
finalNumericGrade =
    midterm * MIDTERM_PERCENTAGE +
    finalExamGrade * FINALEXAM_PERCENTAGE +
    research * RESEARCH_PERCENTAGE +
    presentation * PRESENTATION_PERCENTAGE;
```

"But I'm a big believer in readability. I think the parentheses make the code easier to read for someone else and leave no doubt as to our intentions."

"I understood everything that was going on in this next section," Kate said, "except for the two instances of endl on next-to-last cout statement. What's going on with that?"

Kate was referring to this section of code:

```
cout << "Midterm grade is     : " << midterm << endl;
cout << "Final Exam grade is  : " << finalExamGrade << endl;
```

```
cout << "Research grade is     : " << research << endl;
cout << "Presentation grade is: " << presentation << endl << endl;
cout << "The final grade is: " << finalNumericGrade;
```

"As you learned a little earlier today," I said, "endl causes a carriage return and line feed character to be passed to the cout object. Because we want to print a blank line prior to displaying the final grade in the console, we pass the cout object two instances of endl."

"So that's where that blank line came from," Linda said. "I was wondering about that. Is formatting like this something that we'll concern ourselves with a great deal?"

"Only in this course," I said. "When you take the C++ Intermediate class here at the university, you'll learn how to write C++ programs that present the user with a graphical user interface (GUI)—in other words, windows. At that point, you won't be using the console at all. Finally, this line of code completes the program—the return statement of the integer value zero, followed by the closing right brace."

```
return 0;
}
```

I waited to see if anyone had any questions.

"Next week," I said, "you'll learn how to make our program a lot more intelligent through the use of selection structures."

I then dismissed class for the day—it had been a long, but very valuable one.

Summary

This was quite an exhaustive look at the use of data in C++. In this chapter, you learned about the importance of variables in C++. You learned when, where, and how to use variables and about the different C++ variable types that you can declare. In addition, you discovered how to use a variety of operations to manipulate the data contained in those variables.

Variables are defined in memory to hold data or information. Each variable has a scope, which determines what other parts of your program can see the variable, and a lifetime, which determines when the variable dies. Some variables live for as long as your program runs; others live only for as long as a function executes. We discussed the need to declare and initialize variables.

C++ data types can be categorized in four broad ways:

- **bool**   True or False values only.
- **Numeric**   Numbers only, which can be integer and floating-point data types.
- **char**   A single character.
- **String**   A set of characters, treated as text. Strings can hold the characters representing numbers, but these are not numbers that you can perform arithmetic on.

A constant is like a fixed variable and is declared using the const keyword. Constants should be named in all capital letters so that they stand out in your code. Once a value is assigned to a constant, that value cannot be changed.

Finally, we took a look at arithmetic, comparison, and logical operators. Operators act on expressions and return a result. An example of a mathematical operator is the plus sign. You learned that multiple operators are treated in a defined order called the Order of Operations, where operations in parentheses are performed first, followed by exponentiation, multiplication and division, and finally, addition and subtraction.

An example of a comparison operator is the double equal sign. An example of a logical operator is the And operator, represented by the ampersand (&&).

You should now be familiar, if not totally comfortable, with the ways you can manipulate data in C++ programs. In the next chapter, you'll see how selection structures permit your program to make decisions.

Selection
Structures

I n programming, one of the most important capabilities your program must have is to adapt to conditions that are encountered while it is running. In this chapter, we'll continue to follow my C++ class as we examine selection structures—programming constructs that enable your program to adapt to those runtime conditions. Specifically, you'll learn about the If statement and the Switch statement. Along the way, you'll also get your first taste of writing a program that accepts input from the user.

Selection Structures

I arrived in the classroom a little later than usual and found a bit of a commotion.

"What's wrong?" I asked, noting that there was a group of students surrounding Rose and Jack.

"As you know," Jack said, "Rose and I are both engineers by trade, and we work for the same company. For the last few months, we've been working on our company's biggest account—overseeing the construction of a new cruise ship in the United Kingdom. Construction is way ahead of schedule, and yesterday our supervisor told us that we're being called away to participate in the sea trials. So you see, this will probably be our last class!"

"I'm disappointed," Rose said, "because I had hoped to finish the coding for the Grade Calculation Project before we left for the sea trials, but there's no way we'll be near to that point today."

I told both Rose and Jack that we would all be sorry not to have them present all the way through the project, but we hoped they would be able to return in time to see the final version of the Grade Calculation Project implemented in the English, Math, and Science departments.

"But as far as the Grade Calculation Project is concerned," I said, "I have a surprise for you. By the end of today's class, we'll have coded a working prototype of the Grade Calculation Project. It's not quite what we'll be delivering to Frank Olley in a few weeks, but I think you'll be pleased with it—and pretty amazed at just how full featured it is."

As the obvious shock at my last statement subsided, I began our fourth class by telling everyone that during the next two weeks, they would be learning about the three types of programming structures that form the building blocks of all computer programs.

"Structure?" Ward said. "That sounds like a house or a building."

"The building analogy is a good one, Ward," I said. "You've already learned that the first step in developing a program is to develop a 'blueprint' in the form of a Requirements Statement. Many years ago computer scientists discovered that any program can be written using a combination of three coding structures, much like a house can be constructed using a series of standard components. These three structures—the sequence structure, the selection structure, and the loop structure—will form the basis of our discussions over the next few weeks."

"Will we be writing any code ourselves today?" Rhonda asked. "I know we wrote a bit of code last week, but I'm really getting anxious to get going."

"You'll have a chance to write a lot of code today," I answered. "Whenever possible, I try to have the exercises that we complete here in class ultimately lead to the completion of the Grade Calculation Project. However, from time to time we'll complete some exercises just for practice. So that we don't confuse that work with the Grade Completion Project, if you want to keep your practice exercises, you should save them in the Practice folder you created earlier in the class. Before we get into our examination of the selection structure today, I'd like to give you all a chance to work with code that allows you to 'input' data into your program."

Getting Input into Your Program

"Up to this point," I said, "we have not yet written a program that accepts data from outside of the program while it's running. In the programming world, this is a common need, and there are many ways to accomplish this. For instance, a program can open and read data from a file on the user's PC or network; it can also open and read data from a database, which is a more sophisticated form of a data file. It can also accept data directly from the user."

"Do you mean our program can ask the user a question and do something with their answer?" Rhonda asked.

"Yes, Rhonda, " I said, "that's exactly what I'm getting at. In the next few minutes, I'll demonstrate how we can do that by using the cin object to accept input and the cout object to write to the console window."

I thought for a moment and then wrote and displayed this program on the classroom projector:

```cpp
//Example4_1.cpp
#include <iostream>
#include <string>

int main()
{
    using namespace std;

    string response;

    cout << "What is your favorite programming language? ";
    cin >> response;
    cout << "You have great taste. " <<
        response << " is a great language" << endl;

    return 0;
}
```

I saved the program as Example4_1.cpp, compiled it, and ran it for the class. The following screenshot was displayed on the classroom projector:

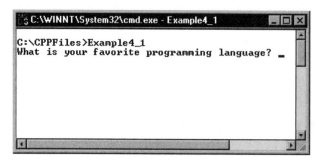

"It's not obvious," I said, "but the program is prompting us to name our favorite programming language. At this point, all we need to do is type our answer and press ENTER." I did so, and the following screenshot was displayed on the classroom projector:

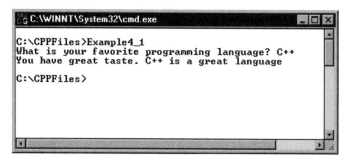

"Let me explain what's going on here," I said. "As we've done with all the programs we've written so far, we begin by telling C++ that we will be including certain libraries in our program. In this case, we are including both the iostream and string libraries, because we will be using the special string object in our program."

```
#include <iostream>
#include <string>
```

"Every program that runs from the command line must have a **main()** function, and these two lines of code begin it. In case you forgot, the word *int* in front of the name of the **main()** function indicates that the function returns an integer value. The pair of empty parentheses indicates that no arguments, or values, are passed to the function. Don't worry about arguments now. We'll be discussing them later."

```
int main(){
```

"After coding the first line of the **main()** function—sometimes called the *procedure header*—we begin the actual coding of the **main()** function by starting off with a bracket, followed by announcing to C++ that we will be using the std namespace in our program. This saves us from having to type the word *std* in front of the objects that are contained in the std namespace, such as cin and cout."

```
using namespace std;
```

"Next, we declare a string variable called *response*. This variable will be used to store the user's response to our question, What is your favorite programming language?"

```
string response;
```

"We need to pose a question to the user, and we do that by passing the question in the form of a quoted string to the cout object. Notice how we insert a space after the question mark. That allows for a space after the question and the user's response."

```
cout << "What is your favorite programming language? ";
```

I waited for questions before continuing.

"This next line of code uses the cin object to 'redirect' the user's response into the variable *response*. In the old days of programming, doing something like this was really tough, but the cin object makes it a snap. Basically, everything that the user types up to the point they hit the ENTER key is placed in the string variable *response*. Notice how the redirection symbol (>>) is in the opposite 'direction' of the redirection symbol we use with the cout object."

```
cin >> response;
```

I paused to see if everyone was still with me. They were.

"Finally, because we now have the user's answer in the *response* variable, we can use its value to confirm the user's great taste in a programming language, using the plus (<<) operator to concatenate the value of the response variable to the string 'You have great taste.'"

```
cout << "You have great taste. " <<
        response << " is a great language" << endl;
```

 NOTE
This code could have been written on a single line. It was broken up in order to 'fit' neatly on the printed page of this book. Remember, in C++, you can break a line of code up in virtually any way you wish—except in the middle of a quoted string.

"Finally, we end the program by executing the return statement. Because we declare the **main()** function to return an integer data type, we return the value 0."

```
return 0;
```

"I'm amazed that I actually understand what's going on here," Rose said.

"I love what this program does," Jack said.

I told my students that I'd like to give them a chance to experiment on their own with obtaining input from the user via the C++ console, so I distributed this exercise for them to complete.

Experimenting with C++ Input

In this exercise, you'll write code to ask the user their first name and then generate a custom response to them. You'll discover that if the user makes no response and then presses ENTER, some unsatisfactory results occur.

1. Create a folder on your hard drive called \CPPFiles\Practice. This will be the home of the C++ programs we create in class that are not part of the Grade Calculation Project.Use Notepad and enter the following code:

```cpp
//Practice4_1.cpp
#include <iostream>
#include <string>

int main()
{
    using namespace std;

    string response;

    cout << "What is your name? ";
    cin >> response;
    cout << "It's nice to meet you, " << response;

    return 0;
}
```

2. Save your source file as Practice4_1 in the \CPPFiles\Practice folder (select File | Save As from Notepad's menu bar). Be sure to save your source file with the filename extension .cpp.

3. Compile your source file into an executable file.

4. Execute the program. When prompted, type your first name only and then press ENTER. A message, including your name, should be displayed in the console.

5. Execute your program again, but this time type your first and last name. What happens? What does C++ display in the console?

6. Execute the program. When prompted, immediately press ENTER. What happens?

Discussion No one had any major problems completing the exercise. By now they were getting pretty good with coding a simple C++ program and having a great time doing it. I ran the program myself, typed my first name, and a message reading "It's nice to meet you, John" was displayed in the C++ console.

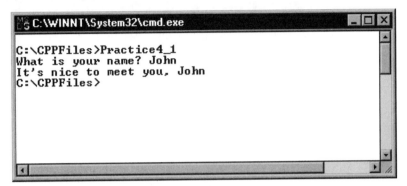

```
C:\WINNT\System32\cmd.exe

C:\CPPFiles>Practice4_1
What is your name? John
It's nice to meet you, John
C:\CPPFiles>
```

A few students had minor problems completing the exercise. One student used the wrong redirection symbol with the cin object, and a couple had problems in formatting their display in the console.

Rhonda indicated that she had a problem. "My cursor didn't stay on the same line as the question. In your version of the program, the cursor stayed on the same line, and there was a space in between the question and your response."

"I suspect," I answered, "that you may have placed the endl object reference on the wrong line of code."

I took a quick walk to Rhonda's PC, and sure enough, that is what she had coded. Not only that, but she had forgotten to include a space after the question mark of her question. This was something Blaine had also done.

```
cout << "What is your name?" << endl;
```

I corrected her code to look like this:

```
cout << "What is your name? ";
```

"Somehow I thought C++ would do that for me automatically," Rhonda said.

"In programming, very little happens automatically," I said. "Especially when you are dealing with string literals like this. Whatever you tell C++ to display, that's exactly what will be displayed—and that includes spaces."

I paused before continuing. "Did everyone notice what happens when you enter both your first and last name?"

I ran the program again, and this time typed both my first and last name and then pressed ENTER. The following screenshot was displayed on the classroom projector:

```
C:\WINNT\System32\cmd.exe                            _ □ ×

C:\CPPFiles>Practice4_1
What is your name? John Smiley
It's nice to meet you, John
C:\CPPFiles>_
```

"Only your first name was displayed," Steve said.

"That's right, Steve," I said. "The cin object is confused. As soon as it encountered a space character, it stopped working. That would be true for any white space, too—like a TAB key or the ENTER key."

"What can we do about this?" Linda asked. "I would think we'll need to be able to have the user input more than a single word into our program."

"Not to worry Linda," I said, "there are a few ways around this. The simplest one is to prompt the user for each element separately. Essentially, we could prompt the user for their first name, store it, and then repeat the process for their last name. If we want to get more input on a single line, though, there is a way around cin's limits, but it involves the use of something called a *character array*. We'll examine arrays later on in the course, and you'll learn that an array is just a collection of something. In this case, a character array is a collection of characters, and using one, in conjunction with the **getline()** method of the cin object, we can deal with this problem. Let me show you."

I then displayed this code on the classroom projector:

```cpp
//Example4_2.cpp
#include <iostream>
#include <string>

int main()
{
   using namespace std;

   char response[256];

   cout << "What is your name? ";
   cin.getline(response,256);
```

```
    cout << "It's nice to meet you, " << response;

    return 0;
}
```

I saved it as Example4_2.cpp, compiled it, and executed it. I then entered both my first and last name at the prompt, and the following screenshot was displayed:

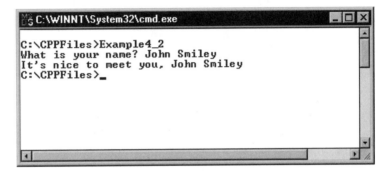

"That's better," I said. "Notice that both my first and last name have been displayed. All we needed to do was change the response variable from a string variable to an array of the char data type."

```
char response[256];
```

"Also, instead of assigning the input of the cin object to a string variable, we executed the **getline()** method of the cin object."

```
cin.getline(response,256);
```

"In case you're wondering, a method is simply another name for a function that is declared in an object. Also, the **getline()** method requires two arguments: the first is the name of the character array, and the second is the maximum number of characters to read. Again, if the concept of an array is baffling you right now, don't be too concerned. We'll cover it in much more detail toward the end of the course."

"You asked us to run our program and immediately hit the ENTER key," Mary said. "When I did that, the program just kept running and running. The only way to stop it was to type something—and then the display was skewed."

"You're absolutely right, Mary," I said. "Both Practice4_1 and the modified version of the program I just coded and ran have a problem dealing with the user immediately hitting the ENTER key without typing any characters. Being able to detect whether the user simply presses the ENTER key will be very important to us later on, and you'll learn how to handle this in just a few moments."

There were no questions on getting input into our program, so I suggested that we take a look at the C++ sequence structure now.

The Sequence Structure—Falling Rock

"As you'll see later on," I said, "both the selection and loop structures require a special syntax to implement, but that's not the case with the sequence structure. Any code that we write is automatically part of a sequence structure. I like to analogize a sequence structure to the behavior of a falling rock."

"Falling rock? What do you mean by that?" Steve said, obviously amused.

"Have you seen signs warning you of falling rock on the highway?" I said. "If you've ever seen rock fall, you know that once it gets rolling, there's no stopping it. The same is true of C++ program code. For instance, let's look at the code we wrote last week that displays the final grade of an English student to the C++ console:

```cpp
//Grades.cpp
#include <iostream>

int main ()
{
  using namespace std;

  const float MIDTERM_PERCENTAGE = .25;
  const float FINALEXAM_PERCENTAGE = .25;
  const float RESEARCH_PERCENTAGE = .30;
  const float PRESENTATION_PERCENTAGE = .20;
  int midterm = 70;
  int finalExamGrade = 80;
  int research = 90;
  int presentation = 100;
  float finalNumericGrade = 0;

  finalNumericGrade =
    (midterm * MIDTERM_PERCENTAGE) +
    (finalExamGrade * FINALEXAM_PERCENTAGE) +
    (research * RESEARCH_PERCENTAGE) +
    (presentation * PRESENTATION_PERCENTAGE);

  cout << "Midterm grade is    : " << midterm << endl;
  cout << "Final Exam grade is : " << finalExamGrade << endl;
  cout << "Research grade is   : " << research << endl;
```

```
cout << "Presentation grade is: " << presentation << endl << endl;
cout << "The final grade is: " << finalNumericGrade;

    return 0;
}
```

"This code is a perfect example of the sequence structure. Last week, we observed that the first line of code in the **main**() function executes, followed by the second line of code, then the third, and so forth, in *sequence*."

"Oh, I see where the term 'sequence structure' comes from now," Valerie said. "You mean each line of code is executed, one after the other. But I guess I have to ask, What else could happen? Isn't every line of code evaluated by C++?"

"Every line of code is evaluated by C++," I said, "but not every line of code is necessarily executed only once—or even one time for that matter. Some lines of code can be skipped based on conditions found when the program is running. In other cases, lines of code may be executed more than once, as you'll see when you learn about coding loops in programs. That's where the C++ selection and loop structures come into play. The selection structure gives 'intelligence' to our program, in the form of decision-making capabilities, which is something the falling rock behavior of a sequence structure simply can't do. The selection structure allows us to *selectively* execute lines of code based on conditions our program finds at runtime. Next week, we'll examine the loop structure, which allows us to execute a line or lines of code *repetitively*."

I paused a moment before adding, "In order to illustrate the alternatives to the falling rock behavior of a sequence structure, I'd like you to complete a series of exercises based on a fictitious collection of seven restaurants in New York City. Pretend, for a few moments, that you have been hired by these seven restaurants to write a program to display their ads on a giant display screen in Times Square, but in our case we're going to use the C++ console as our giant display screen. Here's the second exercise of the day, which will illustrate, I hope, the 'falling rock' behavior of C++ code."

I then distributed this exercise for the class to complete.

Exercise 4-2

Eat at Joe's (The Sequence Structure's Falling Rock Behavior)

In this exercise, you'll write a C++ program that displays information to the C++ console about the days of operation of seven restaurants in New York City. Pretend that the C++ console is actually a giant display screen in New York City's Times Square.

1. Use Notepad and enter the following code (be *extremely* careful of the capitalization—C++ is very picky):

```
//Practice4_2.cpp
#include <iostream>
```

```
int main()
{
    using namespace std;

    cout << "Eat at Joe's" << endl;
    cout << "Eat at Tom's" << endl;
    cout << "Eat at Kevin's" << endl;
    cout << "Eat at Rich's" << endl;
    cout << "Eat at Rose's" << endl;
    cout << "Eat at Ken's" << endl;
    cout << "Eat at Melissa's" << endl;

    return 0;
}
```

2. Save your source file as Practice4_2 in the \CPPFiles\Practice folder (select File | Save As from Notepad's menu bar). Be sure to save your source file with the filename extension .cpp.

3. Compile your source file into an executable file.

4. Execute your program. You should see output similar to this screenshot:

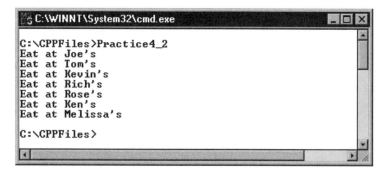

Aside from some students' continued anxiety with writing code and compiling it into an executable file, this exercise went pretty smoothly. Having warned them in the instructions for the exercise, my students were very careful with their capitalization—something that had tripped them up in the previous week's exercise. Only one person had a problem—and that person capitalized the letter *c* in the word *cout*, causing the C++ compiler to generate an error message. I gave everyone a chance to complete the exercise and then began to explain what we had done with this small program.

"This program seemed pretty straightforward," Rhonda said. "What were you trying to illustrate with it?"

"The sequence structure," I answered. "The code that makes up the **main()** function of this class represents something known as a *programming sequence structure*. As I mentioned a little earlier, all that means is that the second line of code executes after the first line of code, the third after the second, and so on."

"Falling rock behavior," Ward chimed in.

"Exactly right, Ward," I said. "Does everyone remember how the cout object works?"

"No problem," Valerie said. "The cout object is used to display output to the C++ console."

"That's right, Valerie," I said.

There where no other questions about the exercise, so I continued.

"Having written this program for the owners of the seven restaurants," I said, "suppose that the owner of Joe's restaurant goes into semi-retirement and decides to open his restaurant only on Sundays. Tom, proprietor of Tom's restaurant, hearing the news about Joe, thinks semi-retirement is a great idea and decides to open his restaurant only on Mondays. Kevin follows suit and opens only on Tuesdays. Soon the rest of the owners hear about this, figure that one day of work a week is a great idea, and the next thing we know, Rich is open only on Wednesdays, Rose only on Thursdays, Ken only on Fridays, and Melissa only on Saturdays. Hoping to save advertising costs in Times Square, each owner contacts us and informs us they want to advertise on our giant display screen only on the days that their restaurant is actually open. How can we handle this with our program?"

I gave everyone a moment or two to think about the problem.

"I suppose," Peter said, "we could write separate C++ programs for different days of the week—although if you tell me there isn't a better way than that, I may need to drop out of the class!"

"Peter is right," I said to the class. "We could write separate C++ programs for each day of the week, and he's also right that there is a better way. We can make our program smart enough to know what the date is—and based on that, the day of the week. Armed with that knowledge, we can then use the C++ selection structure to decide which restaurant advertisement to display on our giant display screen."

The C++ Selection Structure: The If Statement

"Selection structures," I continued, "can alter the default (falling rock) behavior of C++ code, but they are a little more complicated to write. Selection structures require that the programmer specify one or more conditions to be evaluated or tested by the program, along with a statement or statements to be executed if the condition is determined to be true, and optionally, other statements to be executed if the condition is determined to be false. In the next exercise, you'll implement one of the two C++ selection structures: the If statement. The condition that you'll ask C++ to evaluate is the current day of the week, which in this exercise, will be supplied by the operator of the display screen. Based on C++'s determination of the day of the week, a decision as to which restaurant's advertising to display on the console will be made. As you'll see, coding selection structures requires a little more upfront thought than merely coding a plain sequence structure."

I then distributed this exercise for the class to complete.

Exercise 4-3   The If Statement (or Which Restaurant Is Open Today?)

In this exercise, you'll modify the code from Exercise 4-2 to use an If statement to determine which restaurant to advertise in the C++ console.

1. Using Notepad, enter the following code:

```
//Practice4_3.cpp
#include <iostream>
#include <string>

int main()
{
    using namespace std;

    string today;

    cout << "What day of the week is it? ";
    cin >> today;

    if (today == "Sunday")
        cout << "Eat at Joe's";
    if (today == "Monday")
        cout << "Eat at Tom's";
    if (today == "Tuesday")
        cout << "Eat at Kevin's";
    if (today == "Wednesday")
        cout << "Eat at Rich's";
    if (today == "Thursday")
        cout << "Eat at Rose's";
    if (today == "Friday")
        cout << "Eat at Ken's";
```

```
    if (today == "Saturday")
        cout << "Eat at Melissa's";
}
```

2. Save your source file as Practice4_3 in the \CPPFiles\Practice folder (select File | Save As from Notepad's menu bar). Be sure to save your source file with the filename extension .cpp.

3. Compile your source file into an executable file.

4. Execute your program. Enter the current day of the week (be sure to capitalize the first letter of the day of the week). You should see one restaurant advertisement displayed in the C++ console, similar to this screenshot (which one it is will depend on the day of the week you enter at the prompt):

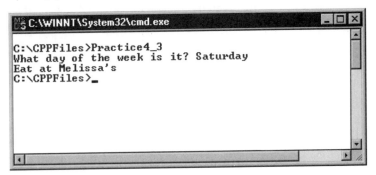

Discussion I gave my students about ten minutes to complete the exercise. They seemed mesmerized with the ability of their program to behave intelligently. Although no one had any trouble completing the exercise, there were still a number of puzzled looks in the classroom.

"This is really cool," Steve said. "I had no idea you could do something like this with a programming language, although I must confess I don't think I understand half the code we just wrote."

"I think you are all comfortable with the first few statements in our program," I said. "These first two lines of code tell C++ that we wish to include the iostream and string libraries in our program."

```
#include <iostream>
#include <string>
```

"The next two lines of code declare the **main()** function."

```
int main()
{
```

"The next line of code tells C++ that we wish to use the std namespace in the program."

```
using namespace std;
```

"This next line of code declares a variable called *today*, which will be used to hold the answer that the 'operator' of our program provides to us when asked what the day of the week is."

```
string today;
```

"Here's the line of code to prompt the user of the program for the day of the week."

```
cout << "What day of the week is it? ";
```

"This is followed by the line of code that takes the user's response and assigns it, via a redirection to the cin object, to the variable *today*."

```
cin >> today;
```

I could see that Jack looked a bit confused, and I asked him if he was okay.

"That makes sense," Jack said. "I think it's just a matter of getting used to all this mention of objects, such as cin and cout."

"It does take some getting used to," I said. "But remember, C++ is very much object oriented. You'll be dealing with objects like this quite often."

I waited for questions before continuing.

"At this point," I said, "the *today* variable contains the current day of the week. Here we are using the C++ If statement in determining whether the day of the week is Sunday."

```
if (today == "Sunday")
```

"Two equal signs?" Rhonda interrupted. "Is that right? Shouldn't it be one?"

"Good question, Rhonda," I said. "In C++, we test for equality by using two equal signs, not a single equal sign. One equal sign is used to assign a value to a variable. Here, we're using the C++ If statement to evaluate an expression to determine whether it is true or false. In this case, the expression is today == "Sunday"."

"The expression that is evaluated as part of the If statement, does it have to be within parentheses?" Chuck asked.

"Good question, Chuck," I said. "The answer is yes. The expression must be enclosed within parentheses, and it must be an expression that can evaluate to a True or False result."

"What happens if the expression evaluates to True?" Kate asked.

"If the expression evaluates to True," I said, "then any imperative statements following it are executed."

"What's an imperative statement?" Rhonda asked.

"Simply speaking," I said, "an imperative statement is a command. In this case, we coded just a single imperative statement to be executed if the day of week happens to be a Sunday."

```
cout << "Eat at Joe's";
```

"What happens if the expression evaluates to False?" Joe asked.

"In that case," I answered, "the imperative statement is skipped—it's not executed."

"Can you execute more than one imperative statement?" Dave asked.

"Yes, you can," I said. "If you want to execute more than one imperative statement if the expression is true, you need to place each statement within a block. In C++, a *block* is code that is placed within curly brackets, like this."

```
if (today == "Sunday")
    {
    cout << "Imperative Statement #1";
    cout << "Imperative Statement #2";
    cout << "Imperative Statement #3";
    }
```

"To save a line of code, it's sometimes written like this."

```
if (today == "Sunday") {
    cout << "Imperative Statement #1";
    cout << "Imperative Statement #2";
    cout << "Imperative Statement #3";
    }
```

NOTE

A block is a group of statements between curly brackets ({ }).

"Provided you understand how our first If statement works, the remainder of the If statements are pretty straightforward. All we're doing is evaluating the value of the variable *today* for the other six days of the week. The other built-in DateTime constants represent the other six days of the week. Because we've covered all our bases here, one of these should evaluate to True, provided the user has typed a valid entry."

```
if (today == "Monday")
    cout << "Eat at Tom's";
if (today == "Tuesday")
    cout << "Eat at Kevin's";
if (today == "Wednesday")
    cout << "Eat at Rich's";
```

```
if (today == "Thursday")
    cout << "Eat at Rose's";
if (today == "Friday")
    cout << "Eat at Ken's";
if (today == "Saturday")
    cout << "Eat at Melissa's";
```

"I know you mentioned earlier," Valerie said, "that if the expression evaluates to False, the imperative statement will be skipped. Is it possible to specify a statement or statements to execute if the expression is False?"

"Optionally, you can do that, yes," I answered, "by using an Else clause of the If statement. In this case, we opted to have the next If statement executed instead."

"So if the If statement evaluates to False," Dave asked, "the imperative statement or statements are skipped, and execution of the program picks up with the next line of code following them?"

"Absolutely correct, Dave," I said. "I couldn't have said it better myself."

"I feel pretty good about If statements," Lou said. "Is that all there is to them?"

"You still have some more to learn about them, Lou," I replied. "There's still the Else clause to consider, plus there's another selection structure called the Switch statement that you need to learn about."

The If...Else Statement

"With the If statements we've seen so far," I said, "we've specified only the imperative statements to execute if the expression evaluates to True. Using the Else clause, we can specify one or more imperative statements to execute if the expression evaluates to False. Let me show you a program that uses a simple If...Else statement."

I then displayed this program on the classroom projector:

```
//Example4_3.cpp
#include <iostream>

int main()
{
    using namespace std;

    string response;
    cout << "What is your favorite programming language? ";
    cin >> response;
```

```
  if (response == "C++")
     cout << "You have great taste. C++ is a great language";
  else
     cout << "It's not as good as C++, but " <<
             response <<
             " is also a great language";

  return 0;
}
```

I saved the program as Example4_3.cpp, compiled it, and ran it for the class. The program asked me what my favorite programming language is. I answered C++ and was congratulated on my good taste.

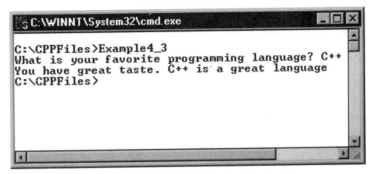

"As you can see, we used an If Statement to determine whether the user entered 'C++'," I said. "Because the If statement found what it was looking for, C++, it executed this imperative statement."

```
if (response == "C++")
   cout << "You have great taste. C++ is a great language";
```

"I see we used the Else clause here," Kate said. "Do I understand that the statement following the word Else will be executed if the user enters anything other than 'C++' as their answer?"

"That's right, Kate," I answered. "If the evaluation of this expression results in a False condition, then the statement or statements following the word *Else* are executed."

```
else
   cout << "It's not as good as C++, but " <<
           response <<
           " is also a great language";
```

"By the way, note that if the user enters 'C++' in any other fashion than with a capital *C*, our program will discern that as a False condition also. For now, let's run this program again and answer the question with another language."

I did exactly that, this time providing an answer of Java as my language of choice. When I did so, the following screenshot was displayed.

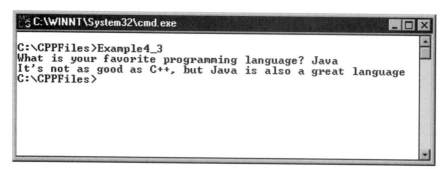

"The display of this message was handled by the Else clause of the If statement," I said. "I should also mention that it's possible to code an If statement as the imperative statement that follows the Else clause."

"Wow, that sounds confusing," Rhonda said. "Why would we want to do that?"

"It allows us to handle situations where we have multiple conditions to test for," I answered. "For instance, if we wanted to display unique messages for a variety of answers that the user might provide to us."

No one had any questions about the If statement or the Else clause, so I suggested that we turn our attention to using an If statement to handle the problems from Exercise 4-1 that arose from the user entering nothing and then pressing ENTER.

Exercise 4-4   ## Using an If Statement to Check for No Entry

In this exercise, you'll modify the code from Exercise 4-1 so that if the user makes no entry and then presses ENTER, an appropriate message will be displayed.

1. Using Notepad, enter the following code:

```
//Practice4_4.cpp
#include <iostream>
#include <string>
```

```
int main()
{
    using namespace std;

    char response[256];

    cout << "What is your name? ";
    cin.getline(response,256);

    if (strlen(response) == 0)
        cout << "You must tell me your name...";
    else
        cout << "It's nice to meet you, " << response;

    return 0;
}
```

2. Save your source file as Practice4_4 in the \CPPFiles\Practice folder (select File | Save As from Notepad's menu bar). Be sure to save your source file with the filename extension .cpp.

3. Compile your source file into an executable file.

4. Execute your program. When prompted, type your full name and then press ENTER. A message, including your full name, should be displayed in the console.

5. Execute your program again, and this time immediately press ENTER. What does C++ display in the console?

Discussion

"This program now exhibits quite a bit of intelligence," I said. "It's basically the same code from Example4_1, but this time we're using a character array in combination with the **getline()** method of the cin object to get the user's input. As it turns out, C++ provides us a function called **strlen()** to determine the number of characters in either a string or character array. All we need to do is execute the **strlen()** function, passing it, as a single argument, the variable name containing the user's response to our question. The return value from the **strlen()** function is the number of characters in the variable. If the return value is 0, we know that the user pressed the ENTER key without typing any other characters, and we display a warning message to that effect."

```
if (strlen(response) == 0)
    cout << "You must tell me your name...";
```

I ran the program myself, immediately pressed ENTER, and the following screenshot was displayed:

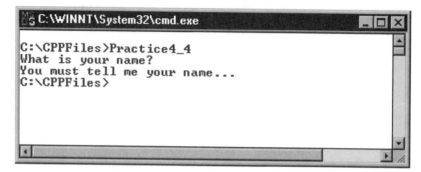

```
C:\CPPFiles>Practice4_4
What is your name?
You must tell me your name...
C:\CPPFiles>
```

"I'm still not absolutely sure about the If statement syntax," Joe said. "Can you show us another example?"

After thinking for a few moments, I said, "To make this all a little more understandable for everyone, let me use pseudocode to illustrate an Else statement intended to display the number of years until an employee is eligible for retirement."

I saw some puzzled looks.

"I think I mentioned pseudocode earlier in the course," I said. "Pseudocode provides a way that programmers use to express complex problems. Instead of coding the problem in a particular language, pseudocode lets us concentrate on expressing the problem in an English-like way. Then, when we have it worked out to our satisfaction, we can translate the pseudocode into whatever language we happen to be working in. Remember, what you see here isn't C++ code, so don't try to type it into a code window!"

I then displayed this pseudocode on the classroom projector:

NOTE
Pseudocode is a way of expressing a complex problem in an English-like way, prior to coding it up in an actual programming language.

```
There is an employee working for a company. According to the rules of company:
If the employee's age is 62 or greater
he/she must be retired
Else If the employee's age is 61
he/she has 1 year until retirement
Else If the employee's age is 60
he/she has 2 years until retirement
Else If the employee's age is 59
he/she has 3 years until retirement
```

```
Else
he/she has a really long time to go
```

I then suggested that we try implementing this pseudocode in C++, but I warned everyone that our code would be a bit unwieldy. "Using a series of If...Else statements can be pretty cumbersome," I said. "After we write the code for this exercise, in Exercise 4-6 we'll look at an alternative selection structure called the Switch statement, which often can be used to streamline If...Else statements."

Exercise 4-5 ## The If...Else...If Statement

In this exercise, you'll create a program to determine how long an employee has until he or she can retire.

1. Using Notepad, enter the following code:

```cpp
//Practice4_5.cpp
#include <iostream>
#include <string>

int main()
{
    using namespace std;

    char response[256];

    cout << "What is your age? ";
    cin.getline(response,256);

    if (strlen(response) == 0)
        cout << "You must tell me your age...";
    else
    if (atoi(response) > 61)
        cout << response << " - You must be retired";
    else
    if (atoi(response) == 61)
        cout << response <<
            " - You have 1 year until retirement";
    else
    if (atoi(response) == 60)
        cout << response <<
            " - You have 2 years until retirement";
    else
    if (atoi(response) == 59)
        cout << response <<
```

```
                         " - You have 3 years until retirement";
             else
                cout << response <<
                         " - You have a long time until retirement";

             return 0;
          }
```

2. Save your source file as Practice4_5 in the \CPPFiles\Practice folder (select File | Save As from Notepad's menu bar). Be sure to save your source file with the filename extension .cpp.

3. Compile your source file into an executable file.

4. Execute your program multiple times, entering **62**, **61**, **60**, **59**, and **40** as answers to your age. Observe the various messages displayed in the console.

5. Execute the program one more time, this time pressing ENTER without making an entry for your age. You should receive a warning message.

Discussion   There was probably more code in this exercise than in any of the others we had done so far, and several of my students became confused and lost their places. Fifteen minutes later, though, I was happy to see that everyone in the class had successfully completed the exercise.

"I don't think we've ever written that much code," Rhonda said.

"I think you're right, Rhonda," I replied. "We haven't written this much code before. When you write code that tests for a variety of conditions like we did here, it can really balloon, but sometimes that's something that just can't be helped. The code you've written for this exercise, though lengthy, is still pretty manageable. Suppose we had a requirement to display a different message for every age between 1 and 100."

"That would really balloon the code," Mary said. "Will the Switch statement you alluded to earlier help cut down on the number of lines of code we have to write to test for multiple conditions?"

"It can," I said, "but before we discuss the Switch statement, I'd like to explain this code first, which, by my count, contains a total of six Else statements."

I displayed the first line of code from the **main()** function on the classroom projector:

```
char response[256];
```

"You've seen this code before," I said. "What we're doing here is declaring a character array of 256 characters. Once again, we'll discuss arrays in more detail later on in the course. For now, all you need to realize is that an array is a type of data storage, similar to a variable, in which a single data type, such as response, can hold multiple values. Next, we prompt the user to enter their age."

```
cout << "What is your age? ";
```

"Then we assign the user's answer to the *response* variable by executing the **getline()** function of the cin object, passing as arguments to the function the name of our character array and the maximum number of characters to accept."

```
cin.getline(response,256);
```

"These next two lines of code," I said, "use the **strlen()** function to check to see whether the user has pressed the ENTER key without entering their age. If that's the case, the return value of the **strlen()** function will be zero, and we display a warning message."

```
if (strlen(response) == 0)
    cout << "You must tell me your age...";
```

"I noticed," Rhonda said, "that as soon as the message is displayed to the user, the program ends. Shouldn't they be given the opportunity to correct their mistake without having to run the program all over again? Is there a way to do that?"

"You're right, Rhonda," I said. "There is a way to do that—and that's something you'll learn how to do next week when we take up the topic of C++ loop structures."

"What's going on with this next line of code?" Ward asked. "What is **atoi()**? I presume that's a function of some kind."

"Good observation, Ward," I said. "**atoi()**, which stands for *ASCII to Integer*, is a function that takes a character array or a string and returns the integer equivalent of it."

Ward (and the other students) seemed thoroughly confused. I reminded the class that the *response* variable is a character array.

"To C++," I said, "characters and strings are not numbers. In order to do the numeric comparisons we need to do in this code, we must work with the user's response as a number, not as a character. To do that, we first need to convert the character value in the *response* variable to an integer data type, and we do that by executing the **atoi()** function. Once that conversion is performed, we can determine whether the value the user has entered is greater than 61 using the greater-than comparison operator."

```
else
if (atoi(response) > 61)
```

"You learned last week that comparison operations return a True or False value, and in this case, if the age the user gives us is greater than 61, a True value is returned from this operation. We then display the user's age, together with the string 'You must be retired' in the console."

```
cout << response << " - You must be retired";
```

"What would have happened if we didn't convert the string value in the *response* variable to an integer?" Kate asked.

"Our program wouldn't compile," I answered. "C++ is very picky. The compiler will prevent us from performing an arithmetic operation against nonnumeric data types."

"What if the user's age is not greater than 61?" Kate asked. "This is where I became confused."

"If the user's age is *not* greater than 61," I said, "the comparison operation returns a False value. Then, because of the Else statement, our code executes the imperative statement following the word *Else*. Of course, it turns out that the imperative statement is another If statement that is then evaluated by C++."

"Can we go back to that line of code where we display the message?" Chuck asked. "Why do we have two sets of redirection (<<) operators?"

I explained that we are joining the string 'You must be retired' with the value of the *response* variable. The redirection operator allows us to 'concatenate' or join one value to another.

```
cout << response << " - You must be retired";
```

"Therefore, if the number 73 is typed by the user, the message we display will read '73 - You must be retired.'"

"That's clever," Steve said. "So we're actually using the value of the variable *response* in the message, not a numeric literal."

"That's right, Steve," I said. "Using the value the user has entered in the message by using the value of the variable *response* gives us a much more flexible and descriptive message. In this way, no matter what age the user types, that age is displayed on the console."

I waited to see if there were any questions before continuing.

"In a similar way," I said, "we can use this code to determine whether the value the user has entered is exactly equal to 61."

```
else
if (atoi(response) == 61)
   cout << response <<
      " - You have 1 year until retirement";
```

"If it is, we then execute the imperative statement to display an appropriate message. If the user's entry is not equal to 61, we execute the imperative statement of the Else clause, which is itself another If statement, to determine whether the user's age is 60."

```
else
if (atoi(response) == 60)
    cout << response <<
        " - You have 2 years until retirement";
```

"I'm okay with this," Linda said. "This is basically the same code we used to determine whether the user's age is 61. If it is, we display a slightly different message."

"That's right," I agreed, "and this next code works in the same way, checking to see whether the user's age is 59."

```
else
if (atoi(response) == 59)
    cout << response <<
        " - You have 3 years until retirement";
```

"Now can you imagine how much code we would have," I said, "if we needed to write individual lines of code for every age from 59 on down to 1. Fortunately, we can take care of all of those possibilities with this single Else statement."

```
else
    cout << response <<
        " - You have a long time until retirement";
```

"By using the Else statement here," I said, "we tell C++ that all the remaining ages fit into one category and to display a generic message indicating that the user has a long time until retirement."

I waited to see whether there were any other questions. To my surprise, everyone in the class seemed pretty comfortable with the If statement. Now it was time to discuss another selection structure—the Switch statement.

The Switch Statement/Structure

"The more alternatives we have in an If...Else...If statement," I said, "the harder the program is to write, read, and modify, and the more likely it is that you'll make a mistake when you code it. I'd like to introduce you to another C++ selection structure, called the Switch statement. Here's the code for a program that asks the user to enter a number between 1 and 3 and then displays a custom message on the console. I displayed this code on the classroom projector:

```
//Example4_4.cpp
#include <iostream>
```

```cpp
int main()
{
    using namespace std;

    char response[256];

    cout << "Pick a number between 1 and 3: ";
    cin.getline(response,256);

    if (strlen(response) == 0)  {
        cout << "You must pick a number...";
        return 1;
    }

    switch (atoi(response))                 //Switch begins
    {
    case 1:
        cout << "You entered the number 1";
        break;
    case 2:
        cout << "You entered the number 2";
        break;
    case 3:
        cout << "You entered the number 3";
        break;
    default:
        cout << "Oops, you entered a number " <<
            "not in the range 1 to 3";
        break;
        }           //Switch ends

    return 0;
}
```

"Let me explain what I've done here," I said. "As has been the case with the programs we've written today, which solicit input from the user, the first thing we do is declare our *response* variable—this time as a character array. Then we display a message prompt and then accept the user's response by executing the **getline()** method of the cin object."

```cpp
char response[256];
```

```
cout << "Pick a number between 1 and 3: ";
cin.getline(response,256);
```

"As we did in the previous exercise, we test the *response* variable to determine whether the user pressed the ENTER key without typing an entry by using the **strlen()** function."

```
if (strlen(response) == 0)  {
```

"This time, instead of merely displaying a warning message to the user if the ENTER key was pressed, we specify two imperative statements to be executed if the condition evaluates to True. One imperative statement will display a message indicating that a number must be entered; the other will end our program by executing the return statement. Notice that instead of returning a value of 0, which traditionally indicates that a program has ended successfully, we return a value of 1. Traditionally, any nonzero value is used to indicate a problem or failure in a program."

```
cout << "You must pick a number...";
   return 1;
}
```

"Why is it," Dave asked, "that we went the extra yard this time by ending the program in addition to displaying the message to the user? That's new, isn't it?"

"We need to end the program at that point because of the falling rock behavior of our code," I said. "If all we did was display a message to the user at this point, our code would continue executing, and within the Switch statement we would wind up evaluating the value of the *response* variable, which really contains nothing at that point. Although the program would still run, ultimately we would display another message indicating that the user entered a number *not* within the range of 1 through 3. At this point, it's much 'cleaner' to simply display the warning message and then end the program."

"What does the number 1 with the return statement signify?" Ward asked. Ward had been working with his version of the program and obviously missed my discussion of it a moment earlier.

"Because we declared the **main()** function to return an integer return value," I said, "some integer value must accompany the return statement. The number zero, by convention, indicates a normal termination of our program. Any nonzero value indicates a problem or a failure. Although we won't do so in this class, it's possible to execute our C++ programs from another program—and the argument we supply with the return statement can be passed back to the program that 'calls' our program, thereby letting the other program know how, or why, our program terminated. Zero, as I mentioned, by convention means the program ended normally."

I waited a moment before continuing.

"With the test for the immediate press of the ENTER key out of the way, we now know that the user typed something. Now it's time to test to see exactly what it is they have typed. For that, we use the C++ Switch statement. Let's concentrate on understanding the Switch statement, which we execute with this line of code."

```
switch (atoi(response))          //Switch begins
```

"The Switch statement," I said, "begins with the word *switch*. The entirety of the Switch statement is enclosed within a pair of curly brackets, which I've marked with comments in this example. The word *switch* is followed by what is called a test expression. The test expression can be a variable, but in actuality it can be anything that evaluates to either a C++ integer or character data type. In this case, the test expression is the return value of the **atoi()** function you learned about earlier. The **atoi()** function returns the integer value of the *response* variable."

"So that's why we were able to use the **atoi()** function within the test expression here," Dave said, "because it returns an integer data type."

"That's right, Dave," I answered. "According to the rules for the Switch statement, the test expression must return a value that is either a character or integer data type. Now, here comes the tricky part. The result of the test expression is then evaluated, in turn, by each one of the successive Case statements. If the result of the test expression matches the first Case statement, then the imperative statement or statements following that Case statement are executed. If the result does not match, then the next Case statement is matched to the test expression result. Once again, if the test expression matches the Case statement, the imperative statement or statements following that Case statement are executed. If the result does *not* match, then each successive Case statement is tested. You can code an optional default case, which if present, is executed if *none* of the Case statements matches the test expression. Here's our first Case statement looking to see whether the test expression evaluates to the number 1. Notice, by the way, the spelling of the word *case*. It's lowercase. If you spell it any other way, your program won't compile at all. Notice also that the line containing the Case statement ends with a colon."

```
case 1:
```

"Once again, if the Case statement finds that the test expression is equal to 1, then the two imperative statements following the Case statement are executed. In this example, what that means is that we display a message to the user and then execute the Break statement."

"What does the Break statement do?" Lou asked.

"The Break statement," I said, "tells C++ to skip the remaining Case statements and to resume execution with the next line of code following the end of the Switch statement."

"You mean after the ending curly bracket?" Rose asked.

"That's right, Rose," I replied. "In this code, we execute the Break statement after a Case statement matches the test expression. If we didn't execute the Break statement, the code in each of the successive Case statements would also execute, regardless of whether the Case statement was true."

```
cout << "You entered the number 1";
break;
```

NOTE
Within a Case statement, there's no need to sandwich multiple imperative statements within curly brackets the way you do with an If statement.

"That's bizarre," Rhonda said, "but I guess it's not the first time I've been surprised by the syntax of a programming language. By the way, why didn't we enclose the number 1 in our Case statement within quotation marks or apostrophes?"

"I bet I know," Dave said. "It's because our test expression is an integer data type. If we had enclosed the number 1 within quotation marks, we would be telling C++ that it's a string. And if we enclose it within apostrophes, we would be telling C++ that it's a character data type?"

"That's excellent, Dave," I said. "In C++, you must always be aware of the data type with which you are working."

I paused a moment before continuing.

"Now at this point, it's just a matter of evaluating the remainder of the Case statements."

```
case 2:
    cout << "You entered the number 2";
    break;
case 3:
    cout << "You entered the number 3";
    break;
```

"The default case," I said, "as I mentioned, is executed if *none* of the other Case statements matches the test expression. Notice that it, too, contains a Break statement. There's really no need to do so, because this is the last Case statement, but most programmers will include it for readability."

```
default:
    cout << "Oops, you entered a number " <<
        "not in the range 1 to 3";
    break;
```

"Finally, this curly bracket marks the end of the Switch statement."

```
}        //Switch ends
```

"If there had been any other code we wanted to execute outside of the Switch statement, we would have placed it beyond the closing curly bracket of the Switch statement."

"What do you mean outside of the Switch statement?" Rhonda asked.

"In theory," I said, "code within the Switch statement—everything within the starting and ending curly brackets—is part of a big selection structure and therefore executes only under certain conditions. If there's some code that you want to execute every time the code runs, regardless of program conditions, place it outside of the Switch statement—that is, following the ending curly bracket of the Switch statement."

"The Switch statement seems pretty powerful," Barbara said. "Are there any limitations to it, other than the fact that the test expression must evaluate to one of the data types you mentioned earlier? Can we use a test expression that evaluates to a string?"

"Unfortunately not, Barbara," I said. "Only a test expression that evaluates to an integer or a character is valid. We can't use a Switch statement to evaluate a string. If you try, you'll receive a compiler error message. If you need to evaluate the contents of a string variable, you'll need to use an If statement."

"Must the Case statement be a string or numeric literal like you've shown so far?" Blaine asked.

"Good question, Blaine," I said. "It must be a literal—either a numeric or character literal—and it must match the data type specified in the test expression. In other words, if the test expression returns an int, then you must use an int literal in your Case statement. And unlike some other languages you may be familiar with, you can't specify a logical Case expression or a range of values. For instance, you can't specify a Case statement that looks like either of these."

```
Case > 5                    // NOT A VALID SYNTAX
```

or

```
Case 1 to 5                 // NOT A VALID SYNTAX
```

There were no questions. I thought it would be a good idea to let everyone take a turn at coding their own Switch statement before taking a break, so I handed out this exercise for the class to complete.

Exercise 4-6   ## The Switch Statement/Structure

In this exercise, you'll work with the program from Exercise 4-5, modifying it to use a Switch statement instead of a series of If...Else statements.

1. Using Notepad, enter the following code:

```
//Practice4_6.cpp
#include <iostream>
```

```cpp
int main()
{
   using namespace std;

   char response[256];

   cout << "What is your age? ";
   cin.getline(response,256);

   if (strlen(response) == 0) {
      cout << "You must tell me your age...";
      return 1;
   }

   if (atoi(response) > 61) {
      cout << response << " - You must be retired";
      return 0;
   }

   switch (atoi(response))
   {
      case 61:
         cout << response <<
            " - You have 1 year until retirement";
         break;
      case 60:
         cout << response <<
            " - You have 2 years until retirement";
         break;
      case 59:
         cout << response <<
            " - You have 3 years until retirement";
         break;
      default:
         cout << response <<
            " - You have a long time until retirement";
         break;
   }

   return 0;
}
```

2. Save your source file as Practice4_6.cpp in the \CPPFiles\Practice folder (select File | Save As from Notepad's menu bar). Be sure to save your source file with the filename extension .cpp.

3. Compile your source file into an executable file.

4. Execute your program multiple times, entering **62**, **61**, **60**, **59**, and **40** at the prompt. Observe the various messages that are displayed.

Discussion

No one seemed to have any great problems completing the exercise, although there were some students who spelled *case* in non-lowercase letters, plus one student entered the 'default' parameter as 'case default' instead.

"Don't forget about the spelling of the word *case*," I said, "and make sure you include a Break statement in each one of the Case statements. Remember, in C++ we need to code the Break statement to prevent the code in each one of the Case statements from executing after one of them is found to be true."

"I can vouch for that," Rhonda said. "I forgot to include it in the Case statement for 'age equal to 61,' and when I executed my program and entered 61, all the messages were displayed—seeing is believing!"

"I really enjoyed this exercise, and I'm glad we took the time to do it," Ward said. "This exercise really helped solidify the concept of the Switch statement in my mind. It's just a shame that we couldn't have expressed every condition we were looking for in the form of a Case statement. I guess there was no way out of having to code an If statement to handle the user simply pressing the ENTER key without typing a number—and also for an age greater than 61."

"That's right, Ward," I said. "Because we are restricted to expressing our Case statements in terms of an equality, we needed to check for an age greater than 61 using an If statement."

```cpp
if (atoi(response) > 61) {
    cout << response <<
        " - You must be retired";
    return 0;
}
```

"I may have missed something somewhere—did we forget to check for an age less than 59?" Rhonda asked.

"We didn't forget. We did it by using the default Case statement," I said.

```cpp
default:
    cout << response <<
        " - You have a long time until retirement";
    break;
```

"How so?" Rhonda asked.

"Because we had already checked for ages greater than 61 and for ages exactly equal to 61, 60, and 59, if we got to the point of executing the code in the default Case statement, it would mean that the age entered was less than 59."

"I see," Rhonda said. "I was a little confused because we didn't explicitly code what we were looking for, but I see the default Case statement is aptly named."

"We could have coded another If statement to be a little more explicit," I said, "like this."

```
if (atoi(response) < 59) {
    cout << response <<
        " - You have a long time until retirement";
    return 0;
}
```

"However, I really wanted to give everyone a chance to work with the default Case statement."

The classroom was pretty quiet; everyone seemed to be okay with the Switch statement. I asked if there were any questions. There were none, so I told them to take a well-earned break.

"When we return from break," I said, "we'll use the selection structures you learned today to enhance the Grade Calculation Project. I think you'll be very pleased with what we're about to do with the project."

Continuing with the Grade Calculation Project

"We now know enough about C++," I said, "to add some intelligence to our Grade Calculation Project we began working on last week. Last week we added code to the project to calculate the grade for a fictitious English student whose midterm grade was 70, final examination grade was 80, research grade was 90, and presentation grade was 100. We displayed the student's final grade of 100 in the C++ console window."

"We hard-coded the component grade pieces in the program code itself," Blaine said.

"That's right, Blaine," I said. "Last week you didn't have the C++ skills to allow the program to accept input from a user, so we had no choice but to hard-code the component grade scores. After what you've learned today about getting input into a program—and the C++ selection structures—we'll be able to ask the user what type of student they wish to calculate and to conditionally accept the component grade scores from the user based on that student type."

"Wow, do you mean we'll be able to calculate the grade for an actual student today?" Ward asked.

"That's right," I replied.

"That's exciting," Rhonda said. "But if I'm not mistaken, based on what you're saying we'll be doing with the project today, won't we be done with it?"

"That's an interesting point you raise, Rhonda," I said. "And strictly speaking, you're correct. By the end of today's class, we will have a working C++ program that basically fulfills the Requirements Statement we developed several weeks ago. You may be wondering what we will be doing for the remainder of the class. You'll spend it learning even more about C++ and enhancing the Grade Calculation Project with your new knowledge."

I then distributed this exercise for the class to complete.

Exercise 4-7   **Enhancing the Grade Calculation Project**

In this exercise, you'll modify the Grade Calculation Project you last worked on last week in Exercise 3-1 by giving it the ability to accept input from the user and calculate grades (both numeric and letter) for an English, math, or science student.

1. Using Notepad, locate and open the Grades.cpp source file you worked on last week. (It should be in the \CPPFiles\Grades folder.)

2. Modify your code so that it looks like this:

```cpp
//Grades.cpp
#include <iostream>

int main ()
{
  using namespace std;

  const float ENGLISH_MIDTERM_PERCENTAGE = .25;
  const float ENGLISH_FINALEXAM_PERCENTAGE = .25;
  const float ENGLISH_RESEARCH_PERCENTAGE = .30;
  const float ENGLISH_PRESENTATION_PERCENTAGE = .20;
  const float MATH_MIDTERM_PERCENTAGE = .5F;
  const float MATH_FINALEXAM_PERCENTAGE = .50;
  const float SCIENCE_MIDTERM_PERCENTAGE = .40;
  const float SCIENCE_FINALEXAM_PERCENTAGE = .40;
  const float SCIENCE_RESEARCH_PERCENTAGE = .20;
  int midterm = 0;
  int finalExamGrade = 0;
  int research = 0;
  int presentation = 0;
```

```cpp
float finalNumericGrade = 0;
char finalLetterGrade;
char response[256];

// What type of student are we calculating?
   cout << "Enter student type " <<
      "(1=English, 2=Math, 3=Science): ";

   cin.getline(response,256);

   if (strlen(response) == 0) {
      cout << "You must select a Student Type";
      return 1;
   }

   if ((atoi(response) < 1) | (atoi(response) > 3)) {
      cout << response <<
         " - is not a valid student type";
      return 1;
   }

// Student type is valid, now let's calculate the grade
   switch(atoi(response))
   {
// Case 1 is an English Student
      case 1:
         cout << "Enter the Midterm Grade: " ;
         cin.getline(response,256);
         midterm = atoi(response);
         cout << "Enter the Final Examination Grade: " ;
         cin.getline(response,256);
         finalExamGrade = atoi(response);
         cout << "Enter the Research Grade: " ;
         cin.getline(response,256);
         research = atoi(response);
         cout << "Enter the Presentation Grade: " ;
         cin.getline(response,256);
         presentation = atoi(response);
         finalNumericGrade =
            (midterm * ENGLISH_MIDTERM_PERCENTAGE) +
            (finalExamGrade *
               ENGLISH_FINALEXAM_PERCENTAGE) +
```

```
                    (research * ENGLISH_RESEARCH_PERCENTAGE) +
                    (presentation *
                       ENGLISH_PRESENTATION_PERCENTAGE);
                if (finalNumericGrade >= 93)
                    finalLetterGrade = 'A';
                else
                if ((finalNumericGrade >= 85) &
                    (finalNumericGrade < 93))
                        finalLetterGrade = 'B';
                else
                if ((finalNumericGrade >= 78) &
                    (finalNumericGrade < 85))
                    finalLetterGrade = 'C';
                else
                if ((finalNumericGrade >= 70) &
                    (finalNumericGrade < 78))
                    finalLetterGrade = 'D';
                else
                if (finalNumericGrade < 70)
                    finalLetterGrade = 'F';
                cout << endl <<
                    "*** ENGLISH STUDENT ***" << endl << endl;
                cout << "Midterm grade is: " <<
                    midterm << endl;
                cout << "Final Exam is: " <<
                    finalExamGrade << endl;
                cout << "Research grade is: " <<
                    research << endl;
                cout << "Presentation grade is: " <<
                    presentation << endl << endl;
                cout << "Final Numeric Grade is: " <<
                    finalNumericGrade << endl;
                cout << "Final Letter Grade is: " <<
                    finalLetterGrade;
                break;

// Case 2 is a Math Student
        case 2:
            cout << "Enter the Midterm Grade: " ;
            cin.getline(response,256);
            midterm = atoi(response);
```

```
        cout << "Enter the Final Examination Grade: " ;
        cin.getline(response,256);
        finalExamGrade = atoi(response);
        finalNumericGrade =
          (midterm * MATH_MIDTERM_PERCENTAGE) +
          (finalExamGrade * MATH_FINALEXAM_PERCENTAGE);
        if (finalNumericGrade >= 90)
            finalLetterGrade = 'A';
        else
        if ((finalNumericGrade >= 83) &
            (finalNumericGrade < 90))
              finalLetterGrade = 'B';
        else
        if ((finalNumericGrade >= 76) &
            (finalNumericGrade < 83))
          finalLetterGrade = 'C';
        else
        if ((finalNumericGrade >= 65) &
            (finalNumericGrade < 76))
          finalLetterGrade = 'D';
        else
        if (finalNumericGrade < 65)
            finalLetterGrade = 'F';
        cout << endl <<
            "*** MATH STUDENT ***" << endl << endl;
        cout << "Midterm grade is: " <<
            midterm << endl;
        cout << "Final Exam is: " <<
            finalExamGrade << endl;
        cout << "Final Numeric Grade is: " <<
            finalNumericGrade << endl;
        cout << "Final Letter Grade is: " <<
            finalLetterGrade;
        break;

// Case 3 is a Science Student
    case 3:
        cout << "Enter the Midterm Grade: " ;
        cin.getline(response,256);
        midterm = atoi(response);
        cout << "Enter the Final Examination Grade: " ;
```

```cpp
            cin.getline(response,256);
            finalExamGrade = atoi(response);
            cout << "Enter the Research Grade: " ;
            cin.getline(response,256);
            research = atoi(response);
            finalNumericGrade =
               (midterm * SCIENCE_MIDTERM_PERCENTAGE) +
               (finalExamGrade *
                   SCIENCE_FINALEXAM_PERCENTAGE) +
               (research * SCIENCE_RESEARCH_PERCENTAGE);
            if (finalNumericGrade >= 90)
                 finalLetterGrade = 'A';
            else
            if ((finalNumericGrade >= 80) &
               (finalNumericGrade < 90))
                   finalLetterGrade = 'B';
            else
            if ((finalNumericGrade >= 70) &
               (finalNumericGrade < 80))
               finalLetterGrade = 'C';
            else
            if ((finalNumericGrade >= 60) &
               (finalNumericGrade < 70))
               finalLetterGrade = 'D';
            else
            if (finalNumericGrade < 60)
               finalLetterGrade = 'F';
            cout << endl <<
                "*** SCIENCE STUDENT ***" << endl << endl;
            cout << "Midterm grade is: " <<
               midterm << endl;
            cout << "Final Exam is: " <<
               finalExamGrade << endl;
            cout << "Research grade is: " <<
               research << endl;
            cout << "Final Numeric Grade is: " <<
               finalNumericGrade << endl;
            cout << "Final Letter Grade is: " <<
               finalLetterGrade;
            break;
      default:
```

```
            cout << response <<
                " - is not a valid student type";
            return 1;
    }
      return 0;
}
```

3. Save your source file as Grades.cpp in the \CPPFiles\Grades folder (select File | Save As from Notepad's menu bar). Be sure to save your source file with the filename extension .cpp.

4. Compile your source file into an executable file.

5. Execute your program and test it thoroughly. See what happens if you immediately hit the ENTER key without making a selection for the student type. What happens if you indicate a student type not equal to 1, 2 or 3, such as 4? What happens if you type the letter a for a student type?

6. Indicate that you wish to calculate the grade for an English student. Enter **70** for the midterm grade, **80** for the final examination grade, **90** for the research grade, and **100** for the presentation grade. A final numeric grade of 84.5 should be displayed with a letter grade of C.

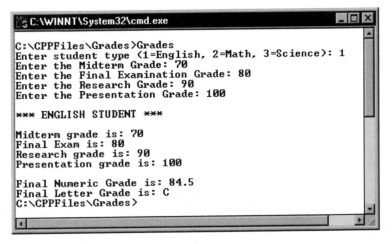

7. Indicate that you wish to calculate the grade for a math student. Enter **70** for the midterm grade and **80** for the final examination grade. A final numeric grade of 75 should be displayed with a letter grade of D.

8. Indicate that you wish to calculate the grade for a science student. Enter **70** for the midterm grade, **80** for the final examination grade, and **90** for the research grade. A final numeric grade of 78 should be displayed with a letter grade of C.

"This exercise was a lot of fun," Rhonda said, "but although I was able to complete it, I must confess I'm not absolutely sure about everything that's going on here."

"I suspect you're not the only one who feels that way, Rhonda," I said. "There's a bunch of code in this exercise. Let's take this a step at a time, and I'm sure you'll be okay. As you now know, each program that writes to the console must have this include statement."

```
#include <iostream>
```

"In addition, each program that is executed from the command-line prompt *must* have a **main()** function."

```
int main ()
```

"And within the **main()** function, we also include the using namespace statement for the std library to eliminate the need for us to preface our C++ statements with the keyword std."

```
using namespace std;
```

"Some of these constants appeared in the previous version of the program we worked on last week, and some are new to this version. Last week, we were only concerned with calculating the grade for an English student. In this version of the program, we're calculating math and science students also, so we need to declare and initialize constants for those student types as well. Constants, by convention, are named in uppercase, and we assign to this group of constants values equating to the relative percentage of the component grade for each one of the three student types we'll be calculating. Constants make your code more readable, and if we need to change the percentage of any one of the component grade pieces, all we need to do is change the value of the constant in the assignment statement."

```
const float ENGLISH_MIDTERM_PERCENTAGE = .25;
const float ENGLISH_FINALEXAM_PERCENTAGE = .25;
const float ENGLISH_RESEARCH_PERCENTAGE = .30;
const float ENGLISH_PRESENTATION_PERCENTAGE = .20;
const float MATH_MIDTERM_PERCENTAGE = .5F;
const float MATH_FINALEXAM_PERCENTAGE = .50;
const float SCIENCE_MIDTERM_PERCENTAGE = .40;
const float SCIENCE_FINALEXAM_PERCENTAGE = .40;
const float SCIENCE_RESEARCH_PERCENTAGE = .20;
```

I paused a moment before continuing.

"We declared these same variables in the previous version of the program," I said, "but this time we're initializing their values to 0."

```
int midterm = 0;
int finalExamGrade = 0;
int research = 0;
int presentation = 0;
float finalNumericGrade = 0;
```

"*finalLetterGrade* is a new string variable for this version of the program. We'll use it to hold the student's calculated letter grade. Notice how we initialize it to an empty string."

```
char finalLetterGrade;
```

"The *response* variable should be familiar to you now. We'll use it to store any responses we get from the user via the **ReadLine()** function of the Console object."

```
char response[256];
```

"This line of code is just a comment. As our programs get larger, using comments is a good idea."

```
// What type of student are we calculating?
```

"At this point, with all our constants and variables declared, it's time to ask the user what type of student they will be calculating a grade for. This is a crucial piece of information for our program, and quite honestly, we're making things a little easier on ourselves by prompting the user to give us a number equating to the student type—1 for an English student, 2 for a math student, and 3 for a science student."

```
cout << "Enter student type " <<
  "(1=English, 2=Math, 3=Science): ";
```

```
cin.getline(response,256);
```

"I was wondering why you did that," Peter said.

"We could have asked the user to type in the actual student type as a string," I said, "but that can be tricky."

"How so?" Kate asked.

"There are two problems," I answered. "You really want to avoid having the user type in anything into your program. Keystrokes lead to typing errors, and typing errors cause program problems. If the user must type, and sometimes it's unavoidable, then reduce their typing to a minimum, which is what we're doing here by having them enter a single number—1, 2, or 3—instead of actually typing out English, math, or science."

"You said there are two problems," Blaine said. "What's the second?"

"A second problem would be this," I said. "Even if the user managed to type in English, math, or science properly, capitalization is an issue as well. For instance, some users might spell their entry in all uppercase, some in lowercase, and some in a combination of both."

"I hadn't thought of that," Linda commented.

"Did you know there are 128 different ways to spell the word *science* if you count the various combinations of upper- and lowercase letters?" I asked. "In theory then, we would need 128 different If statements for each student type—that's why we're prompting for a number instead of a string."

No one had any major objections to my rationale, so I continued.

"These next few lines of code we've dealt with all day long. Here we're checking to see whether the user has hit the ENTER key without telling us the type of student they wish to calculate a grade for. Most likely this is a mistake, so we display a message to the user and end the program by executing the return statement, indicating a failure in our program by returning the integer value of 1."

```
if (strlen(response) == 0) {
    cout << "You must select a Student Type";
    return 1;
}
```

"It really would be great," Ward said, "if instead of just ending the program here we could redisplay the prompt for the student type."

"I totally agree, Ward," I said, "and that's something we'll be able to do after next week's class when you learn about the C++ loop structure. For now though, we just gracefully end the program. Now, provided the user hasn't immediately pressed ENTER, we know that the user has made a response of some kind. Now it's time to determine what it is. You should have noticed, while testing your program, that if the user enters the letter *a*, or any character other than 1, 2, or 3, a message is displayed indicating the entry is not a valid student type. For now, let's assume that the user has entered a valid integer. We now need to determine whether it's outside the range of valid numbers we're looking for. In other words, if it's less than 1 *or* greater than 3, it's not 1, 2, or 3. Last week, we learned about the C++ Or (|) operator. In combination with an If statement, this series of code allows us to determine whether the number entered is outside the range of numbers we're looking for."

```
if ((atoi(response) < 1) | (atoi(response) > 3)) {
    cout << response << " - is not a valid student type";
    return 1;
}
```

"If the number entered is either less than 1 *or* greater than 3 (the < operator means less than, and the > operator means greater than), we display a message to the user indicating that they have entered an invalid student type, and we end the program by executing the return statement."

"Now we're in business!" Kathy said. "If the number entered isn't less than 1 and isn't greater than 3, then it must be 1, 2, or 3."

"You hit the nail right on the head, Kathy," I said. "We now know that the number the user has entered is either a 1, 2, or 3, and that allows us to use a Switch statement to deal with each one of those cases, each of which equates to a different student type."

```
switch(atoi(response))
```

"Case 1 is the English student. Within the Case statement, we prompt the user for the four component pieces that comprise the English student's final grade—midterm, final exam, research, and presentation grades. The user's response to each prompt is assigned to the response variable, and we then assign the value of the response variable to the *midterm, finalExamGrade, research,* and *presentation* variables. Notice how we use the **atoi()** function to 'convert' the character value of the response variable to an integer prior to assigning the value."

```
case 1:
    cout << "Enter the Midterm Grade: " ;
    cin.getline(response,256);
    midterm = atoi(response);
    cout << "Enter the Final Examination Grade: " ;
    cin.getline(response,256);
    finalExamGrade = atoi(response);
    cout << "Enter the Research Grade: " ;
    cin.getline(response,256);
    research = atoi(response);
    cout << "Enter the Presentation Grade: " ;
    cin.getline(response,256);
    presentation = atoi(response);
```

"This next sequence of code calculates the final numeric grade for an English student," I said. "Here, we multiply the value entered by the user for each component piece of the grade by the appropriate constant and then sum them to arrive at the final grade."

```
finalNumericGrade =
    (midterm * ENGLISH_MIDTERM_PERCENTAGE) +
    (finalExamGrade *
```

```
          ENGLISH_FINALEXAM_PERCENTAGE) +
      (research * ENGLISH_RESEARCH_PERCENTAGE) +
      (presentation *
          ENGLISH_PRESENTATION_PERCENTAGE);
```

"Once we have the final numeric grade calculated, we use a series of If...Else statements to calculate the final letter grade. This code is pretty tedious but relatively straightforward."

```
if (finalNumericGrade >= 93)
    finalLetterGrade = 'A';
else
if ((finalNumericGrade >= 85) &
    (finalNumericGrade < 93))
    finalLetterGrade = 'B';
else
if ((finalNumericGrade >= 78) &
    (finalNumericGrade < 85))
    finalLetterGrade = 'C';
else
if ((finalNumericGrade >= 70) &
    (finalNumericGrade < 78))
    finalLetterGrade = 'D';
else
if (finalNumericGrade < 70)
    finalLetterGrade = 'F';
```

"Now that we have the final numeric grade and the final letter grade calculated, it's time to display the results to the C++ console. This also is pretty straightforward. First, we display the type of student for whom we have calculated a grade."

```
cout << endl <<
    "*** ENGLISH STUDENT ***" << endl << endl;
```

"This is followed by the display of the component grade pieces, the final numeric grade, and the final letter grade."

```
cout << "Midterm grade is: " <<
    midterm << endl;
cout << "Final Exam is: " <<
    finalExamGrade << endl;
cout << "Research grade is: " <<
    research << endl;
cout << "Presentation grade is: " <<
    presentation << endl << endl;
```

```
cout << "Final Numeric Grade is: " <<
    finalNumericGrade << endl;
cout << "Final Letter Grade is: " <<
    finalLetterGrade;
```

"Notice at this point that the last line of code in the Case statement we execute is the Break statement," I said. "That's a requirement in C++."

```
break;
```

"Here's the Case statement for the math student," I continued. "It's similar to the Case statement for the English student, with the obvious differences being that math students do not have research and presentation grade components, and, of course, their component percentages are different."

```
case 2:
    cout << "Enter the Midterm Grade: " ;
    cin.getline(response,256);
    midterm = atoi(response);
    cout << "Enter the Final Examination Grade: " ;
    cin.getline(response,256);
    finalExamGrade = atoi(response);
    finalNumericGrade =
        (midterm * MATH_MIDTERM_PERCENTAGE) +
        (finalExamGrade * MATH_FINALEXAM_PERCENTAGE);
    if (finalNumericGrade >= 90)
        finalLetterGrade = 'A';
    else
    if ((finalNumericGrade >= 83) &
        (finalNumericGrade < 90))
        finalLetterGrade = 'B';
    else
    if ((finalNumericGrade >= 76) &
        (finalNumericGrade < 83))
        finalLetterGrade = 'C';
    else
    if ((finalNumericGrade >= 65) &
        (finalNumericGrade < 76))
        finalLetterGrade = 'D';
    else
    if (finalNumericGrade < 65)
        finalLetterGrade = 'F';
    cout << endl <<
        "*** MATH STUDENT ***" << endl << endl;
    cout << "Midterm grade is: " <<
```

```
      midterm << endl;
   cout << "Final Exam is: " <<
      finalExamGrade << endl;
   cout << "Final Numeric Grade is: " <<
      finalNumericGrade << endl;
   cout << "Final Letter Grade is: " <<
      finalLetterGrade;
   break;
```

"Now here's the Case statement for the science student."

```
case 3:
   cout << "Enter the Midterm Grade: " ;
   cin.getline(response,256);
   midterm = atoi(response);
   cout << "Enter the Final Examination Grade: " ;
   cin.getline(response,256);
   finalExamGrade = atoi(response);
   cout << "Enter the Research Grade: " ;
   cin.getline(response,256);
   research = atoi(response);
   finalNumericGrade =
      (midterm * SCIENCE_MIDTERM_PERCENTAGE) +
      (finalExamGrade *
         SCIENCE_FINALEXAM_PERCENTAGE) +
      (research * SCIENCE_RESEARCH_PERCENTAGE);
   if (finalNumericGrade >= 90)
      finalLetterGrade = 'A';
   else
   if ((finalNumericGrade >= 80) &
      (finalNumericGrade < 90))
      finalLetterGrade = 'B';
   else
   if ((finalNumericGrade >= 70) &
      (finalNumericGrade < 80))
      finalLetterGrade = 'C';
   else
   if ((finalNumericGrade >= 60) &
      (finalNumericGrade < 70))
      finalLetterGrade = 'D';
   else
   if (finalNumericGrade < 60)
      finalLetterGrade = 'F';
```

```
cout << endl <<
    "*** SCIENCE STUDENT ***" << endl << endl;
cout << "Midterm grade is: " <<
    midterm << endl;
cout << "Final Exam is: " <<
    finalExamGrade << endl;
cout << "Research grade is: " <<
    research << endl;
cout << "Final Numeric Grade is: " <<
    finalNumericGrade << endl;
cout << "Final Letter Grade is: " <<
    finalLetterGrade;
break;
```

"Finally, here's the code for the default case. This code will execute if the user types a letter as a response to the student type prompt instead of a number."

```
default:
    cout << response <<
        " - is not a valid student type";
    return 1;
```

"This curly bracket marks the end of the Switch statement."

```
}
```

"This is followed by a return statement to end the program, and the closing bracket for the **main()** function."

```
    return 0;
}
```

Great," Ward said. "This is starting to be a lot of fun."

"I just realized," Dave said, "that we don't have any validation for the component grade values that the user enters. Is that a problem?"

"In theory, we would have the same problem with the input of those values as we do with the input of the student type—that is, if the user enters a noninteger value as the student type, we need to be able to handle it. We'll take care of this problem in a few weeks when we start to develop classes and objects to do more of the work in our program."

Dave and the rest of the class seemed content to wait until then to resolve the issue. I waited for questions, but there were none. I had expected my students to be pretty worn out at this point, but instead they were playfully experimenting with a program they seemed genuinely proud of. I dismissed class for the day, telling everyone that next week they would learn about the C++ loop structures.

Summary

In this chapter, we examined selection structures and how they are used to vary the way a program behaves based on conditions found at runtime. You saw that there are several types of selection structures: two varieties of the If statement, and the Switch statement.

Remember the falling rock? You've seen how you can use selection structures to change this behavior, starting with the plain If statement. If a condition evaluates to True, then the imperative statement or statements following the If statement are executed. The If statement can be expanded to include alternative instructions for a False condition as well, using the Else keyword, and even further with a set of Else...If keywords.

After a number of Else statements, your code will begin to look cumbersome. At this point, it's more elegant to use the Switch statement, although it does have some limitations.

We've also come to a significant point in our project: the working prototype of the Grade Calculation Project. This is a very important stage in the development process, because all the key working parts of the program are now in place. From this point on, we'll be adding functionality and code to turn our prototype into a professional-level C++ program.

Chapter

5

Loops

n this chapter, we'll discuss the various types of loop structures available in C++. As you'll see, loop processing can give your programs tremendous power.

Why Loops?

"Last week I mentioned the term *loops* quite often," I said, as I began our fifth class. "In today's class, we'll examine in some detail the loop structures available in C++."

I continued by explaining that a loop allows the programmer to repeatedly execute sections of code without having to type those lines of code over and over again in the source.

"The ability to have parts of your program repeatedly execute," I said, "can give it enormous power to perform many types of operations that would otherwise be impossible."

"Can you give us an example?" Mary asked.

"Sure, Mary," I said. "For instance, a common programming problem is one in which you need to read records from an external disk file into your program. Reading a single record from a disk file isn't difficult. The problem in reading records from an external disk file (or a database) is that you do not know ahead of time how many records the program will need to read. The trick is to write code that reads all of the records in the file—regardless of the number of records in it."

"What do you mean?" Peter asked.

"For instance," I replied, "a file may contain ten records, or it may contain five billion. The point is, when you write your program source file, you don't know how many times to execute the line of code that in C++ is used to read a record from a file. This is where the loop structure comes in handy—with just a few lines of code, it's possible to write code to read every record in a file, regardless of whether there are ten lines or five billion lines."

"Are there different types of loops in C++?" Dave asked. "I know there are in other languages such as Java and Visual Basic."

"Yes, there are, Dave," I said. "C++ has several different types of loop structures, and we'll examine all of them today. One type of loop, called the For loop, executes a section of code, called the *body* of the loop, a definite number of times, and for that reason I call the For loop a *definite* type of loop. Other C++ loop structures are less definite in nature, which means that the number of times the body of the loop is executed is less definite. The number of times that the bodies of these loop are executed is dependent upon the evaluation of a test condition at runtime. Let's go back to that example of reading an external disk file again. If we need to read all the records from the disk file into our program, we do not know ahead of time how many records are in that file—the file could even be empty! This type of programming problem requires the use of an *indefinite* type of loop, of which there are two in C++: the While loop and the Do-While loop."

I suggested that we begin our examination of C++ loops with the For loop.

The For Loop

I displayed the syntax for the For loop on my classroom projector:

```
For (initialization; termination; increment)
statement or statements with statements appearing in a block
```

"This syntax," I said, "is the official syntax for the For loop, but for the time being, you may prefer this translation, which I think is a little easier for beginners to deal with."

```
For (start at this value;
    keep looping as long as this expression is true;
    increment or decrement the value)
statement or statements with statements appearing in a block
```

"I always say a picture is worth a thousand words. Here's the way the code for a C++ For loop would look in a program designed to display the numbers 1 to 10 in the C++ console window," I said, as I displayed this code on the classroom projector:

```cpp
//Example5_1.cpp
#include <iostream>

int main()
{
   using namespace std;

   for (int counter = 1;counter < 11;counter++)
      cout << counter << endl;

   return 0;
}
```

"The For loop," I continued, "begins with the keyword For, in lowercase letters, followed by three arguments that appear in parentheses. Each argument is separated by a semicolon. I think you're familiar with arguments by now—arguments affect or determine the behavior of a C++ statement or function. In the case of the For loop, these three arguments—initialization, termination, and increment—determine the duration of the loop, as you'll see in a just a few moments. In our example program, the first argument declares the variable *counter* as an integer data type and then assigns a value of 1 to it."

```cpp
for (int counter = 1;counter < 11;counter++)
```

"I'm a little confused by that first argument," Rhonda said. "Is there anything special about it, or is it just an ordinary variable declaration?"

"It's really just an ordinary variable declaration," I said. "What makes it seem out of the ordinary is that the variable is declared and initialized as part of the For statement. This variable, sometimes called the *loop-control* variable, is just an ordinary variable, and it should be declared as a numeric data type, as we've done here. You can name the loop-control variable anything you want. Historically, C++ programmers haven't bothered to name their loop-control variables with very meaningful names, preferring instead to name them with single-letter throwaway names, such as *i*, *j*, or *k*. Myself, I prefer to give my loop-control variables more meaningful names, so I've named ours *counter*."

"So both the declaration and assignment of the loop-control variable are done as part of that first argument?" Ward asked. "And that's done only once?"

"That's right, Ward," I replied. "Now, on to the second argument, called the *termination* argument, which is actually a test expression, much like the one you saw last week with the If statement. In a For loop, as long as the test expression evaluates and returns True, the body of the loop (that is, the statement or statements following the For line) is executed."

```
for (int counter = 1;counter < 11;counter++)
```

"In this case, we're telling C++ to continue to execute the statements within the body of the loop for as long as the value of the loop-control variable, *counter*, is less than 11. It's important to understand that in a For loop, the body of the loop will *not* be executed, not even once, until after the test expression is first evaluated. So long as the test expression returns a True value, the body of the loop is executed. If the test expression evaluates to a False value, the next statement following the body of the loop is executed."

"Let me make sure I follow," Barbara said. "The value of *counter* was initialized to 1, and we're telling C++ to execute the body of the loop as long as *counter* is less than 11."

"That's right, Barbara," I answered.

"So what's to keep that from happening forever?" she asked. "If *counter* starts out as 1, and the loop will execute as long as *counter* is less than 11, something needs to make the value of *counter* 11 or greater in order for the loop to stop. Is that right?"

"That's excellent, Barbara," I said, "and that's exactly right. If we don't do anything to increment the value of *counter*, it will remain 1, and this loop will execute forever."

"Is that where the term *endless loop* comes from?" Valerie asked. "I've heard some of the programmers at work use that term."

"That's right, Valerie," I said, "that's exactly what it means. An endless loop is a loop that continues to execute, usually because the programmer forgot to take the necessary steps to ensure that it will eventually stop."

"How will this loop ever stop, then?" Rhonda asked.

"That's where the third argument, the increment argument, comes into play," I said.

```
for (int counter = 1;counter < 11;counter++)
```

"The third argument, the increment argument," I continued, "tells C++ what to do to the loop-control variable. This usually means we add 1 to it, but as you'll see later, we can add to or subtract from it anything we wish. In our example program, we use the C++ increment operator (++) to add 1 to the value of *counter* each time the test expression is evaluated."

"Based on what you're telling us," Peter asked, "does that mean this loop will execute ten times?"

"Excellent, Peter, that's exactly what it means!" I said.

I then compiled and executed the example program, and the following screenshot was displayed on the classroom projector:

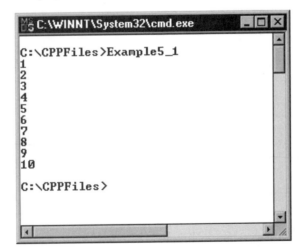

"Hey, that's pretty amazing," Kate said, "considering the fact that we displayed ten numbers in the C++ console window with so little code."

"See what I mean about the power of loops?" I asked. "They can give a program enormous power. This is a great illustration of how computers are excellent at performing repetitive tasks."

"I'm still a little confused about what's happening here," Rhonda said. "I wish we could see this in slow motion."

"Maybe this will help," I said, as I displayed this table on the classroom projector:

Step	Value of counter	counter < 11	Body of Loop Executed?	cout << counter (Number Displayed in C++ Console Window)	New Value of counter after counter ++
1	1	True	Yes	1	2
2	2	True	Yes	2	3
3	3	True	Yes	3	4
4	4	True	Yes	4	5
5	5	True	Yes	5	6
6	6	True	Yes	6	7
7	7	True	Yes	7	8
8	8	True	Yes	8	9
9	9	True	Yes	9	10
10	10	True	Yes	10	11
11	11	False	No		

"Step 1 shows you the value for the *counter* variable as the loop begins to execute," I said. "When the For line is executed for the first time, *counter* is declared and initialized to 1. After that, the test expression is evaluated for the first time. Because the value of *counter* is less than 11 (1 is less than 11), the body of the loop is executed, resulting in the number 1 being displayed in the C++ console window. Next, and it's important to understand the sequence, the value of *counter* is incremented using the C++ increment operator (++)."

"So the incrementation of *counter* actually takes place after the body of the loop is executed?" Dave asked.

"That's right, Dave," I replied. "That fools everyone the first time they see it. Now, in step 2, the current value of *counter*, which is 2, is compared to 11. And 2 is less than 11, which results in the test expression returning a True value, so the body of the loop is executed. Therefore, the value 2 is displayed in the C++ console. *Counter* is incremented by 1, giving it a new value of 3. Some beginners mistakenly believe that *counter* is initialized to 1 all over again, but as you can see, that only happens once—the first time the loop is executed."

"Just to make sure I understand what you're saying, the value of *counter* is incremented after the body of the loop is executed, correct?" Linda asked.

"That's right," I said. "I know that takes some time getting used to: The test expression is evaluated, if it returns a True value, the body of the loop is executed, followed by the increment or decrement of the loop-control variable."

"I think I understand everything that's going on," Blaine said, "but what about when you get to steps 10 and 11 of the table—that's when the loop ends, right?"

"In step 10," I replied, "the value of the variable *counter* is 10. Because 10 is less than 11, the test expression once again evaluates to True; therefore, the body of the loop—the display of the current value of the variable *counter* in the C++ console window—is executed. Then the value of *counter* is incremented by 1, giving it a value of 11."

"Doesn't the loop just end at this point?" Joe asked.

"Not quite, Joe," I answered. "Even though the value of counter has been incremented to 11, the test expression must formally be evaluated once more. At that point, the test expression returns a value of False, because 11 is *not* less than 11, it's equal to it. Once the test expression returns a False value, the loop is exited, meaning that execution now continues with the line of code that follows the For statement or statements. By the way, if you need to execute more than one statement as part of the body of the loop, you need to use curly brackets to form a block, like this."

```cpp
//Example5_2.cpp
#include <iostream>

int main()
{
    using namespace std;

    for (int counter = 1;counter < 11;counter++) {
        cout << "statement1" << endl;
        cout << "statement2" << endl;
    }

    return 0;
}
```

"This is the same technique we had to apply to the If statement that we learned about last week. In general, if you want multiple statements in your control structures, you must enclose them in a block."

Variations on the For Loop Theme

I pointed out that our For loop was a pretty "vanilla" version of what the For loop can do.

"What do you mean by *vanilla?*" Bob asked.

"By vanilla," I said, "I mean that in this example we specified all three arguments for the For loop. Believe it or not, all three arguments are *not* required, and not including them can produce some behavior that is interesting, to say the least. Not providing all three arguments is not something I would recommend, but C++ does permit you to omit any of the three arguments—or all three if you want to. For instance, you can code a For loop that looks like this."

I then displayed the following code on the classroom projector:

```
for ( ; ; )
```

"What will this do?" Rhonda asked.

"This For statement would result in an endless loop," I said.

"An endless loop?" Ward said. "Why would you want to do this?"

"Most likely you wouldn't," I said, "but there are occasions in the programming world where you would want to create an endless loop—and then use the Break statement from inside the body of the loop to 'break out' of it. The point is, with all three arguments of the For statement being optional, it's really easy to do something like this—either because you think it's a good idea or because you accidentally code it that way. The example I showed you earlier is the prototypical example of the For loop, but there are many other ways to code a For loop. Some programmers, for instance, choose to increment their loop-control variable within the body of the loop itself, leaving the third argument—the increment argument—empty, like this."

```
for (int counter = 1;counter < 11;)
```

"Again, this isn't something I would recommend, but you may see some programmers doing this. Still other programmers choose to leave the first argument, the initialization argument, empty, like this."

```
for ( ; counter< 11;counter++)
```

"This is something you can do provided you initialize the loop-control variable elsewhere in your program."

"Again, I presume that's something you don't recommend," Bob said.

"That's right, Bob," I agreed. "I recommend coding all three arguments in the For loop unless you can think of a very persuasive reason for not doing so—and in the beginning stages of your C++ programming career, I don't think you'll think of any."

"Assuming we do code all three arguments for the For loop," Dave asked, "are there any other variations possible with the For loop?"

"That's a great question, Dave," I answered. "It's possible to vary all three arguments in such a way as to produce some very interesting results. For instance, if instead of incrementing your loop-control variable, you decrement it, the value of the loop-control variable will decrease, and you can actually make your loop go backward. And speaking of the loop-control variable, it doesn't have to start out as 1—it can be any value. In fact, it doesn't even have to be a positive number."

I explained that it's possible to simulate real-world situations more accurately if you get a little creative with the arguments of a For loop.

"Last week, we worked with some fictitious restaurants in New York City," I said. "Today, let's suppose you own a Manhattan hotel in which the floors are numbered from 2 to 20. Let's further pretend that the hotel has three elevators: Elevator 1 stops at all the floors of the hotel, elevator 2 stops only at the even-numbered floors, and elevator 3 stops only at the odd-numbered floors. Now, suppose that we want to write a C++ program that displays, in the C++ console window, the floor numbers at which elevator 1 stops. Here's an exercise to do exactly that using the C++ For loop."

Exercise 5-1 Your First For Loop

In this exercise, you'll code a For loop to display the floors at which elevator 1 stops.

1. Use Notepad (if you are using Windows) to enter the following code:

```
//Practice5_1.cpp
#include <iostream>

int main()
{
    using namespace std;

    cout <<
        "Elevator #1 stops at these floors..." << endl;

    for (int counter = 2;counter < 21;counter ++)
        cout << counter << endl;

    return 0;
}
```

2. Save your source file as Practice5_1 in the \C++Files\Practice folder (select File | Save As from Notepad's menu bar). Be sure to save your source file with the filename extension .cpp.

3. Compile your source file into an executable file.

4. Execute your program. You should see the following output in the C++ console window:

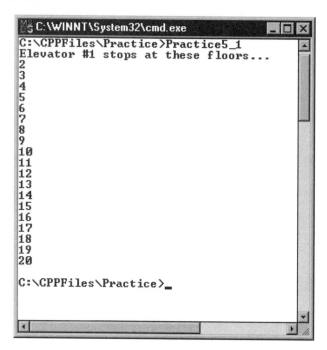

Discussion

No one had any trouble completing this exercise—there wasn't much coding involved.

"Where's the first floor of the hotel?" Kathy asked. "Why did the display start with the number 2?"

"Remember, the floors are numbered from 2 to 20," Mary said. "That's why the loop-control variable was initialized to 2."

"That's right, Kathy," I replied. "This was a good exercise to get your feet wet with the For loop. Now let's get to work on a more challenging problem—elevator 2. That's the elevator that stops only at the even-numbered floors of the hotel. Do you have any ideas on how we should code a For loop to display only the even-numbered floors of the hotel?"

After a few seconds, Dave suggested that we code a For loop, initializing our loop-control variable to 2, that we use a test condition in which we compare the value of the variable to "less than 21," and most importantly, that we increment the value of the loop-control variable by 2 instead of 1.

"Excellent job, Dave," I said, as I distributed this exercise for the class to complete.

| Exercise 5-2 | **Modifying the For Loop to Handle Even-Numbered Floors** |

In this exercise, you'll code a For loop to display the even-numbered floors of the hotel at which elevator 2 stops.

1. Using Notepad, enter the following code:

```
//Practice5_2.cpp
#include <iostream>

int main()
{
    using namespace std;

    cout <<
        "Elevator #2 stops at these floors..." << endl;

    for (int counter = 2;counter < 21;
            counter = counter + 2)
        cout << counter << endl;

    return 0;
}
```

2. Save your source file as Practice5_2 in the \C++Files\Practice folder (select File | Save As from Notepad's menu bar). Be sure to save your source file with the filename extension .cpp.

3. Compile your source file into an executable file.

4. Execute your program. You should see the following output in the C++ console window:

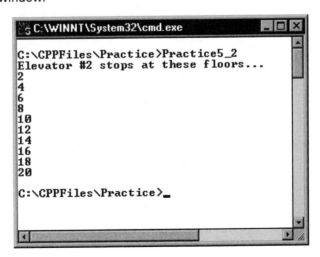

"That was very clever, Dave," Rhonda said, obviously impressed. "I don't think I would have thought of incrementing the loop-control variable by 2."

"Solving programming problems like this requires some imagination," I told Rhonda. "The more programs you work with—whether you read or write them—the easier it will be to envision little tricks like this to solve these types of problems."

"I noticed," Linda said, "that we incremented the value of our loop-control variable *counter* by taking the value of *counter* and adding 2 to it. It sure would be great if there were an increment operator to add 2 to a variable the way the (++) operator adds 1."

"Actually, Linda, there is," I replied. "We used this code to increment the value of the counter variable by 2."

```
counter = counter + 2)
```

"But we can use this code instead, which is a variation of the increment operator (++) you learned about a few weeks ago."

```
counter+=2;
```

"The addition assignment (+=) operator is used to increment the value of a variable by the number that follows it—in this case, +=2 adds 2 to a variable."

"Cool," Chuck said. "Can you increment the variable by any number that way, and is there a way to subtract numbers as well?"

"Yes on both counts, Chuck," I said. "This syntax can be used to add 3 to the variable counter."

```
counter+=3;
```

"And this syntax will subtract 3 from the variable counter."

```
counter-=3;
```

"I've been thinking about elevator 3," Lou said, "the one that stops only at odd-numbered floors in the hotel. I know what you said about using your imagination to solve this problem, but so far, I haven't been able to get it to work. How should we code that loop?"

Linda suggested that a For loop with a loop-control variable initialized to 3, a test condition in which we compare the value of the variable to "less than 21," and once again incrementing the value of the loop-control variable by 2 would be the way to go.

```
for (int counter = 3;counter< 21;counter+=2)
```

"Of course," Lou lamented, "that was my mistake! I kept initializing the value of the loop-control variable to 2 instead of 3."

"Shouldn't the initial value of the loop-control variable be 1?" Rhonda asked.

"Don't forget, Rhonda," I said, "the hotel has no first floor. The first odd-numbered floor is 3, so initializing the loop-control variable to 3 takes care of that."

I then distributed this exercise for the class to complete.

Exercise 5-3   Modifying the For Loop to Handle Odd-Numbered Floors

In this exercise, you'll code a For loop to display the odd-numbered floors at which elevator 3 stops.

1. Using Notepad, enter the following code:

```cpp
//Practice5_3.cpp
#include <iostream>

int main()
{
    using namespace std;

    cout <<
        "Elevator #3 stops at these floors..." << endl;

    for (int counter = 3;counter < 21;counter+=2)
        cout << counter << endl;

    return 0;
}
```

2. Save your source file as Practice5_3 in the \C++Files\Practice folder (select File | Save As from Notepad's menu bar). Be sure to save your source file with the filename extension .cpp.

3. Compile your source file into an executable file.

4. Execute your program. You should see the following output in the C++ console window:

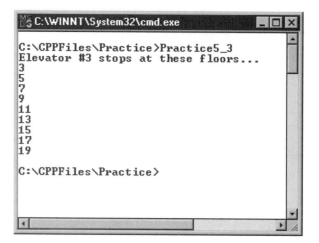

Discussion

By this point, no one seemed to be having any major problems with our elevator exercises.

"This is great fun," Joe said. "I figured there had to be some way to do this kind of thing. Now that I've seen it, it seems pretty easy. I can't wait to apply C++ loops to something practical."

"You'll get a chance to work with loops in the Grade Calculation Project," I said. "But we still have some more work to do before we get to that point."

I continued by saying that all three of the For loop's arguments (initialization, termination, and increment) could be expressed not only as numerical literals (that is, numbers), as we had done in the previous exercises, but also as variables or constants. I then distributed this exercise to demonstrate my point.

Exercise 5-4

Modifying the For Loop to Work with Variables and Constants

In this exercise, you'll code a For loop to display the floors at which elevator 1 stops, but instead of using numeric literals for the initialization, termination, and increment arguments, you'll use a combination of variables and constants.

1. Using Notepad, enter the following code:

```
//Practice5_4.cpp
#include <iostream>
```

```cpp
int main()
{
    using namespace std;

    const int TOP_FLOOR = 20;

    cout << "Elevator #1 stops at these floors..." << endl;

    for (int bottom_floor = 2;
        bottom_floor < TOP_FLOOR+1;bottom_floor++)
        cout << bottom_floor << endl;

    return 0;
}
```

2. Save your source file as Practice5_4 in the \C++Files\Practice folder (select File | Save As from Notepad's menu bar). Be sure to save your source file with the filename extension .cpp.

3. Compile your source file into an executable file.

4. Execute your program. You should see the following output in the C++ console window:

Discussion   "Does everyone see what we're doing here?" I asked.

"It looks like we've done two new things here," Linda said. "First, we used a more meaningful name for the loop-control variable, *bottom_floor*. We also declared a constant called TOP_FLOOR to use as part of the test expression in the termination argument of the For loop."

"That's an excellent analysis, Linda," I said. "Using a constant or constants like this doesn't impact the behavior of the loop, but it does make your code a lot more readable."

I waited to see if there were any questions.

"Now, suppose that we want to display the floors of our hotel backwards?" I continued. "It can be done with a For loop, but I have to warn you, we will have to be careful."

I then distributed this exercise for the class to complete.

Exercise 5-5   ## Displaying the Floors Backwards—but There's a Problem

In this exercise, you'll code a For loop to display the floors of the hotel backwards. But beware: This code has a bug in it and won't behave properly.

1. Using Notepad, enter the following code:

```
//Practice5_5.cpp
#include <iostream>

int main()
{
   using namespace std;

   cout <<
      "Floors in the hotel, listed backwards are..." <<
         endl;

   for (int counter = 20;counter > 20;counter--)
      cout << counter << endl;

   return 0;
}
```

2. Save your source file as Practice5_5 in the \C++Files\Practice folder (select File | Save As from Notepad's menu bar). Be sure to save your source file with the filename extension .cpp.

3. Compile your source file into an executable file.

4. Execute your program. You should see the following output in the C++ console window:

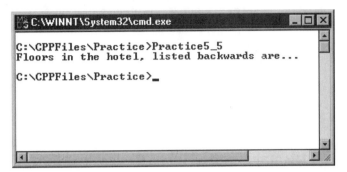

"Nothing happened," Rhonda said. "No floor numbers were displayed. The loop didn't execute, did it?"

Rhonda was correct. Nothing except the heading was displayed in the C++ console window.

"Can anyone tell me what happened?" I asked.

No one had an immediate solution to what had, or hadn't, happened, but then Barbara spoke up.

"I think I know what the problem is," she said. "I know we intended to have the loop go backwards, but in the termination argument the test expression immediately evaluates to False, and that's why the body of the loop never executes."

"What's that, Barbara?" Rhonda asked.

"Take a look at the initial value of our loop-control variable," Barbara continued. "It starts at 20, because that's the top floor of our hotel, and because we want to display the floors backwards, that's where we want to start. But then the test expression asks whether the value of the counter variable is greater than 20. This is where the problem lies. As long as the test expression returns a True value, the body of the loop will execute—but the value of counter is 20, and obviously 20 is not greater than 20. Therefore, the test expression immediately evaluates to False, and the loop terminates."

"Excellent, Barbara," I said. "That's exactly what happened. What we have here is a problem in the way I—and beginning programmers—sometimes miscode loops."

"I would have thought," Ward said, "that C++ would have executed the body of the loop at least once."

"Not with a For loop, Ward," I answered. "Although you'll see in just a few moments that there are some types of C++ loops for which that is the case—that is, the body of the loop is executed at least once—with a For loop, the test expression is always evaluated prior to the body of the loop executing."

"So how can we make this loop count backwards?" Rhonda asked. "What do we need to change?"

"We need to correct our test expression," I said, "to make the loop count backwards."

I then distributed this exercise for the class to complete.

Exercise 5-6   **Displaying the Floors Backwards Correctly**

In this exercise, you'll correct the code from Exercise 5-5 so that the floors of our hotel are correctly displayed backwards.

1. Using Notepad, enter the following code:

```
//Practice5_6.cpp
#include <iostream>

int main()
{
    using namespace std;

    cout <<
        "Floors in the hotel, listed backwards are..." <<
            endl;

    for (int counter = 20;counter > 1;counter--)
        cout << counter << endl;

    return 0;
}
```

2. Save your source file as Practice5_6 in the \C++Files\Practice folder (select File | Save As from Notepad's menu bar). Be sure to save your source file with the filename extension .cpp.

3. Compile your source file into an executable file.

4. Execute your program. You should see the following output in the C++ console window:

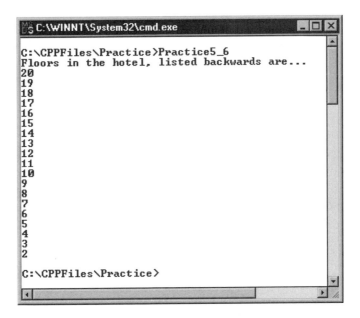

Discussion "That's better," Mary said. "Now the floors are displayed backwards."

"To make the loop count backwards," I said, "you need to specify a test expression that evaluates the value of the loop-control variable against the lower limit of the loop. That's what we did here."

There were no more questions, so I suggested we take a break.

"When we return from break," I said, "we'll examine the indefinite kinds of C++ loops I've mentioned: the While loop family."

While Loops

Resuming after break, I began a discussion of what I call the C++ indefinite loops—the family of While loops.

"Compared to the For loop," I said, "beginners to C++ find the While Loop a bit confusing at first, perhaps because there are actually two variations of it—the While loop and the Do-While loop. But you'll see that the only real difference in the behavior of the two variations is that, like the For loop, the body of the While loop is *not* guaranteed to execute even once. With the Do-While loop, the body of the loop is executed *at least once*. We'll examine both types of While loops during the last half of today's class."

"What are the differences between the While loop and the For loop," Steve asked, "and what are the similarities?"

"Just like the For loop," I said, "the While loop structure permits the programmer to repetitively execute a section of code. But as you'll see, when a While loop ends is not nearly as definite as it is for the For loop."

"How so?" Mary asked.

"With the For loop," I continued, "you saw that we designate a definite endpoint in the way in which we specify our termination argument. With a While loop, there is no built-in loop-control variable as there is with the For loop. Instead, you need to specify an expression in the While statement that is very much like the test expression specified in the For loop. What makes the While loop a bit trickier is that the expression is not written to test the loop-control variable. Instead, the test expression is written to evaluate something else. Unfortunately, when first learning, quite a few beginners miscode the test expression in a While loop, resulting in something we mentioned earlier: an endless or infinite loop."

"What kinds of test conditions can you specify as the expression in the While Loop?" Ward asked.

"You can specify any condition that evaluates to a True or False value," I said, "just as in the test expression you saw in the first For loop we coded today."

"Can we see an example of the While loop?" Mary asked.

The While Loop

"Sure thing, Mary," I said. "Let's take a look at the While loop first; that's the type of While loop in which the test expression is evaluated prior to the body of the loop executing even once."

I then displayed the syntax for the While loop on the classroom projector:

```
while (expression) {
      statement or statements
```

"You're right," Joe said, "this does look a little confusing to me."

"Let's take it a step at a time," I said, "and I'm sure you'll be okay with this. The While loop begins with the word *while*, followed by a test expression, which as I indicated earlier, is much like the test expression in an If statement. Unlike in a For loop, the loop-control variable isn't initialized at the top of the loop structure—there's just this single test expression. There's also no termination argument. As long as the test expression evaluates to True, the body of the loop will be executed. Therefore, it's up to the programmer to ensure that the test expression eventually evaluates to False, and that needs to be done using code within the loop itself, something you'll see in just a few moments. As was the case with the For loop, the test expression is evaluated before the body of the loop is executed. This means that the body of the While loop is not guaranteed to execute even one time: If the text expression immediately evaluates to False, the Loop structure is exited. As you'll see in a few moments, there's a variation of this loop in which the body of the loop is always executed at least once."

"Wouldn't you want every loop you code to execute at least once?" Rhonda asked.

"Not necessarily," I answered. "For instance, suppose you are using a loop to read records from a disk file, and you include the instructions to read the records within the body of the loop. If the file is empty—which can happen—you wouldn't want to execute the body of the loop even once. If you did, you would attempt to read a record from an empty file, which would generate an error."

"Okay," Rhonda answered, "that makes sense to me."

At this point, there were no other questions, and I suggested that we complete an exercise to give everyone a chance to work with the While loop, once again displaying the floors of our hotel.

Exercise 5-7   Using the While Loop to Display the Floors of the Hotel

In this exercise, you'll code a While loop to display the floors of our hotel in the C++ console window.

1. Using Notepad, enter the following code:

```
//Practice5_7.cpp
#include <iostream>

int main()
{
    using namespace std;

    int counter = 2;

    cout << "The floors in the hotel are..." << endl;

    while (counter < 21)    {
       cout << counter << endl;
       counter++;
    }

    return 0;
}
```

2. Save your source file as Practice5_7 in the \C++Files\Practice folder (select File | Save As from Notepad's menu bar). Be sure to save your source file with the filename extension .cpp.

3. Compile your source file into an executable file.

4. Execute your program. You should see the following output in the C++ console window:

Discussion

"As you can see," I said, "we've successfully displayed the floors of our hotel, this time using a While loop to do the job instead of a For loop. I think once you get used to the format, you'll find that working with the While loop—and, specifically, coding the test expression—is somewhat intuitive. Remember, though, we need to do a little more work with the While loop than with the For loop. For instance, because there is no initialization argument, we needed to take care of that ourselves, before the loop structure is encountered, with this line of code."

```
int counter = 2;
```

"Then comes the While loop and its test expression, in which we tell C++ to execute the body of the loop while the value of counter is less than 21 and to display the value of counter in the C++ console window:"

```
while (counter < 21)    {
    cout << counter << endl;
```

"As I mentioned earlier, because the While loop does not have an increment argument of its own, it's imperative that we take care of incrementing the variable we are using to determine the duration of the loop. We do that with this code."

```
counter++;
```

"The variable *counter*," Blaine said, "reminds me of the loop-control variable from the For loop."

"You're right about that, Blaine," I said. "With the While loop, there is no formal loop-control variable as there is in a For loop. In effect, we have to create our own."

"How important is it to increment the value of *counter* inside the loop?" Kathy asked.

"Vitally important," I said. "Beginners typically make two kinds of mistakes with the While loop. Either they initialize the value of a variable they're using in their test expression inside the body of loop, or they increment the value of that variable outside the loop."

"What's wrong with that?" Rhonda asked.

"In our case, if we were to initialize the value of *counter* within the body of the loop," I said, "each time the body of the loop is executed, the value of *counter* is reset to 2. That's not good, in that the value of *counter* never gets to the point where the loop can terminate. Alternatively, if we were to increment the value of *counter* outside the body of the loop, the value of *counter* would always be 2. As a result, the test expression (*counter* < 21) is always true, and the loop never terminates. In both cases, we wind up with an endless loop."

"Why didn't the number 21 display in the C++ console window?" Joe asked. "Why did it stop at 20?"

"Because," I said, "our expression told C++ to execute the body of the loop while *counter* is less than 21. As soon as *counter* is equal to 21, the test expression returns a False value, and the loop immediately terminates."

"You said earlier that While loops have an indefinite nature," Linda said, "but this loop seems pretty definite to me. Can you give us a better example of that?"

"I sure can," I said. "How about a loop that runs until the user tells it to stop?"

I then distributed this exercise for the class to complete.

Exercise 5-8 **An Indefinite Version of the While Loop**

In this exercise, you'll create a While loop structure that displays numbers in the C++ console window. However, the numbers will only be displayed for as long as the user chooses to continue to display them.

1. Using Notepad, enter the following code:

```
//Practice5_8.cpp
#include <iostream>
#include <string>
```

```
int main()
{
    using namespace std;

    int counter = 1;
    string response;

    cout << "Should I start counting? ";
    cin >> response;

    for (int i = 0; i < response.length(); i++) {
        response[i] = toupper (response[i]);
    }

    while (response == "YES") {
        cout << "counter is " << counter << endl;
        counter++;
        cout << "Should I continue? ";
        cin >> response;

        for (int i = 0; i < response.length(); i++) {
            response[i] = toupper (response[i]);
        }
    }

    cout << "Thanks for counting with me!";

    return 0;
}
```

2. Save your source file as Practice5_8 in the \C++Files\Practice folder (select
   File | Save As from Notepad's menu bar). Be sure to save your source file
   with the filename extension .cpp.

3. Compile your source file into an executable file.

4. Execute your program. The program will ask you whether it should start
   counting. Type **Yes** at the C++ console, as shown here:

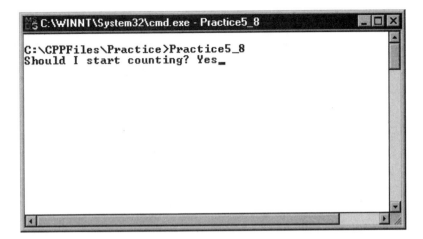

5. The number 1 should appear in the C++ console window, and the program will then ask you whether it should continue counting, as shown here:

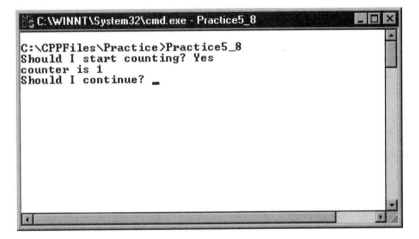

6. Type **Yes** once again. Here's what the screen will look like:

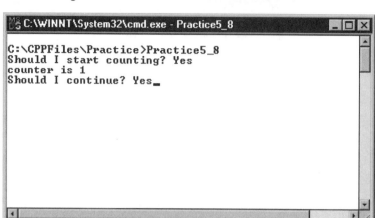

7. The number 2 will then be displayed in the C++ console window, and once again you'll be asked whether the program should continue counting. Numbers will continue to be displayed in the C++ console window for as long as you type **Yes**.

8. Type **No** in answer to the prompt to continue counting. A thank-you message will be displayed in the C++ console, and the program will end, as shown here:

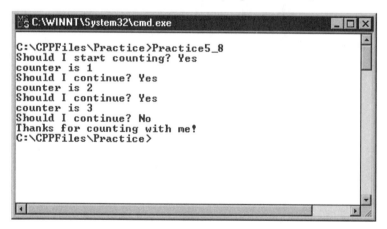

Discussion   There was a fair amount of confusion and problems with this exercise, and it took us about 15 minutes to get through it. The exercise was tedious to type. In addition, not everyone in the class was as attentive to how they typed the word *YES* in their code as they needed to be, which caused some problems when they ran their programs.

"This code is a good example of the indefinite capabilities of the While loop," I explained. "How many times this loop executes is entirely up to the user and is determined at runtime, not when the program is being coded. When we wrote this program, we had no idea how many numbers the user would want displayed in the C++ console window. The While loop gives us a way for the loop to run indefinitely but still with a way to end it. That's the beauty of the While loop. In this case, as soon as the test expression evaluates to False, the loop ends."

I continued by saying that, as we had done in Exercise 5-7, the first thing we did here was to declare the variables we would use in the program.

"Remember," I said, "I can't emphasize this enough: With a While loop there is no built-in loop-control variable, so in order for the loop to eventually end, we need to declare a variable that will be used in a test expression to see whether the loop should be terminated. In the previous exercise, we used the value of *counter* to determine whether the loop should end. This program is a bit different in that we will let the user's response to the question determine when the loop ends. That's the function of the variable *response* here, a variable whose value will be determined by the user. The variable *counter*, as it was in Exercise 5-7, is the number we will display in the C++ console window, and we initialize it to 1."

```cpp
int counter = 1;
string response;
```

"Now it's time," I said, "to use the cout object to display a message to the user, asking them if they wish for the program to start counting, followed by a redirection of the user's input via the cin object to the variable *response*."

```cpp
cout << "Should I start counting? ";
cin >> response;
```

"These next three lines of code are very significant, and some of this may not make much sense to you until we discuss arrays later in the course. The result of this code is that the value of the *response* variable becomes capitalized. Again, this involves the use of arrays, something we'll discuss in more detail later on in the course."

```cpp
for (int i = 0; i < response.length(); i++) {
    response[i] = toupper (response[i]);
}
```

"I was going to ask you about that," Linda said. "What is the **toupper()** function? I presume it's a function."

"Yes it is," I responded. "The **toupper()** function is designed to take a character value and return its uppercase equivalent."

"But the *response* variable isn't a character data type," Dave said, "it's a string."

"That's true, Dave," I replied, "but you may remember last week when I was discussing the String data type, I indicated that it's really a collection of characters. Because of that, we can use a For loop to examine each character in a string variable, execute the **toupper()** function on it, and return its uppercase equivalent."

"In other words," Ward chimed in, "if the character is a lowercase *a*, **toupper()** will return a capital *A*."

"That's right, Ward," I said. "In terms of a string variable, if the user were to enter the string j-o-h-n, the For loop would replace it with J-O-H-N."

"Why are we doing this?" Kate asked.

"In short," I said, "because we want to make our test expression manageable. In this way, no matter how the user spells the word *YES*—all lowercase, all uppercase, or something in between, ultimately their response is converted to YES, in all uppercase letters, and that will make determining whether the user answered 'yes' or something else much easier."

"I guess I'm missing something here," Chuck said, "but how can converting the user's response to uppercase make the comparison easier?"

"Did you realize," I answered, "that the user can type the word *yes* in eight different ways?"

"What do you mean eight different ways?" asked Barbara.

"Each letter of the word *yes* can be entered by the user in either upper- or lowercase," I explained. "And although it's nice to believe that the user would enter 'YES' in all caps if we asked them to, in reality, some users mix and match case as they're entering values into an input box or a text field. Let's take a moment to come up with all the possible combinations of the word *yes*, and you'll see that there are eight different ways of writing it."

YES	yES
YEs	yEs
YeS	yeS
Yes	yes

"So you see," I said, "if we 'convert' the user's response to all uppercase characters, that means we only need to perform the comparison in our test expression to the word *YES*, in all capital letters. The alternative would be to write code using a series of Or operations that would look like this."

```
while (
    response == "YES" | response == "YEs" |
    response == "YeS" | response == "Yes" |
```

```
response == "yES" | response == "yEs" |
response == "yeS" | response == "yes") {
```

"I see what you mean now," Ward said. "That makes sense, and it makes even more sense if we ask the user a question whose answer requires 13 characters."

"That's right, Ward," I said. "A word of 13 characters can be entered 8,192 different ways by the user—that's a comparison I wouldn't want to make using the Or operator. Let's get back to that first line of the While loop, in which we tell C++ to execute the body of the loop provided the variable response is equal to the uppercase value YES."

```
while (response == "YES") {
```

"Oh, so that's the benefit of having converted the user's response to uppercase," Rhonda said. "The light bulb just went on!"

"Is this the type of loop in which the body of the loop is *not* necessarily executed once?" Blaine asked.

"That's right, Blaine," I said. "Because the test expression in a While loop is evaluated at the top of the loop structure, the body of the loop will be executed only if the test expression evaluates to True, something that can only happen if the user answers 'yes' to the question, Should I start counting? Provided the user answers using any of the eight varieties of 'yes,' this next line of code will display the value of the counter variable in the C++ console window."

```
cout << "counter is " << counter << endl;
```

"And then this line of code will increment the value of *counter*."

```
counter++;
```

"Incrementing the value of *counter* is important, but it's not as important as it was in Exercise 5-7, because it's not the value of *counter* that determines if and when the loop ends. The responsibility for ending the loop belongs to the response the user gives to the question, Should I continue? And this response is stored in the *response* variable. That's the key to the loop eventually ending. Notice how we must 'uppercase' the user's response to this question, once again executing the For loop to do the job."

```
cout << "Should I continue? ";
cin >> response;
    for (int i = 0; i < response.length(); i++) {
    response[i] = toupper (response[i]);
    }
```

"So the loop will continue until the user answers 'no'?" Ward asked.

"Not exactly, Ward," I said. "The loop will continue as long as the user types any of the eight variations of the word *yes*. That means the loop will end if the user types anything else, at which time we will then display this message to the user thanking them for counting with us and end the program."

```
cout << "Thanks for counting with me!";
```

Prior to moving on, I repeated my earlier assertion that one of the biggest mistakes beginners make with the While loop is to forget to include code within the body of the loop that enables the loop to end.

"Because the test condition we set up is to compare the value of the response variable to YES," I said, "if we forget to give the user the opportunity to change the value of that variable, we'll wind up with an endless loop condition."

Do-While Loop

No one had any questions about the While loop, so it was time to move on to a discussion of the Do-While loop. I displayed the syntax for the Do-While loop on the classroom projector:

```
do {
    statement(s)
    } while (expression);
```

"This variation of the While loop is called the Do-While loop," I said, "because the first line of the loop structure begins with the single word *do*, and the last line of the loop contains the While statement. Everything else in between is considered the body of the loop."

"How is this Do-While loop different from the While loop we just worked with?" Mary asked.

"Unlike the While loop and the For loop," I answered, "in which the body of the loop is *not* guaranteed to execute even once, with the Do-While loop, the body of the loop will execute at least one time."

"Is it the location of the word *while* that causes that behavior?" Linda asked. "I notice that the test expression is located after the body of the loop."

"Great observation, Linda," I said. "In the While loop structure we just examined, because the word *while* appeared as the first line of the loop structure, the test expression was evaluated prior to the body of the loop executing. With the Do-While loop, because the test expression appears as the last line of the loop structure, the body of the loop is guaranteed to execute at least once, even if the test expression is always false."

No one had any other questions, so I suggested that we complete an exercise in which we implement the functionality from Exercise 5-8 using a Do-While loop instead.

Exercise 5-9 **The Do-While Loop**

In this exercise, you'll create a Do-While loop structure that displays numbers in the C++ console window. However, the numbers will only be displayed for as long as the user chooses to continue to display them.

1. Using Notepad, enter the following code:

```cpp
//Practice5_9.cpp
#include <iostream>
#include <string>

int main()
{
    using namespace std;

    int counter = 1;
    string response;

    cout << "Should I start counting? ";

    cin >> response;

    for (int i = 0; i < response.length(); i++) {
        response[i] = toupper (response[i]);
    }

    do   {
        cout << "counter is " << counter << endl;
        counter++;
        cout << "Should I continue? ";
        cin >> response;

        for (int i = 0; i < response.length(); i++) {
            response[i] = toupper (response[i]);
        }                              // end of for
    } while (response == "YES");        // end of while

    cout << "Thanks for counting with me!";

    return 0;
}
```

2. Save your source file as Practice5_9 in the \C++Files\Practice folder (select File | Save As from Notepad's menu bar). Be sure to save your source file with the filename extension .cpp.

3. Compile your source file into an executable file.

4. Execute your program. The program will ask you whether it should start counting. Type **Yes** at the C++ console. As was the case with Exercise 5-8, the number 1 should appear in the C++ console window, and the program will then ask you whether you wish it to continue counting.

5. Answer **Yes** once again. The number 2 will then be displayed in the C++ console window, and once again you'll be asked whether you wish for the program to continue counting. Numbers will continue to be displayed in the C++ console window for as long as you answer Yes.

6. Answer **No** (or anything other than Yes) to the prompt to stop counting. A thank-you message will be displayed in the C++ console, and the program will end.

Discussion

No one had any major problems completing the exercise.

"It looks like this program is behaving the same way as the program from Exercise 5-8," Rhonda said.

"You're right, Rhonda," I said. "We've proven we can implement the same functionality using a Do-While loop as we did when we coded the program using a While loop."

"So what's the difference?" Joe asked.

"The difference in the behavior," I said, "won't become apparent unless the user answers 'no' to the first question asked of them, Should I start counting? If the user answers 'no' to this question in the Exercise 5-8 version of the program, the body of the loop will *never* execute. That's not the case with the Exercise 5-9 version of the program. Because the test expression is at the bottom of the Do-While structure, the body of the loop will always execute at least once. Let me show you what I mean."

I then ran the code from Exercise 5-8 and answered 'no' to the question asking me if I wanted the program to start counting. The program immediately ended without displaying any numbers in the C++ console window.

"That's what I would expect," Ward said.

"Now let's see what happens," I said, "when we run the code from Exercise 5-9."

I then ran the code from Exercise 5-9 and answered 'no' to the question asking me if I wanted the program to start counting. Despite my answer of 'no,' the program displayed the number 1 in the C++ console window, as shown here:

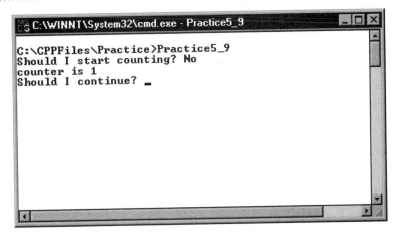

"I see the difference now," Rhonda said. "The program ignored our answer."

"It's not so much that the program ignored our answer," I answered, "but that it didn't check our answer until the body of the loop had already executed once. In Exercise 5-8, the answer was evaluated at the beginning of the loop. Because the test condition evaluated immediately to False, the body of the loop was never executed. In Exercise 5-9, the test condition was evaluated after the body of the loop had already executed and displayed the number 1 in the C++ console window."

I asked if there were any questions about the While family of loops. There were none, so I asked everyone to take a break.

"When we return from break," I said, "we'll be working on a modification to the Grade Calculation Project to include loop processing."

Adding a Loop to the Grade Calculation Project

When my students returned from break, a couple of them immediately asked what we would be doing with the Grade Calculation Project that involved a loop.

"Right now," I said, "as the project stands, it properly calculates the grade for an English, math, or science student, but it only performs one calculation before ending."

"That's right," Blaine said. "One grade calculation, and the program ends. By using loop processing, will we be able to make the program perform multiple calculations before ending?"

"You hit the nail right on the head, Blaine" I said.

"How will we do that?" Chuck asked.

"What we'll do," I said, "is 'sandwich' the code that performs the grade calculation within a loop structure so that we can calculate the grades for many students instead of just one. Can anyone suggest the kind of loop we should use to do that?"

"I suppose we could use a For loop," Rhonda suggested, "but from what we've learned today, a For loop is the best choice when we know for certain the number of times we want the body of the loop to execute. That wouldn't be the case here because each time the program runs, there's likely to be a different number of grades to be calculated. I guess, for that reason, the While loop is the way to go."

"Great thinking, Rhonda," I said, "and I agree, a While loop makes sense to use. Now another question: Should we use the While loop or the Do-While variety?"

"I would vote for the While loop," Valerie answered. "I think we should evaluate the test expression we code at the top of the loop structure, not at the end of it. That way, if the user decides that they don't actually want to calculate a grade, they don't have to. They can just exit the program."

"I agree, Valerie," I said. "Although it's not likely that the user will run the program and then have no grades at all to calculate, it is possible. I think it's safer to ask the user whether they have grades to calculate, and if so, execute the body of the loop to calculate the grades."

I saw some confusion in the eyes of my students, but I knew this would be cleared up when they started to code the modifications to the Grade Calculation Project. I then distributed this exercise for the class to complete.

Exercise 5-10   Adding a Loop to the Grade Calculation Project

In this exercise, you'll modify the Grade Calculation Project you last worked on last week in Exercise 4-7 by giving it the ability to calculate more than one student's grade before ending.

1. Using Notepad, locate and open the Grades.cpp source file you worked on last week. (It should be in the \C++Files\Grades folder.)

2. Modify your code so that it looks like this:

```
//Grades.cpp
#include <iostream>
#include <string>

int main ()
{
    using namespace std;

    const float ENGLISH_MIDTERM_PERCENTAGE = .25;
    const float ENGLISH_FINALEXAM_PERCENTAGE = .25;
```

```
const float ENGLISH_RESEARCH_PERCENTAGE = .30;
const float ENGLISH_PRESENTATION_PERCENTAGE = .20;
const float MATH_MIDTERM_PERCENTAGE = .5F;
const float MATH_FINALEXAM_PERCENTAGE = .50;
const float SCIENCE_MIDTERM_PERCENTAGE = .40;
const float SCIENCE_FINALEXAM_PERCENTAGE = .40;
const float SCIENCE_RESEARCH_PERCENTAGE = .20;
int midterm = 0;
int finalExamGrade = 0;
int research = 0;
int presentation = 0;
float finalNumericGrade = 0;
char finalLetterGrade;
char response[256];
string moreGradesToCalculate;

cout << "Do you want to calculate a grade? ";
cin >> moreGradesToCalculate;

for (int i = 0;
   i < moreGradesToCalculate.length(); i++) {
   moreGradesToCalculate[i] =
      toupper (moreGradesToCalculate[i]);
}

while (moreGradesToCalculate == "YES") {


// What type of student are we calculating?
   cout << "Enter student type " <<
      "(1=English, 2=Math, 3=Science): ";

   cin.getline(response,256);

   if (strlen(response) == 0) {
      cout << "You must select a Student Type";
      return 1;
   }

   if ((atoi(response) < 1) | (atoi(response) > 3)) {
      cout << response <<
         " - is not a valid student type";
      return 1;
```

```
          }

          // Student type is valid, now let's calculate the grade
          switch(atoi(response))
          {
          // Case 1 is an English Student
              case 1:
                  cout << "Enter the Midterm Grade: " ;
                  cin.getline(response,256);
                  midterm = atoi(response);
                  cout << "Enter the Final Examination Grade: " ;
                  cin.getline(response,256);
                  finalExamGrade = atoi(response);
                  cout << "Enter the Research Grade: " ;
                  cin.getline(response,256);
                  research = atoi(response);
                  cout << "Enter the Presentation Grade: " ;
                  cin.getline(response,256);
                  presentation = atoi(response);
                  finalNumericGrade =
                    (midterm * ENGLISH_MIDTERM_PERCENTAGE) +
                    (finalExamGrade *
                        ENGLISH_FINALEXAM_PERCENTAGE) +
                    (research * ENGLISH_RESEARCH_PERCENTAGE) +
                    (presentation *
                        ENGLISH_PRESENTATION_PERCENTAGE);
                  if (finalNumericGrade >= 93)
                      finalLetterGrade = 'A';
                  else
                  if ((finalNumericGrade >= 85) &
                     (finalNumericGrade < 93))
                        finalLetterGrade = 'B';
                  else
                  if ((finalNumericGrade >= 78) &
                     (finalNumericGrade < 85))
                     finalLetterGrade = 'C';
                  else
                  if ((finalNumericGrade >= 70) &
                     (finalNumericGrade < 78))
                     finalLetterGrade = 'D';
                  else
```

```
    if (finalNumericGrade < 70)
        finalLetterGrade = 'F';
    cout << endl <<
        "*** ENGLISH STUDENT ***" << endl << endl;
    cout << "Midterm grade is: " <<
        midterm << endl;
    cout << "Final Exam is: " <<
        finalExamGrade << endl;
    cout << "Research grade is: " <<
        research << endl;
    cout << "Presentation grade is: " <<
        presentation << endl << endl;
    cout << "Final Numeric Grade is: " <<
        finalNumericGrade << endl;
    cout << "Final Letter Grade is: " <<
        finalLetterGrade;
    break;

// Case 2 is a Math Student
    case 2:
        cout << "Enter the Midterm Grade: " ;
        cin.getline(response,256);
        midterm = atoi(response);
        cout << "Enter the Final Examination Grade: " ;
        cin.getline(response,256);
        finalExamGrade = atoi(response);
        finalNumericGrade =
            (midterm * MATH_MIDTERM_PERCENTAGE) +
            (finalExamGrade * MATH_FINALEXAM_PERCENTAGE);
        if (finalNumericGrade >= 90)
            finalLetterGrade = 'A';
        else
        if ((finalNumericGrade >= 83) &
            (finalNumericGrade < 90))
            finalLetterGrade = 'B';
        else
        if ((finalNumericGrade >= 76) &
            (finalNumericGrade < 83))
            finalLetterGrade = 'C';
        else
        if ((finalNumericGrade >= 65) &
```

```
            (finalNumericGrade < 76))
          finalLetterGrade = 'D';
      else
      if (finalNumericGrade < 65)
          finalLetterGrade = 'F';
      cout << endl<<
          "*** MATH STUDENT ***" << endl << endl;
      cout << "Midterm grade is: " <<
          midterm << endl;
      cout << "Final Exam is: " <<
          finalExamGrade << endl;
      cout << "Final Numeric Grade is: " <<
          finalNumericGrade << endl;
      cout << "Final Letter Grade is: " <<
          finalLetterGrade;
      break;

// Case 3 is a Science Student
    case 3:
        cout << "Enter the Midterm Grade: " ;
        cin.getline(response,256);
        midterm = atoi(response);
        cout << "Enter the Final Examination Grade: " ;
        cin.getline(response,256);
        finalExamGrade = atoi(response);
        cout << "Enter the Research Grade: " ;
        cin.getline(response,256);
        research = atoi(response);
        finalNumericGrade =
            (midterm * SCIENCE_MIDTERM_PERCENTAGE) +
            (finalExamGrade *
                SCIENCE_FINALEXAM_PERCENTAGE) +
            (research * SCIENCE_RESEARCH_PERCENTAGE);
        if (finalNumericGrade >= 90)
            finalLetterGrade = 'A';
        else
        if ((finalNumericGrade >= 80) &
            (finalNumericGrade < 90))
              finalLetterGrade = 'B';
        else
        if ((finalNumericGrade >= 70) &
```

```
                (finalNumericGrade < 80))
               finalLetterGrade = 'C';
         else
           if ((finalNumericGrade >= 60) &
               (finalNumericGrade < 70))
               finalLetterGrade = 'D';
         else
           if (finalNumericGrade < 60)
               finalLetterGrade = 'F';
           cout << endl <<
               "*** SCIENCE STUDENT ***" << endl << endl;
           cout << "Midterm grade is: " <<
               midterm << endl;
           cout << "Final Exam is: " <<
               finalExamGrade << endl;
           cout << "Research grade is: " <<
               research << endl;
           cout << "Final Numeric Grade is: " <<
               finalNumericGrade << endl;
           cout << "Final Letter Grade is: " <<
               finalLetterGrade;
           break;
       default:
           cout << response <<
               " - is not a valid student type";
           return 1;
   }                                       // end of switch

   cout << endl<< endl<<
       "Do you have another grade to calculate? ";
   cin >> moreGradesToCalculate;
   for (int i = 0;
       i < moreGradesToCalculate.length(); i++) {
       moreGradesToCalculate[i] =
           toupper (moreGradesToCalculate[i]);
   }                                      // end of for
   }                                 // end of while
   cout <<
       "Thanks for using the Grades Calculation program!";

   return 0;
}                                       // end of main
```

3. Save your source file as Grades.cpp in the \C++Files\Grades folder (select File | Save As from Notepad's menu bar). Be sure to save your source file with the filename extension .cpp.

4. Compile your source file into an executable file.

5. Execute your program and test it thoroughly. We need to verify that the looping behavior of the program is working correctly. After you start up your program, it should ask you whether you have a grade to calculate.

6. Answer **Yes** and calculate the grade for an English student. Enter **70** for the midterm, **80** for the final examination, **90** for the research grade, and **100** for the presentation. A final numeric grade of 84.5 should be displayed with a letter grade of C.

7. After the grade is displayed, the program should ask whether you have more grades to calculate.

8. Answer **Yes** and calculate the grade for a math student. Enter **70** for the midterm and **80** for the final examination. A final numeric grade of 75 should be displayed with a letter grade of D.

9. After the grade is displayed, the program should ask whether you have more grades to calculate.

10. Answer **Yes** and calculate the grade for a science student. Enter **70** for the midterm, **80** for the final examination, and **90** for the research grade. A final numeric grade of 78 should be displayed with a letter grade of C. After the grades is displayed with the calculated grade, the program should ask whether you have more grades to calculate.

11. Answer **No**. You should be thanked for using the program, and the program should end.

Discussion

Making the modifications to the code in the Grades class required careful attention to detail, but in the end, everyone was able to complete the exercise without a great deal of trouble.

"I have to say I'm really impressed with the practical use for this loop," Ward said.

"Me, too," Rhonda said. "In a way, this program kind of reminds me of an Automated Teller Machine in that once you are done withdrawing your money, it asks whether you have any more transactions to complete before giving you your card back."

"Can you go over the code?" Mary asked. "I think I understand what's going on here, but I want to be absolutely sure."

"I'd be glad to do that, Mary," I said. "We made just a few enhancements to the code from last week's version of the Grade Calculation Project, the major one being to sandwich in a While loop, the code that actually does the calculations. Prior to that, we needed to declare a variable to store the value of the user's answer to the question we are going to pose: Do you want to calculate a grade? Because we already had a variable in the program called *response* that we use to accept the individual grade component values from the user, we declared a new variable called *moreGradesToCalculate* for the answer to the question."

```
string moreGradesToCalculate;
```

"Having declared that variable to hold the user's response to our question, it's now time ask the question and accept a response."

```
cout << "Do you want to calculate a grade? ";
cin >> moreGradesToCalculate;
```

"Again, we uppercase the user's response by executing the **toupper()** function within a For loop against each character of the response string."

```
for (int i = 0;
    i < moreGradesToCalculate.length(); i++) {
        moreGradesToCalculate[i] =
            toupper (moreGradesToCalculate[i]);
}
```

"Now here's the critical line of code," I said. "It's where we set up the While loop structure, using the user's response in the test expression."

```
while (moreGradesToCalculate == "YES") {
```

"If the user has answered 'Yes' to the question that they have a grade to calculate, the value of *moreGradesToCalculate* is 'YES,' and we execute the body of the loop—the code that we wrote last week to calculate the student's final numeric and letter grades."

"So really, not all that much has changed with this code," Joe said.

"That's right, Joe," I said. "The really difficult code to calculate the grade was written last week. All we've done by placing it within the body of the loop is give our program the ability to calculate more than one student. We do that by asking the user the question using this code."

```
cout << endl<< endl<<
    "Do you have another grade to calculate? ";
cin >> moreGradesToCalculate;
for (int i = 0;
    i < moreGradesToCalculate.length(); i++) {
    moreGradesToCalculate[i] =
```

```
              toupper (moreGradesToCalculate[i]);
     }                                          // end of for
     }                                          // end of while
```

"If the user answers anything other than 'yes' or its many varieties," I said, "our test expression will evaluate to False, and the loop will terminate, followed by this code, which thanks the user for using our program and gracefully ends the program."

```
     cout <<
        "Thanks for using the Grades Calculation program!";
```

"If the user answers 'yes,' the body of the loop will execute once more, permitting a second student's grade to be calculated."

"I have a problem," Rhonda said. "When I run my program, it's thanking me for using the program after each student I calculate. Shouldn't it do that only when I say I'm finished?"

"That's right, Rhonda," I said, "it should only thank the user once."

I already had a feeling I knew what the problem was as I strode to Rhonda's workstation. Sure enough, she had placed the message thanking the user within the body of the loop, not outside of it. Here's what her code looked like:

```
     for (int i = 0;
        i < moreGradesToCalculate.length(); i++) {
        moreGradesToCalculate[i] =
           toupper (moreGradesToCalculate[i]);
     }                                          // end of for
     cout <<
        "Thanks for using the Grades Calculation program!";
     }                                          // end of while
     return 0;
     }                                          // end of main
```

"I see what you mean," Rhonda said, after I pointed out the problem. "By placing that line of code within the While loop, I ensured it ran each time I calculated a student's grade."

Ward expressed some concern over the growing length and complexity of the code in the Grade Calculation Project.

"The code just keeps growing and growing," he said. "I realize there isn't much we can do about its length. However, it's getting so complex that I'm having a harder and harder time following it."

"I agree," Rhonda added, "and as I said last week, aren't we just about done with this project? I think we've fulfilled all the requirements for the project, haven't we?"

"I think we have, Rhonda," I replied. "From a functional point of view, there really isn't much that we'll be adding to the project. In the remainder of the course, we will streamline and fine-tune the program and take advantage of some of the object-oriented characteristics of the C++ programming language. I think in doing so we'll be addressing Ward's concerns about the growing complexity of the code, although you'll see the overall number of lines of code in the project won't decrease. Object-oriented programs have a way of simplifying the complex nature of code, and we'll start doing that next week when we create some functions and methods of our own, which should make our program a little easier to follow."

It had been a long class. I could see that everyone was feeling proud of the product they were producing week by week. I could also see that they were pretty worn out; it had been an intense session. I dismissed class for the day.

Summary

In this chapter, we discussed how loop processing can make programming a lot easier as well as adding a lot of power to our programs.

Here's a summary of some of the different loop structures we discussed:

- **For loops**   These loops execute a definite number of times. The number of times that the loop runs is determined by the start, end, and step parameters set in the "for" line of the loop control.

- **While loops**   These loops execute an indefinite number of times, determined by a test condition. The While loop continues to run while a specified condition is true. In a While loop, the test expression is evaluated prior to the body of the loop executing even one time. Therefore, in a While loop, there is the possibility that the code in the body of the loop will not execute even one time.

- **Do-While loops**   Like the While loop, the Do-While loop executes an indefinite number of times, determined by a test condition. The Do-While loop continues to run while the test expression evaluates to True. In a Do-While loop, the test expression is evaluated after the body of the loop executes. Therefore, in a Do-While loop, the body of the loop is always executed at least one time.

We also modified the Grade Calculation Project so that it can calculate more than one student's grade.

In the next chapter, we'll take a first look at how C++ allows us to create classes that simulate real-world objects.

Creating Your Own Functions

I n this chapter, we'll discuss how to make our programs more readable and efficient by creating our own functions. As you'll see during the course of the chapter, functions are pieces of code that perform a single task, and they promote a concept called *modularity*.

Modular Programs Are Easier to Maintain and Understand

"Starting today," I said, as I began our sixth class, "and continuing for the next three weeks or so, we'll be examining ways in which we can use some of C++'s object-oriented features to make programs that are more readable, more efficient, and easier to maintain. Even more importantly, you'll discover that object-oriented programming languages such as C++ promote the concept of *software reuse*, which means that a piece of code, once written, doesn't have to be tossed away or rewritten for another program but can be incorporated into classes for use in other programs. In other words, the same piece of code can be used in multiple programs. We'll look at that in more detail next week when you see how you can create classes of your own. In today's class, we'll take the first step along the path of software reuse when you learn how to write functions of your own."

"But haven't we already written functions of our own?" Kate asked.

"To a degree that's true, Kate," I said. "Every one of the programs we've written has contained a **main**() function."

"If I'm correct," Dave said, "I believe that every program we've written in this class has had only one function—the **main**() function. Isn't that right?"

"That's right, Dave," I answered, "and you have probably noticed that as our programs have gotten more complex, the number of lines of code in the **main**() function has grown and grown. Today, you'll learn how to create functions of your own that reside in the same file as the one in which the **main**() function is contained. Then, next week, you'll learn how to create functions that reside in something known as a *class*. These functions can then be executed or called from other programs."

"You said that the number of lines of code in the **main**() function of our Grades Calculation Program has grown and grown," Kate said. "Is that bad? Is there a limit to the number of lines of code that can go into the **main**() function? Why do we need to write other functions?"

"There's no limit to the number of lines of code that can be placed in the **main**() function, or in any function for that matter," I said. "However, the more lines of code contained in a function, the more difficult the program is to follow, understand, and maintain."

"What do you mean by *maintain*?" Rhonda asked. "Is that like car maintenance?"

"Maintaining a program," I answered, "means changing or modifying the program. Programs need to be maintained for a number of different reasons. Some programs need to be modified because of a change in the business environment for which the program is written. Other programs need to be modified due to new governmental regulations. Still other programs need to be modified because of requests from users. Regardless of the reason, you can be almost certain that any program you write will eventually need to be modified, if not by you, then by someone else. Even if all you need to change is a single line of code, if that line of code happens to appear in a **main**() function with hundreds or thousands of other lines of code, you're going to have a heck of a time finding that line of code unless the program was written in a modular fashion."

"Modular?" Lou asked.

"You'll see a little later on, Lou," I said, "that modular programs are programs that are written in distinct, logical units."

"Do programs need to be changed all that often that we need to worry about this?" Blaine asked.

"Most programs that are written for commercial purposes will at one time or other need to be changed." I answered. "In fact, it has been estimated that the programming staff in a large corporation may spend up to 85 percent of its time modifying the code in already existing programs."

"That's incredible," Chuck said. "So making programs easier to read and maintain is really very important."

"Absolutely," I said. "In fact, it's pretty likely that the program we're writing for Frank Olley will need to be changed at some point. If the English, Math, and Science departments change the formula for the way a student's final grade is calculated, we'll need to change the Grade Calculation program."

"I see why programs need to be changed," Valerie said, "but how can creating functions of our own in addition to the **main**() function make that process easier?"

"So far," I answered, "in all the code you've written for this class, I've pretty much told you exactly what line or lines of code to write and where to place them. In the real world, however, this won't be the case. You're more likely to be asked by a supervisor or project leader to make a functional change to a program. In other words, you'll be told what change to make in terms such as 'Change the federal tax withholding rate from 18 percent to 22 percent.' It will be up to you to find the appropriate C++ file, locate the line or lines of code in that file that performs that calculation, decide upon the necessary changes, and then apply them. From experience, I can tell you that if all the code in your program is located within the **main**() function of a single C++ program file, finding and making changes to that code can be pretty tough."

"And this is where having more than one function will come in handy?" Rhonda asked. "I'm afraid I just don't see why."

"I think I can help," Dave chimed in. "I work in a department that gets a tremendous amount of mail. We have a super-efficient secretary, Millie, who by the time I sit down in my cubicle each morning, has separated everyone's mail and placed it on each individual's desk. On those days when Millie isn't in, the place is chaos. Anyone who is expecting an important piece of correspondence sifts through a huge pile of mail. Eventually they find the piece they're looking for, but it's a painstaking job, and sometimes they accidentally pull out a piece of mail belonging to someone else."

"So that huge pile of mail, Dave," Rhonda said, "is like having one big **main**() function?"

"That's right," Dave replied. "Millie, by sorting and distributing the mail each morning, produces logical 'modules' of mail. It makes the whole process much easier."

"That's a great analogy, Dave, thanks," I said. "In terms of modular programming, this means that when we write code, we should place code that performs a single task into a function of its own. For instance, if we write a program to calculate payroll, all the code to calculate the federal withholding tax should be placed in a function of its own, ideally named in such a way that conveys the meaning of what the function does. Similarly, the code to calculate the state withholding tax should be placed in a function of its own. This process has traditionally been described as *modular programming*, although the concepts and techniques have been enhanced quite a bit by modern object-oriented programming languages such as C++."

What Is a Function?

"So in theory," Bob said, "a function is code that performs a single task."

"That's right, Bob," I said. "For instance, last week, all the code we wrote for the Grade Calculation Project went into the **main**() function of the Grades.cpp file. By the end of today's class, we'll have taken that code and redistributed much of it into separate functions. For instance, all the code that performs the calculation for the final grade of an English student will be placed in a function of its own called **CalculateEnglishGrade**(). In a similar way, the code to perform the calculation for the final grade of a math student will be placed in a function of its own called **CalculateMathGrade**(), and the code to perform the calculation for the final grade of a science student will be placed in a function of its own called **CalculateScienceGrade**()."

"I see what you're getting at now," Ward said. "If the code to calculate the final grade for a math student is in a function of its own, I would think finding it and making the correct changes to it would be much easier."

"Right on the mark, Ward," I said. "Not only is code that is broken down and placed in functions easier to find and modify, but when it's also bundled in the form of an object—something we'll do next week—it can be easily reused in other applications."

"How's that?" Peter asked.

"Do you remember the **toupper**() function we used last week?" I asked. "It's a perfect example of code reusability. It's probably no exaggeration to say that millions of C++ programs use the code in the **toupper**() function to do exactly what we did last week—convert characters to uppercase characters—yet the code in the **toupper**() function was written just once. The same thing can be said of the cout and cin objects that we have been using since our first week of class."

I gave everyone a chance to take in what I was saying.

"Are there any rules or guidelines for writing functions?" Steve asked. "Do you write them from scratch right away, or do you place all your code in the **main**() function and then at some point move the code out of there into separate functions as we're doing today?"

"With a little experience, Steve," I said, "you'll find yourself writing functions of your own right from the very start of your program. It seems strange to you now because for the last five weeks we've dealt with just the single **main**() function, but the more programs you write, the more natural placing code in your own functions will become. Just remember, place code that performs a single task into a function of its own. Needless to say, we haven't done that yet with the Grade Calculation Project, but that's because we needed to concentrate on learning the fundamentals of the C++ language and how to create a working program before we worry about making our program more readable, efficient, and easy to modify. For the remainder of today's class we'll worry about all that, and in next week's class and the one after that, you'll learn how the functions we create today can be placed in C++ classes of their own that can then be incorporated into programs written by other programmers."

"Just like the **toupper**() function?" Kate asked.

"You hit the nail on the head, Kate," I said. "Programmers who write good code and are insightful enough to place that code into classes are rewarded by having their code used by hundreds of other programmers—not only by programmers in their own companies but by programmers all over the world. You'll learn more about how to create code and place it in those types of classes next week."

"I can imagine that's quite an ego trip," Ward said, "having your code used like that—and it's also quite an incentive for me to learn this language."

"I have just one question," Mary said. "If we take all the code out of our **main**() function and place it in those other functions you mentioned, what will be left in the **main**() function?"

"We won't take *all* the code out of the **main**() function," I answered. "We know that only a C++ file containing a **main**() function can be executed from a command prompt, so the **main**() function can't disappear entirely. What will happen is that the **main**() function will 'shrink' so that it contains the code that 'calls' or requests the execution of the code contained in those other functions. The code in the **main**() function frequently resembles the outline or table of contents of a book, with each call to a function appearing as a chapter heading."

Creating Your Own Functions

"This all sounds very exciting," Rhonda said. "So how do we create functions of our own, and what do we name them?"

"You can name your functions virtually anything you want, Rhonda," I said, "but be sure to pick a meaningful name. As far as how to create them, in today's class the functions you write will be typed into the same C++ file as the **main()** function. By convention, they should follow the **main()** function, and although this is not required, it's a good idea to separate any functions you write from the **main()** function with a blank line. Let's examine a now-familiar C++ program containing just a single **main()** function and then modify it to include another function of our own."

I then displayed this code on the classroom projector:

```
//Example6_1.cpp

#include <iostream>

int main()
{
  using namespace std;
  cout << "I Love C++";
  return 0;
}
```

"Look familiar?" I asked. "This is the first C++ program we wrote in the course. As you know, it displays the message 'I love C++!' in the C++ console window. Let's see how we can take the code to display that message out of the **main()** function and place it in a function of its own, which we'll call **DisplayMessage()**."

I then modified the code to look like this:

```
//Example6_2.cpp

#include <iostream>

void DisplayMessage();   // Function Prototype

int main()
{
  using namespace std;

  DisplayMessage();       // Call to Custom Function
  return 0;
}

void DisplayMessage()    // Custom Function
```

```
{
  using namespace std;

  cout << "I Love C++";
}
```

I then saved the code as Example6_2.cpp, compiled it, and executed it. The message "I love C++!" was displayed in the C++ console window.

"This program behaves in the same manner as the previous version did," I said, "but in this version of the program, the C++ instruction to display the message 'I love C++!' is no longer being executed directly from the **main**() function. Instead, the instruction is executed from a function called **DisplayMessage**(). C++ requires that we include something called a *function prototype* at the 'top' of our code. A function prototype tells C++ the name of the function we'll be using, its return type, and the number and type of arguments—called its *signature*—that it accepts."

Function Prototype

"Notice how we included the function prototype for the **DisplayMessage**() function right after the include statement," I continued.

```
void DisplayMessage(); // Function Prototype
```

"I was wondering what that was," Blaine said. "So that's not the function itself?"

"That's right, Blaine," I said. "Each function contained in the file—other than the **main**() function—must have a function prototype specified. The function prototype doesn't contain any instructions. It just announces to C++ our intention to create a function with that name and 'signature.'"

I waited a moment before continuing.

"Here is the code that tells C++ to execute the code in the **DisplayMessage**() function."

```
DisplayMessage(); // Call to Custom Function
```

"Notice," I continued, "that the code to call or execute the **DisplayMessage**() function references the name of the function precisely because function names, like variable names, are case sensitive. Notice also that the **DisplayMessage**() function follows the **main**() function."

"Do we need to use the parentheses when we call the function?" Peter asked.

"I think we do," Kate said. "I accidentally coded this program without them, and although the program compiled okay, nothing seemed to happen when I ran it."

"A good question Peter," I said, "and a good answer Kate. Failing to include the parentheses in the function call can lead to all sorts of problems—although as you discovered, the program will compile cleanly. Let's take a closer look at the first line of the **DisplayMessage()** function now."

Function Header

"I see that the first line of the **DisplayMessage()** function is different from the **main()** function," Kathy said. "I think at some point in the class you promised to explain that first line of the **main()** function in more detail. Is now the time?"

"You're right, Kathy," I said. "The first line in each function—which is sometimes called the function header, the function definition, or the function signature—is different. And you're also right that now is a great time to discuss what that first line means in some detail."

```
int main()
```

"That looks so complicated to me!" Rhonda said, looking at the **main()** function header on the classroom projector in a bewildered manner.

"Let's see if this will help," I said, as I displayed this graphic on the classroom projector. "This is a schematic of the **main()** function header."

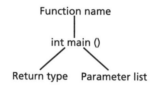

"For comparison purposes," I said, "here's the header for the **DisplayMessage()** function we just created."

```
void DisplayMessage()
```

"It looks to me," Rhonda said, "that apart from the obvious difference in the names of the two functions, that **main()** has the word *int* in front of it, and **DisplayMessage()** has the word *void*. Is the **main()** function somehow special?"

"The only 'special' quality of the **main()** function," I said, "is that its code is automatically executed when we execute a C++ executable file from the command-line prompt. Refer to the chart on the classroom projector as we take a closer look at the declaration for the **main()** function. Here is what you see, reading left to right."

- The return type of the function (in this case, int)
- The name of the function

■ A pair of parentheses within which any parameters to the function are specified, with both a type and name

"So far in this class," I said, "the parentheses have been empty, but shortly you'll learn how to pass parameters to a function."

"What's a parameter?" Bob asked.

"A parameter is a piece of information," I said, "that in some way provides additional instructions to the function about how it should behave. A function that is defined with one or more parameters is seeking qualifying information from the code that calls it, and any code that executes that function is required to supply that qualifying information. Parameters are specified in the function header within parentheses. If the parentheses are empty, as is the case with the **DisplayMessage**() function, that means the function is defined without parameters, so the code calling the function need not worry about supplying it with qualifying information. By the way, you will also hear the term *arguments* used interchangeably with parameters. Technically, functions are defined with parameters, and the qualifying information itself is passed to the header as an argument when the function is called. There's a subtle difference."

"Can we see an example of a function header with parameters?" Linda asked.

"Sure thing, Linda," I answered. "Here's a preview of the **DisplayMessage**() function header with a single string argument."

```
void DisplayMessage(string language)
```

"Is the word *language* in the **DisplayMessage**() function header the name of the parameter?" Dave asked.

"That's right, Dave," I said. "Parameters are named in the function header, and language is my choice for a meaningful parameter name. In actuality, the parameter name can be virtually anything."

"I know we've covered this before," Valerie said, "but does every program need to have a **main**() function?"

"I was about to ask that myself," Rhonda said. "Now that we have a function of our own—**DisplayMessage**() in Example6_2—is it really necessary to have a **main**() function also?"

"Yes, it is, Rhonda." I said. "The **main**() function must be included in every C++ executable file that is to be executed from the command prompt. However, only the executable file is required to have a **main**() function, and it's important to note that there can be only one **main**() function in your program. Next week, we'll create C++ classes that have no **main**() function, but they won't be executed directly from the command prompt. Instead, they'll be used as 'templates' from which we'll create objects."

The Return Type

"In the **main**() function definition, what is *void*?" Chuck asked. "That's a strange-sounding word."

"In C++," I said, "functions perform some sort of processing, and many of them then return a value of some kind to the program that calls them. The return value can be used to inform the calling program as to the success or failure of the operation, or something along those lines. Ordinarily, the return type is a C++ data type, such as int or double. You'll also learn that the return type can also be an object. When the function, by design, returns no value, C++ needs to know this, and the return type of void is designated."

> **NOTE**
> *The return type void indicates that the function does not return a value.*

> **NOTE**
> *Void functions do not require a 'return' statement. If a function indicates a return type, it must contain a return statement that passes back a value of the indicated type.*

"So both the **main**() and **DisplayMessage**() functions perform some kind of processing—**main**() returns an integer value, but **DisplayMessage**() returns no value to the code that calls it. Is that right?" Dave asked.

"That's exactly right, Dave," I said.

"I'm a bit confused," Rhonda said.

"Sometimes," I said, "I analogize functions to favors that you ask a friend to do for you. Perhaps you ask your friend to feed your fish while you're away on vacation, and because you tend to be a worrier, you request a 'return value' in the form of a phone call or an e-mail from your friend to confirm that she actually fed the fish. On the other hand, your friend may be the type of person who never forgets to do anything, in which case, your mind is at ease, and no 'return value' is necessary."

"So functions always do something," Kate said, "but sometimes they return a value, and sometimes they do not."

"That's right, Kate," I said, "and it's entirely up to the designer of the function to decide. In the case of the **DisplayMessage**() function we wrote in Example6_2, did we return a value?"

Kate checked for a minute and then said, "No, the function header specifies void, and there's also no return statement within the body of the function."

"That's right, we didn't return a value from the **DisplayMessage**() function," I said, "but we could have. In the case of **DisplayMessage**(), I didn't think it was really necessary."

"So will the return type be one of the C++ data types we've already learned about?" Mary asked. "Such as int, single, or double?"

"To name a few," I said. "The return data type can also be an object such as a string, or even an object of your own design, the kind we'll create next week."

"I'm trying to recall whether we've executed functions that return a value." Lou said.

"I think we have, Lou," Linda said. "When we executed the **toupper**() function last week, it returned a value that we then assigned to a variable."

"That's right, I forgot about that," Lou said.

"Can we see how to write a function of our own that returns a value?" Barbara asked.

"Sure thing, Barbara," I said. "We can modify the **DisplayMessage**() function we wrote in Example6_2 to return a value—in this case, a bool data type."

I then displayed this code on the classroom projector:

NOTE

Long lines of code in this book (such as the ones in Example6_3.cpp to display output to the C++ console) have been broken up into several lines for formatting reasons. You may type the code on a single line if you wish.

```cpp
//Example6_3.cpp

#include <iostream>

bool DisplayMessage();              // Function Prototype

int main()
{
   using namespace std;

   bool messageDisplayed;

   messageDisplayed = DisplayMessage();

   cout << endl << "The value of messageDisplayed is "
     << boolalpha << messageDisplayed;
   return 0;
}

bool DisplayMessage()                    // Custom Function
{
```

```
using namespace std;

cout << "I Love C++! ";
return true;
}
```

I saved the program as Example6_3.cpp and then compiled and executed it. The following screenshot was displayed on the classroom projector:

"To return a value from a function," I said, "we need to do two things. First, we need to tell C++ that the function will return a Boolean value, which is either True or False. Because we need to include a function prototype in our program, we first change the return type of the function's prototype from void to bool."

```
bool DisplayMessage(); // Function Prototype
```

"And we also change the function header itself."

```
bool DisplayMessage() {
```

"You said we need to do two things," Chuck said. "What's the second?"

"Having told C++ that the function returns a value by declaring it as bool in both the function prototype and function header," I said, "we must now actually return the value from the **DisplayMessage()** function. We do that by coding a return statement somewhere within the body of the function—usually the last statement. C++ is pretty smart about this. If we forget to code the return statement, the program simply won't compile. Here's the statement that returns the bool return value we committed to returning when we declared the function."

```
return true;
```

CAUTION

Be sure to spell 'true' in lowercase letters in your C++ code. Spelling it 'True' will generate a compiler error.

"As you can see, all we need to do is execute the return statement, followed by an appropriate value for the declared data type of the return value. In this case, because we committed to returning a bool data type, we need to return the C++ value True or the value False."

"What does the program that calls the function do with the return value?" Kate asked.

"The code calling the **DisplayMessage**() function," I said, "can do one of three things with the return value. It can store the return value in a variable; it can use the return value in an expression—for instance, by redirecting it to cout object; or, interestingly enough, it can choose to ignore the return value simply by executing the function and not doing anything at all with the return value. In this example, we declared a bool variable called *messageDisplayed* in which we store the return value from the function call. Remember, because we declared the **DisplayMessage**() function with a return type of bool, the variable we declare to store the return value should also be declared as a bool data type."

```
bool messageDisplayed;
```

"Having declared the *messageDisplayed* variable, we now execute the **DisplayMessage**() function, but notice how we place the call to the function to the right of the assignment operator (=). In this way, after the **DisplayMessage**() function executes, its return value is immediately stored in the variable *messageDisplayed*."

```
messageDisplayed = DisplayMessage();
```

"Finally, we display the return value stored in the *messageDisplayed* variable to the C++ console."

```
cout << endl << "The value of messageDisplayed is "
    << boolalpha << messageDisplayed;
```

"I should mention here," I said, "that instead of storing the return value of **DisplayMessage**() in a variable the way we did here, we could have used the return value directly, like this."

```
//Example6_4.cpp

#include <iostream>

bool DisplayMessage();          // Function Prototype
```

```
int main()
{
  using namespace std;

  cout << endl << "The value of messageDisplayed is "
     << boolalpha << DisplayMessage();
  return 0;
}

bool DisplayMessage()                    // Custom Function
{
  using namespace std;

  cout << "I Love C++! ";
  return true;
}
```

"This version of the code is a bit trickier to follow, but many C++ programmers love the compact nature of this style of code—just something to watch out for."

"I noted that you included the 'using namespace std;' statement in both the **main()** and the **DisplayMessage()** functions," Chuck said. "Is that because both of them use cout?"

"Great point, Chuck," I replied. "That's exactly right."

"I'm surprised," Rhonda said. "I actually understand what's going on here."

"Can a function return more than one value?" Chuck asked.

"Excellent question, Chuck," I replied. "The answer is no. A function is limited to returning just a single return value. However, it is possible to return an array. An *array* is a data structure that's actually a collection of variables. So there is a way around the limitation of returning just a single return value."

Function Parameters and Arguments

We were making some pretty good progress in examining the function header. "What's next in the function header?" I asked.

"After the word *int* in the **main()** function," Steve said, "comes the name of the function—no problem there. But then comes the part that confuses me—the parentheses."

I displayed the **main()** function header on the classroom projector once again:

```
int main()
```

"Let me assure you, Steve," I said, "the parentheses confuse everyone at first. I still remember the first time I saw them. I just couldn't understand what they were there for. Just remember, the parentheses are used to designate the parameter list, and if the parentheses are empty, that means the function will be accepting no parameters. As is the case with the **main**() function, no parameters defined are with the **DisplayMessage**() function either, and that's why there's just an empty set of parentheses."

```
bool DisplayMessage()               // Custom Function
```

"What are parameters, anyway?" Linda asked. "Have we executed any functions containing them?"

"I think we have," Dave chimed in. "Aren't parameters the same as arguments, like the one we've passed to some of the functions we've executed, such as **atoi**() and **toupper**()?"

"You're right, Dave," I said. "Arguments are the actual values that we pass to a function. Many programmers use the terms *arguments* and *parameters* interchangeably, and really, only a computer scientist would argue with you. In theory, parameters are the names that appear in a function header, and arguments are the actual values that are passed to the function by the code that calls it. For each parameter in the function's header, there must be a corresponding argument passed to it."

"So parameters appear in the function header, and arguments are the actual values passed to the function when it is called. Is that correct?" Dave asked.

"Perfect, Dave," I said. "I—"

"I know," Rhonda said, laughing. "You couldn't have said it any better yourself!"

"Can we modify the **DisplayMessage**() function to include a parameter?" Linda asked.

"I don't see why not," I answered. "Let's do this: Let's modify the **DisplayMessage**() function to allow the programmer to pass an argument specifying his favorite programming language."

I thought for a moment and then displayed this code on the classroom projector:

```
//Example6_5.cpp

#include <iostream>
#include <string>

using namespace std;

void DisplayMessage(string language);      // Function Prototype

int main()
{
  DisplayMessage("Java");
  DisplayMessage("Visual Basic");
```

```
   DisplayMessage("C++");

   return 0;
}

void DisplayMessage(string language)          // Custom Function
{
   cout << "I Love " << language << endl;
}
```

I saved the program as Example6_5.cpp, compiled it, and then executed it. The following screenshot was displayed on the classroom projector:

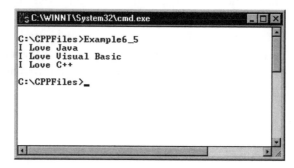

"Let's take a look at the new header for the **DisplayMessage()** function," I said. "I decided in this version of the program to go back to a void return type because returning a value from this function doesn't really add anything to the program. Here's the original function header."

```
void DisplayMessage()                    // Custom Function
```

"And here's the new function header declared with a parameter."

```
void DisplayMessage(string language)     // Custom Function
```

"Within the parentheses," I continued, "we are telling C++ that the **DisplayMessage()** function will accept a single parameter, called language, and that the parameter will be a string data type."

I could see some confusion in the eyes of my students, but I knew that would be cleared up momentarily.

"Let's see the code to call the **DisplayMessage()** function." I said. "Calling a function that requires a parameter is easy, provided you know the function's signature."

"Signature?" Joe asked.

"The function's signature is the function name, along with the number and type of arguments required," I said. "Here we know that we need to pass **DisplayMessage()** just a single string argument, and we do that—actually executing it three times—with this code."

```
DisplayMessage("Java");
DisplayMessage("Visual Basic");
DisplayMessage("C++");
```

"And because the function requires a string argument, we enclose the argument within quotation marks. This is required for a string literal."

"I'm a little confused as to what the **DisplayMessage()** function does with the argument once it receives it from the calling code," Barbara said. "Can you clear that up?"

"I'll try, Barbara," I answered. "Let's look at the code from the body of the Example6_4 program, which was hard-coded to display C++ as the favorite language."

```
cout << "I Love C++! ";
```

"Here's the modified code, which uses the parameter language in conjunction with the cout object to write to the display of the C++ console."

```
cout << "I Love " << language << endl;
```

"Is language a variable?" Lou asked. "And if so, why isn't it declared within the body of the function?"

"Parameters are a lot like variables," I said, "but they don't need to be declared within the body of the function because they are declared within the function header."

"That makes sense," Barbara said.

"I just noticed something," Dave said. "You took the 'using namespace' statement out of the **main()** function and put it right after the include statements. It isn't inside either of the two functions. Why is that?"

"Good observation, Dave," I replied. "It's because of our use of the string type parameter in the function header for **DisplayMessage()**. C++ needs the help of the std namespace in order to work with the string data type, and because the function prototype and function header appear 'outside' of the **main()** function, we need to include the 'using namespace' statement outside of the **main()** function as well. One side benefit of this is that we no longer need to include the using namespace statement inside of the **main()** function—or within the **DisplayMessage()** function either. Technically, we've given the std namespace global scope. The alternative is to write the function prototype and the function header like this."

```
void DisplayMessage(std::string language)
```

NOTE

Some C++ programmers prefer not to use global namespace references like this and instead opt for the longer function prototype and header. In the interest of saving space, for the remainder of the book we'll code global namespace references.

"I have another question," Barbara said. "Is it possible to create a function that accepts more than one argument, and if so, how does C++ know which parameter is which when the code that calls the function passes the arguments?"

"Another good question," I said. "Yes, it is common to design a function that accepts more than one argument. In C++, arguments are passed *positionally*, which means that if the function's header specifies two parameters, C++ assumes that the first argument passed to the function is the first parameter and that the second argument passed to the function is the second parameter. Let me show you exactly what I mean by modifying the code we just wrote to accept two parameters."

I then modified the code from Example6_5 to look like this, saved it as Example6_6.cpp, and displayed it on the classroom projector:

```cpp
//Example6_6.cpp

#include <iostream>
#include <string>

using namespace std;

void DisplayMessage(string language, string howMuch);

int main()
{
  DisplayMessage("Java", "a bunch");
  DisplayMessage("Visual Basic", "lots");
  DisplayMessage("C++", "a lot more");

  return 0;
}

void DisplayMessage(string language, string howMuch)
{
  cout << "I Love " << language << " " << howMuch << endl;
}
```

"Notice the difference in both the function prototype and the function header for **DisplayMessage()**," I said. "They are both now defined with two string parameters: language and howMuch. Both of these parameters are used in the body of the function along with the cout object."

```
void DisplayMessage(string language, string howMuch)
{
    cout << "I Love " << language << " " << howMuch << endl;
}
```

"Also, as you would expect, if the function header now specifies two string parameters, the call to the function must specify two string arguments, which appear after the function name within parentheses, separated by a comma. Notice that because these are string arguments, they are enclosed within quotation marks."

```
DisplayMessage("Java", "a bunch");
DisplayMessage("Visual Basic", "lots");
DisplayMessage("C++", "a lot more");
```

I then compiled and executed the modified program, and the following screenshot appeared on the classroom projector:

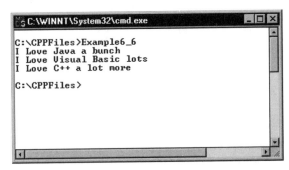

"Now, not only can the calling program designate a favorite language, it can also provide an assessment as to how much the user likes the language," I said.

"I can see," Ward said, "that using two parameters makes this function even more flexible. This stuff is pretty neat."

"You're right, Ward," I said. "The more parameters a function accepts, the more flexible it can be. Of course, the more parameters a function accepts, the more complex the code in the function needs to be to handle the multiple arguments that it will receive. Later on today, we'll create functions for the Grade Calculation Project that will accept several parameters, and you'll see what I mean."

"Suppose we had forgotten to supply the function call with two arguments." Lou said. "What would have happened? Would the program bomb when we ran it?"

"That depends," I said, "on a number of things. When we compile a C++ program, the C++ compiler will always check the function call against the function header, and if there's something wrong with the number and type of arguments being used in the function call, the compiler simply won't compile an executable file. However, sometimes programs are executed, referencing a function outside of the program itself that has been changed since the program was compiled. In that case, the program can bomb at runtime."

"How is it possible to call a function outside of the actual program?" Kate asked.

"We've been doing this during the entire course." I said, "For instance, the **toupper()** function we coded last week in our Grade Calculation program wasn't included in the Grades.cpp file—it's a function that's included in the iostream library we reference via the include statement. If the **toupper()** function's number and type of arguments are changed after we compile a program using this function, the program would bomb at runtime. That's why when you change a function definition the way we just did here, you have to be very careful, especially in a corporate or commercial environment, where many other programs can be using your function."

"What do you mean?" Valerie asked.

"If you change the function's signature," I said, "which is the number and type of parameters— or even order of the parameters—programs that have already been written to call this function may bomb with runtime errors. Even worse, they could execute with incorrect results."

"Do changes to a function's signature happen a lot in the real world?" Blaine asked.

"Functions do change in the real world," I said, "and it's vitally important *not* to change a function's signature when making changes. When you do that, in programming talk, you have 'broken' the client's code. However, sometimes changing a function like this just can't be helped. A function that you designed and coded last year may, in some cases, require more information from the calling program in order to do its job."

"How can you implement a change like that without changing the function's signature?" Bob asked.

"Frequently you can't," I said. "But fortunately, in C++, it's possible to have more than one function with the same name but with different signatures. This is called *function overloading*, and it enables existing programs that call the function with its old signature to run fine and at the same time permits new programs to be written calling the function with its new signature. But let's put off the topic of function overloading for just a few minutes longer. Right now, I'd like to discuss an alternative way of passing arguments to a function."

"What do you mean?" Rhonda asked.

"So far," I replied, "we've passed string literals to the **DisplayMessage()** function we've designed."

"What else can we pass?" Chuck asked.

"We can pass a variable," I said. "Let me show you."

I then displayed this code on the classroom projector:

```
//Example6_7.cpp

#include <iostream>
#include <string>
```

```
using namespace std;

void DisplayMessage(string language, string howMuch);

int main()
{
  string favorite = "C++";
  string intensity = "enormously";
  DisplayMessage(favorite, intensity);

  return 0;
}

void DisplayMessage(string language, string howMuch)
{
  cout << "I Love " << language << " " << howMuch << endl;
}
```

I saved the program as Example6_7.cpp, compiled it, and then executed it. The following screenshot was displayed on the classroom projector:

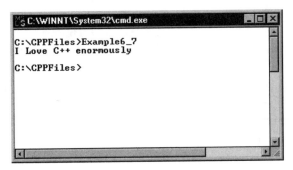

"This version of the program," I said, "displays just a single message in the C++ console window, but aside from that, it behaves in the same manner as the other version. However, we've changed the code by first declaring two string variables called *favorite* and *intensity* and then assigning them values."

```
string favorite = "C++";
string intensity = "enormously";
```

"Then we passed them as arguments to the **DisplayMessage()** function."

```
DisplayMessage(favorite, intensity);
```

"Doing this has no impact on the execution of the function. The function doesn't really care whether a string literal or a variable is passed to it as an argument."

By Default, Arguments Are Passed by Value in C++

"Suppose," Linda said, "that for some reason within the body of the function, we change the value of the passed argument. Does that have any effect on the value of the variable in the code that called it?"

"I'm not sure I know what Linda is asking," Rhonda said.

"Let me try to explain, Rhonda" I said. "In some programming languages, when a change is made to the value of a parameter that is passed to a procedure or function via a variable, as we did here, the value of the variable itself, back in the code that called it, is also changed."

I gave everyone a moment to think about that.

"Is that good?" Joe asked.

"Some programmers find this a convenient way of arriving at a programming solution," I said. "In most programming languages, variables can be passed as arguments to a procedure or function either by value or by reference. *By value* simply means that the actual value of the variable is passed to the function as an argument, and in that case, changing the parameter within the body of the function has no impact on the variable in the calling code. When a variable is passed as an argument to a function *by reference*, it isn't the actual value of the variable that is passed to the function but rather the address of the variable in the computer's memory. This means that when the function changes the value of the parameter, it directly updates the value of the variable back in the calling code."

"What happened here?" Mary asked.

"In C++," I said, "by default, variables are passed 'by value' only, which means that although a variable is passed as an argument to a function, unless we want to, there's no way that changing the value of the parameter within the body of the function can impact the value of the variable in the code that calls the function."

"Can we see an example of both?" Mary asked.

"Sure thing, Mary," I answered. "Let's start by passing a variable as an argument by value."

I then displayed this code on the classroom projector:

```
//Example6_8.cpp

#include <iostream>
#include <string>

using namespace std;

void DisplayMessage(string language, string howMuch);
```

```
int main()
{
  string favorite = "C++";
  string intensity = "enormously";
  DisplayMessage(favorite, intensity);
  cout << "The value of favorite in main() is " << favorite << endl;

  return 0;
}

void DisplayMessage(string favorite, string intensity)
{
  cout << "The value of favorite in DisplayMessage() is "
    << favorite << endl;
  favorite = "VB";
  cout << "The value of favorite in DisplayMessage() is now "
    << favorite << endl;
}
```

I saved the program as Example6_8.cpp and then compiled and executed it. The following screenshot was displayed on the classroom projector:

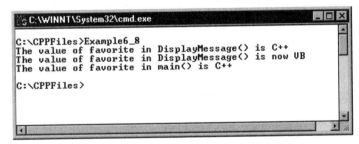

"Let me explain what's going on here," I said. "As we did in Example6_7, within the **main()** function we declared two variables called *favorite* and *intensity* and initialized both of them with values."

```
string favorite = "C++";
string intensity = "enormously";
```

"We then passed the variables as arguments to the **DisplayMessage()** function."

```
DisplayMessage(favorite, intensity);
```

"We didn't need to do this to prove that, by default, C++ passes variables by value," I said, "but notice that we've changed the names of the parameters within the function's header. We're still accepting two string parameters, but in this version of the program we've named them with the same names as the variables in the **main()** function."

```cpp
void DisplayMessage(string favorite, string intensity)
```

"Can we do that?" Ward asked. "Shouldn't the names of the parameters be different from the variables in the **main()** function?"

"They don't have to be," I said. "I know that in Example6_6 and Example6_7, the parameter names are different from the names of the variables in the **main()** function, but there's no rule that they have to be. The variables declared in the **main()** function are local to the **main()** function, and the parameters in the **DisplayMessage()** function are local to that function. C++ considers each of these variables to be different animals. We prove that by executing this line of code within the **DisplayMessage()** function, which displays, in the C++ console, the original value of the argument passed to it as the favorite parameter, which is C++."

```cpp
cout << "The value of favorite in DisplayMessage() is "
    << favorite << endl;
```

"With this line of code, we change the value of the favorite parameter to VB."

```cpp
favorite = "VB";
```

"You might be inclined to believe that we have also changed the value of the *favorite* variable in the **main()** function, but you'll see in a moment that we haven't. First, we prove that the value of the favorite parameter has indeed been changed by executing this line of code."

```cpp
cout << "The value of favorite in DisplayMessage() is now "
    << favorite << endl;
```

"This displays, in the C++ console, the altered value of the favorite parameter, which is now VB. The **DisplayMessage()** function ends, and this line of code is then executed from the body of the **main()** function, proving that the value of the *favorite* variable in the **main()** function has not changed."

```cpp
cout << "The value of favorite in main() is " << favorite << endl;
```

"We've proven," I concluded, "that changing the value of the favorite parameter within the **DisplayMessage**() function has no impact on the value of the *favorite* variable in the **main**() function."

"I think I understand what's going on here," Linda said. "Even though the variables in the **main**() function and the parameters in the **DisplayMessage**() function have the same names, they're really separate things, aren't they?"

"That's right, Linda," I said. "Both the variables and the parameters are declared 'local' to each function in which they appear."

To Pass Arguments by Reference, Use the Ampersand (&)

"Now what about that other way of passing arguments?" Kate asked. "You said that it's possible to pass a variable as an argument to a function and have the function change the value of the variable back in the code that called it."

"That's right, Kate," I said. "Take a look at this code, which is basically the same as the code from Example6_8, except this time we are passing variables as arguments to **DisplayMessage**() by *reference*, not by *value*."

```cpp
//Example6_9.cpp

#include <iostream>
#include <string>

using namespace std;

void DisplayMessage(string &language, string &howMuch);

int main()
{
  string favorite = "C++";
  string intensity = "enormously";
  DisplayMessage(favorite, intensity);
  cout << "The value of favorite in main() is " << favorite << endl;

  return 0;
}

void DisplayMessage(string &favorite, string &intensity)
{
  cout << "The value of favorite in DisplayMessage() is "
```

```
  << favorite << endl;
favorite = "VB";
cout << "The value of favorite in DisplayMessage() is now "
  << favorite << endl;
}
```

"In order to pass a variable 'by reference,'" I continued, "we need to preface the name of the variable in both the function prototype and the function header with an ampersand. In a few weeks, we'll learn that this is called a C++ reference."

```
void DisplayMessage(string &language, string &howMuch);
```

"Let's see the difference," I said, as I saved the program as Example6_9.cpp, compiled it, and then executed it.

```
C:\CPPFiles>Example6_9
The value of favorite in DisplayMessage() is C++
The value of favorite in DisplayMessage() is now VB
The value of favorite in main() is VB

C:\CPPFiles>
```

"I see what happened," Linda said excitedly. "This time, the **DisplayMessage()** function changed the value of the variables *favorite* and *intensity* in the **main()** function."

NOTE

A little later on in the book, you'll learn that it's also possible to get the same results by working with C++ pointers.

"That's right, Linda," I said. "That's because this time, by specifying an ampersand along with the parameter names in the function header and prototype, the memory address of the *favorite* and *intensity* variables were passed to the **DisplayMessage()** function. When the **DisplayMessage()** function changed the value of the favorite parameter, C++ was given direct access to the value of the *favorite* variable back in the **main()** function."

```
favorite = "VB";
```

"I think I understand what's going on here," Rhonda said. "Now, did you say that there are certain types of problems that can be more easily be solved by passing a variable by reference?"

"That's true, Rhonda," I said, "but you needn't concern yourself with those in this course. While you're learning C++, don't worry about passing arguments by reference. The default, by value, will be just fine."

Variable Scope

"You've used the term *local* several times this morning," Blaine said. "Can you tell us exactly what it means?"

"Local is a term that refers to the scope of a variable," I said. "A variable's scope describes what other parts of your program can 'see' the variable. In C++, there are three types of variables: instance, class, and local variables. We'll discuss both instance variables and class variables next week. Local variables are variables declared within a function. A variable declared within a function can be seen or accessed only by code within that same function."

"So a local variable is one declared within a function?" Kate asked.

"That's basically correct, Kate," I said. "Technically, a local variable is one declared within a block—that is, within a pair of brackets. This means that if you declare a variable within the brackets of an If statement, the variable can only be seen by the code within the If statement."

"I think at work I've seen some variables declared just above the **main**() function," Linda said. "They don't appear to belong to any function."

"Those are global, static, or class variables," I said. "We examined a global variable a few weeks ago in Example3_8. We'll talk more about static and class variables next week."

Variable Lifetime

"I've heard some programmers at work refer to the *lifetime* of a variable," Valerie said. "Is lifetime the same as scope?"

"No, but they are related," I replied. "Scope affects what parts of your program can see the variable. Lifetime, on the other hand, affects how long your variable lives. A variable declared as a local variable within a function has local scope and can only be seen by other code within the function. It's also 'born' when its declaration statement within the function is executed, and it 'dies' after the last line of code in the function is executed. Next week, you'll see that the lifetimes for global, static, and class variables are different. In the case of a global variable, it exists for as long as the program is running. In the case of a class variable, it exists as long as an object created from its class exists. Static variables may live even longer—as long as *any* object created from its class exists. More on that next week."

We had been working for quite some time, so I suggested we all take a break before completing our first hands-on exercise of the day.

Using Functions to Fine-tune Your Code

Fifteen minutes later, when we returned from break, I resumed class by reminding my students that the main benefit to creating functions of our own—*custom functions,* as I call them—is that it promotes program modularity.

"Remember," I said, "modularity means that, as much as possible, you should create functions in your programs that perform one function and one function only. In the long run, this makes your programs easier to read, understand, and modify in the future. Creating custom functions and placing them in instantiable classes allows our code to be easily used by other programmers. That's something we'll do next week. Today, I have a pretty extensive first exercise for you to complete. There's a lot of code to it, and as you write it, you'll find that all of it is being placed within the **main**() function of the class. As you complete the exercise, try to think of ways you could use custom functions to make the program modular, because that's exactly what we'll be doing in the next exercise."

I then distributed the exercise for the class to complete.

Exercise 6-1	**The Smiley National Bank Program with All of the Code in the main() Function**

In this exercise, you'll write a program that allows the user to display their bank balance or make deposits and withdrawals from their account.

1. Using Notepad, enter the following code:

```cpp
//Practice6_1.cpp
#include <iostream>
#include <string>
using namespace std;
int main()
{
    float balance = 0;
    float newBalance = 0;
    float adjustment = 0;
    char response[256];
    string moreBankingBusiness;

    cout << "Do you want to do some banking? ";
    cin >> moreBankingBusiness;

    for (int i = 0;
       i < moreBankingBusiness.length(); i++) {
       moreBankingBusiness[i] =
```

```
           toupper (moreBankingBusiness[i]);
   }

   while (moreBankingBusiness == "YES") {

//What type of business are we doing?
       cout << "What would you like to do? " <<
               "(1=Deposit, 2=Withdraw, 3=Get Balance): ";
       cin.getline(response,256);

       if (strlen(response) == 0) {
          cout << "You must make a selection";
          return 1;
       }
       else
       if (atoi(response) < 1 |
           atoi(response) > 3) {
           cout << response <<
              " - is not a valid banking function";
           return 1;
       }

//1 is a Deposit
       if (atoi(response) == 1) {
          cout << "Enter the Deposit Amount: ";
          cin >> adjustment;
          newBalance = balance + adjustment;
          cout << endl << endl <<
             "*** SMILEY NATIONAL BANK ***" <<
                endl << endl;
          cout << "Old Balance is: " << balance << endl;
          cout << "Adjustment is: +" << adjustment << endl;
          cout << "New Balance is: " << newBalance <<
                endl <<endl;
       }

//2 is a Withdrawal
       if (atoi(response) == 2) {
          cout << "Enter the Withdrawal Amount: ";
          cin >> adjustment;
          newBalance = balance - adjustment;
          cout << endl << endl <<
             "*** SMILEY NATIONAL BANK ***" <<
```

```
                            endl << endl;
                cout << "Old Balance is: " << balance << endl;
                cout << "Adjustment is: -" << adjustment << endl;
                cout << "New Balance is: " << newBalance <<
                    endl <<endl;
            }


    // 3 is a Balance Inquiry
            if (atoi(response) == 3) {
                cout << endl << endl <<
                    "*** SMILEY NATIONAL BANK ***" <<
                        endl << endl;
                cout << "Your current Balance is: " <<
                    newBalance << endl <<endl;
            }

            balance = newBalance;
            cout << "Do you have more banking business? ";
            cin >> moreBankingBusiness;

            for (int i = 0;
              i < moreBankingBusiness.length(); i++) {
              moreBankingBusiness[i] =
                    toupper (moreBankingBusiness[i]);
            }


        }                               // end of while

      cout << endl << endl << "Thanks for banking with us!";
      return 0;
    }
```

2. Save your source file as Practice6_1.cpp in the \CPPFiles\Practice folder (select File | Save As from Notepad's menu bar). Be sure to save your source file with the filename extension .cpp.

3. Compile your source file into an executable file.

4. Execute your program. The program will ask whether you wish to do some banking. Type **Yes** at the C++ console.

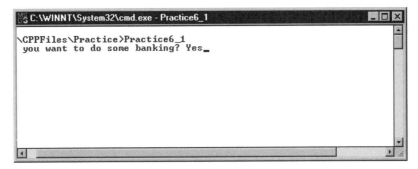

5. You will then be asked what you wish to do: make a deposit, make a withdrawal, or get a balance. Type **1** at the C++ console.

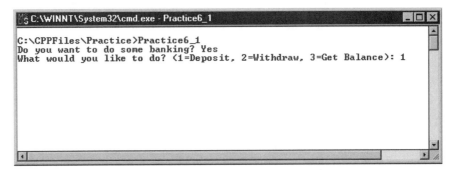

6. The program will then ask you how much you wish to deposit into your account. Type **50** at the C++ console to indicate your deposit amount.

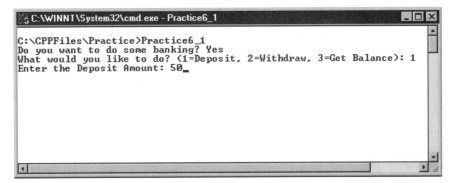

7. The program will display a confirmation message, indicating your deposit amount and your old and new balances.

```
C:\WINNT\System32\cmd.exe - Practice6_1                          _ □ X

C:\CPPFiles\Practice>Practice6_1
Do you want to do some banking? Yes
What would you like to do? (1=Deposit, 2=Withdraw, 3=Get Balance): 1
Enter the Deposit Amount: 50


*** SMILEY NATIONAL BANK ***

Old Balance is: 0
Adjustment is: +50
New Balance is: 50

Do you have more banking business? _
```

8. Notice that the program is asking whether you have more banking business. Type **Yes** at the C++ console.

9. Once again, the program will ask you what you wish to do: make a deposit, make a withdrawal, or get a balance. Type **2** at the C++ console to indicate you wish to make a withdrawal.

10. The program will then ask you how much you wish to withdraw. Type **20** at the C++ console to indicate your withdrawal amount.

11. The program will display a confirmation message, indicating your transaction (withdrawals are designated with a negative transaction amount) and your old and new balances.

12. Once again, the program will whether you have more banking business. Type **Yes** at the C++ console.

13. The program will then ask you what you wish to do: make a deposit, make a withdrawal, or get a balance. Type **3** at the C++ console to indicate you wish to display the current balance.

14. The program will then display the current balance of your account.

15. Once again, the program will ask whether you have more banking business. Type **No** at the C++ console.

16. The program will display a message thanking you for using it and then end.

Discussion

Although this program was very tedious to type, everyone was pretty comfortable with the code in it. There really wasn't anything new in the program, and in about 15 minutes, all my students had successfully coded the exercise.

"This program," I said, "is one we'll be working with in quite a few exercises and is a good example of the type of program you may be asked to develop in the future. It's also a good example of the type of program that can be enhanced significantly by writing custom functions. As you undoubtedly noticed while you keyed in the program, there's a lot of code, and all of it is in the **main()** function. As I mentioned earlier, having all your code in the **main()** function makes reading and understanding the code difficult, and it toughens the task of making modifications to this program if they are ever required."

"I agree with that," Kate said. "I made a mistake or two while coding it, and trying to find these mistakes was certainly compounded by the length of the code and the fact that it's all in one place. Will we be able to break the **main()** function into other functions?"

"I think so, Kate," I said. "If we examine the code in the **main()** function, we'll find that we're performing three distinct tasks: making a deposit, making a withdrawal, and displaying a balance. Those three tasks, according to what you've learned today about program modularity, should be in three separate custom functions, and that's what we'll be doing in the next exercise. Before we start with that, do you have any questions about anything in this code?"

"I think just about everything in this program is something we've done before," Steve said, "but I was a little confused about the two variables, *balance* and *newBalance*. Was the reason we needed to have these two variables because we chose to display both the old balance and the new balance whenever the user made a transaction?"

"That's exactly the case, Steve," I answered. "It isn't until after we display a confirmation of the user's transaction that we actually calculate a new balance. For that reason, we need to keep both the old balance and the new balance in memory to display both in the C++ console. The old balance is no problem—it's stored in the *balance* variable. To calculate the new balance, we execute one of two lines of code, depending on the transaction type. If a deposit was made, we perform this calculation."

```
newBalance = balance + adjustment;
```

"And if the user makes a withdrawal, we perform this calculation."

```
newBalance = balance - adjustment;
```

"Regardless of the type of transaction, though, just before asking the user whether they have more banking business, we must set the value of the *balance* variable equal to the value of the *newBalance* variable."

```
cout << "Do you have more banking business? ";
cin >> moreBankingBusiness;
```

"Makes sense to me," Steve answered. "Thanks for the explanation."

I waited to see if there were more questions before continuing.

"Okay," I said, "let's take a shot at modifying this program to use three custom functions: one for a deposit, one for a withdrawal, and one to display a balance. There will still be some code in the **main()** function—we're not moving it *all* into custom functions—but the **main()** function will appear more condensed this time around when we add the calls to the three other functions. When all is said and done, the new version of the program should behave identically to the one we just wrote, but you should find the program easier to read and much easier to modify if necessary. In fact, we'll be doing just that next week when we move the code in the three functions you are about to create and place them into instantiable classes."

No one had any questions about what we were about to do, so I distributed this exercise for my class to complete.

<table>
<tr><td>**Exercise 6-2**</td><td>### The Smiley National Bank Program with Three Custom Functions</td></tr>
</table>

In this exercise, you'll modify the program you wrote in Exercise 6-1, taking much of the code in the **main()** function and placing it in one of three custom functions you'll create.

1. Using Notepad, enter the following code:

```
//Practice6_2.cpp
#include <iostream>
#include <string>

using namespace std;

void MakeDeposit();
void MakeWithdrawal();
void GetBalance();

float balance = 0;
float newBalance = 0;
float adjustment = 0;

int main()
{
    char response[256];
    string moreBankingBusiness;

    cout << "Do you want to do some banking? ";
    cin >> moreBankingBusiness;
```

```
for (int i = 0; i < moreBankingBusiness.length(); i++) {
   moreBankingBusiness[i] =
      toupper (moreBankingBusiness[i]);
}

while (moreBankingBusiness == "YES") {

   cout << "What would you like to do? " <<
           "(1=Deposit, 2=Withdraw, 3=Get Balance): ";
   cin.getline(response,256);

   if (strlen(response) == 0) {
      cout << "You must make a selection";
      return 1;
   }
   else
   if (atoi(response) < 1 |
       atoi(response) > 3) {
         cout << response <<
            " - is not a valid banking function";
         return 1;
   }

   if (atoi(response) == 1) {
   MakeDeposit();
   }

   if (atoi(response) == 2) {
   MakeWithdrawal();
   }

   if (atoi(response) == 3) {
   GetBalance();
   }

   balance = newBalance;
   cout << "Do you have more banking business? ";
   cin >> moreBankingBusiness;

   for (int i = 0;
      i < moreBankingBusiness.length(); i++) {
```

```
            moreBankingBusiness[i] =
                toupper (moreBankingBusiness[i]);
        }

    }                                    // end of while

  cout << endl << endl << "Thanks for banking with us!";
  return 0;
}


void MakeDeposit()
{
   cout << "Enter the Deposit Amount: ";
   cin >> adjustment;
   newBalance = balance + adjustment;
   cout << endl << endl <<
      "*** SMILEY NATIONAL BANK ***" << endl << endl;
   cout << "Old Balance is: " << balance << endl;
   cout << "Adjustment is: +" << adjustment << endl;
   cout << "New Balance is: " << newBalance
      << endl <<endl;
}

void MakeWithdrawal()
{
   cout << "Enter the Withdrawal Amount: ";
   cin >> adjustment;
   newBalance = balance - adjustment;
   cout << endl << endl <<
      "*** SMILEY NATIONAL BANK ***" << endl << endl;
   cout << "Old Balance is: " << balance << endl;
   cout << "Adjustment is: -" << adjustment << endl;
   cout << "New Balance is: " << newBalance
      << endl <<endl;
}

void GetBalance()
{
   cout << endl << endl <<
      "*** SMILEY NATIONAL BANK ***" << endl << endl;
```

```
cout << "Your current Balance is: " <<
    newBalance << endl <<endl;
}
```

2. Save your source file as Practice6_2 in the \CPPFiles\Practice folder (select File | Save As from Notepad's menu bar). Be sure to save your source file with the filename extension .cpp.

3. Compile your source file into an executable file.

4. Execute your program. The program will ask whether you wish to do some banking. Type **Yes** at the C++ console.

5. You will then be asked what you wish to do: make a deposit, make a withdrawal, or get a balance. Type **1** at the C++ console.

6. The program will then ask you how much you wish to deposit into your account. Type **50** at the C++ console to indicate your deposit amount.

7. The program will display a confirmation message, indicating your deposit amount and your old and new balances.

8. Notice that the program is asking whether you have more banking business. Type **Yes** at the C++ console.

9. Once again, the program will ask you what you wish to do: make a deposit, make a withdrawal, or get a balance. Type **2** at the C++ console to indicate you wish to make a withdrawal.

10. The program will then ask you how much you wish to withdraw. Type **20** at the C++ console to indicate your withdrawal amount.

11. The program will display a confirmation message, indicating your transaction (withdrawals are designated with a negative transaction amount) and your old and new balances.

12. Once again, the program will ask whether you have more banking business. Type **Yes** at the C++ console.

13. The program will then ask you what you wish to do: make a deposit, make a withdrawal, or get a balance. Type **3** at the C++ console to indicate you wish to display the current balance.

14. The program will then display the current balance of your account.

15. Once again, the program will ask whether you have more banking business. Type **No** at the C++ console.

16. The program will display a message thanking you for using it and then end.

Discussion   During the completion of this exercise, the question as to the most efficient way to modify the code from the previous exercise came up. Many of my students created a new C++ file and copied and pasted the old code into the new file. Then they modified the old code for the new exercise. Copying and pasting is not without its perils, however, and doing so in order to create the Practice6_2.cpp file was probably no quicker than just creating the code from scratch.

"This program should behave the same as the previous version, is that right?" Rhonda asked.

"That's right, Rhonda," I said, but I could tell from her face that something wasn't right. I paid a quick visit to her PC and discovered that even though she had properly created the three custom functions, she had failed to call them from the **main()** function of the class. Therefore, the program wasn't permitting her to do any banking business.

"The behavior of the program hasn't changed," I said, after getting Rhonda on the right track. "What we've done is take the code to make a deposit, a withdrawal, and display a balance out of the **main()** function and move it into three custom functions called **MakeDeposit()**, **MakeWithdrawal()**, and **GetBalance()**, respectively."

"In addition to those obvious changes," Dave said, "I did notice a few other subtle modifications in the program. Can you go over those?"

"Sure thing, Dave," I said. "I suspect you're talking about the three variables, *balance*, *newBalance*, and *adjustment*, that are declared outside of any of the four functions that we now have in the class."

"Why are they there?" Blaine asked. "Are these the global variables you were talking about?"

"That's excellent, Blaine," I said. "As I mentioned before our break, variables declared within a function have local scope, which means that a variable that is declared within the **MakeDeposit()** function cannot be seen by code outside of it. Also, when the **MakeDeposit()** function ends, the variable and its value die. All three of these variables have values that need to be seen by code in the three custom functions. The only way to give the code in all three of those functions access to the value in a variable is to declare the variable as a global variable, which is what happens when the variable is declared outside of a function."

```
static float balance = 0;
static float newBalance = 0;
static float adjustment = 0;
```

"Global variables," I said, "are accessible by every function in the program, and their values live for as long as our program is running. Aside from these changes and the creation of our three custom functions, I believe the program is now pretty much identical to the previous version."

No one seemed to disagree, so I continued.

Function Overloading

"In a few minutes," I said, "we'll be modifying the Grade Calculation Project by creating custom functions. Before we do that, however, there's one more concept we need to go over, and that's function overloading. Earlier in today's class, I mentioned that function overloading allows you to define multiple functions with the same name, as long as each one of the functions has a different signature."

"A signature, as I recall you saying," Linda said, "is the combination of the function name along with the number and type of parameters in the function header."

"That's right, Linda," I said. "So long as the number and type of parameters are different in the function header, you can have any number of functions with the same name. You'd be surprised how comfortable you'll get with function overloading as you use it more and more, and we'll be creating some overloaded functions of our own."

"So C++ knows which of the overloaded functions to execute by examining the arguments that are passed to it?" Kate asked.

"That's exactly right, Kate," I said. "Let me show you an example of an overloaded function. I think you'll find it pretty interesting."

I thought for a moment and then displayed the following code on the classroom projector:

```cpp
//Example6_10.cpp

#include <iostream>
#include <string>

using namespace std;

void DisplayMessage(string favorite);
void DisplayMessage(string favorite, string intensity);

int main()
{
  DisplayMessage("C++");
  DisplayMessage("C++", "a lot");

  return 0;
}

void DisplayMessage(string favorite)
{
  cout << "I love " << favorite << endl;
```

```
}

void DisplayMessage(string favorite, string intensity)
{
   cout << "I love " << favorite << " " << intensity << endl;
}
```

I then saved the program as Example6_10.cpp, compiled it, and then executed the program. The following screenshot was displayed on the classroom projector:

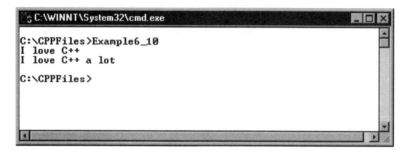

```
C:\WINNT\System32\cmd.exe

C:\CPPFiles>Example6_10
I love C++
I love C++ a lot

C:\CPPFiles>
```

"That's impressive," Ward said. "I think I can see a lot of practical applications for function overloading at my work."

"This is a pretty simple example," I said, "but I think it illustrates the concept of function overloading quite nicely. What we've done here is define two custom functions, each one with the same name—**DisplayMessage**()—but with different signatures. The first function accepts a single string argument called favorite."

```
void DisplayMessage(string favorite)
{
   cout << "I love " << favorite << endl;
}
```

"And the second function accepts two string arguments called favorite and intensity."

```
void DisplayMessage(string favorite, string intensity)
{
   cout << "I love " << favorite << " " << intensity << endl;
}
```

"C++ determines which one of the two functions to execute," I said, "by matching up the number and type of arguments supplied with the function call. This line of code tells C++ to execute the **DisplayMessage**() function that requires just a single string parameter."

```
DisplayMessage("C++");
```

"And this line of code tells C++ to execute the **DisplayMessage**() function that requires two string parameters."

```
DisplayMessage("C++", "a lot");
```

"Somehow," Rhonda said, "with the term *overloading*, I thought this would be a lot more difficult than it turned out to be. This isn't bad at all. In this case, a picture really was worth a thousand words."

"Are the names of the parameters within the function header considered when C++ determines which function to execute?" Dave asked. "For instance, suppose you have two identically named functions, requiring the same number and types of parameters, but the names of the parameters are different."

"That's a good question, Dave," I said. "The names of the parameters in the header are *not* considered by C++, only the numbers and types of parameters. For instance, if we were to define two functions named **DisplayMessage**() and specify that each one accept a single string parameter, the fact that we name the string parameter in the first function Elton and the string parameter in the second function Elvis doesn't matter. When we compiled the program, C++ would generate a compiler error, informing us that we attempted to define a duplicate function."

"Does the order of the parameters in the header affect whether the compiler detects a duplicate function header?" Barbara asked.

"That's a great question, Barbara," I answered. "The order of the parameters is significant. For instance, C++ does permit us to write two identically named functions, both of which accept an integer and a string parameter, but with the parameters in opposite orders."

"Could you clarify that?" Bob asked.

"Sure," I replied. I then displayed these two similar looking functions on the classroom projector.

```
void DisplayMessage(string favorite, string intensity);
void DisplayMessage(string intensity,string favorite);
```

I explained to the class that the compiler recognizes these as two distinct overloaded functions, since the parameter types, although the same number and type, are in a different order.

"What about the return value of the function?" Linda asked. "Is that considered to be part of the function's signature?"

"Another good question," I said, "and the answer is no. The return value is not considered to be part of the function's signature and is not used by C++ when determining whether the function can be overloaded."

"I'm not sure I understand what Linda means about the return value being considered part of the function's signature," Chuck said.

"In other words, Chuck," I said, "let's say you have two identically named functions, both requiring the same number and type of arguments, but one has a return value of void and the other a return value of string. Does C++ consider them to be unique? The answer is no. When you compile the class in which these two functions appear, C++ will tell you that you're trying to define two identical functions. The bottom line is that only the number and type of parameters affect the uniqueness of an overloaded function in the eyes of C++. If you declare two functions with the same signature, you'll generate a compiler error."

I waited for more questions, but everyone seemed satisfied with the concept of function overloading.

"With the remaining time we have left today," I said, as I glanced at the classroom clock, "I'd like to make changes to the Grade Calculation program we wrote last week by adding several custom functions to it. You'll also have a chance to work with an overloaded function."

I then distributed the final exercise of the day for the class to complete.

Exercise 6-3

The Grade Calculation Project with Custom Functions

In this exercise, you'll modify the Grade Calculation program by taking some of the code currently residing in the **main()** function and creating several custom functions—**WhatKindOfStudent()**, **CalculateEnglishGrade()**, **CalculateMathGrade()**, and **CalculateScienceGrade()**—and three overloaded versions of **DisplayGrade()**.

1. Using Notepad, locate and open the Grades.cpp source file you worked on last week. (It should be in the \CPPFiles\Grades folder.)

2. Modify your code so that it looks like this:

```
//Grades.cpp
#include <iostream>
#include <string>

using namespace std;

int WhatKindOfStudent();
void CalculateEnglishGrade();
void CalculateMathGrade();
void CalculateScienceGrade();

void DisplayGrade(int midterm, int finalExamGrade,
                  int research, int presentation,
```

```
                    float finalNumericGrade,
                    char finalLetterGrade);

void DisplayGrade(int midterm, int finalExamGrade,
                    float finalNumericGrade,
                    char finalLetterGrade);

void DisplayGrade(int midterm, int finalExamGrade,
                    int research,
                    float finalNumericGrade,
                    char finalLetterGrade);

const float ENGLISH_MIDTERM_PERCENTAGE = .25;
const float ENGLISH_FINALEXAM_PERCENTAGE = .25;
const float ENGLISH_RESEARCH_PERCENTAGE = .30;
const float ENGLISH_PRESENTATION_PERCENTAGE = .20;
const float MATH_MIDTERM_PERCENTAGE = .50;
const float MATH_FINALEXAM_PERCENTAGE = .50;
const float SCIENCE_MIDTERM_PERCENTAGE = .40;
const float SCIENCE_FINALEXAM_PERCENTAGE = .40;
const float SCIENCE_RESEARCH_PERCENTAGE = .20;
int midterm = 0;
int finalExamGrade = 0;
int research = 0;
int presentation = 0;
float finalNumericGrade = 0;
char finalLetterGrade;
char response[256];
string moreGradesToCalculate;

int main ()
{
   int lresponse;

   cout << "Do you want to calculate a grade? ";
   cin >> moreGradesToCalculate;

   for (int i = 0;
      i < moreGradesToCalculate.length(); i++) {
      moreGradesToCalculate[i] =
         toupper (moreGradesToCalculate[i]);
```

```
                }

                while (moreGradesToCalculate == "YES") {
                   lresponse = WhatKindOfStudent();
                   switch(lresponse)
                   {
                      case 1:
                         CalculateEnglishGrade();
                         DisplayGrade (midterm, finalExamGrade,
                                       research, presentation,
                                       finalNumericGrade,
                                       finalLetterGrade);
                         break;
                      case 2:
                         CalculateMathGrade();
                         DisplayGrade (midterm, finalExamGrade,
                                         finalNumericGrade,
                                         finalLetterGrade);
                         break;
                      case 3:
                         CalculateScienceGrade();
                         DisplayGrade (midterm, finalExamGrade,
                                        research, finalNumericGrade,
                                        finalLetterGrade);
                         break;
                   }        // end of switch

                cout << endl<< endl<<
                   "Do you have another grade to calculate? ";
                cin >> moreGradesToCalculate;
                for (int i = 0;
                   i < moreGradesToCalculate.length(); i++) {
                   moreGradesToCalculate[i] = toupper
                      (moreGradesToCalculate[i]);
                }                              // end of for
                }                   // end of while
                cout <<
                   "Thanks for using the Grades Calculation program!";
                return 0;
             }
```

```cpp
int WhatKindOfStudent()
{
   int lresponse;

   cout << "Enter student type " <<
       "(1=English, 2=Math, 3=Science): ";

   cin.getline(response,256);

   if (strlen(response) == 0) {
      cout << "You must select a Student Type";
      exit(1);
   }

   if ((atoi(response) < 1) | (atoi(response) > 3)) {
      cout << response <<
          " - is not a valid student type";
      exit(2);
   }

   return atoi(response);
}

void CalculateEnglishGrade()
{
   cout << "Enter the Midterm Grade: " ;
   cin.getline(response,256);
   midterm = atoi(response);
   cout << "Enter the Final Examination Grade: " ;
   cin.getline(response,256);
   finalExamGrade = atoi(response);
   cout << "Enter the Research Grade: " ;
   cin.getline(response,256);
   research = atoi(response);
   cout << "Enter the Presentation Grade: " ;
   cin.getline(response,256);
   presentation = atoi(response);
   finalNumericGrade =
       (midterm *
        ENGLISH_MIDTERM_PERCENTAGE) +
        (finalExamGrade * ENGLISH_FINALEXAM_PERCENTAGE) +
```

```
            (research * ENGLISH_RESEARCH_PERCENTAGE) +
            (presentation * ENGLISH_PRESENTATION_PERCENTAGE);
      if (finalNumericGrade >= 93)
          finalLetterGrade = 'A';
      else
      if ((finalNumericGrade >= 85) &
          (finalNumericGrade < 93))
         finalLetterGrade = 'B';
      else
      if ((finalNumericGrade >= 78) &
          (finalNumericGrade < 85))
         finalLetterGrade = 'C';
             else
      if ((finalNumericGrade >= 70) &
          (finalNumericGrade < 78))
         finalLetterGrade = 'D';
      else
      if (finalNumericGrade < 70)
          finalLetterGrade = 'F';
}


void CalculateMathGrade()
{
   cout << "Enter the Midterm Grade: " ;
   cin.getline(response,256);
   midterm = atoi(response);
   cout << "Enter the Final Examination Grade: " ;
   cin.getline(response,256);
   finalExamGrade = atoi(response);
   finalNumericGrade =
       (midterm * MATH_MIDTERM_PERCENTAGE) +
       (finalExamGrade * MATH_FINALEXAM_PERCENTAGE);
   if (finalNumericGrade >= 90)
      finalLetterGrade = 'A';
   else
   if ((finalNumericGrade >= 83) &
       (finalNumericGrade < 90))
      finalLetterGrade = 'B';
   else
```

```
   if ((finalNumericGrade >= 76) &
       (finalNumericGrade < 83))
     finalLetterGrade = 'C';
   else
   if ((finalNumericGrade >= 65) &
      (finalNumericGrade < 76))
     finalLetterGrade = 'D';
   else
   if (finalNumericGrade < 65)
     finalLetterGrade = 'F';
}

void CalculateScienceGrade()
{
   cout << "Enter the Midterm Grade: " ;
   cin.getline(response,256);
   midterm = atoi(response);
   cout << "Enter the Final Examination Grade: " ;
   cin.getline(response,256);
   finalExamGrade = atoi(response);
   cout << "Enter the Research Grade: " ;
   cin.getline(response,256);
   research = atoi(response);
   finalNumericGrade =
      (midterm * SCIENCE_MIDTERM_PERCENTAGE) +
      (finalExamGrade *
          SCIENCE_FINALEXAM_PERCENTAGE) +
      (research * SCIENCE_RESEARCH_PERCENTAGE);
   if (finalNumericGrade >= 90)
             finalLetterGrade = 'A';
   else
   if ((finalNumericGrade >= 80) &
      (finalNumericGrade < 90))
     finalLetterGrade = 'B';
   else
   if ((finalNumericGrade >= 70) &
      (finalNumericGrade < 80))
     finalLetterGrade = 'C';
   else
   if ((finalNumericGrade >= 60) &
      (finalNumericGrade < 70))
```

```
            finalLetterGrade = 'D';
        else
        if (finalNumericGrade < 60)
            finalLetterGrade = 'F';
}

void DisplayGrade(int midterm, int finalExamGrade,
                  int research, int presentation,
                  float finalNumericGrade,
                  char finalLetterGrade)
{
    cout << endl <<
        "*** ENGLISH STUDENT ***" << endl << endl;
    cout << "Midterm grade is: " <<
        midterm << endl;
    cout << "Final Exam is: " <<
        finalExamGrade << endl;
    cout << "Research grade is: " <<
        research << endl;
    cout << "Presentation grade is: " <<
        presentation << endl << endl;
    cout << "Final Numeric Grade is: " <<
        finalNumericGrade << endl;
    cout << "Final Letter Grade is: " <<
        finalLetterGrade;

}               // end of DisplayGrade with 6 parameters

void DisplayGrade(int midterm, int finalExamGrade,
                  float finalNumericGrade,
                  char finalLetterGrade)
{
    cout << endl<<
        "*** MATH STUDENT ***" << endl << endl;
    cout << "Midterm grade is: " <<
        midterm << endl;
    cout << "Final Exam is: " <<
        finalExamGrade << endl;
    cout << "Final Numeric Grade is: " <<
        finalNumericGrade << endl;
    cout << "Final Letter Grade is: " <<
```

```
                  finalLetterGrade;
    }               // end of DisplayGrade with 4 parameters



    void DisplayGrade(int midterm, int finalExamGrade,
                      int research,
                      float finalNumericGrade,
                      char finalLetterGrade)
    {
        cout << endl <<
            "*** SCIENCE STUDENT ***" << endl << endl;
        cout << "Midterm grade is: " <<
            midterm << endl;
        cout << "Final Exam is: " <<
            finalExamGrade << endl;
        cout << "Research grade is: " <<
            research << endl;
        cout << "Final Numeric Grade is: " <<
            finalNumericGrade << endl;
        cout << "Final Letter Grade is: " <<
            finalLetterGrade;

    }               // end of DisplayGrade with 5 parameters
```

3. Save your source file as Grades.cpp in the \CPPFiles\Grades folder (select File | Save As from Notepad's menu bar). Be sure to save your source file with the filename extension .cpp.

4. Compile your source file into an executable file.

5. Execute your program and test it thoroughly. We need to verify that the looping behavior of the program is working correctly. After you start up your program, it should ask whether you have a grade to calculate.

6. Answer **Yes** and calculate the grade for an English student. Enter **70** for the midterm, **80** for the final examination, **90** for the research grade, and **100** for the presentation. A final numeric grade of 84.5 should be displayed with a letter grade of C.

7. After the grade is displayed, the program should ask whether you have more grades to calculate.

8. Answer **Yes** and calculate the grade for a math student. Enter **70** for the midterm and **80** for the final examination. A final numeric grade of 75 should be displayed with a letter grade of D.

9. After the grade is displayed, the program should ask whether you have more grades to calculate.

10. Answer **Yes** and calculate the grade for a science student. Enter **70** for the midterm, **80** for the final examination, and **90** for the research grade. A final numeric grade of 78 should be displayed with a letter grade of C. After the grades are displayed with the calculated grade, the program should ask whether you have more grades to calculate.

11. Answer **No**. You should be thanked for using the program, and the program should end.

Discussion

"Wow, that was intense," Rhonda said. "My program works, and amazingly, I think I actually understand what we did here. Essentially, we've taken a bunch of code out of the **main()** function and put it into one of several custom functions."

"Exactly right, Rhonda," I said. "We created several custom functions— **WhatKindOfStudent()**, **CalculateEnglishGrade()**, **CalculateMathGrade()**, and **CalculateScienceGrade()**—and three overloaded functions called **DisplayGrade()**. As much as possible, I think the program is now pretty modular, although I'm sure some of you might be able to suggest the creation of some additional functions."

"I think the program is very modular," Kate said. "We have a function to determine the type of student for whom the user wishes to calculate a final grade, three functions for the calculation for each one of the three different student types, plus three overloaded functions for the display of the grade."

"The number of lines of code in the **main()** function has really been reduced," I said. "The first thing we did was move the variable and constant declarations out of the **main()** function and convert them to global variables and constants so that their values could be accessible to the code in each of the custom functions we created. Something else that was important is that we declared a local response variable called *lresponse*. This variable will be used to store an integer value—either 1, 2 or 3—passed to us from the **WhatKindOfStudent()** function representing the student type selected by the user."

```
int lresponse;
```

"Could we have named this variable *response* also," Ward asked, "or would that in some way have conflicted with the global variable *response*?"

"Good question, Ward," I answered. "We could have named both variables *response*—variables that are declared in a function take precedence over the same named global variable—meaning that C++, if it finds a local variable with the same name as a global variable, will use the local variable. But C++ code can be confusing enough to follow—that's why I gave the variable a different name here."

I waited a moment before continuing.

"All that really remains in the **main()** function," I said, "is a loop that asks the user whether they want to calculate a grade. Based on their response, the **WhatKindOfStudent()** function is executed. After it's finished executing, the local variable *lresponse* contains the user's valid answer."

```
while (moreGradesToCalculate == "YES") {
    lresponse = WhatKindOfStudent();
```

"Why did you say *valid answer*?" Mary asked.

"The **WhatKindOfStudent()** function prompts the user for a number from 1 to 3, indicating the type of student for which they wish to calculate a grade," I said. "As it did when it was in the **main()** function, this code evaluates the user's response by using the **WhatKindOfStudent()** function, and it prompts the user if they just press the ENTER key without typing 1, 2, or 3."

```
if (strlen(response) == 0) {
        cout << "You must select a Student Type";
```

"In addition, we now do something we didn't do before—we immediately end the program by executing the C++ **exit()** function with a return value of 1."

```
exit(1);
```

"In a similar way, we evaluate the user's response to see whether the number entered is less than 1 or greater than 3. If it is, we warn the user that their response is invalid, and once again immediately end the program. Notice how we use an exit code of 2 in this case to designate a different abnormal termination condition."

```
if ((atoi(response) < 1) | (atoi(response) > 3)) {
    cout << response <<
        " - is not a valid student type";
exit(2);
```

"As a result, the only remaining alternative is a valid response of 1, 2, or 3, and we pass that back to the **main()** function via this return statement, first executing the **atoi()** function against the value of the *response* variable."

```
return atoi(response);
```

"I understand now," Mary said, "what you meant by a valid response."

"Now," I continued, "based on the value of the *lresponse* variable, we then call one of the three custom functions we wrote to calculate the student's grade and execute the overloaded **DisplayGrade()** function. C++ decides which one of the three overloaded functions to execute by the number and type of arguments supplied as arguments."

```
switch(lresponse)
{
    case 1:
        CalculateEnglishGrade();
        DisplayGrade (midterm, finalExamGrade,
                      research, presentation,
                      finalNumericGrade,
                      finalLetterGrade);
        break;
```

"Each one of the three **Calculate** functions is fairly well encapsulated," I said.

"Encapsulated?" Kathy asked.

"Encapsulated," I said, "means that everything that is needed to perform the calculations, including prompting the user for the component pieces of the grade, is included in the function. Not all programmers would write these functions like this. Some might very well include a separate function to prompt the user for the grade components and then execute one of the calculate functions, followed by the display functions."

"Why is that?" Ward asked. "Is there something wrong with the way we've done it?"

"There's a science and art to designing functions," I said. "No two people are likely to write their program in the same way, which is one of the things I love about teaching programming. For instance, some programmers would argue that our use of global variables is wrong. The problem is that the techniques we need to use to avoid using global variables we are a week or two away from learning. Our ultimate use of C++ objects will make our program much more efficient—and stylistically more pleasing to the C++ programming purists."

"Something I found pretty interesting," Joe said, "is how you chose to create overloaded functions to display the grades. Why didn't you just display the grades from within the various **Calculate** functions?"

"Calculating a grade and displaying a grade are different tasks," I said. "Separating the code for each task makes sense, especially if you consider the fact that the manner in which we are displaying the information for Frank Olley is completely arbitrary. He doesn't really care how the display of the information looks."

"In other words," Dave said smiling, "he may want it changed as soon as he sees it. Placing the code to display the grades in functions separate from the calculation code will make modifying the code easier."

"But why not just go with three uniquely named functions?" Ward asked. "Why did you use overloaded functions to display the grades?"

"That's simple, Ward," I said. "I wanted to give you experience working with overloaded functions. That experience will come in handy later on in the course."

It had been an extremely long and interesting class. No one had any further questions, so I dismissed class for the day.

Summary

In this chapter, you learned about the concept of program modularity and the benefits of creating custom functions in our C++ programs. We discussed details of creating our own functions, including the four types of access modifiers, the return types of functions, and how to define functions to accept one or more parameters. You also learned how overloaded functions permit you to define more than one function with the same name, provided the function headers are unique in terms of the number and type of arguments supplied. We finished the chapter by modifying the Grade Calculation Project to include several custom functions, including an overloaded function.

Creating Objects from Instantiable Classes

I n Chapter 6, you began to learn how to introduce modularity into the programs you write by creating custom functions in our Startup program module. Once defined, these functions are then called from the **main**() function. In this chapter, we take modularity several steps further by creating what C++ calls *instantiable classes*—that is, classes from which objects can be created by the programs you've learned how to write so far, called *client programs*, and sometimes by other classes. Creating objects from classes is the name of the game in object-oriented programming languages such as C++, and by the end of today's class, you'll see why. The data and code in your startup programs, as well as the number of lines of code, will shrink. Overall, your programs will become easier to follow, maintain, and modify. Plus, the code you place in instantiable classes is available to hundreds, even thousands, of other programmers in your company or throughout the world. This is truly object-oriented programming.

Creating Objects from Instantiable Classes

"Early on in our course," I said, as I began our seventh class, "I mentioned to you that C++ is an object-oriented programming language in which in we work with standard packages of classes and objects that make the job of writing a program much easier. I also told you that at some point, you would be able to design classes of your own from which objects could be created. However, I warned you that it would be some time before you could do this. Well, today's the day. Up until now, we've used functions of objects created from classes provided to us in what are known as the standard C++ libraries—functions such as the **toUpper**() function and the **atoi**() function. In today's class, you'll learn how to design and create classes from which other programs will be able to instantiate objects."

"Instantiate?" Rhonda asked.

"*Instantiate* is a term that means to create an object from a class," I said. "In C++, an instantiable class is a model for an object, much like an architectural blueprint is a model for a house or a building. Just as from one blueprint, many 'instances' of a house can be built, from one instantiable class, many instances of an object can be created. I know what you're probably thinking. The programs we've created so far haven't been used like that. That's because they've been startup programs, which are programs intended to be executed from the command prompt. Instantiable classes are different. They are not intended to be run from the command prompt; in fact, they can't be. Instantiable classes are meant to enable startup programs (and other classes) to create objects from them. Today you'll learn how to create these instantiable classes, and by the end of today's class, you'll have designed and coded several classes that model real-world objects."

"This sounds exciting!" Ward said. "What kind of real-world objects can be modeled using instantiable classes?"

"In the real world of programming," I said, "we can use instantiable classes to model many things, such as employees, students, and inventory, to name a few. In today's class, we'll create an instantiable class to model a bank transaction—and, of course, we'll also be creating a class to model the English, math, and science students here at the university."

"This process sounds to me like it may not be all that easy," Rhonda said.

Creating Classes Is an Extension of Modular Programming

"I don't want to make creating instantiable classes sound too easy," I said, "but I think you'll find it's just an extension of the modular programming process you learned about and practiced last week when we broke up our code into modules by creating custom functions. Creating instantiable classes is a matter of determining what real-world objects need to be represented in your program and apportioning variables and functions to each one. In many ways, this is nearly complete with the Grade Calculation Project. I think you all realize by now that the project is modeling a real-world student. In the Grade Calculation Project, that's one object, and there may be more. The bottom line is that if you are comfortable with what we did last week concerning function creation, you'll have no trouble going through the mechanics of creating instantiable classes. Experience will help you identify the objects you need to model in your program, along with the characteristics and behavior of the objects you need to simulate."

"Do instantiable classes look like the startup programs we've written so far?" Peter asked.

"Startup programs require a **main()** function so that they can be executed from a command prompt," I said. "Instantiable classes do not contain a **main()** function, and for that reason, instantiable classes cannot be executed directly from a command prompt the way the programs we've written so far can. Instantiable classes provide their blueprint to your program's functions or to other classes so that objects can be created from them. Instantiable classes are designed in such a way that the objects created from them simulate the characteristics and behavior of a real-world object, such as an employee or a piece of inventory."

"You've used the terms 'classes' and 'instantiable classes'," Kate pointed out. "Is there a difference?"

"Good point, Kate," I said, "Not all classes are instantiable—that is, not every class is meant to be used directly as a blueprint to create objects. For now, we'll deal only with instantiable classes. We'll see those other kinds of classes later on in the course."

Objects Have Properties That Simulates Their Characteristics

"What do you mean by 'characteristics of an object'?" Blaine asked. "Can you give us an example of an object's characteristics?"

"Yes I can, Blaine," I said. "For instance, if we create an instantiable class designed to represent a real-world employee in a corporation, we would want to create a class capable of representing the employee's name, address, social security number, and salary, to name a few. The characteristics of the Employee object are represented and stored inside the object using the instance and static variables I briefly mentioned last week. The characteristics are also called properties of the object."

NOTE

Remember, a class is a template or model for the object that is instantiated from it, just like a house is an object created from an architectural blueprint.

Objects Have Behavior (Methods)

"That makes sense to me," Linda said, "but what about an object's *behavior*, which you also mentioned? What kind of behavior can an object possess?"

"Well," I said, thinking for a moment, "an employee has certain kinds of behaviors, such as working on a particular task, attending meetings, traveling to a customer site, and taking a vacation day. These kinds of behavior can be simulated in an object through the implementation of a class function. Class functions are very similar to the kind we wrote last week. Class functions are also called methods."

"I see," Kate said, "but wouldn't the code for that be pretty complex? I'd hate to have to write it."

"You're right, Kate," I said. "I bet that code would be pretty complex to write, but the beauty of instantiable classes is that if you want to use an Employee object in one of your programs, you don't have to write a bit of that code. It's the designer of the Employee class who needs to worry about the details of the code to model that behavior, and once it's written, it can be used over and over again by hundreds, even thousands, of other programmers. You see, all the really difficult code necessary to implement the behavior of the object resides within the class itself. A programmer who wants to use the Employee object, just like we've been using the cout object to direct output to the console, only needs to execute the object's function in order to implement the behavior."

"So you're saying that the programmer who designs the class from which an object is created isn't necessarily the programmer who will later use the object in a program?" Ward asked.

"That's right, Ward," I said. "It's usually senior-level programmers and designers who design the classes from which objects in a corporate environment are created. I know C++ programmers who spend all their time designing instantiable classes just like that and never write any code that actually creates any of those objects."

"So what happens after the instantiable class is designed?" Steve asked.

"Usually," I answered, "the class is placed in a package, advertised, and made available to other programmers in the company or corporation. Some companies make their living by designing such classes for commercial sale to programmers in other companies. And if the instantiable class you design is really good, it may be used by other programmers all over the world, like the C++ cout object is."

"I think you mentioned this a minute ago, but I may have missed it," Mary said. "If characteristics of an object are implemented via class and member variables, how is the behavior of an object implemented?"

"Behavior in an object is implemented via functions," I said, "just like the functions we wrote last week."

"I'm anxious to see one of these instantiable classes," Linda said. "Can you show us one?"

"Sure thing, Linda," I said. "Let's create an instantiable class, called Banner, designed to display the user's favorite programming language in the C++ console. The class will contain just a single attribute, called *favoriteProgram*, implemented via a member variable, and it will possess just one kind of behavior, Display, designed to display that single attribute. This behavior will be implemented via a function.

I then displayed this code on the classroom projector:

```
//Banner.cpp
#include <iostream>
#include <string>

using namespace std;

class Banner
{
  public: string favoriteProgram;
  public: void Display()
  {
     cout << "I love " << favoriteProgram << endl;
  }
};
```

"Where's the **main()** function?" Rhonda asked. "I don't see it anywhere."

"Instantiable classes aren't required to have a **main()** function," I said, "because they are not intended to be executed directly from a command prompt. Instantiable classes are meant to serve as blueprints for objects that are created from another class—you'll see that in a moment. Before we do that, however, let's take a closer look at the code in the Banner instantiable class. The first lines of the class contain the include and using statements you've seen in the other programs we've written. These are necessary because the code in this class will use the C++ cout object."

```
#include <iostream>
#include <string>

using namespace std;
```

"This next line of code, however, is like nothing you've seen before," I continued. The word 'class' tells C++ that this is the definition for a class, and the name of the class follows everything in between the braces is the class definition."

```
class Banner
{
```

"By the way, notice that there's a semicolon following the closing brace of the class definition."

```
};
```

"That next line of code," Valerie said, "looks like a variable declaration. Is that the class variable you were telling us about earlier in the course?"

"That's right, Valerie," I said. "A class variable—technically known as a member variable—is a variable declared within a class but not within any function of the class. That way, the variable is visible, or *scoped*, to all the functions in the class. The string variable *favoriteProgram* is used to implement the one and only attribute of the Banner class."

```
public: string favoriteProgram;
```

"Let me make sure I understand why this is a member variable," Dave said. "It's the fact that the declaration does *not* appear within the **Display()** function, is that right? Otherwise, it appears to be an ordinary variable declaration to me."

"That's right, Dave," I said. "Member variables are variables that are declared outside of any function. Member variables, by convention, appear at the top of the class, just after the left bracket denoting the beginning of the class."

"I notice the Public keyword in front of the declaration of the member variable," Kate said. "Is that necessary?"

"Yes, it is," I said. "Without the keyword Public, the *favoriteProgram* member variable would only be accessible by code within the Banner class. In other words, no program using the Banner object would be able to access or update the attribute. Notice how the word 'public' and the data type 'string' are separated by a colon."

I waited to see if anyone had any more questions before continuing.

"Now, let's take a look at the one and only behavior of the Banner class, Display, which is implemented via a function."

```
public: void Display()
{
    cout << "I love " << favoriteProgram << endl;
}
```

"As I think you can see," I said, "this function is very much like the functions you learned to code last week. The **Display()** function merely displays the value of the member variable *favoriteProgram* to the C++ console using the cout object. What makes this special is that it isn't code from the Banner class itself that will execute the **Display()** function, but rather code from another program that will first create an instance of the Banner object, which will then execute this function."

"When you say an object is created from the Banner class," Dave said, "does that mean that each object gets its own copy of each of the member variables and functions to work with?"

"That's right, Dave," I said. "Later in today's class, you'll see that it's possible to create in a program more than one object from the same class. When that happens, each object has separate copies of each of the member variables and functions defined in the class. In this way, there's no danger of one object stepping on the foot of another."

"Are we going to execute this class?" Rhonda asked. "I can't wait to see how this works."

"Because it has no **main()** function, we can't directly execute this Banner class from the command prompt," I said. "In fact, if we save this class as Banner.cpp and then try to compile it using the C++ compiler, we wind up with a problem. Let me show you."

I then saved the class as Banner.cpp and attempted to compile it. The following screenshot was displayed:

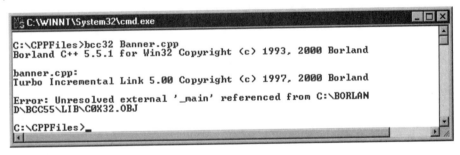

"What does that mean?" Kate asked.

"C++ is telling us," I answered, "that this class, the Banner class, does not have a **main()** function, which is required for programs to run from the command prompt. Actually, it's the linker program that runs after the compilation is complete that is giving us this error."

"Is that a problem?" Lou asked.

"It's not a big deal," I said. "We don't intend to run this class from the command prompt anyway. Classes, which do not have a **main()** function, are designed to have their objects created from other programs, called startup programs, that contain a **main()** function."

NOTE

*Sometimes objects are created from other classes. Ultimately, however, a program run from the command prompt must contain a **main()** function.*

"Each C++ application should have one of these startup programs. In a moment, we'll create a startup program called Example7_1, which will create an instance of the Banner class object."

"Does that mean we won't be able to compile the classes that don't contain a **main**() function?" Peter asked. "Suppose we have an error? How will we know?"

"We can still compile the source code in these classes and the compiler will still display any other errors it encounters," I said. "Most C++ compilers, including the one we're using here in class, will display warnings as well as errors. Warnings are potential coding problems that the compiler discovers. The compiler will still compile your program despite warnings. On the other hand, it will terminate compilation if it encounters just a single error. In general, warnings are showing you poor or dangerous programming practices that might work well for now, but that you should think about fixing to avoid problems down the road."

"I was wondering about those warning messages I've been receiving," Rhonda said. "I've pretty much been ignoring them."

"Just bear in mind," I said, "that we'll always receive the linker error we just saw—unresolved external '_main' referenced. Treat this error—which doesn't halt compilation—as if it were a warning. In this case, it's a warning that we expect to receive, since we omitted the **main**() function on purpose. If that's our only problem, we're fine. I'll be showing you how in a minute. Once we have the startup program coded, we can then compile both the startup program and the class into a single executable file."

"Are you saying that code from both the startup program and the class will be contained in the final EXE?" Dave asked.

"Yes, Dave," I replied. "The final .exe file will contain the code from both the startup program and the class. However, in terms of the code files, we have several choices here. Something that you see frequently in C++ textbooks is the actual inclusion of the other class into the startup program. In the real world of programming, this is seldom the case. Classes typically are included in files of their own, sometimes ending in the filename extension .cpp, and sometimes ending in the filename extension .hpp, indicating something known as a *header file*. C++ purists like to create a class prototype—like a function prototype, a class prototype contains the class function signatures—in a header file and place the actual definition of the class into what is known as an *implementation file*, ending with a .cpp file extension."

"What will we be doing in this course?" Linda asked.

"I prefer," I answered, "to create the class in a file of its own, name it with an extension of .cpp, then use an include statement to refer to it in the startup program. Of course, how exactly you do this is up to you. In the beginning of your C++ learning, there's certainly nothing wrong with including the code for your class in the same file as the program that uses it."

NOTE

To simplify our discussion in this book, after this week, I'll be creating just a single file, with the .hpp file extension, for each class. Creating two files for each class, although the preferred method among C++ programmers, will "balloon" the size of the book and complicate the completion of our Grade Calculation Project case study.

"Getting back to the **Display**() function," Dave persisted. "This function doesn't seem very dynamic. Suppose you need to make a change to the code in the Banner class. Does that mean you need to recompile the startup program in order for the changes to the Banner class to take effect?"

"In most cases," I said, "if code in the class changes, you won't need to recompile the startup program, but you will need to 'relink' it to the modified class."

I could see some confusion in the eyes of my students.

"In the course so far," I continued, "we haven't made a distinction between compiling and linking, because our compiler takes care of both steps for us with a single command-line statement. However, the two processes are distinct, and it is possible to link already compiled programs to produce an executable."

"What's the advantage there?' Linda asked. "Why not recompile and link?"

"Linking is the 'glue' that puts compiled pieces of our program together," I said. "In a real-world program, you might have hundreds of component pieces that together form a single executable. In that case, compiling each and every piece could take hours, whereas just linking them together can be much faster."

Creating Objects from Your Classes

I waited a moment before continuing.

"To create an instance of a Banner object from our Banner class," I said, "we must first create a startup program. This startup program will look like the others we've coded in the course so far. What you'll find strange, I'm sure, is the code necessary to create, or *instantiate*, the Banner object. Take a look."

I then displayed this code on the classroom projector:

```
//Example7_1.cpp

#include "Banner.cpp"

int main()
{
  Banner x;
  x.favoriteProgram = "C++";
```

```
   x.Display();

   return 0;
}
```

I could see a lot of confusion on the faces of many of my students.

"Let's break down this code line by line," I said. "As you can see, this startup program begins like the others we've seen, with an include statement. However, this time, instead of including the C++ studio library, we're including the Banner class we just coded."

```
#include "Banner.cpp"
```

"Didn't we just try to compile Banner.cpp?" Blaine asked. "I though the compile failed? How can we include the Banner class like this?"

"That's not quite true, Blaine," I replied. "We did compile and link the Banner class—and the compile phase ran fine. It was the linker that reported that Banner.cpp had no **main()** function. Because the compiler reported no errors, it's perfectly fine to include the class in this startup program."

NOTE

Enclose the names of your own custom classes in quotes, not brackets. The include statements we've seen so far enclose the name of the C++ libraries in angle brackets, indicating that the libraries are contained in the C++ compiler standard libraries. When using the include statement with your own classes, the filename must be enclosed within quotation marks to indicate that the class can be found in the same directory as the startup program.

I waited a moment before continuing.

"The include statement is then followed by the **main()** function, which is required of every program that is executed from a command prompt."

```
int main()
{
```

"What's going on with that next line of code?" Kathy asked. "I don't recall you discussing a Banner data type a few weeks back."

"This line of code looks like a variable declaration, doesn't it?" I said.

```
Banner x;
```

"In fact, it is. However, instead of seeing a familiar C++ data type of int or string, what you see instead is a variable declaration that begins with the class name Banner."

"Can we do that?" Ward asked.

"Yes, we can," I said. "When you declare a type int variable , C++ associates that variable name with an integer type, allocates enough space in the computer's memory for an integer data type, and associates the variable name with that newly allocated memory. When you declare a type Banner variable, C++ does the same thing—except that it allocates space in the computer's memory for both the Banner object's member variables and for its function definitions."

"That's right," Dave said excitedly. "You did say that each object gets a copy of the class's member variables and functions. So that's how it's done."

"That's right, Dave," I said. "This syntax looks very confusing at first, but that's what's going on. We're telling C++ to allocate enough room in the PC's memory for a Banner object."

"What's *x*?" Lou asked.

"It's just the name of the banner-type variable, in this case an object variable," I said. "Hereafter, the instance of the Banner object we're about to create will be referred to by this name. In almost every way, you can think of this as a 'normal' variable, except for the fact that we, not C++, have defined its type."

I gave everyone a further chance to study the line of code that declares and then creates an instance of a Banner object. It had been my experience that this single line of code is sometimes the most confusing single concept for beginning C++ programmers.

"You're right, this syntax is pretty confusing," Kate said. "I'm just so used to seeing a data type specified for a variable declaration. Seeing a class name that we've defined ourselves specified as the type declaration is strange."

"I agree, Kate," I said. "It's strange at first, but believe me, once you get used to it, declaring variables to refer to instances of your own classes will become second nature to you. As I think I've mentioned before, that's the name of the game in C++, and C++ programmers are forever defining classes with attributes and behaviors and then instantiating objects from these classes in their programs."

"Could you go over the idea of instantiating an object again," Rhonda asked. "I'm still a little unsure of the difference between creating the class and instantiating it."

"Sure," I replied. "It's a very important point, and very basic to understanding classes. When we created the banner.cpp file, we defined the class—much like drawing up the blueprint for a house. We haven't produced anything from the blueprint, yet—you might say we haven't yet built any houses from it. When we declare a variable to refer to an object, C++ takes the blueprint and makes a house from it—that is, it creates the object for us."

"There's actually a difference between declaring a variable and instantiating an object to associate with it. In this code, they happen at the same time, but that doesn't always have to be true. We'll look at the other case later in the course when we discuss pointers, but for now, you can be comfortable with the object getting created when you declare the variable."

Changing an Object's Attributes

"Can you go over how to change an object's attributes?" Mary asked. "It seemed like you used an assignment statement, but I was a little confused by the syntax."

"Good question, Mary," I said. "Once you've declared an instance of your class's object, you can easily set—by that I mean *change*—one of its attributes just by changing the value of the member variable that implements that attribute. Remember, behind the scenes, the attributes or characteristics of an object are really just member variables defined in the object's class. Changing the attributes of an object is easy, but we can't just assign a value to the member variable. We need to assign a value to the member variable associated with this particular object. Because of that, we need to use a special notation called *object dot notation.*"

"Object dot notation?" Rhonda asked. "This is getting more complicated."

"It's not bad at all, Rhonda," I replied. "Object dot notation is just a way of telling C++ the name of the object whose member variable we wish to update. With object dot notation, we first specify the name of the variable that we used to declare an instance of our object, followed by a dot, or period, followed by the name of the member variable that implements the attribute. After that, we're basically working with an ordinary C++ assignment statement, in that we use the equal sign assignment operator, followed by the value we wish to assign to the member variable."

```
x.favoriteProgram = "C++";
```

"So what we've done here is change the value of the member variable *favoriteProgram* inside the Banner class?" Steve asked.

"That's close, Steve," I said. "But more specifically, we've changed the value of the member variable *favoriteProgram* within the particular instance of the Banner object referenced by the variable *x*. Remember, each object has its own copy of every member variable and function in memory. It's a subtle distinction, I know, but the distinction will become important later today when you learn that we can create another type of variable within a class called a *static variable*. A static variable is a variable that is shared by every instance of an object instantiated from that class."

"So can we can retrieve the value of an object's attribute using the same object dot notation?" Ward asked.

"That's right, Ward," I said. "We could display the value of the *favoriteProgram* attribute using this syntax."

```
cout << x.favoriteProgram;
```

"I see," Linda said. "Really, except for the name of the object variable and the dot, this syntax is just like working with an ordinary variable."

"That's a good way of thinking about it," I said.

Everyone seemed to understand how to change and view the value of an object's attribute, so I proceeded to describe calling an object's functions.

Calling an Object's Functions

"Calling the function for an object that we've declared," I said, "should be familiar to you. It's similar to the way we've executed functions so far in the class—the only difference here is that we need to reference the object variable name we used to instantiate the object. Once again, as was the case when we referred to the object's attributes, we use object dot notation, specifying the name of our object variable, followed by a dot, followed by the name of the function we wish to execute."

```
x.Display();
```

"What's the purpose of the empty set of parentheses following the function name?" Mary asked.

"Any arguments required by the function appear within the parentheses," I said. "We defined the **Display**() function of the Banner class to require no parameters. The empty set of parentheses are required even when no arguments are required."

"I'm anxious to see the Banner class in action," Rhonda said. "What do we need to do?"

"In order to create an instance of a Banner object," I said, "all we need to do is create and compile a startup program that references the Banner class."

"Do we need to compile the Banner class first?" Peter asked.

"No we don't," I said. "Simply referencing the name of the Banner class via the include statement in the startup program is enough for the compiler—provided the Banner class is found in the same directory or folder as the startup program."

I saved the startup program as Example7_1.cpp and then compiled and executed it. The following screenshot was displayed on the classroom projector:

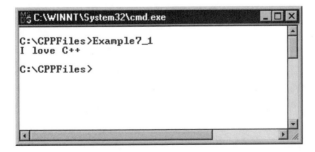

"Does everyone realize what has happened here?" I asked. "The code in Example7_1 created an instance of a Banner object from the Banner class, set the value of its *favoriteProgram* attribute, and executed its **Display**() function."

"One program executing code in another," Kate said. "Pretty cool."

"I don't want to be a downer about all of this," Rhonda said, "but couldn't we have just executed all this code from a single startup program? What has all this extra code really bought us? Quite honestly, I think it just complicated things."

"That's usually the first reaction beginners have," I said. "You're right in that we could have placed all the code we just executed in a single file, like this."

```cpp
#include <iostream>
#include <string>

using namespace std;

class Banner
{
  public: string favoriteProgram;
  public: void Display()
  {

    cout << "I love " << favoriteProgram;
  }
};

int main()
{
  Banner x;
  x.favoriteProgram = "C++";
  x.Display();
  return 0;
}
```

"And as you know, we also could have placed all the code within the **main()** function of a single startup program. But many years of experience has shown that modular programming—and in C++, that means creating objects—leads to better programs. While the benefits of this approach are greatest when a separate program reuses the class code, modular programming methods do a lot for the clarify and readability of a single program too. I think as the day progresses you'll begin to understand that placing code in classes whose objects are then instantiated within other classes actually *un*complicates programs."

"You said you would show us three methods for coding a startup program and the class from which it creates objects," Dave said. "If I'm not mistaken, we've seen two methods—one where the class is included in the same file as the startup program, and one where the startup program uses an include statement to refer to the class. Can you show us the third method?"

"Sure thing, Dave," I said. "But if it's okay with you, I'll wait until next week to do so. That will give you a little more time to get comfortable with classes. For now, let's keep things as simple as possible by creating a single file to represent our classes as well as a single startup program to create objects from them."

Creating Multiple Objects from Your Classes

"You told us that it's possible to create more than one instance of the same object in the startup program," Bob said. "How would we do that? For example, suppose I was creating an instance of that Employee object you were describing earlier, and I wanted to instantiate an object for every employee in a particular department?"

"Yes, it is possible, and quite common," I said. "You just need to declare more than one object variable, like this."

I then displayed the following code on the classroom projector:

```
//Example7_2.cpp

#include "Banner.cpp"

int main()
{
  Banner x;
  Banner y;
  x.favoriteProgram = "C++";
  x.Display();
  y.favoriteProgram = "Java";
  y.Display();

  return 0;
}
```

I saved the program as Example7_2.cpp and then compiled and executed it. The following screenshot was displayed on the classroom projector:

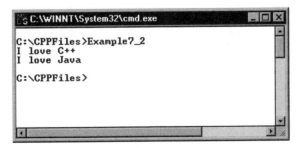

"What we've done here," I said, "is declare two instances of the Banner object."

```
Banner x;
Banner y;
```

"How is it possible to have two object instances of the same class in a program?" Blaine asked.

"It's no problem," I said, "because as I mentioned earlier, each instance of an object is maintained separately in the computer's memory. Keeping the object and its attributes in separate locations of memory keeps one object from being confused with another. When we modify the attribute value of an object, C++ knows exactly which object to act upon by the object variable name we use."

```
x.favoriteProgram = "C++";
x.Display();
y.favoriteProgram = "Java";
y.Display();
```

"That's pretty amazing," Rhonda said. "Is there a limit to the number of objects you can instantiate?"

"The only limit," I said, "is the available memory in your computer because that's where the objects are maintained. In some large commercial applications, it's not unusual to have thousands of objects in memory at one time."

Class Constructors

"I think working with instantiable classes like this to create objects is great," Ward said, "and I really can't wait to start working with them back at my office. Is there anything else we need to know about creating instantiable classes?"

"There are some more features of instantiable classes that I want to discuss with you that can give your programs tremendous power," I said. "For instance, we can write code in something called a *constructor function* that is automatically executed each time an instance of our object is created."

"Kind of like a startup macro in Microsoft Word," Valerie added.

"Constructor functions are very similar," I said. "If you have code that you want to be executed when an instance of an object is created from a class, you place it inside a special function called a constructor function. Constructor functions are named with the same name as the class."

"What kind of code goes into a constructor function?" Joe asked.

"Any kind of code that in some way initializes our object," I said.

"Initializes?" Rhonda asked.

"That's right, Rhonda," I said. "For instance, if the class is used to gain access to records in a database, the constructor function is an ideal location to place code that finds and opens the database. Other types of initialization code are for setting attributes of the object—that is, member variables—to default values, if that's appropriate. For instance, if your class has a *currentDate* member variable, you could place code in its constructor function to find out the system date on the user's PC and set the value of the *currentDate* member variable accordingly."

"I see," Kate said. "That makes sense."

"Speaking of member variables," I said, "take a look at this code."

I then displayed the following code on the classroom projector:

```
//Example7_3.cpp

#include "Banner.cpp"

int main()
{
  Banner x;
  x.Display();

  return 0;
}
```

I saved the program as Example7_3.cpp and then compiled and executed it. The following screenshot was displayed on the classroom projector:

"What happened?" Blaine asked. "What's up with that message?"

"What happened here," I said "is that we created an instance of a Banner object, but prior to assigning a value to the member variable *favoriteProgram*, we immediately executed the Banner object's **Display()** function. We displayed in the C++ console the value of the *favoriteProgram* member variable, which is an empty string."

"I didn't notice that we hadn't initialized the value of *favoriteProgram*," Dave said. "I thought that in C++ you have to initialize your variables."

"That's only the case with local variables," I said. "C++ doesn't require us to initialize member variables. As a result, accidents like this can easily happen. The bottom line is that it's a good idea to initialize all our member variables, either at the time we declare them or as part of the class's constructor function. In fact, initializing member variables is perhaps the most common programming task in a class constructor."

"Can you show us how to code a constructor function?" Ward asked. "Is it complicated?"

"Creating a constructor function is very easy, Ward," I said. "A class constructor function is just an ordinary function with the same name as the class. For instance, a basic constructor function for the Banner class would look like this."

I then displayed the following code on the classroom projector:

```cpp
public: Banner()
   {
      cout << "Banner's Constructor" << endl;
   }
```

NOTE
A constructor is a function of the class, having the same name as the class, that is automatically executed when an object of the class is created.

"Coding a constructor function looks easy," Linda said. "I notice you didn't specify a return type for the function. Isn't a return type always required?"

"That's a good point, Linda," I answered. "Return types for functions are required *except* in the case of a constructor function. In fact, constructor functions may *not* return a value of any kind, not even the void return type. That's why no return type is permitted here."

"I'm going to have to remember that," Rhonda said. "That's the type of thing I'm likely to forget, but I guess the compiler will warn me."

"That's right, Rhonda," I said. "The compiler will tell you that a constructor function may not have a return type."

NOTE
A constructor function may not specify a return type of any kind, not even void.

"I bet that can have you scratching your head for hours," Kate said. "Can we see the constructor function in action?"

"Sure thing, Kate," I said. "Let's modify the Banner class to include a constructor function. All we'll do is display a message in the C++ console that tells us the constructor function has been executed."

I then modified the Banner class to look like this, and displayed its code on the classroom projector:

```cpp
//Banner.cpp
#include <iostream>
#include <string>

using namespace std;

class Banner
{
  public: string favoriteProgram;

  public: Banner()
  {
    cout << "Banner's Constructor" << endl;
  }

  public: void Display()
  {
    cout << "I love " << favoriteProgram << endl;
  }
};
```

"Does everyone see the constructor function?" I asked. "It's the function called **Banner()**."

```cpp
public: Banner()
  {
    cout << "Banner's Constructor" << endl;
  }
```

"Notice that the name of the constructor function is identical to the class name, and also notice that no return value is specified for the function."

"So when an object of this class is created, the code in the constructor function will automatically be executed, correct?" Steve asked.

"That's right, Steve," I said. "Here's some simple code that will illustrate the behavior of the constructor function. All we're doing here is creating an instance of the Banner object, nothing else."

I then displayed the following code on the classroom projector:

```cpp
//Example7_4.cpp

#include "Banner.cpp"
```

```
int main()
{
  Banner x;

  return 0;
}
```

I saved the program as Example7_4.cpp and then compiled and executed it. The following screenshot was displayed on the classroom projector:

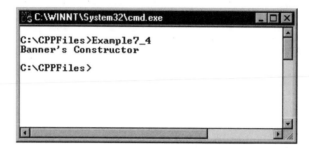

"As you can see," I said, "when we executed this line of code in Example7_4, the Banner object was created, and its constructor function was automatically executed."

```
Banner x;
```

"That resulted in the message we see in the C++ console."

"What did you say earlier about using a constructor to initialize member variables?" Rhonda asked.

"Constructors are also an ideal place to initialize any member variables in your class with default or startup values," I said. "Let me show you."

I displayed this modified code on the classroom projector:

```
//Banner.cpp
#include <iostream>
#include <string>

using namespace std;

class Banner
{
  public: string favoriteProgram;

  public: Banner()
```

```
   {
      cout << "Banner's Constructor" << endl;
      favoriteProgram = "C++";
   }

   public: void Display()
   {
      cout << "I love " << favoriteProgram << endl;
   }
};
```

"Do you remember what happened when we executed Example7_3 a few minutes ago?" I asked.

"I do," Kate said. "Because we didn't set the *favoriteProgram* attribute prior to executing the Banner object's **Display**() function, we displayed the message 'I love' in the C++ console window."

"Right on the mark, Kate," I said. "Having changed the Banner class to initialize the value of *favoriteProgram* in its constructor function, let's recompile Example7_3 to include the latest version of the Banner class. Then we'll execute it and see what happens."

I did exactly that, and the following screenshot was displayed on the classroom projector:

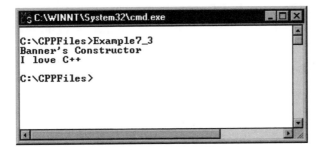

"That's better, isn't it?" I asked. "Now if the user forgets to tell us with an assignment statement what their favorite program is, we'll just display the default value of the *favoriteProgram* member variable."

Class Contracts

I noticed that Dave seemed very pensive. "What's wrong, Dave?" I asked.

"I'm just pondering what we've done here," he said. "We changed the Banner class to include a constructor function, and although we had to recompile Example7_3 to include the new version of the Banner class, none of the code in Example7_3 needed to be changed. Is that true in all cases? For instance, suppose we had changed the name of the **Display**() function in the Banner class."

"You raise a good point, Dave," I said. "In the world of object-oriented programming, there is a presumed 'contract' between the designer of the object and the many users—actually other programmers—who use the object. Because of this, there's a hard-and-fast rule: *Don't break the contract.* This means that a class should not be modified in such a way as to cause programs already using objects from that class to bomb. In the case you cite, where a class function name is changed, we would have discovered that we 'broke' the contract when we attempted to recompile a program that uses the modified class. But sometimes changes to a class can escape the watchful eye of the compiler and instead bomb at runtime."

"What could cause programs using the class to bomb?" Bob asked.

"The C++ compiler," I said, "does thorough checking to ensure that a class function or attribute referenced in a program actually exists. It will also verify that the number and type of arguments supplied to the class function, when it is called, are correct. However, if the code within the function is changed so that it no longer operates the way the programmer calling the function believes it does, that could potentially cause a runtime error."

"Something like that happened to me a few months ago at work," Dave said. "I called a function designed to calculate and return the unit cost for one of our part numbers—unknown to me, someone had modified the function to return the inventory on hand. For one of our part numbers, we had zero inventory, and I wound up dividing by zero, which caused a runtime error in my program. As you can see, the violation of the 'contract' between me and one of my fellow programmers caused me big problems."

CAUTION
Division by zero is a big programming no-no. We'll cover this error later in the book.

"That's a great real-world example, Dave. Thanks," I said.

"Obviously, adding a constructor function to the class had no detrimental impact on Example7_3," Ward said. "The program compiled okay, and it ran fine."

"That's right, Ward," I said, "and that's a big benefit to modularizing code into objects like this. A minor change like this to the code in a class has no impact on the program using it."

"I understand," Peter said, "that if we change the name of a function, or change the signature of a function in a class, the program using its object will fail to compile. And I see that adding a new function to the class is not a problem. But suppose we change some of the code in an existing function, the way the programmer did at Dave's work. Is that always a problem?"

"That's the beauty of object-oriented programming," I said. "By hiding the details of exactly how a function does its work and simply having the client program execute it, in theory, a change to the function, in most cases, has no impact on the client program. For instance, when we add classes to the Grade Calculation Project later today, the code for the calculation of an English student will reside in the **Calculate**() function of an EnglishStudent class. If Frank Olley should request a change in the way the final grade for an English student is calculated, all we need to do is change the code in the function, and any client program using the function won't have a problem."

"How often are the signatures of functions changed in the commercial world?" Valerie asked.

"They're usually not," I said. "If something requires a change to the function signature, it's better to create an...."

"Overloaded function," Kate yelled out. "Now I understand why we would want to use one."

"You took the words right out of my mouth, Kate," I said. "That's one good reason to create an overloaded function. By maintaining a function with the old signature and creating a function with the new signature, you ensure that older programs will still run, while new programs can take advantage of the functionality in the new function."

"I just thought of something," Chuck said. "In our first version of the Banner class, we didn't code a constructor function. I assume that means that classes don't have to have a constructor? Is that correct?"

"That's right, Chuck," I answered. "Constructor functions are not required in a class, but as you'll learn as you progress in your C++ career, coding a constructor function is usually a good idea. In fact, it's possible, and often a good idea, to code more than one constructor function for a class."

"You mean an overloaded constructor?" Dave asked.

Overloaded Constructors

"Exactly right, Dave," I said. "When your class has two or more constructor functions with the same name but with different function signatures, you have overloaded constructors."

"I didn't realize you could pass arguments to a constructor function," Kate said.

"Yes, you can, Kate," I said. "I'll show you an example of a constructor function that accepts arguments in a minute or two."

"Why would you want to create more than one constructor function?" Rhonda asked.

"Because constructor functions are automatically executed whenever an object of your class is created," I said, "coding overloaded constructor functions gives the user of your class more flexibility in the way they create objects from your class. For example, as the designer of your class, you might create a constructor function with no arguments. This constructor, when executed, would create a no-frills object from your class, perhaps initializing member variables to default values. But you might also want to code a constructor function that does much more than this—maybe permitting the program creating an object from your class to specify values for one or more member variables at the time the object is created."

NOTE

Overloaded constructors are similar to the overloaded functions we have already encountered. When you have overloaded constructors, or any function, the compiler keeps track of each one, along with their function signatures. When the function is called, the compiler executes the one whose full signature matches the parameters passed in the function call. To the compiler, they are truly different functions. All we have to remember is that the only difference between a regular overloaded function and an overloaded constructor is in the way you actually call them.

I could see some confusion in the classroom, so I suggested that we modify the Banner class to provide two constructor functions.

"The first constructor function," I said, "is the one we have already written. It will accept no arguments and will simply initialize the value of the *favoriteProgram* member variable to 'C++'. The second constructor function will accept a single argument, and it will initialize the value of the *favoriteProgram* member variable to whatever value is passed as an argument to the constructor."

I then displayed the modified code for the Banner class containing two constructor functions on the classroom projector:

```cpp
#include <iostream>
#include <string>

using namespace std;

class Banner
{
  public: string favoriteProgram;

  public: Banner()
  {
     cout << "Banner's Constructor" << endl;
     favoriteProgram = "C++";
  }

  public: Banner(string param1)
  {
     cout << "Banner's Overloaded Constructor" << endl;
     favoriteProgram = param1;
  }

  public: void Display()
  {
     cout << "I love " << favoriteProgram << endl;
  }
};
```

"Do you see that we now have two constructor functions?" I asked. "Both are named Banner. The first requires no arguments, but the second requires a single string argument called param1."

```
public: Banner(string param1)
{
   cout << "Banner's Overloaded Constructor" << endl;
   favoriteProgram = param1;
}
```

"I was pretty comfortable with creating overloaded functions last week," Steve said, "and I see what you're doing here in the Banner class to create the overloaded constructor functions. But how do you call an overloaded constructor?"

"Let me show you," I said, as I displayed this program on the classroom projector:

```
//Example7_5.cpp

#include "Banner.cpp"

int main()
{
  Banner x;           // Call Constructor
  x.Display();

  Banner y("Java");        // Call Overloaded Constructor
  y.Display();

  return 0;
}
```

I saved the program as Example7_5.cpp and then compiled and executed it. The following screenshot was displayed on the classroom projector:

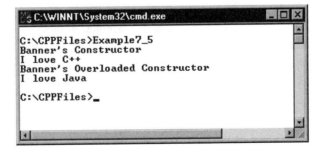

"Does everyone see what happened?" I said. This code created an instance of the Banner object, and because there were no arguments supplied, C++ automatically executed the constructor function requiring no arguments:"

```
Banner x;          // Call Constructor
```

"When that constructor function is executed, the value of the *favoriteProgram* Member variable is set to 'C++', which is why when we executed this code, 'I love C++' was displayed in the C++ console window."

```
x.Display();
```

"This code also creates an instance of the Banner object. Notice that this time we pass a single string argument, which is the word 'Java' contained within the parentheses. When C++ see this string argument, it automatically executes the constructor function requiring a single string argument."

```
Banner y("Java");     // Call Overloaded Constructor
```

"When that constructor function is executed, the value of the *favoriteProgram* member variable is set to the value of the passed argument, which is 'Java'. That's why, when we executed this code, 'I love Java' was displayed in the C++ console window."

```
y.Display();
```

"This is really neat," Ward said. "I would imagine you could come up with quite a few different constructor functions."

"That's right, Ward," I said. "Programmers frequently have more than one. The important thing to remember is that constructor functions are an ideal place for code to initialize the state of your object at the time of its creation."

Static Variables

"I mentioned earlier," I said, "that each object and its attributes, or member variables, are maintained in separate locations in the computer's memory. This protects the data in one object from being confused with the data of another object. There's another type of variable you can declare in a class called a *static* variable that allows you to share its value with every instance of an object created from that class."

"I was just about to ask if such a thing was possible," Dave said. "I've worked with other languages where I could do that, and it can be a pretty beneficial feature."

"When you say *share*," Kate asked, "do you mean that every object created from the same class can see the value of the variable and update it as well?"

> **NOTE**
> *Static variables share their values with every instance of the object created from the class.*

"That's right, Kate," I said. "As Dave said, this can be a very beneficial feature. Static variables are a great way for objects of the same class to share data."

"Is that important?" Mary asked. "Is that something that's commonly required?"

"It can be," I said. "For instance, have you ever worked with an accounting program? One part of an accounting program typically is used to generate invoices for your customers, and it's customary to assign a unique number to each invoice. If you write the accounting program using C++, each invoice can be an object, and you could create a static variable called *nextInvoiceNumber* that would enable each object to access the next available invoice number when the invoice object is created."

"I see what you mean," Valerie said. "That makes sense. By storing the value of the next invoice number in a static variable, each instance of the object can get at the value, plus increment the value by one after it's used."

"Excellent, Valerie," I said. "The alternative is to force your **main**() function or startup program to keep track of the next invoice number, and that's contrary to the good practice of encapsulation we are trying to develop."

"Can we add a static variable to the Banner class to see how it works?" Steve asked.

"Sure, Steve," I said. "Remember in Example7_2, we created two Banner objects, both of which were alive at the same time. Suppose we want each object to be able to know how many Banner objects are currently alive. A static variable is an ideal way to do that."

"How exactly would we do that?" Peter asked.

"We can declare an integer static variable in the Banner class," I said, "and then, within its constructor function, increment the value of that static variable by one. Because the constructor function is automatically executed each time an object of the class is created, the value of the static variable should always reflect the number of Banner objects currently in existence."

I then modified the Banner class to look like this, and displayed it on the classroom projector:

```
#include <iostream>
#include <string>
```

```
using namespace std;

class Banner
{
  public: string favoriteProgram;
  public: static int numberOfBannerObjects;

  public: Banner()
  {
    cout << "Banner's Constructor" << endl;
    numberOfBannerObjects++;
    favoriteProgram = "C++";
  }

  public: Banner(string param1)
  {
    cout << "Banner's Overloaded Constructor" << endl;
    numberOfBannerObjects++;
    favoriteProgram = param1;
  }

  public: void HowMany()
  {
    cout << "The number of Banner objects is " <<
        numberOfBannerObjects << endl;
  }

  public: void Display()
  {
    cout << "I love " << favoriteProgram << endl;
  }
};
```

"Let's take a look at the new code in the Banner class," I said. "We added a static variable called *numberOfBannerObjects*, added a line of code in each of the two constructor functions, and created a new function called **HowMany()**. Let's take a look at the declaration of the static variable first. A static variable is like a member variable in that it is declared outside any functions in the class. What differentiates a static variable from an member variable is that it is declared with the Static keyword."

```
public: static int numberOfBannerObjects;
```

"Static means that *numberOfBannerObjects* is a static variable and not an member variable, right?" Blaine asked.

"That's right, Blaine," I said. "By the way, you can also write the declaration of our two public member variables like this, everything following the Public keyword is assumed to be public."

```
public:
    string favoriteProgram;
    static int numberOfBannerObjects;
```

I waited a moment before continuing.

"We also needed to modify both constructor functions to increment the value of the *numberOfBannerObjects* static variable by using the increment (++) operator. Here's the code for the first constructor function."

```
public: Banner()
{
    cout << "Banner's Constructor" << endl;
    numberOfBannerObjects++;
    favoriteProgram = "C++";
}
```

"And here's the code for the second."

```
public: Banner(string param1)
{
    cout << "Banner's Overloaded Constructor" << endl;
    numberOfBannerObjects++;
    favoriteProgram = param1;
}
```

"Finally, here's the code for the new function called **HowMany**(). This function will be used by client programs to display the number of Banner objects currently alive."

```
public: void HowMany()
{
    cout << "The number of Banner objects is " <<
        numberOfBannerObjects << endl;
}
```

"Now let's write the code to see the effect of the static variable in action." I said. "What we'll do is create two Banner objects and then execute the **HowMany**() function of each one."

I then displayed this code on the classroom projector:

```
//Example7_6.cpp

#include "Banner.cpp"

int Banner::numberOfBannerObjects;

int main()
{
  Banner x;          // Call Constructor
  x.Display();
  x.HowMany();

  Banner y("Java");       // Call Overloaded Constructor
  y.Display();
  y.HowMany();

  return 0;
}
```

"It's easy to miss," I said, "but notice how in order to use a static variable, we must declare it in our program—that's what this code does. Notice how we prefix the name of the static variable with the name of the class, followed by two colons (:: called the scoping operator)..."

```
int Banner::numberOfBannerObjects;
```

"I thought we declared the static variable in the class," Mary said.

"We didn't declare it," I said. "We *defined* it. In C++ there's a fine distinction. We need to declare the static variable in the program that will be accessing it in order to create storage space for the variable."

CAUTION

Failure to declare a static variable in the program that uses it will result in a compiler error.

I saved the program as Example7_6.cpp and then compiled and executed it. The following screenshot was displayed on the classroom projector:

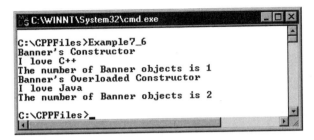

"Do you see what happened here?" I asked. "After we create the first instance of the Banner object using this syntax, the value of the static variable *numberOfBannerObjects* is incremented by one when the no-arguments constructor function is executed, thus giving us 1. Remember, integer variables, when uninitialized, are automatically set to zero."

```
Banner x;          // Call Constructor
```

"Executing the **HowMany()** function displays the value of the static variable, 1, on the C++ console."

```
x.HowMany();
```

"This syntax is then used to create a second instance of the Banner object."

```
Banner y("Java"); // Call Overloaded Constructor
```

"The call to the single parameter version of the constructor also results in the value of the static variable *numberOfBannerObjects* being incremented by one, thus giving us 2. Executing the **HowMany()** function displays the value of the static variable, 2, on the C++ console."

```
y.Display();
```

"From this example," Dave said, "I can see that both of our Banner objects can 'see' the value of the static variable *numberOfBannerObjects*, but can both of them modify its value?"

"Good question, Dave," I said, "and the answer is yes. Each object can modify the value of the static variable, although the syntax is different from that used to modify a member variable. Take a look."

I then modified the code from Example7_6 to look like this:

```
//Example7_7.cpp

#include "Banner.cpp"

int Banner::numberOfBannerObjects;
```

```
int main()
{
   Banner x;
   x.HowMany();
   Banner y;
   y.HowMany();
   Banner::numberOfBannerObjects = 0;
   x.HowMany();
   y.HowMany();

   return 0;
}
```

I saved the program as Example7_7.cpp and then compiled and executed it. The following screenshot was displayed on the classroom projector:

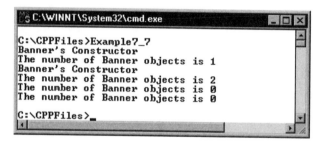

"I know this code is a bit confusing," I said, "but it does illustrate the capability of an object to modify the value of a static variable. As we did in Example7_6, here we've also created two Banner objects. The first Banner object is created by this code:"

```
Banner x;
```

"As a result, the no-arguments version of the constructor function is executed, incrementing the value of the static variable *numberOfBannerObjects* from its initial value of 0 to 1. Executing the **HowMany()** function of the first object results in the message 'The number of Banner objects is 1' being displayed on the C++ console."

```
x.HowMany();
```

"The second Banner object is then created by this code."

```
Banner y;
```

"Once again, the no-arguments version of the constructor function is executed, incrementing the value of the static variable *numberOfBannerObjects* from 1 to 2. Executing the **HowMany**() function of the second object results in the message 'The number of Banner objects is 2' being displayed on the C++ console."

```
y.HowMany();
```

"With this line of code, we gain direct access to the static variable *numberOfBannerObjects* and update it to 0 using an assignment statement with the first object. Because there is just one copy of a static variable, shared across all instances of objects derived from the class, we use the class name Banner, and not the name of the object variable, to update it."

```
Banner::numberOfBannerObjects = 0;
```

"Has the value of the static variable really been updated? Yes, it has, and we can prove that by executing the **HowMany**() function of the second Banner object, which results in the message 'The number of Banner objects is 0' being displayed on the C++ console."

```
x.HowMany();
```

"Not surprisingly, because both objects have access to the same static variable, we get the same results in the C++ console when we execute the **HowMany**() function of the second Banner object."

```
y.HowMany();
```

"I'm convinced there really is just the single static variable called *numberOfBannerObjects* shared among all the objects created from the class," Rhonda said. "I think I'm really beginning to understand this. But isn't there a potential problem here?"

"How so, Rhonda?" I asked.

"Well," she continued, "the static variable *numberOfBannerObjects* was intended to keep track of the number of Banner objects in existence, and one of our objects was able to subvert that by resetting the value to 0. If other objects are dependent on the value of *numberOfBannerObjects*, a program being able to directly change the value the way we did here seems more than a little dangerous to me."

"You raise some good points, Rhonda," I said "Actually, this topic is one that we'll cover next week when we discuss ways to protect the data—that is, variables—in our classes from intentional and unintentional updates."

"Is there any way to validate the types of updates that a program like our startup program can make to an object's member and static variables?" Dave asked.

"The answer is yes," I said, "and again, next week, we'll spend the entire class examining ways to protect the data within our objects. For example, you'll learn there are techniques we can use to prevent an object from directly updating a member or static variable by forcing all updates to be performed through special validation functions—but more on that next week."

Destroying an Object

"I've got to say that I feel pretty confident about working with objects," Ward said. "Now that you've shown us how to create classes of our own and create objects from them, is there anything special we need to know to destroy them? What happens to the objects we create in our program? Do they just go away when the program that creates them ends?"

"There's no need in C++ to explicitly destroy an object when you're done working with it," I said. "Objects are automatically destroyed for us when they go out of scope."

> **NOTE**
>
> *This statement is true, unless we happen to be working with something called pointers, which you'll learn about later on in the course. Pointers to an object must be explicitly destroyed, in order to ensure that all the object's resources are freed up, but again, that's something we'll talk about later.*

"Out of scope?" Rhonda said. "What does that mean?"

"Just like any local variable, an object goes out of scope when the function that is using it ends," I said.

"Does that mean," Joe asked, "that when Example7_7 finished, the two Banner objects we created were destroyed?"

"That's right, Joe," I said, "and with them all the space in our computer's memory that they were consuming. Of course, when the program ends, C++ frees up that memory anyway. If we declare Banner objects in a function, however, C++ destroys the objects after the function finishes executing—freeing up the memory they used while the program continues to execute."

"Based on what you just said, I understand there's nothing we need to do when we're done with an object," Linda said, "but suppose we would like to have code execute when the program using our object is done with it. Is there a way to do that?"

Class Destructors

"C++ provides objects with a *destructor function*," I said. "The destructor function is an optional function that is guaranteed to be executed just before the object is destroyed."

"The destructor function sounds similar to the constructor function," Kate said, "except that instead of executing when the object is born, it's executed just before it dies. How do we create a destructor function?"

"The destructor function is pretty easy to code," I said. "Like the constructor function, it's just a procedure with some code in it. The rules for creating the Destructor function's header are a bit strict though: You take the name of the class and precede it with a tilde; use no keyword, such as Public or Private; and include no parameters nor a return type, like this."

```
~Banner()
```

"What kind of code would we place in the destructor function?" Bob asked.

"Any kind of code that needs to be executed when the object dies," I said. "For instance, you might want to store the object's data in a database or file of some kind when the client program is done with it. Placing code in the object's destructor function is one way to ensure that the data is saved prior to the object dying, when the values of its member variables would be lost. Let's modify the Banner class we've been using this morning to see the destructor function in action."

I then displayed this modified code for the Banner class on the classroom projector:

```cpp
#include <iostream>
#include <string>

using namespace std;

class Banner
{
  public: string favoriteProgram;
  public: static int numberOfBannerObjects;

  public: Banner()
  {
     cout << "Banner's Constructor" << endl;
     numberOfBannerObjects++;
     favoriteProgram = "C++";
  }

  public: Banner(string param1)
  {
     cout << "Banner's Overloaded Constructor" << endl;
     numberOfBannerObjects++;
     favoriteProgram = param1;
```

```
      }

      ~Banner() {
         cout << "Banner's Destructor" << endl;
      }

      public: void HowMany()
      {
         cout << "The number of Banner objects is " <<
            numberOfBannerObjects << endl;
      }

      public: void Display()
      {
         cout << "I love " << favoriteProgram << endl;
      }
};
```

"Here's the code for the destructor function," I said. "Nothing fancy here. We're just writing a message to the C++ console to let us know that the Banner object is about to be destroyed."

```
~Banner() {
   cout << "Banner's Destructor" << endl;
}
```

"Now let's write some code to see the destructor function in action," I said. I then displayed this code on the classroom projector:

```
//Example7_8.cpp

#include "Banner.cpp"

int Banner::numberOfBannerObjects;

int main()
{
   Banner x;
   x.favoriteProgram = "C++";
   Banner y("Java");

   return 0;
}
```

I saved the program as Example7_8.cpp and then compiled and executed it. The following screenshot was displayed on the classroom projector:

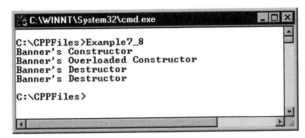

"Does everyone see what happened here?" I asked. "We created two Banner objects, triggering their constructor functions. That's all we did with them, and when the code in the **main**() function of Example7_8 finished, both objects were no longer being used by it. That's when our objects were about to be destroyed, and the destructor function of each one of the objects was triggered.

"This process—of objects going out of scope and being destroyed—happens on its own, right?" Kathy asked.

"That's right, Kathy," I said. "As I said earlier, we don't need to explicitly destroy the objects. That happens for us."

Working with Objects

"This is all great stuff," Rhonda said. "I'm finding the whole concept of objects and how to work with them quite fascinating, but I'd be lying if I didn't say that I would feel a lot more confident about creating my own classes and objects if I had a chance to work with them a little bit. Will we have time to do that today?"

"Absolutely," I said. "I have a series of exercises for you to complete that will give you plenty of practice in creating classes and objects. We'll start by taking the Smiley National Bank program we created last week and modifying it to use objects. Then, toward the end of today's class, you'll modify the Grade Calculation Project to use objects also."

We had been working a long time without a break, and so I asked everyone to take 15 minutes. When my students returned, I distributed this exercise for them to complete.

Exercise 7-1	Create the BankTransaction Instantiable Class for the Smiley National Bank

In this exercise, you'll take the code you wrote last week in Practice6_2 and include it in a BankTransaction class. This class will then be used by a client program you'll write in Exercise 7-2 to instantiate BankTransaction objects that will handle the details of making deposits, withdrawals, and displaying bank balances.

1. Using Notepad, enter the following code:

```cpp
//BankTransaction.cpp

#include <iostream>
#include <string>
using namespace std;

class BankTransaction
{
   private:
       static float balance;
       float newBalance;
       float adjustment;


   public: BankTransaction()
   {
      cout << "BankTransaction's Constructor" << endl;
   }


   ~BankTransaction() {
      cout << "BankTransaction's destructor" << endl;
   }

   public: void MakeDeposit()
   {
    cout << "Enter the Deposit Amount: ";
    cin >> adjustment;
    newBalance = balance + adjustment;
    cout << endl << endl <<
       "*** SMILEY NATIONAL BANK ***" << endl << endl;
    cout << "Old Balance is: " << balance << endl;
    cout << "Adjustment is: +" << adjustment << endl;
    cout << "New Balance is: " << newBalance << endl <<
       endl;
    balance = newBalance;
   }

   public: void MakeWithdrawal()
```

```
     {
       cout << "Enter the Withdrawal Amount: ";
       cin >> adjustment;
       newBalance = balance - adjustment;
       cout << endl << endl <<
           "*** SMILEY NATIONAL BANK ***" << endl << endl;
       cout << "Old Balance is: " << balance << endl;
       cout << "Adjustment is: -" << adjustment << endl;
       cout << "New Balance is: " << newBalance << endl <<
           endl;
       balance = newBalance;
     }

     public: void GetBalance()
     {
       cout << endl << endl <<
           "*** SMILEY NATIONAL BANK ***" << endl << endl;
       cout << "Your current Balance is: " << balance <<
           endl << endl;
     }
};
```

2. Save your source file as BankTransaction.cpp in the \CPPFiles\Practice folder (select File | Save As from Notepad's menu bar). Be sure to save your source file with the filename extension .cpp.

3. Compile your source file. Look for any compiler error messages. If you receive one, correct the problem so that the compiler runs cleanly. Because your source file contains a class, once the class compiles cleanly, you will still receive an error from the linker program indicating that you don't have a **main()** function. If that's the only error you receive, don't worry. In Exercise 7-2, you'll create a startup program to instantiate objects from this class.

Discussion   Creating the BankTransaction instantiable class took us about 15 minutes to complete. Much to my surprise, most of the students seemed comfortable completing the exercise. I think they were beginning to feel comfortable working with objects.

"Somehow I thought this would be more confusing," Rhonda said, "but I think I've surprised myself by more or less understanding what's going on here. Not only that, but I'm beginning to get the sense that the changes we've made to the Smiley National Bank application are doing exactly what you said they would do. They'll make the program easier to read, follow, and modify in the future. If I'm correct, what we've done in this exercise is take a bunch of code out of Practice6_2 and include it in an instantiable object called BankTransaction. Is that right?"

"That's right, Rhonda," I said. "We've taken some but not all the code we had in written in Practice6_2 and included it in a BankTransaction class, from which we will create objects in a client program. The BankTransaction class contains three variables. Two of the variables, *adjustment* and *newBalance*, are member variables, which means that each object created from the class has a separate copy of them. One variable, however, *balance*, was designated with the Static keyword, and that means it's a static variable."

"I got it! A static variable can be seen by every object of that class," Ward said, "plus, it exists for as long as any object of that class is alive."

"That's excellent, Ward," I said.

"Why is *balance* declared as a static variable?" Peter asked.

"We have elected to have BankTransaction take on the responsibility of tracking the value of the account balance," I said. "The alternative would to be to declare and track it from within the startup program, but that would have been less encapsulated. If another object needs to access the current balance, we can add a function to the BankTransaction class to retrieve that value. We'll discuss that kind of function next week. Ultimately, designating *balance* as a static variable will enable our client program to keep a running total of the bank account balance as it is updated by various objects."

"I notice," Mary said, "that our three variables, *balance*, *newBalance*, and *adjustment*, aren't defined as public like the variables were in the examples you worked up earlier. What's the difference here?"

"That's an excellent question, Mary," I answered. "In the examples we worked up earlier, our client program was updating the member variables of the object directly, so the access modified for the variables needed to be public. In this case, the member variables of the object are private in scope. Private means that only code within the class itself can access or modify the variables. That's fine in this case because, as you'll see in a minute, our client program will only be executing functions of this object, not directly accessing its attributes."

"How many functions are there in the BankTransaction class?" Chuck asked.

"The BankTransaction class has three functions," I said. "**MakeDeposit()**, **MakeWithdrawal()**, and **GetBalance()**. The code in each of these functions hasn't changed from that found in the functions in Practice6_2. All we've done is move the functions from a startup program to an instantiable class called BankTransaction. Plus, in order to illustrate the lifetime of our BankTransaction object, we've written code for a constructor and destructor function."

"You're right," Valerie said. "I was a little amazed at that myself. It seems that the work we did last week creating custom functions for this application enabled us to create the BankTransaction class pretty easily."

"That's good design," I said. "When you start to get more experienced with C++, you'll create classes like this right from scratch."

I waited a moment to see if there were any questions. No one had any, so I distributed this exercise to create the client program in which we would instantiate objects from the BankTransaction class we just created.

Exercise 7-2   **The Smiley National Bank Client Program Using BankTransaction Objects**

In this exercise, you'll create a client program to instantiate objects from the BankTransaction class you created in Exercise 7-1.

1. Using Notepad (if you are using Windows), enter the following code:

```cpp
//Practice7_1.cpp

#include <iostream>
#include <string>
#include "BankTransaction.cpp"

using namespace std;

float BankTransaction::balance;

int main()
{
   char response[256];
   string moreBankingBusiness;

   cout << "Do you want to do some banking? ";
   cin >> moreBankingBusiness;

   for (int i = 0; i < moreBankingBusiness.length();
      i++) {
      moreBankingBusiness[i] =
         toupper (moreBankingBusiness[i]);
   }

   while (moreBankingBusiness == "YES") {

      cout << "What would you like to do? " <<
            "(1=Deposit, 2=Withdraw, 3=Get Balance): ";
      cin.getline(response,256);

      if (strlen(response) == 0) {
         cout << "You must make a selection";
```

```
            return 1;
        }
        else
        if (atoi(response) < 1 |
            atoi(response) > 3) {
            cout << response
               << " - is not a valid banking function";
            return 1;
        }

        if (atoi(response) == 1) {
            BankTransaction transaction;
            transaction.MakeDeposit();
        }

        if (atoi(response) == 2) {
            BankTransaction transaction;
            transaction.MakeWithdrawal();
        }

        if (atoi(response) == 3) {
            BankTransaction transaction;
            transaction.GetBalance();
        }

        cout << "Do you have more banking business? ";
        cin >> moreBankingBusiness;

        for (int i = 0;
          i < moreBankingBusiness.length(); i++) {
          moreBankingBusiness[i] =
              toupper (moreBankingBusiness[i]);
        }

    }                                    // end of while

    cout << endl << endl << "Thanks for banking with us!";
    return 0;
}
```

2. Save your source file as Practice7_1 in the \CPPFiles\Practice folder (select File | Save As from Notepad's menu bar). Be sure to save your source file with the filename extension .cpp.

3. Compile your source file into an executable file.

4. Execute your program. The program will ask whether you wish to do some banking. Type **Yes** at the C++ console.

5. You will then be asked what you want to do: make a deposit, make a withdrawal, or get a balance. Type **1** at the C++ console.

6. The program will then ask how much you wish to deposit into your account. Type **50** at the C++ console to indicate your deposit amount.

7. The program will display a confirmation message, indicating your deposit amount and your old and new balances.

8. Notice that the program is asking whether you have more banking business. Type **Yes** at the C++ console.

9. Once again, the program will ask what you wish to do: make a deposit, make a withdrawal, or get a balance. Type **2** at the C++ console to indicate you want to make a withdrawal.

10. The program will then ask how much you wish to withdraw. Type **20** at the C++ console to indicate your withdrawal amount.

11. The program will display a confirmation message, indicating your transaction (withdrawals are designated with a negative transaction amount) and your old and new balances.

12. Once again, the program will ask whether you have more banking business. Type **Yes** at the C++ console.

13. The program will then ask what you wish to do: make a deposit, make a withdrawal, or get a balance. Type **3** at the C++ console to indicate you want to display the current balance.

14. The program will then display the current balance of your account.

15. Once again, the program will ask whether you have more banking business. Type **No** at the C++ console.

16. The program will display a message thanking you for using it and then end.

Discussion

"This program behaves in an identical manner to the code in Practice6_2," I said. "The difference is in the way the code is implemented, with this version using a client program to create instances of the BankTransaction object we created in Exercise 7-1. In this version of the program, it's the BankTransaction object that does the majority of the work. This client program creates objects, and based on the type of banking business the user wishes to do, executes one of the three functions of the BankTransaction class."

```
if (atoi(response) == 1) {
    BankTransaction transaction;
    transaction.MakeDeposit();
}
```

```
if (atoi(response) == 2) {
   BankTransaction transaction;
   transaction.MakeWithdrawal();
}

if (atoi(response) == 3) {
   BankTransaction transaction;
   transaction.GetBalance();
}
```

"We've really taken the notion of modular programming to its extreme by creating classes and objects, haven't we?" Dave commented.

"That's right, Dave," I said. "By encapsulating the code for making deposits and withdrawals and displaying balances within the BankTransaction object, all the client program using our object needs to know is how to instantiate the object and what functions to execute. It's pretty easy, isn't it?"

"Will we be modifying the Grade Calculation Project to use objects today?" Joe asked.

"That's our next step, Joe," I said. "Right now, the Grade Calculation Project contains a single startup program called Grades. Grades contains eight functions: **main()**, **WhatKindOfStudent()**, **CalculateEnglishGrade()**, **CalculateMathGrade()**, **CalculateScienceGrade()**, and three overloaded functions called **DisplayGrade()** to handle each of the three different types of student grade calculations. Any suggestions as to how we can turn this code into an instantiable class?"

"I guess we could create a single class called Student," Mary said, "having the same eight functions we created last week. That's essentially what we just did with the banking program."

"That's a possibility," I agreed.

"From what I've been reading about object-oriented programming," Dave said, "I think we need at least three classes, one for each of the three different types of students."

"Is that right?" Rhonda said, turning to Dave, but addressing her question to me.

"Dave's on the right track," I said. "Object design will start to go more smoothly for you when we discuss a concept called *inheritance* in two weeks, but it makes the most sense to create a separate class for each type of student."

Getting back to Mary's suggestion, I said. "Mary, I'd have no objection if you created a single class called Student. You wouldn't really be wrong, but I think you'll see that creating three student classes is the better approach of the two."

"Sounds great," Rhonda said. "I'm ready to start!"

"Before we begin," I said, "I'd also like to suggest that we create one other class called DisplayGrade. We currently have three overloaded functions called DisplayGrade, and I think that tells us that displaying grades is a distinct function in this program. Creating an object to handle the display of the grades will make things even easier on us."

"If the EnglishStudent, MathStudent, and ScienceStudent objects do the work of prompting the user for information and calculating a grade," Dave said, "and the DisplayGrade object takes care of displaying the student's grade, I think we have ourselves a very modular program."

"Yes, we do," I agreed.

"Is there more than one way to design the classes in this project?" Blaine asked. "I hadn't thought of a DisplayGrade class at all."

"That's a good question, Blaine," I said. "I want to emphasize that although there are some agreed-upon rules for the construction of objects, believe me, if we asked five programmers to review the requirements for this project and design classes based on these requirements, we would come up with five different object models. As I frequently say, in the world of programming, there are many ways to paint a picture, and there's rarely a single correct solution to a problem."

"Can we get going on this?" Rhonda repeated impatiently. "This sounds like great fun to me, and I'm anxious to get started."

I then distributed this exercise for the class to complete.

Exercise 7-3   Create the EnglishStudent Instantiable Class

In this exercise, you'll create the EnglishStudent class for the Grade Calculation Project. This class will allow a client program to create an object that will prompt the user for information necessary to calculate the final grade for an English student.

1. Using Notepad, enter the following code:

```
//EnglishStudent.cpp
#include <iostream>
#include <string>

using namespace std;

class EnglishStudent
{
  public:
    int midterm;
    int finalExamGrade;
```

```
   int research;
   int presentation;
   float finalNumericGrade;
   char finalLetterGrade;
   float ENGLISH_FINALEXAM_PERCENTAGE;
   float ENGLISH_RESEARCH_PERCENTAGE;
   float ENGLISH_PRESENTATION_PERCENTAGE;
   float ENGLISH_MIDTERM_PERCENTAGE;

public: EnglishStudent()
{
 cout << "English Student's Constructor" << endl;
 midterm = 0;
 finalExamGrade = 0;
 research = 0;
 presentation = 0;
 finalNumericGrade = 0;
 ENGLISH_FINALEXAM_PERCENTAGE = .25;
 ENGLISH_RESEARCH_PERCENTAGE = .30;
 ENGLISH_PRESENTATION_PERCENTAGE = .20;
 ENGLISH_MIDTERM_PERCENTAGE = .25;
}

public: void Calculate()
{
 char response[256];
 string moreGradesToCalculate;

 cout << "Enter the Midterm Grade: " ;
 cin.getline(response,256);
 midterm = atoi(response);
 cout << "Enter the Final Examination Grade: " ;
 cin.getline(response,256);
 finalExamGrade = atoi(response);
 cout << "Enter the Research Grade: " ;
 cin.getline(response,256);
 research = atoi(response);
 cout << "Enter the Presentation Grade: " ;
 cin.getline(response,256);
 presentation = atoi(response);
 finalNumericGrade =
    (midterm *
```

```
                        ENGLISH_MIDTERM_PERCENTAGE) +
                    (finalExamGrade * ENGLISH_FINALEXAM_PERCENTAGE) +
                    (research * ENGLISH_RESEARCH_PERCENTAGE) +
                    (presentation * ENGLISH_PRESENTATION_PERCENTAGE);
            if (finalNumericGrade >= 93)
                finalLetterGrade = 'A';
            else
            if ((finalNumericGrade >= 85) &
                (finalNumericGrade < 93))
                finalLetterGrade = 'B';
            else
            if ((finalNumericGrade >= 78) &
                (finalNumericGrade < 85))
                finalLetterGrade = 'C';
                    else
            if ((finalNumericGrade >= 70) &
                (finalNumericGrade < 78))
                finalLetterGrade = 'D';
            else
            if (finalNumericGrade < 70)
                finalLetterGrade = 'F';
    }
    };
```

2. Save your source file as EnglishStudent.cpp in the \CPPFiles\Grades folder (select File | Save As from Notepad's menu bar). Be sure to save your source file with the filename extension .cpp.

3. Compile your source file. Look for any compiler error messages. If you receive one, correct the problem so that the compiler runs cleanly. Because your source file contains a class, once the class compiles cleanly, you will still receive an error from the linker program indicating that you don't have a **main()** function. If that's the only error you receive, don't worry. You'll be creating an EnglishStudent object from this class via the startup Grades class, which you'll modify in Exercise 7-7.

Discussion   No one had any trouble creating the EnglishStudent class, although I did notice a student or two trying to execute the class from the command prompt, which is something that can't be done because EnglishStudent is an instantiable class.

"Just a couple of things to note here," I said. "First, you may have noticed that we changed the constants we formerly had in the Grades Calculation program to member variables here."

"I was wondering about that," Dave said. "Why is that?"

"In a C++ class," I said, "you can't assign values to member variables or constants—that is, those declared outside of class functions. Because a constant *must* have a value assigned to it when it's declared, it's therefore impossible to declare a constant in a class that is outside of a function."

NOTE

The latest C++ standards permit constants to be declared and assigned values outside of a class function, but not all compilers (including the one we're using here in the class) support this new feature yet.

"And if we declare a constant within a function," Dave added, "it has only local scope, meaning all the other functions won't be able to see it. Isn't that right?"

"You hit the nail on the head," I said. "That's why we changed our constants to member variables and assigned values to them via our constructor function."

"I noticed that you changed the name of the function **CalculateEnglishGrade()** to **Calculate()**," Dave said. "Is there a reason for that?"

"There's an object-oriented programming term called *polymorphism*," I said, "which means it's okay—even preferable—to have identically named functions in different classes, provided the functions perform the same task. Because each one of our Student classes has a function to perform a calculation, I thought it made sense to give each one of them the same name. Therefore, we'll have a **Calculate()** function in each one of the three Student classes."

"I noticed that we have a constructor function in the class," Linda said. "Is that really necessary?"

"You're right, Linda," I said. "We coded a constructor function, and as you can see, we use it to assign initial values to our member variables, including the variables that were formerly declared as constants."

NOTE

Remember, the class constructor function is the perfect place to initialize values for the object's use.

```cpp
public: EnglishStudent()
  {
    cout << "English Student's Constructor" << endl;
    midterm = 0;
    finalExamGrade = 0;
    research = 0;
    presentation = 0;
    finalNumericGrade = 0;
    ENGLISH_FINALEXAM_PERCENTAGE = .25;
    ENGLISH_RESEARCH_PERCENTAGE = .30;
```

```
    ENGLISH_PRESENTATION_PERCENTAGE = .20;
    ENGLISH_MIDTERM_PERCENTAGE = .25;
}
```

"Why are we displaying a message to the console?" Linda asked.

"Whenever I'm developing a new application, I like to code constructor functions that write a message out to the C++ console. That way, when I run the program, I can see if and when my objects are being created. This can sometimes help you understand how your programming is behaving. At any rate, it can't hurt, provided we remember to remove the code from the constructor functions prior to delivering the final version of the program to Frank Olley."

There were no other questions, so we moved on to creating the MathStudent class.

Exercise 7-4   ## Create the MathStudent Instantiable Class

In this exercise, you'll create the MathStudent class for the Grade Calculation Project. This class will allow a client program to create an object that will prompt the user for information necessary to calculate the final grade for a math student.

1. Using Notepad, enter the following code:

```cpp
//MathStudent.cpp
#include <iostream>
#include <string>

using namespace std;

class MathStudent
{
   public:
      int midterm;
      int finalExamGrade;
      float finalNumericGrade;
      char finalLetterGrade;
      float MATH_MIDTERM_PERCENTAGE;
      float MATH_FINALEXAM_PERCENTAGE;

   public: MathStudent()
   {
      cout << "Math Student's Constructor" << endl;
      midterm = 0;
      finalExamGrade = 0;
      finalNumericGrade = 0;
```

```
                    MATH_MIDTERM_PERCENTAGE = .50;
                    MATH_FINALEXAM_PERCENTAGE = .50;
                 }

              public: void Calculate()
              {
               char response[256];
               string moreGradesToCalculate;

               cout << "Enter the Midterm Grade: " ;
               cin.getline(response,256);
               midterm = atoi(response);
               cout << "Enter the Final Examination Grade: " ;
               cin.getline(response,256);
               finalExamGrade = atoi(response);
               finalNumericGrade =
                    (midterm * MATH_MIDTERM_PERCENTAGE) +
                    (finalExamGrade * MATH_FINALEXAM_PERCENTAGE);
               if (finalNumericGrade >= 90)
                    finalLetterGrade = 'A';
               else
               if ((finalNumericGrade >= 83) &
                    (finalNumericGrade < 90))
                    finalLetterGrade = 'B';
               else
               if ((finalNumericGrade >= 76) &
                     (finalNumericGrade < 83))
                    finalLetterGrade = 'C';
               else
               if ((finalNumericGrade >= 65) &
                    (finalNumericGrade < 76))
                    finalLetterGrade = 'D';
               else
               if (finalNumericGrade < 65)
                    finalLetterGrade = 'F';
              }
              };
```

2. Save your source file as MathStudent.cpp in the \CPPFiles\Grades folder
   (select File | Save As from Notepad's menu bar). Be sure to save your source
   file with the filename extension .cpp.

3. Compile your source file. Look for any compiler error messages. If you receive one, correct the problem so that the compiler runs cleanly. Because your source file contains a class, once the class compiles cleanly, you will still receive an error from the linker program indicating that you don't have a **main()** function. If that's the only error you receive, don't worry. You'll be creating a MathStudent object from this class via the startup Grades class, which you'll modify in Exercise 7-7.

| Discussion | Again, there were no major problems in completing the exercise, and to my surprise, absolutely no questions. We then moved on to the next exercise: the creation of the ScienceStudent class. |

| Exercise 7-5 | **Create the ScienceStudent Instantiable Class** |

In this exercise, you'll create the ScienceStudent class for the Grade Calculation Project. This class will allow a client program to create an object that will prompt the user for information necessary to calculate the final grade for a science student.

1. Using Notepad, enter the following code:

```cpp
//ScienceStudent.cpp
#include <iostream>
#include <string>

using namespace std;


class ScienceStudent
{
  public:
    int midterm;
    int finalExamGrade;
    int research;
    float finalNumericGrade;
    char finalLetterGrade;
    float SCIENCE_MIDTERM_PERCENTAGE;
    float SCIENCE_FINALEXAM_PERCENTAGE;
    float SCIENCE_RESEARCH_PERCENTAGE;

  public: ScienceStudent()
  {
    cout << "Science Student's Constructor" << endl;
```

```
   midterm = 0;
   finalExamGrade = 0;
   research = 0;
   finalNumericGrade = 0;
   SCIENCE_MIDTERM_PERCENTAGE = .40;
   SCIENCE_FINALEXAM_PERCENTAGE = .40;
   SCIENCE_RESEARCH_PERCENTAGE = .20;
}

public: void Calculate()
{
 char response[256];
 string moreGradesToCalculate;

 cout << "Enter the Midterm Grade: " ;
 cin.getline(response,256);
 midterm = atoi(response);
 cout << "Enter the Final Examination Grade: " ;
 cin.getline(response,256);
 finalExamGrade = atoi(response);
 cout << "Enter the Research Grade: " ;
 cin.getline(response,256);
 research = atoi(response);
 finalNumericGrade =
     (midterm * SCIENCE_MIDTERM_PERCENTAGE) +
     (finalExamGrade *
         SCIENCE_FINALEXAM_PERCENTAGE) +
     (research * SCIENCE_RESEARCH_PERCENTAGE);
 if (finalNumericGrade >= 90)
             finalLetterGrade = 'A';
 else
 if ((finalNumericGrade >= 80) &
     (finalNumericGrade < 90))
    finalLetterGrade = 'B';
 else
 if ((finalNumericGrade >= 70) &
     (finalNumericGrade < 80))
    finalLetterGrade = 'C';
 else
 if ((finalNumericGrade >= 60) &
     (finalNumericGrade < 70))
    finalLetterGrade = 'D';
```

```
            else
            if (finalNumericGrade < 60)
                finalLetterGrade = 'F';
        }
    };
```

2. Save your source file as ScienceStudent.cpp in the \CPPFiles\Grades folder (select File | Save As from Notepad's menu bar). Be sure to save your source file with the filename extension .cpp.

3. Compile your source file. Look for any compiler error messages. If you receive one, correct the problem so that the compiler runs cleanly. Because your source file contains a class, once the class compiles cleanly, you will still receive an error from the linker program indicating that you don't have a **main()** function. If that's the only error you receive, don't worry. You'll be creating a ScienceStudent object from this class via the startup Grades class, which you'll modify in Exercise 7-7.

Discussion

"All three of these classes are very similar," I said, "with just minor differences in the way the final grade is calculated. This is something that will come into play when we discuss inheritance in two weeks."

There were no questions, so I distributed this exercise for the class to complete.

Exercise 7-6

Create the DisplayGrade Instantiable Class

In this exercise, you'll create the DisplayGrade class for the Grade Calculation Project. This class will allow a client program to create an object that will display the final grade for an English, math, or science student. This class has three overloaded constructor functions to code, so be careful while entering them.

1. Using Notepad, enter the following code:

```
//DisplayGrade.cpp
#include <iostream>
#include <string>

using namespace std;

class DisplayGrade
{
// This function accepts 6 parameters for the
// English Student
    public: DisplayGrade(int midterm, int finalExamGrade,
                    int research, int presentation,
                    float finalNumericGrade,
                    char finalLetterGrade)
```

```
      {
        cout << endl <<
          "*** ENGLISH STUDENT ***" << endl << endl;
        cout << "Midterm grade is: " <<
          midterm << endl;
        cout << "Final Exam is: " <<
          finalExamGrade << endl;
        cout << "Research grade is: " <<
          research << endl;
        cout << "Presentation grade is: " <<
          presentation << endl << endl;
        cout << "Final Numeric Grade is: " <<
          finalNumericGrade << endl;
        cout << "Final Letter Grade is: " <<
          finalLetterGrade;
      }           // end of DisplayGrade with 6 parameters

// This function accepts 4 parameters for the Math student
public: DisplayGrade(int midterm, int finalExamGrade,
                     float finalNumericGrade,
                     char finalLetterGrade)
      {
        cout << endl<<
          "*** MATH STUDENT ***" << endl << endl;
        cout << "Midterm grade is: " <<
          midterm << endl;
        cout << "Final Exam is: " <<
          finalExamGrade << endl;
        cout << "Final Numeric Grade is: " <<
          finalNumericGrade << endl;
        cout << "Final Letter Grade is: " <<
          finalLetterGrade;
      }           // end of DisplayGrade with 4 parameters


// This function accepts 5 parameters for the
// Science Student
public: DisplayGrade(int midterm, int finalExamGrade,
                     int research,
                     float finalNumericGrade,
                     char finalLetterGrade)
```

```
{
    cout << endl <<
        "*** SCIENCE STUDENT ***" << endl << endl;
    cout << "Midterm grade is: " <<
        midterm << endl;
    cout << "Final Exam is: " <<
        finalExamGrade << endl;
    cout << "Research grade is: " <<
        research << endl;
    cout << "Final Numeric Grade is: " <<
        finalNumericGrade << endl;
    cout << "Final Letter Grade is: " <<
        finalLetterGrade;

}               // end of DisplayGrade with 5 parameters

};
```

2. Save your source file as DisplayGrade.cpp in the \CPPFiles\Grades folder (select File | Save As from Notepad's menu bar). Be sure to save your source file with the filename extension .cpp.

3. Compile your source file. Look for any compiler error messages. If you receive one, correct the problem so that the compiler runs cleanly. Because your source file contains a class, once the class compiles cleanly, you will still receive an error from the linker program indicating that you don't have a **main()** function. If that's the only error you receive, don't worry. You'll be creating a DisplayGrade object from this class via the startup Grades class, which you'll modify in Exercise 7-7.

<table>
<tr><td>**Discussion**</td><td>No one seemed to have any problems completing the exercise, but I could sense some confusion.</td></tr>
</table>

"Does everyone understand what's going on here?" I asked. "We've created a class that has three overloaded constructor functions."

"Constructor functions have the same name as the class, is that right?" Rhonda asked. "And they are automatically executed when an object from the class is created."

"That's excellent, Rhonda," I said. "Constructor functions are guaranteed to execute when an object of the class is created. Furthermore, you can create more than one constructor function with the same name. These are called *overloaded* constructor functions, and C++ decides which one of them to execute based on the number and type of arguments passed to the constructor when the object is created. I'll give you a preview of the code change we're about to make in the Grades class. This is the code that will instantiate a DisplayGrade object and pass the constructor function six arguments to display the final grade for an English student."

```
DisplayGrade x(eStudent.midterm,
               eStudent.finalExamGrade,
               eStudent.research,
               eStudent.presentation,
               eStudent.finalNumericGrade,
               eStudent.finalLetterGrade);
```

No one had any other questions, so we moved on to the final exercise of the day: modifying the Grades class to create objects from the instantiable classes we had just created.

Exercise 7-7 | ### Modify the Grade Calculation Program to Use Instantiable Objects

In this exercise, you'll modify the Grades class from last week to create objects from the instantiable classes you just created.

1. Using Notepad, locate and open the Grades.cpp source file you worked on last week. (It should be in the \CPPFiles\Grades folder.)

2. Modify your code so that it looks like this:

```
//Grades.cpp

#include <iostream>
#include <string>
#include "EnglishStudent.cpp"
#include "MathStudent.cpp"
#include "ScienceStudent.cpp"
#include "DisplayGrade.cpp"

using namespace std;

int WhatKindOfStudent();
char response[256];
string moreGradesToCalculate;

int main ()
{
    int lresponse;

    cout << "Do you want to calculate a grade? ";
```

```
cin >> moreGradesToCalculate;

for (int i = 0;
   i < moreGradesToCalculate.length(); i++) {
   moreGradesToCalculate[i] =
      toupper (moreGradesToCalculate[i]);
}

while (moreGradesToCalculate == "YES") {
   lresponse = WhatKindOfStudent();

   switch(lresponse)
   {
      case 1:  // English Student
        {
         EnglishStudent eStudent;
         eStudent.Calculate();
         DisplayGrade x(eStudent.midterm,
                     eStudent.finalExamGrade,
                     eStudent.research,
                     eStudent.presentation,
                     eStudent.finalNumericGrade,
                     eStudent.finalLetterGrade);
        }
        break;
      case 2:     // Math Student
        {
         MathStudent mStudent;
         mStudent.Calculate();
         DisplayGrade y(mStudent.midterm,
                     mStudent.finalExamGrade,
                     mStudent.finalNumericGrade,
                     mStudent.finalLetterGrade);
        }
        break;
      case 3:     // Science Student
        {
         ScienceStudent sStudent;
         sStudent.Calculate();
         DisplayGrade z(sStudent.midterm,
                     sStudent.finalExamGrade,
                     sStudent.research,
```

```
                              sStudent.finalNumericGrade,
                              sStudent.finalLetterGrade);
              }
           break;
      }          // end of switch

      cout << endl << endl <<
         "Do you have another grade to calculate? ";
      cin >> moreGradesToCalculate;
      for (int i = 0;
         i < moreGradesToCalculate.length(); i++) {
         moreGradesToCalculate[i] = toupper
            (moreGradesToCalculate[i]);
      }                           // end of for
   }                              // end of while
   cout <<
        "Thanks for using the Grades Calculation program!";
   return 0;
}


int WhatKindOfStudent()
{
   cout << "Enter student type " <<
      "(1=English, 2=Math, 3=Science): ";

   cin.getline(response,256);

   if (strlen(response) == 0) {
      cout << "You must select a Student Type";
      exit(1);
   }

   if ((atoi(response) < 1) | (atoi(response) > 3)) {
      cout << response <<
         " - is not a valid student type";
      exit(1);
   }

   return atoi(response);
}
```

3. Save your source file as Grades.cpp in the \CPPFiles\Grades folder (select File | Save As from Notepad's menu bar). Be sure to save your source file with the filename extension .cpp.

4. Compile your source file into an executable file.

5. Execute your program and test it thoroughly. Verify that the looping behavior of the program is working correctly. After you start up your program, it should ask whether you have a grade to calculate.

6. Answer **Yes** and calculate the grade for an English student. Enter **70** for the midterm, **80** for the final examination, **90** for the research grade, and **100** for the presentation. A final numeric grade of 84.5 should be displayed with a letter grade of C.

7. After a message is displayed with the calculated grade, the program should ask whether you have more grades to calculate.

8. Answer **Yes** and calculate the grade for a math student. Enter **70** for the midterm and **80** for the final examination. A final numeric grade of 75 should be displayed with a letter grade of D.

9. After a message is displayed with the calculated grade, the program should ask whether you have more grades to calculate.

10. Answer **Yes** and calculate the grade for a science student. Enter **70** for the midterm, **80** for the final examination, and **90** for the research grade. A final numeric grade of 78 should be displayed with a letter grade of C. After the message is displayed with the calculated grade, the program should ask whether you have more grades to calculate.

11. Answer **No**. You should be thanked for using the program, and the program should end.

Discussion   Changing the Grades class to use instantiable objects was pretty tedious, and it took most of my students about 15 minutes to complete the exercise. Despite that, there were no major problems (one or two students forgot the include statement for the four classes; however, for the most part, I think most everyone understood what was going on).

"In the final analysis," Ward said, "we took a bunch of the code from the Grades class and placed it in the EnglishStudent, MathStudent, ScienceStudent, and DisplayGrade classes. Is that right?"

"That's right, Ward," I said. "Notice that the code in the Grades class itself has been drastically reduced because so much of it was moved into one of four other classes. Most importantly, the code is easier to read, understand, and maintain, although the overall code is larger when you consider all the classes that comprise it."

"How so?" Rhonda asked. "I mean, how is it easier to maintain?"

"Let me ask you this question," I said. "If Frank Olley walked into our classroom right now and told you that the calculation of the final grade for an English student needs to be changed, could you tell me what class we would need to change?"

"That's easy," Dave said. "That code is in the EnglishStudent class. In fact, it's in the **Calculate()** function of the EnglishStudent class."

"I couldn't have said it better myself, Dave," I replied.

"Can you review the code that instantiates the various student objects?" Barbara asked.

"Sure thing, Barbara," I said. "Here it is:"

```cpp
switch(lresponse)
    {
        case 1:  // English Student
            {
            EnglishStudent eStudent;
            eStudent.Calculate();
            DisplayGrade x(eStudent.midterm,
                           eStudent.finalExamGrade,
                           eStudent.research,
                           eStudent.presentation,
                           eStudent.finalNumericGrade,
                           eStudent.finalLetterGrade);
            }
            break;
        case 2:  // Math Student
            {
            MathStudent mStudent;
            mStudent.Calculate();
            DisplayGrade y(mStudent.midterm,
                           mStudent.finalExamGrade,
                           mStudent.finalNumericGrade,
                           mStudent.finalLetterGrade);
            }
            break;
        case 3:   // Science Student
            {
```

```
        ScienceStudent sStudent;
        sStudent.Calculate();
        DisplayGrade z(sStudent.midterm,
                       sStudent.finalExamGrade,
                       sStudent.research,
                       sStudent.finalNumericGrade,
                       sStudent.finalLetterGrade);
    }
    break;
}          // end of switch
```

"All the code necessary to instantiate the EnglishStudent, MathStudent, and ScienceStudent objects is contained within this Switch structure. The test condition for the Switch structure is the user's response of 1, 2, or 3. If the user's response is 1, we declare an instance of the EnglishStudent object using the object variable eStudent."

```
EnglishStudent eStudent;
```

"We then execute the **Calculate()** function of the EnglishStudent object using this code."

```
eStudent. Calculate();
```

"This is followed by an instantiation of the DisplayGrade object. Depending on the number and type of arguments supplied, one of the three constructor functions we created is executed."

```
DisplayGrade x(eStudent.midterm,
               eStudent.finalExamGrade,
               eStudent.research,
               eStudent.presentation,
               eStudent.finalNumericGrade,
               eStudent.finalLetterGrade);
```

"What's the significance of sandwiching the Case statements within curly braces?" Dave asked. "We haven't done that before."

"We need to put curly braces around the Case statement," I said, "because one of the imperative statements declares an object. Without the braces, C++ will complain that there's a conditional variable declaration occurring here—something that, for technical reasons beyond the scope of this course, it won't allow. The braces give the Case statements local scope, allowing the code to compile."

"I probably should have asked this earlier," Linda said, "but why didn't we place the code for the grade calculation in a constructor function of the EnglishStudent class, like we did with the DisplayGrade class, instead of creating a separate function called **Calculate()**?"

"That's a good question, Linda," I said. "We certainly could have done that. It's another case of there being more than one way to paint a picture. In theory, constructor functions should be used to initialize the state or data variables of an object. I stretched the intended purpose of the constructor functions for the DisplayGrade object just a bit, in part because I wanted to give you all a chance to work with one."

I waited to see if anyone had any questions, but there were none.

"This class has been a very productive one," I said, "in that you learned how to code classes and create objects from them, which gives us access to the object's data and behavior. Next week, you'll learn that sometimes in our haste to give a client program access to an object's data, we permit too much access, which can have some pretty nasty effects on the data integrity of our objects. You'll learn how to correct that problem next week."

With that, I dismissed the class for the day.

Summary

In this chapter, you learned how to create instantiable classes—that is, classes from which objects can be created. These objects can have attributes, which are implemented via member and static variables within the class, and behaviors, which are implemented via class functions.

Instantiable classes cannot be executed via a command prompt; their objects must be created from within another class, typically a startup program possessing a **main**() function. Instantiable objects can be created using a syntax very similar to those for the fundamental data types. Instantiable objects created in this way are destroyed by C++ when they go out of scope, so there is no need to explicitly destroy a C++ object as there is in other programming languages.

Instantiable classes have two special types of functions. The first, the constructor function, has the same name as the class, and its code is guaranteed to execute when an object of the class is first created. Constructor functions may be overloaded—that is, you may have more than one constructor function with the same name, provided each one has a different signature (the number and type of arguments).

The second special function is called a destructor function, and its code is guaranteed to execute when a C++ object is about to be destroyed. Destructor functions are named with the class name and prefixed with a tilde (~). Neither constructor nor destructor functions may accept any parameters.

Controlling Access to the Data in Your Object

In Chapter 7, you learned how to create instantiable classes, which are classes from which other objects can be created. These objects are just like the standard C++ objects, such as cout, that we've been working with all along. Instantiable objects possess characteristics or attributes that are created via instance and member variables. An instantiable object's attributes can be read or updated by the C++ program (or other class) that creates the object. Instantiable objects also possess certain types of behavior, which are created via functions (functions with classes are called *methods*). An instantiable object's methods can be executed by the C++ program (or other class) that creates it.

In this chapter, you'll learn that although it's great that the C++ class that creates an instantiable object can access and update the object's member variables, it's not always desirable for these variables to be directly updateable by the client program. The same can be said of client programs that execute the object's methods. There may be cases where some methods of the instantiable class need to be hidden from the client program. You'll learn that there are ways to deal with these potential problems.

Controlling Access to Your Object's Data

"Last week," I said, as I began our eighth class, "you learned how to create instantiable classes, which are classes from which objects can be created. You learned how we can design an instantiable class to model a real-world object, complete with characteristics or attributes and behaviors. When an object is created from an instantiable class, the C++ program creating the object can read and update the object's attributes and trigger its behavior by executing its methods. In today's class, we'll continue studying instantiable class creation, which we began last week."

"I wouldn't have thought there was a lot more to cover with instantiable classes," Mary said. "I thought we were pretty much done with this topic last week."

"In terms of instantiable classes," I said, "what we've done so far has been fine, but in today's class, you'll learn that the instantiable classes we created last week, although fully functional, may have some potential data problems."

"Data problems?" Rhonda asked. "That sounds serious. Do you mean that there are problems with the classes we created last week?"

"There's no need to be alarmed, Rhonda," I said. "In terms of the mechanics of creating instantiable classes, everything we did last week was just fine. But in our excitement about learning how to use a C++ class to model an object, we didn't consider in the least whether the data in the object needs to be protected, and if so, how to protect it."

"Protecting the data?" Peter asked. "I'm afraid I don't understand. From whom do we need to protect data?"

"That's a great question, Peter," I said. "It may be difficult for you to fathom right now, but the C++ programs you will write later, particularly if you are writing programs to run in a commercial environment, have the potential for exposing data that is sensitive."

"Such as?" Ward asked.

"In a Customer object, customer account numbers and social security numbers are sensitive data," I said. "In an Employee object, employee salary information or employee performance appraisals are sensitive data. These are examples of data that, if the designer of the instantiable class is not careful, can wind up in the hands of the wrong person. It seems that nearly every week there's a story in the newspaper about sensitive data finding its way into the wrong hands. This is something we need to consider when we design our instantiable classes."

"How do we do that?" Blaine asked. "Can you give us an example?"

"Sure thing, Blaine," I said. "Every class we've created so far in the course has been created as a public class, with public methods and public member variables. Let's take a look at the code we wrote last week to implement the attributes of the EnglishStudent class."

```
public:
    int midterm;
    int finalExamGrade;
    int research;
    int presentation;
    float finalNumericGrade;
    char finalLetterGrade;
```

"The Public keyword is in front of these member variables," Rhonda said.

"That's my point exactly, Rhonda," I said. "When we created the EnglishStudent class last week, we specified the keyword Public. That tells C++ to give these variables public access."

"What does public access mean?" Steve wondered.

"In terms of a member variable," I said, "public access means that code in other classes and in the startup program can directly access the member variables in the class."

"What do you mean by 'directly access'?" Valerie asked.

"When I say directly access," I replied, "I mean that a class can create an instance of the EnglishStudent object and, using object dot notation, directly update the value of an instance or a member variable, like this."

I then showed the following example on the classroom projector:

```
//Example8_1.cpp

#include "EnglishStudent.cpp"
```

```
int main()
{
  EnglishStudent x;
  x.midterm = 99;        // Update the member variable
  cout << x.midterm;     // Access the member variable

  return 0;
}
```

"Is that a problem?" Steve asked. "Don't we want the program that creates our object to be able to work directly with the object's attributes and methods?"

"In some cases," I said, "but perhaps not all. Updating the midterm attribute of EnglishStudent may be fine, but suppose one of the programmers using the EnglishStudent class discovers he or she can directly update the finalNumericGrade attribute, like this."

I then showed the following example on the classroom projector:

```
//Example8_2.cpp

#include "EnglishStudent.cpp"

int main()
{
  EnglishStudent x;
  x.finalNumericGrade = 99;

  return 0;
}
```

"Now we're starting to get into dangerous territory," I said. "Allowing a program to create an object and then update the component pieces of the English student's final grade is fine, but by design, only the **Calculate()** method of the EnglishStudent object should determine the final numeric grade. To allow a programmer to directly update the finalNumericGrade or finalLetterGrade attribute of the EnglishStudent object is to invite problems."

"Like what?" Rhonda asked.

"The only way a final grade should be calculated," I said, "is via the code that the designer of the object wrote. By permitting the user of the object to directly update the finalNumericGrade or finalLetterGrade attribute, we've allowed them to bypass the correct calculation. This can lead to results that are incorrect at best and fraudulent at worst."

"In other words," Dave said, "an unscrupulous programmer could update the final grade for a student by bypassing the code in the **Calculate()** method of the EnglishStudent object."

"That's right, Dave," I said, "and it has happened. But as I said before, fraudulent activity like this is the worst-case scenario. In this case, since the examination and other final grade components are public, an unscrupulous programmer could also fraudulently update the examination or other grade components, achieving a similar effect. However, even if the programmer doesn't intend to do something like that, allowing the programmer to directly update an attribute that can properly only be updated by complex code is a big mistake. Remember, one of the great things about objects is that they allow the developer of the object to shield the complexities of a task from the programmer who needs to use the object. In the real world of programming, programmers work with objects like this all the time, and the objects are many times more complex than that of an English student at a university. Programmers are developing object-oriented programs today to monitor switches in nuclear power plants or values on the space shuttle just before launch. Can you imagine the dire effects if the designer of one of these objects accidentally permitted the programmer using the object to directly update one of its attributes?"

"I think I get the point," Valerie said. "Certain attributes of an object shouldn't be updateable by the programmer using the object."

"That's right, Valerie," I said, "and some attributes are best not seen as well. My point is that whether or not to allow access to an object's attributes and methods is something to which the designer of the class needs to give careful thought before distributing the class for use by other programmers."

I waited a moment before continuing.

"I'm not sure there is a consensus among class designers," I said, "but I think it's safe to say that some attributes, but not all, can be directly accessible by the program creating the object and therefore should be designated with the Public keyword. Other attributes can be visible to the program creating the object but should not be directly updateable by it. Other attributes should be invisible to certain users of the program creating the object, and still others should be totally invisible to the program creating the object—accessible only by code within the methods of the object itself. These attributes should be designated with the Private access keyword."

"Can you give us an example of each one of these categories?" Kate asked. "I'm afraid I'm still not getting it."

"Let's imagine," I said, "that a programmer at XYZ University designs a Student class to model the university's real-world student, and that the Student class has this list of attributes."

I then showed the following example on the classroom projector:

```cpp
//Student.cpp
#include <iostream>
#include <string>

using namespace std;

class Student
{
  public:
```

```
string studentID;
string name;
string address;
int age;
string SSN;
float GPA;
```

"SSN is the student's social security number, and GPA is the student's grade point average. Let's further suppose that the designer of the Student class coded a constructor method so that when a Student object is created, the value of the studentID attribute is used to locate student information in a database record and to assign values to the rest of the Student class attributes. Finally, let's suppose that another programmer at the university finds the Student class and decides to use it in a program they are writing, which is designed to permit a work-study student to update student address and age information."

"I see some potential problems with this Student class right away!" Dave said. "There's nothing stopping the program from creating a Student object that then exposes private information about the student, such as social security number and grade point average."

"I agree," Steve added. "I think that the client program using the Student object should have full access—by that I mean read and update—to just two attributes, the address and age attributes. Furthermore, I would suggest read-only access to the studentID and name attributes. We don't want either of those attributes being changed by accident. Finally, I would suggest that both SSN and GPA be totally invisible to the user of the Student object, at least in this particular case."

"I agree with both Dave and Steve," Rhonda said. "But how can we hide some attributes and make others invisible in C++? Is that what you were talking about earlier when you were discussing access keywords?"

"That's part of it, Rhonda," I said. "By specifying a Private access keyword, we can prevent the client program from being able to access the attribute at all, and in a moment, you'll see that we can also use special methods to selectively restrict what the client program using our object can do with the data inside of it. Let's create a Student class with the attributes I just listed and create a method called **Display**() to display its data."

"Will we be accessing data in a database today?" Rhonda asked excitedly.

"No, Rhonda," I replied. "Working with data from a database within C++ is beyond the scope of this introductory course. Instead of looking up the student's information in a database record, we'll simulate its lookup by assigning a set of default values to the object's attributes via its constructor method."

I displayed this code for the Student class on the classroom projector:

```
//Student.cpp
#include <iostream>
#include <string>
```

```cpp
using namespace std;

class Student
{
  public:
    string studentID;
    string name;
    string address;
    int age;
    string SSN;
    float GPA;

  public: Student()        //Constructor Method
  {
    studentID = "123";
    name = "Mary Smith";
    address = "22 Twain Drive";
    age = 22;
    SSN = "111-22-3333";
    GPA = 2.12;
  }

  public: void Display()
  {
      cout << "Student ID:  " << studentID << endl <<
          "Name: " << name << endl <<
          "Address: " << address << endl <<
          "Age: " << age << endl <<
          "SSN: " << SSN << endl <<
          "GPA: " << GPA << endl;
  }
};
```

I then saved the code as Student.cpp and compiled it. Except for the message from the compiler complaining that the class lacked a **main()** function (remember, an object of the class needs to be created from a client program), the program compiled fine.

"As you can see," I said, "the Student class contains the six attributes we discussed. Notice that all six member variables are defined with the Public keyword. Notice also that the Student class has two methods: The constructor method, called **Student()**, is given the same name as the class. In it, we placed code to assign a set of default values to each one of the six attributes of the class so that we can experiment a bit with Student objects created from the class. As I mentioned earlier, ordinarily we would obtain this information from a data source, such as a database, but that's beyond the scope of this introductory course, so we'll just 'pretend' to do so via the constructor method. Besides, the constructor method is the proper place to initialize the object's attributes anyway. The second method is the **Display()** method, which displays the values of the attributes to the C++ console. Now let's create a client program and write the code necessary to instantiate a Student object from this class."

I displayed this code on the classroom projector:

```
//Example8_3.cpp

#include "Student.cpp"

int main()
{
  Student x;
  x.Display();

  return 0;
}
```

I saved the program as Example8_3.cpp and then compiled and executed it. The following screenshot was displayed on the classroom projector:

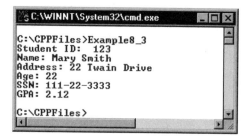

```
C:\CPPFiles>Example8_3
Student ID:  123
Name: Mary Smith
Address: 22 Twain Drive
Age: 22
SSN: 111-22-3333
GPA: 2.12

C:\CPPFiles>
```

"Can anyone tell me what this code did?" I asked.

"What you've done here," Chuck said, "is create a Student object, initialize the values of all six attributes via its constructor method, and display those values in a message box via the Object's **Display()** method."

"That's excellent, Chuck," I said. "Any other comments?"

"Right now," Dave said, "the data in this class is very much unprotected. The user of the Student object can directly access every Student attribute."

"Absolutely right, Dave," I said, "We previously agreed that we didn't want a client program to have access to the student's social security number or grade point average, and both of these are now prominently displayed in the message box. Worse yet, the user of this Student object can directly update both of those attributes, something we also said we didn't want to happen. Let's change the grade point average for Mary Smith."

I displayed this modified code on the classroom projector:

```
//Example8_4.cpp

#include "Student.cpp"

int main()
{
  Student x;
  x.GPA = 3.99;
  x.Display();

  return 0;
}
```

I saved the program as Example8_4.cpp and then compiled and executed it. The following screenshot was displayed on the classroom projector:

"Wow," Kate said. "We've really done that Mary Smith a favor: her grade point average went from 2.12 to 3.99. I see what you mean by allowing the client program full access to the GPA attribute of the Student class."

"It didn't occur to me that we could use the object dot-notation to directly update these attributes," Ward said, "and with the access control keyword of Public, the member variables in the class can be updated by the client program."

NOTE

Access control keywords are typed in lowercase (for example, public and private).

"Besides public access," Mary asked, "what are the other access control keywords again?"

"Public access," I said, "which is what we have here, gives full access to the member variable to code in any other client class. There's also private and protected access. Protected access applies only when inheritance is a factor. Inheritance is something we'll be discussing next week."

"What about private access?" Steve asked. "Did you skip that?"

"Private access," I said, "means that the member variable can be used only by code located within the same class as the member variable."

I gave everyone a chance to ponder that statement for a moment.

"In the case of the Student class," I said, "that means that if the member variable GPA is defined with a Private access control keyword, only code in the methods of the Student class itself will be able to access the member variable."

 NOTE
As a reminder, a method is the name given to a function in a class.

"That seems pretty worthless, doesn't it?" Mary said. "What's the use of having an attribute if it can't be seen or updated from outside the instantiable class?"

"You'll see in a moment," I said, "how the Private access control keyword is the perfect way to protect data within our object. What we do is make the member variables private but provide public methods to access and modify them. Right now, I'd like to show you what happens if we define our member variables with the Private access control keyword."

I then modified the code in the Student class to look like this:

```cpp
//Student.cpp
#include <iostream>
#include <string>

using namespace std;

class Student
{
  private:
    string studentID;
    string name;
    string address;
    int age;
    string SSN;
    float GPA;

  public: Student()      //Constructor Method
  {
    studentID = "123";
```

```
      name = "Mary Smith";
      address = "22 Twain Drive";
      age = 22;
      SSN = "111-22-3333";
      GPA = 2.12;
   }

   public: void Display()
   {
       cout << "Student ID:  " << studentID << endl <<
          "Name: " << name << endl <<
          "Address: " << address << endl <<
          "Age: " << age << endl <<
          "SSN: " << SSN << endl <<
          "GPA: " << GPA << endl;
   }
};
```

"By specifying an access control keyword of Private for the member variables of the Student class," I said, "we're now preventing the code from the Example8_4 class from being able to access the values of these member variables. Look at what happens when we try to recompile the code from Example8_4."

I then attempted to recompile Example8_4. The following screenshot was displayed:

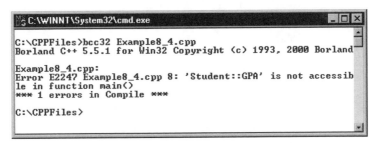

"What happened?" I heard Rhonda say.

"The C++ compiler has recognized that the code in Example8_4 is trying to access the private member variable GPA in the Student class and has flagged that line of code as an error," I said. "With the Private access control keyword, access to these member variables from code outside the class is no longer possible."

"I see that private access means we can't update the value of the member variable," Rhonda said. "Does it also mean we can't see the value?"

"That's right, Rhonda," I said. "We can neither see nor update private member variables directly. However, and this is where the trick comes in, we can indirectly see and update private member variables, provided that a public method of the Student class is written to do that. Remember, private access allows methods within the same class to 'get at' the private member variables. We can modify the code in Example8_4 to look like this:"

```
//Example8_5.cpp

#include "Student.cpp"

int main()
{
  Student x;
  x.Display();

  return 0;
}
```

"This code will compile and run just fine, with the public **Display()** method of the Student class taking care of allowing our program to see the values of the Student object's attributes."

I saved the program as Example8_5.cpp and then compiled and executed it. The following screenshot was displayed on the classroom projector:

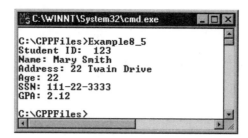

```
C:\WINNT\System32\cmd.exe

C:\CPPFiles>Example8_5
Student ID:  123
Name: Mary Smith
Address: 22 Twain Drive
Age: 22
SSN: 111-22-3333
GPA: 2.12

C:\CPPFiles>
```

"I see what you mean now," Mary said. "Even though the member variables are declared as private, the public **Display()** method allows us to see the values of the Student class's member variables."

"Exactly, Mary," I answered.

"But suppose," Mary continued, "we want to be able to update the member variables as well as see them?"

"Then we write a public method to enable us to do that as well," I said. "The point is that instead of allowing a client program to directly view or update a member variable, we write a public method that permits either the view or the update, or both. At this point, that approach may not seem like much of an improvement over simply having a public attribute, but I think you'll see the benefits of doing so in just a few minutes."

Member Variables: Public or Private?

"Are you saying that all our member variables should be declared as private?" Linda asked.

"That's a good question, Linda," I said. "In the C++ world, it's considered best to create private member variables, and many programmers follow this guideline, declaring all their member variables as private and writing public methods to provide access to the member variables and their values. On the other hand, you will find some programmers who declare all their member variables as public. You'll also find programmers who pick and choose, declaring some member variables as public and some as private, depending on the particular attribute of an object the member variable represents."

"What's your recommendation?" Steve asked.

"My recommendation," I said, "is that you declare your member variables as private and write public methods to access them, and that's the consensus opinion. However, the bottom line is that the C++ language allows you to create public member variables. If you choose to do so, that's up to you. However, bear in mind that this practice may be something that a prospective employer frowns upon, because public member variables can cause data integrity problems, the type we just saw with the Student class example. Certainly, you should at least think twice before you declare a member variable as public."

"I'm still having problems with this concept of private member variables and public methods," Chuck said. "In the Student class we just wrote, is the **Display**() method the type of public method you are talking about?"

"Good question, Chuck," I said. "More typically, the public methods I'm referring to are functions or methods normally called **Get**() and **Set**() methods. *Get()* methods are public methods that permit a client program to get or retrieve the value of a private member variable. *Set()* methods are public methods that permit a client program to set or update the value of a private member variable. By the way, **Get**() methods are also called *accessor* methods, and **Set**() methods are also called *mutator* methods.

NOTE

*C++ terminology can be confusing. In some cases, you will see both the **Set()** and **Get()** methods referred to collectively as accessor methods. You will sometimes see the **Set()** method referred to as a mutator method (because it changes the value of a private member variable) and the **Get()** method referred to as an accessor method (because it accesses the value of a private member variable). For the purposes of our discussion, I'll refer to the **Set()** method as the mutator method and the **Get()** method as the accessor method.*

"So we should code a pair of **Get**() and **Set**() public methods for each member variable?" Linda asked.

"If you declare your member variables as private," I said, "you will need a public **Get**() method to retrieve an attribute's value and a public **Set**() method to change it. Without them, there's no way the client program can access the object's attribute represented by that member variable. There are also times where you may choose *not* to code either one, thereby preventing the attribute from either being seen, updated, or both."

"What kind of code do we put in the **Get()** method?" Valerie asked. "Just the code to update the private member variable."

"As you'll see in a minute," I said, "you can place code in the **Get()** method to determine whether the client program requesting the value of the private member variable really should have access to it, and you can place code in the **Set()** method to determine whether the client program attempting to update the value of the private member variable should be able to do so."

"That would come in very handy with the SSN and GPA attributes of the Student class," Mary said.

"Absolutely," I said. "The **Set()** method is a great place to put code to verify whether the client program has the authority to update the private member variable. Code in the **Set()** method can also be used to perform validation on the proposed update before the member variable is actually changed and the object is set to an invalid state."

"Validation code?" Rhonda asked. "Invalid state? What do you mean?"

"The 'state' of an object refers to the values of the data that represent the object," I said. "An object must always maintain its data in a valid state, and a well-written object should test any changes to its data, ensuring that each one of its attribute's values doesn't violate its set of legal values. For instance, in Example8_4, you saw how a client program can inappropriately change the value of the GPA member variable. Still, the value of GPA was set to a value that is consistent with a grade point average. With a public member variable, it's easy for a client program to make a mistake and cause the object's state to become invalid, like this:"

```
//Example8_6.cpp

#include "Student.cpp"

int main()
{
  Student x;
  x.age = -6;
  x.Display();

  return 0;
}
```

 NOTE

If you try to compile this code, the class won't compile cleanly because the age attribute is currently defined with private access.

Using the Get() and Set() Methods

"Does anyone see a problem here?" I asked.

"I do," Rhonda called out. "You've assigned a negative number to the Student object's age attribute. I'm sure you didn't mean to do that."

"Is that what you mean by 'invalid state'?" Ward asked.

"You're both absolutely right," I said. "I didn't intend to do that, but if the age member variable is declared with public access, there's absolutely no way to prevent this. And now the Student object does have an invalid state: One of its attributes makes no sense. The student's age cannot be negative."

"A Set() method could prevent this from happening?" Lou asked.

"That's right, Lou," I said. "Using a Set() method, we can alert the user if the update they've attempted to make to a private member variable is invalid. Let's code Set() and Get() methods for two of the attributes in the Student class. Take a look at this code."

I then modified the code in the Student class to look like this:

```
//Student.cpp
#include <iostream>
#include <string>

using namespace std;

class Student
{
  private:
    string studentID;
    string name;
    string address;
    int age;
    string SSN;
    float GPA;

  public: Student()       //Constructor Method
  {
    studentID = "123";
    name = "Mary Smith";
    address = "22 Twain Drive";
    age = 22;
    SSN = "111-22-3333";
    GPA = 2.12;
  }

  public: void Display()
```

```
    {
        cout << "Student ID:  " << studentID << endl <<
            "Name: " << name << endl <<
            "Address: " << address << endl <<
            "Age: " << age << endl;
    }


    public: void SetAddress(string temp)
    {
        address = temp;
    }

    public: string GetAddress()
    {
        return address;
    }

    public: void SetAge(int temp)
    {
        if (temp < 1)
        {
            cout << "Invalid Age " << temp << " Program Terminating" << endl;
            exit(1);
        }
        else
            age = temp;
    }

    public: int GetAge()
    {
        return age;
    }

};                              //end of class
```

"What we've done here," I said, "is declare a **Get()** and **Set()** method for two of our member variables: address and age."

"Are those the accessor and mutator methods you mentioned earlier?" Valerie asked.

"That's right, Valerie," I answered. "**Get()** methods are also called accessor methods, and they permit the client program to retrieve the value of a private member variable. **Set()** methods are also called mutator methods, and they permit the client program to update the value of a private member variable."

"Why didn't we create **Get**() and **Set**() methods for each one of the private member variables?" Kate asked. "Didn't you say that was your recommendation?"

"Not quite, Kate," I replied. "My recommendation is to create private member variables for every attribute of the object but to create **Get**() and **Set**() methods only where necessary. Remember, I mentioned that there may be times when we choose not to create accessor or mutator methods for some attributes. This is a good example of that. We are not interested in providing our client program with access to the Student object's other four attributes, so those values would be initialized by the constructor method, perhaps from a database file, and then remain the same for the life of the object. By providing no **Get**() or **Set**() methods for those member variables, there's no way the client program can view them or update them."

"Except through the public **display**() method," Dave said, "and I notice that you've modified that method, and it no longer displays the SSN or GPA member variables."

"That's right, Dave," I said. "Does everyone see the benefits of declaring our member variables as private?"

"I think I do," Linda said, "but isn't providing **Get**() and **Set**() methods the same as making the member variable public in the first place?"

"That's the argument that some programmers make," I said, "but that's only true if no validation or access rights check is being performed in the **Get**() or **Set**() method. You have to remember that when a direct retrieval or update is made to a public member variable by a client program, there's nothing that the object can do to stop it. **Get**() and **Set**() methods, on the other hand, can be coded to be much 'smarter' than that. For instance, code in a **Get**() method can determine the identity of the user of the client program and make a decision as to whether the user should be permitted to see the data. Code in a **Set**() method can validate the proposed update *before* it occurs."

"I'm convinced," Linda said. "Can we take a closer look at the **Get**() and **Set**() methods before we test this code?"

"Sure thing, Linda," I said. "Let's take a look at the **Set**() methods first. Remember, we created **Set**() methods only for the age and address private member variables."

"Does that mean the other four private member variables can't be updated?" Linda asked.

"That's right," I said. "If we declare a member variable as private, without a mutator method or some other public method that can update it, the member variable is shut off from the client program."

"So it's up to the designer of the object to decide whether a **Get**() or **Set**() method will be written for each private member variable, right?" Joe asked.

"Exactly," I answered. "If no access to the private member variable is required, then we don't write either a **Get**() or **Set**() method. If the private member variable's value needs to be seen but not updated, we only write a **Get**() method."

Set() Mutator Methods

"Where's the mutator method for the address attribute?" Blaine asked. "Is that the **SetAddress()** method?"

"That's right, Blaine," I said, as I displayed it on the classroom projector. "Mutator methods by convention begin with the prefix 'Set'. Notice also that we have specified the Public keyword."

```cpp
public: void SetAddress(string temp)
{
    address = temp;
}
```

"Is there anything special about a mutator method?" Barbara asked. "**SetAddress()** looks like an ordinary method to me."

"Barbara's right," I said. "**Set()** methods are just ordinary methods with code that permits the user of the object to update the value of a private member variable. This is accomplished by the client program passing the proposed updated value of the private member variable as an argument to the **Set()** method. Notice that **SetAddress()** is declared to accept a single string argument called temp. This argument, when passed to **SetAddress()**, is then assigned to the private member variable *address*."

"So that's how it works," Rhonda said. "The *address* member variable is declared private, but even so, code within the class itself has full access to it."

"You have the idea now, Rhonda," I said. "Notice that there was no validation code in the **SetAddress()** method. However, the mutator method for the age attribute is a bit more complicated."

```cpp
public: void SetAge(int temp)
{
    if (temp < 1)
    {
        cout << "Invalid Age " << temp << " Program Terminating" << endl;
        exit(1);
    }
    else
        age = temp;
}
```

"As was the case with the **SetAddress()** mutator method, **SetAge()** also accepts a single argument, although this one is an integer, because the passed argument must match the data type of the private member variable. **SetAddress()** contains validation code, using an If statement, to handle the negative number that we 'accidentally' assigned to the age attribute in Example 8_4. If the value of the passed argument is less than 1, we display a message to the user and execute the **exit()** method to immediately end the program. Otherwise, we assign the value of the passed argument to the private member variable called age."

"What's the impact of executing the **exit**() method within the mutator method?" Dave asked. "Will it end the program or just destroy the Student object?"

"Executing the **exit**() method immediately terminates the entire program," I said.

"Is there a more elegant way of handling the error than that?" Linda asked.

"Yes, there is," I said. "We could have defined the mutator method to return a predetermined value to the client program and then have the client program react to that return value."

"So mutator methods can return a value?" Bob asked.

"Absolutely," I said. "Mutator methods can return a value just like any other method. In the case of **SetAge**(), we could have chosen to return a value to the client program indicating the success or failure of the update. Traditionally, a return value of 0 indicates success, and some other value, such as −1, indicates failure."

Everyone seemed anxious to see the mutator method of the Student class in action by executing a client program, but first, we needed to quickly examine the accessor methods.

Get() Accessor Methods

"Let's take a look at the two accessor methods we created, **GetAddress**() and **GetAge**(). As you can see, by convention, accessor methods are named beginning with the prefix 'Get'. Accessor methods return the value of the private member variable as a return value to the client program that calls them. Here's the **GetAddress**() accessor method:"

```
public: string GetAddress()
   {
      return address;
   }
```

"And here's the **GetAge**() accessor method:"

```
public: int GetAge()
   {
      return age;
   }
```

"We had no reason to do so," I continued, "but it's within the accessor method that we can write code to determine whether the client program should have access to the value of the private member variable. One way to do so would be to require the client program to supply, as an argument to the accessor method, some kind of password."

I waited to see if there were any questions, but there were none.

"I'm anxious to see how the mutator and accessor methods work," Rhonda said.

"Rhonda's right," I said. "It's time to test the accessor and mutator methods of the Student class. Let's see if we can assign a negative value to the age attribute of the Student object."

I then displayed this code on the classroom projector:

```
//Example8_7.cpp

#include "Student.cpp"

int main()
{
  Student x;
  x.SetAddress("222 Elm Street");
  x.SetAge(-6);
  x.Display();

  return 0;
}
```

"Here's code that creates an instance of a Student object," I said, "and then uses the mutator methods **SetAddress()** and **SetAge()** to update the private member variables of address and age. Notice how we're passing values for both of the mutator methods via arguments to the respective mutators."

"I was about to say," Kate mentioned, "that there is no assignment statement in the code. I forgot that we no longer assign a value directly to a member variable and that instead we pass a value as an argument to the mutator method."

"Does everyone notice that I've repeated the mistake that I made earlier," I asked, "by 'accidentally' passing a negative number as an argument to the **SetAge()** mutator method? Let's see if the mutator catches it."

I saved the program as Example8_7.cpp and then compiled and executed it. The following screenshot was displayed:

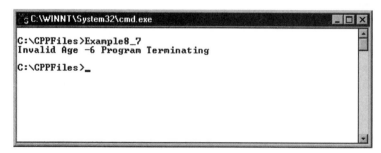

"Looks like the mutator worked," I heard Steve say.

"Indeed it did," I replied. "The **SetAge()** mutator detected a passed value less than 1, displayed a message to the user, and then ended the program. Now, let's see how the program behaves if we pass it a legal value for the age attribute."

I then displayed the following code on the classroom projector:

```cpp
//Example8_8.cpp

#include "Student.cpp"

int main()
{
  Student x;
  x.SetAddress("222 Elm Street");
  x.SetAge(46);
  x.Display();

  return 0;
}
```

I saved the program as Example8_8.cpp and then compiled and executed it. The following screenshot was displayed on the classroom projector:

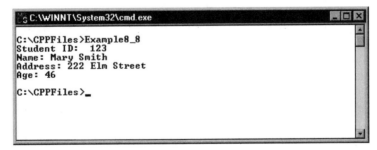

"Does everyone see how the two mutator methods have allowed us to update the private member variables address and age?" I asked.

"I'm fine with that," Linda said, "but we haven't used the accessor methods, have we? We used the public **Display()** method of the Student object to display the values for the address and age member variables. Can we see their accessor methods in action?"

"That's a good point, Linda," I said. "Let's do that."

I then displayed the following code on the classroom projector:

```cpp
//Example8_9.cpp

#include "Student.cpp"

int main()
{
  Student x;
  x.SetAddress("222 Elm Street");
  x.SetAge(46);
  cout << "The value of age is: " << x.GetAge() << endl;
  cout << "The value of address is: " << x.GetAddress() << endl;

  return 0;
}
```

"Where are we executing the accessor methods for age and address?" Rhonda asked. "I'm afraid I'm just not seeing them."

"They're in these two lines of code," I said. "You may have missed them because their return values are being used as an argument to the cout object."

```cpp
cout << "The value of age is: " << x.GetAge() << endl;
cout << "The value of address is: " << x.GetAddress() << endl;
```

"I see now," Rhonda said.

I saved the program as Example8_9.cpp and then compiled and executed it. The following screenshot was displayed on the classroom projector:

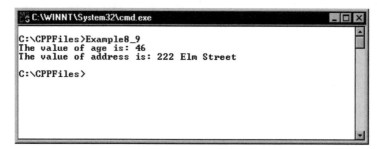

We had been working for some time, so I suggested we take a break prior to examining the Grade Calculation Project for data integrity issues. While my class was out of the room, I placed a quick phone call to coordinate a visit with a special guest.

Analyzing the Grades Calculation Project for Data Integrity

Fifteen minutes later I resumed class by explaining that it was now time to examine the Grade Calculation Project for data integrity concerns, the type that we had been studying all morning.

"Does anyone see any data integrity problems with the Grade Calculation Project?" I asked. "Don't forget, you'll need to examine all the classes in the project."

I gave everyone a few minutes to find and load their own versions of the Grade Calculation Project on their PCs.

"The first thing that strikes me as being suspect, at least based on what we learned this morning," Dave said, "is that the member variables in the EnglishStudent, MathStudent, and ScienceStudent classes are currently defined with the Public keyword. From what we learned today, that means a client program can, in theory, directly access those member variables—and also modify them."

"Absolutely correct," I replied. "That's definitely something we'll need to correct."

"Does that mean we'll need to write **Get()** and **Set()**methods for each of the member variables?" Joe asked.

"Almost all of them Joe," I replied. "We'll need to write **Set()** methods for each member variable we want our client program to update, and **Get()** methods for each member variable we want our client program to be able to access."

"I think," Linda said, "that the **Set()** mutator methods will be a great place to put the validation code we'll need for the *midterm, finalExamGrade, research,* and *presentation* member variables. Just like the negative number we assigned to the age attribute a few minutes ago, each one of the member variables of the various Student classes in the Grades Calculation Project can have an invalid number assigned to it by the user. Isn't the **Set()** mutator method the place for that code?"

"Absolutely, Linda," I said. "You're right. At this point, the user can specify a negative number for a student's midterm, and our program will calculate a final grade anyway. We'll definitely need to correct that. One more thing: I'd suggest coding the **Set()** methods with an access control keyword of Private. This will ensure that only code within the class can update the member variables."

"Can we do that?" Ward asked, "I mean, code a method with an access keyword of Private, just like our member variables? I thought all our methods needed public access."

"Yes, we can code a private method," I said. "It works the same way as with a member variable. A private method is one that can only be executed by code within the same class."

"But if we code the **Set()** mutator method as private, how will the private member variable be updated?" Barbara asked.

"I was just about to ask," Kate said, "whether anything we do in the next few minutes will require a change to the Grades class itself. I notice that, right now, the Grades program, when it creates a DisplayGrade object, directly references the member variables in each one of the Student objects.

"You both hit the nail on the head," I said. "Our program will no longer be directly updating the member variables in the various Student objects as it does now. Instead, we'll be coding and executing **Set()** mutator methods of the Student classes. In fact, as you'll see shortly, it will be the constructor methods of the Student classes that ultimately will execute the **Set()** mutator methods for each one of the member variables."

We then spent the next few minutes agreeing on what everyone believed would be the final versions of the various Student classes (the students didn't realize they would be changing these classes again after they learned about inheritance the following week). We agreed that for every Student class we would do the following:

- Modify all the member variables to have Private access keywords
- Create **Get()** accessor and **Set()** mutator methods for the *midterm, finalExamGrade, research,* and *presentation* member variables. We agreed to incorporate validation code in the **Set()** mutator methods of each, with valid grades ranging from 0 to 100. Because these **Set()** mutator methods would be executed only by code within the Student classes themselves, we agreed to specify an access keyword of Private for these methods.

We agreed that there was no need to code a **Set()** mutator method for either the *finalNumericGrade* or the *finalLetterGrade* member variables—the Student classes would update these variables directly, which is okay because the update is not being performed by a client program. I further suggested that it would be a good idea to code a **Get()** accessor method for both the *finalNumericGrade* and *finalLetterGrade* member variables."

"I just thought of something," Rhonda said. "What about the DisplayGrade class? Are any changes required of it?"

Rhonda's question was a good one, but after a quick analysis of the DisplayGrade class, we saw that it contained no member variables of any kind. Therefore, no changes were required there. With no more questions, I then distributed the first exercise of the day to complete the modification of the EnglishStudent class.

Exercise 8-1   Modify the EnglishStudent Class

In this exercise, you'll modify the EnglishStudent class you created last week.

1. Using Notepad (if you are using Windows), locate and open the EnglishStudent.cpp source file you worked on last week. (It should be in the \CPPFiles\Grades folder.)

2. Modify your code so that it looks like this:

```
//EnglishStudent.cpp
#include <iostream>
#include <string>

using namespace std;
```

```cpp
class EnglishStudent
{
   private:
      int midterm;
      int finalExamGrade;
      int research;
      int presentation;
      float finalNumericGrade;
      char finalLetterGrade;
      float ENGLISH_FINALEXAM_PERCENTAGE;
      float ENGLISH_RESEARCH_PERCENTAGE;
      float ENGLISH_PRESENTATION_PERCENTAGE;
      float ENGLISH_MIDTERM_PERCENTAGE;

   public: EnglishStudent()
   {
      cout << "English Student's Constructor" << endl;
      midterm = 0;
      finalExamGrade = 0;
      research = 0;
      presentation = 0;
      finalNumericGrade = 0;
      ENGLISH_FINALEXAM_PERCENTAGE = .25;
      ENGLISH_RESEARCH_PERCENTAGE = .30;
      ENGLISH_PRESENTATION_PERCENTAGE = .20;
      ENGLISH_MIDTERM_PERCENTAGE = .25;
   }

   private: void SetMidterm(int temp)
   {
      if (temp < 0 || temp > 100)
      {
         cout << "Invalid Midterm Grade (" <<
            temp << ") " <<
            "Program Terminating" << endl;
         exit(1);
      }
      else
         midterm = temp;
   }

   public: int GetMidterm()
   {
```

```
      return midterm;
}

private: void SetFinalExamGrade(int temp)
{
   if (temp < 0 || temp > 100)
   {
      cout << "Invalid Final Exam Grade (" <<
         temp << ") " <<
         "Program Terminating" << endl;
      exit(1);
   }
   else
      finalExamGrade = temp;
}

public: int GetFinalExamGrade()
{
   return finalExamGrade;
}

private: void SetResearch(int temp)
{
   if (temp < 0 || temp > 100)
   {
      cout << "Invalid Research Grade (" <<
         temp << ") " <<
         "Program Terminating";
      exit(1);
   }
   else
      research = temp;
}

public: int GetResearch()
{
   return research;
}

private: void SetPresentation(int temp)
{
   if (temp < 0 || temp > 100)
   {
```

```
            cout << "Invalid Presentation Grade (" <<
                temp << ") " <<
                "Program Terminating";
            exit(1);
        }
        else
            presentation = temp;
    }

public: int GetPresentation()
{
    return presentation;
}

public: float GetFinalNumericGrade()
{
    return finalNumericGrade;
}

public: char GetFinalLetterGrade()
{
    return finalLetterGrade;
}

public: void Calculate()
{
    char response[256];
    string moreGradesToCalculate;

    cout << "Enter the Midterm Grade: " ;
    cin.getline(response,256);
    SetMidterm(atoi(response));
    cout << "Enter the Final Examination Grade: " ;
    cin.getline(response,256);
    SetFinalExamGrade(atoi(response));
    cout << "Enter the Research Grade: " ;
    cin.getline(response,256);
    SetResearch(atoi(response));
    cout << "Enter the Presentation Grade: " ;
    cin.getline(response,256);
    SetPresentation(atoi(response));
        finalNumericGrade =
            (midterm *
                ENGLISH_MIDTERM_PERCENTAGE) +
```

```
                (finalExamGrade * ENGLISH_FINALEXAM_PERCENTAGE) +
                (research * ENGLISH_RESEARCH_PERCENTAGE) +
                (presentation * ENGLISH_PRESENTATION_PERCENTAGE);
        if (finalNumericGrade >= 93)
            finalLetterGrade = 'A';
        else
        if ((finalNumericGrade >= 85) &
            (finalNumericGrade < 93))
            finalLetterGrade = 'B';
        else
        if ((finalNumericGrade >= 78) &
            (finalNumericGrade < 85))
            finalLetterGrade = 'C';
        else
        if ((finalNumericGrade >= 70) &
            (finalNumericGrade < 78))
            finalLetterGrade = 'D';
        else
        if (finalNumericGrade < 70)
            finalLetterGrade = 'F';
    }
};
```

3. Save your source file as EnglishStudent.cpp in the \CPPFiles\Grades folder (select File | Save As from Notepad's menu bar). Be sure to save your source file with the filename extension .cpp.

4. Compile your source file. Look for any compiler error messages. If you receive one, correct the problem until the compiler runs cleanly. Because your source file contains a class, once the class compiles cleanly, you will still receive an error from the linker program indicating that you don't have a **main()** function. If that's the only error you receive, don't worry. You won't be testing your modified EnglishStudent class until we have completed the work on the other classes in the project.

Discussion   "Let's take a look at what we've done in the EnglishStudent class," I said. "We made three major types of changes. First, we changed the access keywords for our member variables from public to private"

```
private:
    int midterm;
```

"Second," I continued, "we created private mutator, or **Set()** methods, for each one of the member variables. As Linda pointed out earlier, the **Set()** method is a great place to put validation code for our member variables. Here's the **Set()** method for the *midterm* member variable."

```
private: void SetMidterm(int temp)
{
   if (temp < 0 || temp > 100)
   {
      cout << "Invalid Midterm Grade (" <<
         temp << ") " <<
         "Program Terminating" << endl;
      exit(1);
   }
   else
      midterm = temp;
}
```

"Notice that within the **Set()** method," I said, "we are accepting a midterm grade from the user and validating it to ensure that it's a value between 1 and 100. If it is, we then assign the value to the private member variable *midterm*. If it's not, we display a message to the C++ console and end the program."

"Tell me again why these are private methods." Blaine said.

"By making the **Set()** methods private," I said, "we prevent our client program from updating the member variables, even via the **Set()** method. Only code within the English class itself will be able to execute the various **Set()** methods, and they will be triggered only after the user is prompted for their appropriate values."

I waited for questions, but everyone seemed fine.

"Finally," I said, "we created accessor, or **Get()** methods, for each one of the member variables. In comparison to the **Set()** methods, these are relatively simple. Here's the **Get()** method for the *midterm* member variable."

```
public: int GetMidterm()
{
   return midterm;
}
```

"We won't be able to see the **Get()** and **Set()** methods in action until we modify the Grades class to use them," I said.

"I noticed we also made a change to the **Calculate()** method," Dave said.

"Thanks Dave," I said. "I almost forgot about that. Because we are now updating the value of the EnglishStudent member variables by executing the various **Set()** methods, the **Calculate()** method has changed slightly. Here's the code that prompts the user to enter the midterm grade."

```
cout << "Enter the Midterm Grade: " ;
cin.getline(response,256);
SetMidterm(atoi(response));
```

Notice how we use the return value of the **atoi()** function as an argument to the **SetMidterm()** function."

There were no questions on the modifications we had made to the EnglishStudent class, so we moved on to the next exercise.

| Exercise 8-2 | **Modify the MathStudent Class** |

In this exercise, you'll modify the MathStudent class you created last week.

1. Using Notepad (if you are using Windows), locate and open the MathStudent.cpp source file you worked on last week. (It should be in the \CPPFiles\Grades folder.)

2. Modify your code so that it looks like this:

```
//MathStudent.cpp
#include <iostream>
#include <string>

using namespace std;

class MathStudent
{
    private:
       int midterm;
       int finalExamGrade;
       float finalNumericGrade;
       char finalLetterGrade;
       float MATH_MIDTERM_PERCENTAGE;
       float MATH_FINALEXAM_PERCENTAGE;

    public: MathStudent()
    {
      cout << "Math Student's Constructor" << endl;
      midterm = 0;
      finalExamGrade = 0;
      finalNumericGrade = 0;
      MATH_MIDTERM_PERCENTAGE = .50;
      MATH_FINALEXAM_PERCENTAGE = .50;
    }
```

```
public: void Calculate()
{
 char response[256];
 string moreGradesToCalculate;

 cout << "Enter the Midterm Grade: " ;
 cin.getline(response,256);
 SetMidterm(atoi(response));
 cout << "Enter the Final Examination Grade: " ;
 cin.getline(response,256);
 SetFinalExamGrade(atoi(response));
 finalNumericGrade =
     (midterm * MATH_MIDTERM_PERCENTAGE) +
     (finalExamGrade * MATH_FINALEXAM_PERCENTAGE);
 if (finalNumericGrade >= 90)
    finalLetterGrade = 'A';
 else
 if ((finalNumericGrade >= 83) &
     (finalNumericGrade < 90))
    finalLetterGrade = 'B';
 else
 if ((finalNumericGrade >= 76) &
     (finalNumericGrade < 83))
    finalLetterGrade = 'C';
 else
 if ((finalNumericGrade >= 65) &
     (finalNumericGrade < 76))
    finalLetterGrade = 'D';
 else
 if (finalNumericGrade < 65)
    finalLetterGrade = 'F';
}
   private: void SetMidterm(int temp)
   {
      if (temp < 0 || temp > 100)
      {
         cout << "Invalid Midterm Grade (" <<
            temp << ") " <<
            "Program Terminating" << endl;
         exit(1);
      }
      else
```

```
            midterm = temp;
      }

      public: int GetMidterm()
      {
         return midterm;
      }

      private: void SetFinalExamGrade(int temp)
      {
         if (temp < 0 || temp > 100)
         {
            cout << "Invalid Final Exam Grade (" <<
               temp << ") " <<
               "Program Terminating" << endl;
            exit(1);
         }
         else
            finalExamGrade = temp;
      }

      public: int GetFinalExamGrade()
      {
         return finalExamGrade;
      }

      public: float GetFinalNumericGrade()
      {
         return finalNumericGrade;
      }

      public: char GetFinalLetterGrade()
      {
         return finalLetterGrade;
      }

   };               // end of class
```

3. Save your source file as MathStudent.cpp in the \CPPFiles\Grades folder
   (select File | Save As from Notepad's menu bar). Be sure to save your
   source file with the filename extension .cpp.

4. Compile your source file. Look for any compiler error messages. If you
   receive one, correct the problem until the compiler runs cleanly. Because
   your source file contains a class, once the class compiles cleanly, you will still

receive an error from the linker program indicating that you don't have a **main()** function. If that's the only error you receive, don't worry. You won't be testing your modified MathStudent class until we have completed the work on the other classes in the project.

Again, there were no major problems completing the exercise—the changes we made to the MathStudent class were nearly identical to those we made in the EnglishStudent class. Rhonda did attempt to add a **Get()** and **Set()** method for both the *presentation* and *research* member variables, which the math student does not possess. But she quickly realized her mistake, and we then moved on to updating the ScienceStudent class.

Modify the ScienceStudent Class

In this exercise, you'll modify the ScienceStudent class you created last week.

1. Using Notepad (if you are using Windows), locate and open the ScienceStudent.cpp source file you worked on last week. (It should be in the \CPPFiles\Grades folder.)

2. Modify your code so that it looks like this:

```cpp
//ScienceStudent.cpp
#include <iostream>
#include <string>

using namespace std;


class ScienceStudent
{
  private:
    int midterm;
    int finalExamGrade;
    int research;
    float finalNumericGrade;
    char finalLetterGrade;
    float SCIENCE_MIDTERM_PERCENTAGE;
    float SCIENCE_FINALEXAM_PERCENTAGE;
    float SCIENCE_RESEARCH_PERCENTAGE;

  public: ScienceStudent()
  {
    cout << "Science Student's Constructor" << endl;
    midterm = 0;
    finalExamGrade = 0;
```

```
     research = 0;
     finalNumericGrade = 0;
     SCIENCE_MIDTERM_PERCENTAGE = .40;
     SCIENCE_FINALEXAM_PERCENTAGE = .40;
     SCIENCE_RESEARCH_PERCENTAGE = .20;
   }

public: void Calculate()
{
 char response[256];
 string moreGradesToCalculate;

 cout << "Enter the Midterm Grade: " ;
 cin.getline(response,256);
 SetMidterm(atoi(response));
 cout << "Enter the Final Examination Grade: " ;
 cin.getline(response,256);
 SetFinalExamGrade(atoi(response));
 cout << "Enter the Research Grade: " ;
 cin.getline(response,256);
 SetResearch(atoi(response));
 finalNumericGrade =
    (midterm * SCIENCE_MIDTERM_PERCENTAGE) +
    (finalExamGrade *
        SCIENCE_FINALEXAM_PERCENTAGE) +
    (research * SCIENCE_RESEARCH_PERCENTAGE);
 if (finalNumericGrade >= 90)
              finalLetterGrade = 'A';
 else
 if ((finalNumericGrade >= 80) &
     (finalNumericGrade < 90))
    finalLetterGrade = 'B';
 else
 if ((finalNumericGrade >= 70) &
     (finalNumericGrade < 80))
    finalLetterGrade = 'C';
 else
 if ((finalNumericGrade >= 60) &
     (finalNumericGrade < 70))
    finalLetterGrade = 'D';
 else
 if (finalNumericGrade < 60)
    finalLetterGrade = 'F';
}
```

```cpp
private: void SetMidterm(int temp)
{
   if (temp < 0 || temp > 100)
   {
      cout << "Invalid Midterm Grade (" <<
         temp << ") " <<
         "Program Terminating" << endl;
      exit(1);
   }
   else
      midterm = temp;
}

public: int GetMidterm()
{
   return midterm;
}

private: void SetFinalExamGrade(int temp)
{
   if (temp < 0 || temp > 100)
   {
      cout << "Invalid Final Exam Grade (" <<
         temp << ") " <<
         "Program Terminating" << endl;
      exit(1);
   }
   else
      finalExamGrade = temp;
}

public: int GetFinalExamGrade()
{
   return finalExamGrade;
}

private: void SetResearch(int temp)
{
   if (temp < 0 || temp > 100)
   {
      cout << "Invalid Research Grade (" <<
         temp << ") " <<
```

```
                    "Program Terminating";
                exit(1);
            }
            else
                research = temp;
        }

        public: int GetResearch()
        {
            return research;
        }

        public: float GetFinalNumericGrade()
        {
            return finalNumericGrade;
        }

        public: char GetFinalLetterGrade()
        {
            return finalLetterGrade;
        }

    };
```

3. Save your source file as ScienceStudent.cpp in the \CPPFiles\Grades folder (select File | Save As from Notepad's menu bar). Be sure to save your source file with the filename extension .cpp.

4. Compile your source file. Look for any compiler error messages. If you receive one, correct the problem until the compiler runs cleanly. Because your source file contains a class, once the class compiles cleanly, you will still receive an error from the linker program indicating that you don't have a **main()** function. If that's the only error you receive, don't worry. You won't be testing your modified ScienceStudent class until we have completed the work on the other classes in the project.

Discussion

"I know you told us that we would need to make changes to the Grades class in order to see the impact of the changes we just made," Barbara said. "What kinds of changes will we need to make to the Grades class?"

"All we really need to do," I said, "is find any code that directly references a member variable of any of the Student classes, and then modify the code to use the newly created **Get()** methods instead. In the case of the Grades class, there are currently references to private member variables that are passed as arguments to the DisplayStudent object's constructor method. We'll need to reference the **Get()** methods of those member variables instead."

I then distributed this exercise for the class to complete.

Modify the Grades Class

In this exercise, you'll modify the Grades class to include **Get()** and **Set()** methods.

1. Using Notepad (if you are using Windows), locate and open the Grades.cpp source file you worked on last week. (It should be in the \CPPFiles\ Grades folder.)

2. Modify your code so that it looks like this (changed code appears in bold):

```cpp
//Grades.cpp

#include <iostream>
#include <string>
#include "EnglishStudent.cpp"
#include "MathStudent.cpp"
#include "ScienceStudent.cpp"
#include "DisplayGrade.cpp"

using namespace std;

int WhatKindOfStudent();
char response[256];
string moreGradesToCalculate;

int main ()
{
   int lresponse;

   cout << "Do you want to calculate a grade? ";
   cin >> moreGradesToCalculate;

   for (int i = 0;
      i < moreGradesToCalculate.length(); i++) {
      moreGradesToCalculate[i] =
         toupper (moreGradesToCalculate[i]);
   }

   while (moreGradesToCalculate == "YES") {
      lresponse = WhatKindOfStudent();

      switch(lresponse)
      {
```

```
        case 1:
          {
          EnglishStudent eStudent;
          eStudent.Calculate();
          DisplayGrade x(eStudent.GetMidterm(),
                         eStudent.GetFinalExamGrade(),
                         eStudent.GetResearch(),
                         eStudent.GetPresentation(),
                         eStudent.GetFinalNumericGrade()
                         eStudent.GetFinalLetterGrade());
          }
          break;
        case 2:
          {
          MathStudent mStudent;
          mStudent.Calculate();
          DisplayGrade y(mStudent.GetMidterm(),
                         mStudent.GetFinalExamGrade(),
                         mStudent.GetFinalNumericGrade(),
                         mStudent.GetFinalLetterGrade());
          }
          break;
        case 3:
          {
          ScienceStudent sStudent;
          sStudent.Calculate();
          DisplayGrade z(sStudent.GetMidterm(),
                         sStudent.GetFinalExamGrade(),
                         sStudent.GetResearch(),
                         sStudent.GetFinalNumericGrade(),
                         sStudent.GetFinalLetterGrade());
          }
          break;
      }        // end of switch

  cout << endl<< endl <<
      "Do you have another grade to calculate? ";
  cin >> moreGradesToCalculate;
  for (int i = 0;
     i < moreGradesToCalculate.length(); i++) {
     moreGradesToCalculate[i] =
```

```
            toupper (moreGradesToCalculate[i]);
    }                                  // end of for
    }                      // end of while
    cout <<
        "Thanks for using the Grades Calculation program!";
    return 0;
}


int WhatKindOfStudent()
{
    cout << "Enter student type " <<
        "(1=English, 2=Math, 3=Science): ";

    cin.getline(response,256);

    if (strlen(response) == 0) {
        cout << "You must select a Student Type";
        exit(1);
    }

    if ((atoi(response) < 1) || (atoi(response) > 3)) {
        cout << response <<
            " - is not a valid student type";
        exit(1);
    }

    return atoi(response);
}
```

3. Save your source file as Grades.cpp in the \CPPFiles\Grades folder (select File | Save As from Notepad's menu bar). Be sure to save your source file with the filename extension .cpp.

4. Compile your source file into an executable file.

5. Execute your program and test it thoroughly. Verify that the looping behavior of the program is working correctly. After you start up your program, it should ask whether you have a grade to calculate.

6. Answer **Yes** and calculate the grade for an English student. Enter **70** for the midterm, **80** for the final examination, **90** for the research grade, and **100** for the presentation. A final numeric grade of 84.5 should be displayed with a letter grade of C.

7. After a message is displayed with the calculated grade, the program should ask whether you have more grades to calculate.

8. Answer **Yes** and calculate the grade for a math student. Enter **70** for the midterm and **80** for the final examination. A final numeric grade of 75 should be displayed with a letter grade of D.

9. After a message is displayed with the calculated grade, the program should ask whether you have more grades to calculate.

10. Answer **Yes** and calculate the grade for a science student. Enter **70** for the midterm, **80** for the final examination, and **90** for the research grade. A final numeric grade of 78 should be displayed with a letter grade of C. After the message is displayed with the calculated grade, the program should ask whether you have more grades to calculate.

11. Answer **No**. You should be thanked for using the program, and the program should end.

12. Now execute the program again and verify that the code in the **Set()** methods of the Student classes is properly handling invalid entries for the midterm, final exam, research, and presentation grades. This will take several iterations of the program, because each time you enter an invalid grade, the program will display a message and end.

Discussion   I gave everyone in the class a chance to make their changes to the Grades class—and to experiment with their own versions of the Grades program. All in all, this took about half an hour. Some students discovered, while compiling the Grades.cpp program, that they still had 'errors' in some of the various Student classes.

"Did everyone notice the changes we made to the program?" I asked.

"I did," Blaine said. "We modified the sections of code that created instances of the DisplayGrade class. Previously, we directly referenced member variables of each of the Student classes in the constructor method of the DisplayGrade class. Now we've made those member variables private and we're executing the various **Get()** methods of the Student classes instead."

"Excellent, Blaine," I said. "Here's the modified code that is executed to display the grade for an English student."

```
DisplayGrade x(eStudent.GetMidterm(),
               eStudent.GetFinalExamGrade(),
               eStudent.GetResearch(),
               eStudent.GetPresentation(),
               eStudent.GetFinalNumericGrade(),
               eStudent.GetFinalLetterGrade());
```

"In a similar way," I continued, "we execute the accessor methods for the math and science students as well."

I waited to see if anyone had any questions, but there were none.

A Surprise Visit from Frank Olley

Just then, I heard a voice call from outside my classroom door. Unknown to the students in the class, Frank Olley had been outside and had just witnessed the execution of the Grade Calculation Project from the hallway. I had phoned Frank during the break to confirm some aspects of the validation of the component grades (I wanted to be sure that valid grades ranged from 0 to 100), and when I found out he was on campus, I invited him down for a demo.

"I've got to tell you," Frank said, "I'm most impressed with the progress you've made with the program in such a short time. In fact, I like it so much, I'd like nothing better than for you to install it on my PC today—but John tells me you still have some work to do on it."

I could see that the students in the class were just about to burst with pride.

Frank then spent some time admiring the work of the individual students. About 10 minutes later, I dismissed class for the day.

Summary

This chapter dealt with a topic that is extremely important in the world of C++: protecting the data in your objects from accidental or willful manipulation that can cause unauthorized changes, or even cause the state of your objects to become invalid.

You learned that the primary way to protect your data is to declare your member variables with the Private access keyword, which allows only code within the class itself to view or update the variables. Having done that, if you want client programs (those creating instances of your object) to be able to see or update these member variables, you need to write accessor and mutator methods.

Accessor, or **Get**(), methods enable a client program to see the values of your member variables. Mutator, or **Set**(), methods enable a client program to update the values of your member variables.

Chapter

9

Inheritance

n the last two chapters, you learned how to create instantiable classes that permit client programs (other classes) to create objects from them. You saw that a C++ programmer does more than just write code; a C++ programmer is also a class architect who designs classes that can be used by other programmers. This is an illustration of the software reusability of C++: One class and the object it represents can be used in thousands of other programs.

In this chapter, you'll learn how a C++ programmer can design a class that can then be used as the basis for other new classes, which will once again illustrate how an object-oriented programming language can help you avoid reinventing the wheel. This feature of object-oriented programming languages is called *inheritance*, and it can be an enormous timesaver when creating classes in the programs you write.

Inheritance

"Today's topic is inheritance," I said, as I began our ninth class. "In object-oriented programming languages, inheritance means that a new class can be coded based on (or derived from) an already existing class. The new class is called the *derived class*, and the already existing class is called the *base class*. Deriving one class from an already existing class can be an enormous timesaver for programmers, especially if the base class already has features—member variables and methods— that the derived class can use."

"Sounds complicated," Rhonda said.

"Inheritance, as a concept, isn't unique to object-oriented programming," I said. "I have a friend who is a structural engineer who designs bathroom shower doors. I didn't know this until it came up in conversation, but there are many different styles and types of bathroom shower doors and, as in the fashion industry, each year hundreds of new styles are introduced. My friend is constantly designing new shower doors, and much to my surprise, I learned recently that structural engineers use something similar to class inheritance in their own work."

"How does an engineer implement the type of inheritance you're talking about with C++?" Barbara asked. "Does an engineer work with classes?"

"Not quite," I said, "but an engineer does work with blueprints. Blueprints, as I think I mentioned in our first class meeting, are to an architect or engineer what classes are to a C++ programmer. A blueprint is the model for something that is built, just like a class is a blueprint for an object. Ultimately, both blueprints and classes are nothing more than designs. My friend the structural engineer turns her completed blueprints over to a manufacturing facility that produces the actual shower doors. As C++ programmers, we turn our classes over to other programmers who then create objects from them."

"I'm okay with your analogy about blueprints and classes," Kate said, "but where does this notion of inheritance come into play with your friend the structural engineer?"

"I'm getting to that," I said, smiling. "Just last week I was talking to my friend the engineer, and I commented how frustrating it must be to have to design a shower door from scratch every year to produce a new door with a different style or with slightly different features. That's when she told me that she doesn't design every shower door from scratch. The blueprints for her previous years' designs are stored on the hard drive of her personal computer, and she can derive the design for a new shower door based on a previous model."

"In other words," Dave said, "she's not reinventing the wheel."

"That's right, Dave," I said. "The basic features of last year's door very likely will be identical to the basic features of this year's door, with some stylistic differences. Perhaps it may be the color of the chrome on the door that is different or the style of the glass or even the location of the door handles. However, the shape and thickness of the supporting steel structure may be identical, the dimensions of the door, as well as the size and location of the glass may be identical—my point is that there are a lot more similarities than there are differences."

"I see where you're coming from," Steve said. "By starting her design of a new shower door with the blueprints from a previous one, she saves herself a whole bunch of work. But I don't quite see how this will work in C++. Are you saying that if one class is similar to another, we can copy and paste the code from that first class into Notepad as a starting point for the new class?"

"That's not quite it, Steve," I said, "although we could certainly do that—copy and paste, I mean. But copying and pasting doesn't quite give us the software reusability that I'm talking about. Instead of copying and pasting code from one class to another, we can tell C++ that the class we're coding is derived from another class—that is, the new class should be considered to have variables and methods found in another class—without having to explicitly code those variables and methods in the class itself. We can then add attributes and methods to the derived class to provide it with its own unique features."

"So are you saying," Valerie asked, "that if an existing class already has most of the functionality you need in your new class, you can derive or 'inherit' variables and methods from that existing class and then add some functionality of its own to the new class?"

"That's exactly right, Valerie," I said. "Technically, the existing class is called the *base* class, and the class that is inherited from it is called the *derived* class. Think of the base class as a parent of the child derived class. At the risk of oversimplifying this, all that's really required is that we tell C++ that our derived class wishes to inherit from the base class to derive the functionality (variables and methods) from it. But you'll see that in just a few minutes."

"From the way you're describing it," Dave said, "I bet that inheritance would have made the work of creating the three Student classes in the Grade Calculation Project a little easier."

"How so?" Rhonda asked, directing her attention to Dave.

"Well," Dave said, "if you think about it, all three Student classes—EnglishStudent, MathStudent, and ScienceStudent—have a lot in common in terms of member variables and methods. In fact, some of their code is even duplicated. I would think that being able to derive one class from another would have come in very handy there."

"Dave's absolutely right about the Student classes," I said. "In fact, we'll be modifying these classes later on to incorporate the concepts of inheritance that you'll learn today."

"I wish we had learned about inheritance last week," Chuck said. "Coding those classes has been a real pain in the neck for me. Why did we wait until now to discuss inheritance?"

"We first needed to learn how to create classes and protect their data before we could start to learn about inheritance," I said.

"Inheritance sounds like something I can really use back at work," Ward said. "It seems like I'm forever reinventing the wheel there—I can't wait to get started. Can you show us an example of inheritance in C++?"

Before Inheritance Came Along...

"Sure thing, Ward," I said. "Let me demonstrate inheritance by first creating an ordinary C++ class, and then we'll derive other classes from it."

I thought for a moment before continuing.

"Let's pretend that after completing this introductory C++ course, you're hired by a small consulting firm as a C++ programmer. In your first week on the job, you are asked to write what appears to be a simple program to calculate the payroll for a relatively large plumbing company in the area. Having learned about the benefits of the Systems Development Life Cycle in this class, you then spend some time working with the client in determining the requirements for the payroll system. During the Analysis phase of the SDLC, it becomes obvious to you that you should create a C++ class called Employee to model the company's employees. You decide that the Employee class will have the following five attributes, implemented as member variables."

I then displayed these variables on the classroom projector:

- empID
- name
- hourlyRate
- hoursWorked
- grossPay

"You also decide to implement a **Display**() method to output the employee's gross pay to the C++ console (to keep things simple for our demonstration, that's the only value we'll calculate). Within the **Display**() method, you include a calculation of grossPay equal to the multiplication of hourlyRate by hoursWorked."

"Sounds simple enough," Rhonda said, smiling. "I bet I could code that up in no time."

I was tempted to take Rhonda up on her offer, but since I had already coded up the Employee class myself prior to class, I displayed the code for this class on the classroom projector:

```cpp
//Employee.cpp
#include <iostream>
#include <string>

using namespace std;

class Employee
{
  private:
    string empID;
    string name;
    float hourlyRate;
    int hoursWorked;
    float grossPay;


  public: Employee()      //Constructor Method
  {
     cout << "Employee's Constructor" << endl;
  }

  public: void Display()
  {
     cout << "*** EMPLOYEE RECORD ***" << endl << endl;
     cout << "Employee ID: " << empID << endl;
     cout << "Name: " << name << endl;
     cout << "Hourly Rate: $" << hourlyRate << endl;
     cout << "Hours Worked: " << hoursWorked << endl;
     cout << "Gross Pay: $" << GetGrossPay() << endl;
  }
```

```
public: void SetEmpID(string temp)
{
    empID = temp;
}

public: string GetEmpID()
{
    return empID;
}

public: void SetName(string temp)
{
    name = temp;
}

public: string GetName()
{
    return name;
}

public: void SetHourlyRate(float temp)
{
    hourlyRate = temp;
}

public: float GetHourlyRate()
{
    return hourlyRate;
}

public: void SetHoursWorked(int temp)
{
    hoursWorked = temp;
}

public: int GetHoursWorked()
{
    return hoursWorked;
}

public: float GetGrossPay()
```

```
   {
      grossPay = hourlyRate * hoursWorked;
      return grossPay;
   }

};                          //end of class
```

"I don't think there's anything in this Employee class that you haven't seen before," I said. "We have the five attributes of the Employee class, each implemented as private member variables. Also, based on what you learned last week, we've created **Get**() and **Set**() methods for four of the five attributes—empID, name, hourlyRate, and hoursWorked. We don't want any client programs using our Employee object to be able to directly update the grossPay attribute, so we have created a **Get**() method for it called **GetGrossPay**(), but no **Set**() method. Notice that the **GetGrossPay**() method does the work of calculating the employee's gross pay. Finally, we also have the public **Calculate**() method, which outputs the employee's information to the C++ console. To keep things simple, we have no validation in this class. Obviously, in something other than a demo like this, we would have plenty of validation code."

"I noticed that we created a constructor method," Kate said. "Is that really necessary here? Isn't this class going to be used as a base class for other classes? Is a constructor required?"

"Good question, Kate," I said. "A constructor isn't required, but I thought it would be a good idea to code one here. When we create an object from a class derived from this base class, we'll be able to see when the constructor of the base class is executed—I think you'll find that pretty fascinating when you see it in action."

"I'm a little confused with a line of code in the **Display**() method," Rhonda said. "What's going on with that line of code to display the gross pay?"

"This can be a little confusing," I said. "Here we're using the return value of the accessor method **GetGrossPay**() as an argument to the **cout** object."

```
cout << "Gross Pay: " << GetGrossPay() << endl;
```

"Okay," Rhonda answered, "I think I remember you doing that before."

I waited to see if there were any more questions before continuing. There were none.

"Remember," I said, "all we've done so far is create a simple class—we haven't done any inheritance yet. Now let's write code in a client program that will create an instance of an Employee object and calculate the gross pay for that employee."

I then displayed this code on the classroom projector:

```
//Example9_1.cpp

#include "Employee.cpp"
```

```
int main()
{
    Employee x;
    x.SetEmpID("086");
    x.SetName("John Smith");
    x.SetHourlyRate(12.50);
    x.SetHoursWorked(40);
    x.Display();

    return 0;
}
```

"Nothing too fancy here," I said. "All we're doing is creating an instance of an Employee object."

```
Employee x;
```

"We then use its mutator, or **Set**(), methods to assign values to its attributes (member variables). Notice that we indicate that the pay rate for this employee is $12.50 per hour and that his total number of hours worked is 40."

```
x.SetEmpID("086");
x.SetName("John Smith");
x.SetHourlyRate(12.50);
x.SetHoursWorked(40);
```

"Then we execute the **Display**() method."

```
x.Display();
```

I saved this program as Example9_1.cpp and then compiled and executed it. The following screenshot was displayed on the classroom projector:

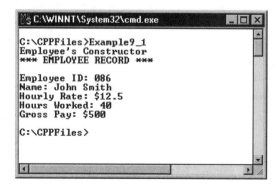

"Nothing surprising here," I said. "We created an instance of the Employee object, updated the empID, name, hourlyRate, and hoursWorked attributes via the mutator methods of the class, and then executed the **Display**() method of the class to display the employee's pay information to the C++ console, complete with the calculated gross pay of $500. Notice that a message was also displayed in the C++ console to let us know that the constructor method of the Employee class was executed."

"How did the grossPay attribute of the Employee class get updated?" Rhonda asked.

"That was done as part of the **Display**() method," I said. "The **Display**() method concatenated the return value of the **GetGrossPay**() accessor method of the Employee class to the string 'Gross Pay:'."

```
cout << "Gross Pay: $" << GetGrossPay() << endl;
```

"The **GetGrossPay**() accessor method is where the grossPay attribute was updated when the actual calculation was performed."

```
public: float GetGrossPay()
{
    grossPay = hourlyRate * hoursWorked;
    return grossPay;
}
```

"Okay, that makes sense," Rhonda said.

"I understand what we just did," Chuck said, "but how does this relate to inheritance?"

Creating Classes from Other Classes Using Inheritance

"It doesn't, yet," I said, "That will be our next step. Before I show you how to implement inheritance in your program, I need to clue you in a little bit about real-world programming, but I don't think you'll be at all surprised about what I have to tell you. In the real-world of C++ programming, there are two ways that inheritance comes into play. First, you meticulously plan it. That is, right from the start you design a class, known as a base class, possessing the most basic common functionality—attributes and methods—from which you will derive other classes. For a number of reasons, this structured approach to building base classes and derived classes—like the structured approach of the Systems Development Life Cycle—is ideal."

"I can see why this structured approach is the way to go," Kate said. "An organized approach is always best. But what's the other way in which inheritance comes about—you said there were two."

"The second approach is what I call the evolutionary approach to inheritance," I replied. "What happens is that one day you have the need to create a class to model a real-world object, and you realize that you already have a class that is very close to what you need—but not quite. I should tell you that real-world C++ classes may have hundreds of attributes and methods—so you see, the last thing you want to do is to 'start from scratch' by creating a new class."

"So in this case," Steve said, "you would borrow the functionality of the existing class by deriving the new class from it."

"Exactly, Steve," I said. "If you—or another programmer—already have a class that is 'close enough' in functionality to the class you need to create, you can save yourself a bunch of work by deriving the new class from it. This process isn't nearly as efficient as planning a base class and later deriving classes from it, but in the real world, that's not always possible."

"I'm not sure I'm fully understanding this." Blaine said.

"Let's try it this way, Blaine," I said. "Suppose that two months after we create the Employee class we just coded, the plumbing company asks us to modify the program to calculate payroll for biweekly salaried employees as well as hourly ones."

"I sense a problem here," Ward said. "The calculation for an hourly employee is nothing like that of a salaried employee."

"That's right, Ward," I agreed. "Salaried employees draw a straight salary, regardless of the number of hours they work. The hoursWorked and hourlyRate attributes of the Employee class have no meaning for a salaried employee."

"Will we be able to use the Employee class for the salaried employee calculation," Rhonda asked, "or will we need to create a Salaried class to do the job?"

"Without inheritance, Rhonda," I said, "that's exactly what we would need to do—create a new class entirely from scratch. But using inheritance, we can 'borrow' the functionality of the Employee class. It's not a perfect fit. After all, remember that the existing Employee class contains two attributes—hourlyRate and hoursWorked—that don't make any sense for a salaried employee. However, the remaining three attributes—empID, name, and grossPay—are fine for the salaried employee."

"We will also need to add a new attribute to the derived class to represent the salaried employee's annual salary," Dave said. "The calculation of the gross pay for a salaried employee is different from that of an hourly employee, which means that the **GetGrossPay()** accessor method of the derived class will have to be different. Because the employee is paid every other week, the pay will be equal to the annual salary divided by 26."

"That was really an excellent analysis, Dave," I said. "It really illustrates why inheritance can be useful in our programming. The Employee class probably has 20 to 30 lines of code, and a new Salaried class would probably have a similar number of lines of code—much of it duplicating that found in the Employee class. Why bother writing that code from scratch—and therefore reinventing the wheel—if we already have a class that is very close to what we need. For that reason, we'll create a derived class called SalariedEmployee and base it on the Employee class."

"I'd like to get back to something Dave mentioned," Barbara said. "He said that the **GetGrossPay**() method in the derived class will need to be different from the one in the base class. Does that mean we can have a method in the derived class with the same name as one in the base class? Isn't that an overloaded method?"

"You make a good point, Barbara," I said. "What I'm describing is very similar to an overloaded method in which two identically named methods, but with different signatures, appear in the same class. In this case, we have identically named methods with identical signatures—one appearing in the base class and the other in the derived class. The method in the derived class 'overrides' the identically named method in the base class. What this means is that if a client program creates an object from the derived class, the code in the method of the derived class will be executed, not the code in the method of the base class. However, a client program could always choose to use the base class in its program, in which case the code in the method of the base class will execute."

The Base (Parent) Class

"Will the Employee class become a base class then?" Mary asked. "If so, what will we need to change in the Employee class?"

"That's an excellent question, Mary," I said. "The beauty of inheritance is that nothing needs to be done to a class in order for it to be used as a base class. We can design the class to facilitate inheritance, ensuring that certain features—attributes and methods—are present. However, the only thing that makes a class a base class is the fact that other classes—derived classes—choose to be derived from it."

The Derived (Child) Class

"How does C++ know that a derived class wishes to be derived from a base class?" Chuck asked.

"That's done by following the name of the class with a colon," I said, "followed by the name of the class that is to be used as the base class. In addition, it's necessary to add an include compiler directive for the base class. Let me show how we do this by creating the SalariedEmployee derived class, using the Employee class as a base class."

NOTE
In C++, it's possible to derive a class from more than one base class. This is called multiple inheritance. To invoke multiple inheritance, separate the name of each base class with a comma.

I then displayed this code on the classroom projector:

```
//SalariedEmployee.cpp

#include <iostream>
```

```cpp
#include <string>
#include "EmployeeBase.cpp"

using namespace std;

class SalariedEmployee : public EmployeeBase
{
  private:
    float annualSalary;


  public: SalariedEmployee()      //Constructor Method
  {
     cout << "Salaried Employee's Constructor" << endl;
  }

  public: void SetAnnualSalary(float temp)
  {
     annualSalary = temp;
  }

  public: float GetAnnualSalary()
  {
     return annualSalary;
  }

   public: float GetGrossPay()
  {
     grossPay = annualSalary / 26;
     return grossPay;
  }

  public: void Display()
  {
      cout << endl<< "*** SALARIED EMPLOYEE RECORD ***" << endl << endl;
      cout << "Employee ID: " << empID << endl;
      cout << "Name: " << name << endl;
      cout << "Annual Salary: $" << annualSalary << endl;
      cout << "Gross Pay: $" << GetGrossPay() << endl;
  }

};                              //end of class
```

"Aren't we missing some attributes?" Rhonda asked. "I don't see empID or name—yet we're referring to them in the **Display()** method."

"That's the point, Rhonda," I said. "By deriving SalariedEmployee from the already existing Employee class, we don't need to define those attributes here in this class. Notice how we include a reference to the base class using the include compiler directive."

```
#include "EmployeeBase.cpp"
```

"Then we tell C++ that we're using the Employee class as the starting point for SalariedEmployee. The keyword Public, followed by the name of our base class, tells C++ to use the Employee class as the starting point for SalariedEmployee."

```
class SalariedEmployee : Public Employee
```

 NOTE
Failure to include the keyword Public will cause your derived class not to be able to "see" public methods of the base class. Always be sure to include it.

"Every variable and method that Employee has is automatically made a part of the SalariedEmployee derived class. In other words, the derived class derives the member variables and methods of its base class. This means that, without any coding, the SalariedEmployee derived class automatically possesses the five member variables of the Employee class, as well as its 11 methods."

"So are you saying that all we need to code in the derived class are any new member variables and methods?" Dave asked.

"That's basically correct, Dave," I said, "but let's take it a step further. When it comes to deriving a new class from a base class, there are four things you can choose to 'do' with the existing member variables and methods of the base class parent.

"First, you can accept the member variable or method 'as is' because it fits the needs of the derived class. For example, the member variable empID and its accessor method getEmpID of the base class Employee are also necessary in the derived class SalariedEmployee. Accepting a member variable or method requires absolutely no action on the part of the programmer—these are automatically included when you 'inherit' from the base class.

"Second, you can ignore the member variable or method derived from the base class because it is not required in the derived class. Ignoring the member variable or method again requires no extra 'effort' on the part of the programmer. For example, in the derived class SalariedEmployee, we have no need for either the member variable hourlyRate or its accessor method getHourlyRate. We 'ignore' them simply by not using them anywhere in the derived class or client programs using the derived class.

"Third, you can add new member variables or methods to the derived class. Member variables and methods are added to the derived class to give it the unique behavior that differentiates it from the base class. In the case of SalariedEmployee, we added one new member variable, annualSalary, which is required by the derived class because it needs an annual salary to properly calculate a biweekly gross pay for a salaried employee.

"Fourth, you can override the derived member variables or methods in the derived class, in effect 'hiding' the definition of these member variables or methods in the base class. For instance, both the base class Employee and the derived class SalariedEmployee need to possess a **GetGrossPay()** method and a **Display()** method, but the code for these methods in the two classes needs to be different. To override a member variable or method, place the definition in the derived class, and the derived member variable or method of the base class will be overridden."

"So in short," Kate said, "we can accept, ignore, add, or override member variables or methods derived from the base class."

"That's perfect, Kate," I said, "Here's a table detailing the actions we took with the member variables and methods of the Employee base class in the derived SalariedEmployee class."

Employee Base Class	SalariedEmployee Derived Class Action
empID	Accepted
name	Accepted
hourlyRate	Ignored
hoursWorked	Ignored
	annualSalary added to derived class
Employee()	Accepted
SetEmpID()	Accepted
GetEmpID()	Accepted
SetName()	Accepted
GetName()	Accepted
SetHourlyRate()	Ignored
GetHourlyRate()	Ignored
SetHoursWorked()	Ignored
SetHoursWorked()	Ignored
GetGrossPay()	Overridden
Display()	Overridden
	SetAnnualSalary() added to derived class
	GetAnnualSalary() added to derived class

"As you can see," I said, "in the derived class SalariedEmployee, we accepted two member variables (empID and name) and five methods (Employee, SetEmpID, GetEmpID, SetName, and GetName) of the base class Employee. We ignored two member variables (hourlyRate and hoursWorked) and four methods (SetHourlyRate, GetHourlyRate, SetHoursWorked, and GetHoursWorked) of the base class Employee. All these pertained to an hourly employee, and we had no need for these in our derived class. It's important to note that even though we are ignoring these member variables and methods in our derived class, they're still part of the derived class, and a client program could still use them. Finally, we 'hide' two methods in the base class—**GetGrossPay**() and **Display**()—by writing new code, unique to the derived class SalariedEmployee."

"I see we also added one member variable (annualSalary) and two methods (SetAnnualSalary and GetAnnualSalary) to the derived class that don't exist in the base class," Mary said.

"That's right, Mary," I answered. "annualSalary is a member variable we need to store the employee's annual salary, and **SetAnnualSalary**() and **GetAnnualSalary**() are its mutator and accessor methods. We also use annualSalary in the **GetGrossPay**() and **Display**() methods we overrode."

"Do we compile a derived class the same way we compile any other class?" Blaine asked after a few seconds of silence.

"Yes, Blaine," I said, "that's right. We compile a derived class the same way we compile any other class—of course, the base class must be included in the derived class via an include statement."

I then compiled the SalariedEmployee derived class—but with less-than-satisfactory results. The following screenshot was displayed:

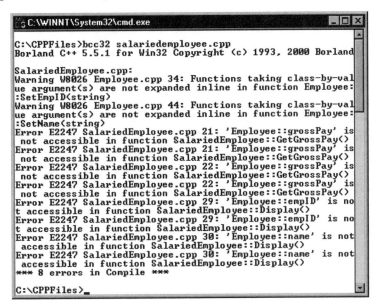

"Uh-oh," I heard Rhonda say, "what happened? The SalariedEmployee derived class didn't compile."

I had to take a close look at the error messages for a few moments before I realized the problem myself.

"Oh, I see what happened," I said. "The problem is that we defined the member variables in the Employee class with private access."

"Last week we learned that only code in the same class can access member variables defined with the private access specifier," Blaine said. "Is that the problem? Our derived class can't 'see' the member variables in the base class."

"That's right, Blaine," I said. "We can't derive private member variables from a base class."

"Does this mean we can't create a derived class from a base class unless the member variables are declared as public?" Barbara asked. "From what we learned last week, won't that impact the data integrity of the Employee class? How would the designer of the base class feel about that?"

"You're right, Barbara," I agreed. "Changing the member variables from private to public would fix this problem, but that's not a step the original designer would be in favor of—just so we can derive a class from it. Fortunately, we don't need to do that to fix this problem. Does anyone remember last week, when we we're discussing access specifiers, that in addition to the Private and Public keywords, there's another one that I told you wouldn't mean much to you until you learned about inheritance?"

"I do," Dave quickly volunteered. "I think it's the Protected keyword, isn't it?"

"Dave's absolutely right," I said. "Protected access comes into play only when we are dealing with a class used as a base class. Protected access is just like private access—except that member variables and methods defined with protected access can be derived and used in a derived class with no problem."

"So all we need to do is go back and change the access specifiers in the Employee base class from Private to Protected, and our SalariedEmployee derived class will compile okay?" Peter asked.

"Absolutely," I said.

I then made these changes to the Employee class, changing every private member variable in Employee from Private to Protected, and displayed the modified code on the classroom projector:

```
//Employee.cpp
#include <iostream>
#include <string>

using namespace std;
```

```
class Employee
{
  protected:
    string empID;
    string name;
    float hourlyRate;
    int hoursWorked;
    float grossPay;


  public: Employee()      //Constructor Method
  {
     cout << "Employee's Constructor" << endl;
  }

  public: void Display()
  {
      cout << "*** EMPLOYEE RECORD ***" << endl << endl;
      cout << "Employee ID: " << empID << endl;
      cout << "Name: " << name << endl;
      cout << "Hourly Rate: $" << hourlyRate << endl;
      cout << "Hours Worked: " << hoursWorked << endl;
      cout << "Gross Pay: $" << GetGrossPay() << endl;
  }


  public: void SetEmpID(string temp)
  {
     empID = temp;
  }

  public: string GetEmpID()
  {
     return empID;
  }

  public: void SetName(string temp)
  {
     name = temp;
  }
```

```
public: string GetName()
{
   return name;
}

public: void SetHourlyRate(float temp)
{
   hourlyRate = temp;
}

public: float GetHourlyRate()
{
   return hourlyRate;
}

public: void SetHoursWorked(int temp)
{
   hoursWorked = temp;
}

public: int GetHoursWorked()
{
   return hoursWorked;
}

public: float GetGrossPay()
{
   grossPay = hourlyRate * hoursWorked;
   return grossPay;
}

};                                //end of class
```

I then recompiled the SalariedEmployee class. This time SalariedEmployee compiled with no errors (except, of course, for the warning message that it contained no **main**() function).

"That's better," I said. "Now that we have changed the member variables in the Employee class from private to protected access, SalariedEmployee can derive those member variables with no problem. Now let's write some code to use the SalariedEmployee derived class in a client program."

I then displayed this code on the classroom projector:

```
//Example9_2.cpp

#include "SalariedEmployee.cpp"
```

```
int main()
{
    SalariedEmployee x;
    x.SetEmpID("337");
    x.SetName("Mary Jones");
    x.SetAnnualSalary(52000);
    x.Display();

    return 0;
}
```

I saved the program as Example9_2.cpp and then compiled and executed it. The following screenshot was displayed on the classroom projector:

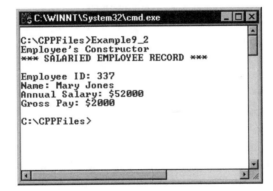

"I'm still not quite sure what's going on here," Rhonda said. "Can you explain it to us?"

"Sure thing, Rhonda," I said. "What we've done is create an instance of a SalariedEmployee object using the SalariedEmployee derived class."

```
SalariedEmployee x;
```

"We then executed the SetEmpID and SetName mutator methods of the empID and name member variables."

```
x.SetEmpID("337");
x.SetName("Mary Jones");
```

"Take note that both of those methods don't explicitly appear in the SalariedEmployee derived class but are actually public methods of the Employee base class. We never defined them ourselves in the SalariedEmployee derived class."

"I just realized that myself," Chuck said. "I don't think I really understood this whole concept of inheritance until just now. Now I see exactly how much time and effort deriving one class from another class can save us."

"Exactly. Chuck," I said, waiting for more questions and comments. "Now, with this line of code, we execute one of the two 'new' methods in the SalariedEmployee class, **SetAnnualSalary()**."

```
x.SetAnnualSalary(52000);
```

"This is followed by the execution of the overridden **Display()** method."

```
x.Display();
```

"So this code is executing the **Display()** method of the derived class SalariedEmployee, not the **Display()** method of the base class Employee?" Linda asked.

"That's right, Linda," I said. "Because we created an instance of the SalariedEmployee class, it's the **Display()** method of SalariedEmployee we're executing here."

"Very impressive," Ward said, "very impressive. I can see a lot of practical applications for inheritance back at the office. I think this can save me a lot of work."

"I have a question," Dave said. "I just noticed the message in the C++ console indicating that the constructor method of the base class Employee had been run. I know we didn't code a constructor method for the SalariedEmployee derived class, so I'm presuming that without a constructor method in the derived class, the constructor method for the base class executes. Is that correct?"

"Good observation, Dave," I said, "and you're right. The constructor method for the Employee base class was executed when an instance of the SalariedEmployee derived class was created. A derived class automatically 'inherits' the constructor method of its base class."

"Suppose we code a constructor method in the derived class." Kathy said. "What happens then? Do they both execute?"

"Let's see," I said.

I then modified the code for the SalariedEmployee derived class by adding a constructor method of its own. In other words, now both the Employee base class and the derived class SalariedEmployee have constructor methods of their own.

```
//SalariedEmployee.cpp

#include <iostream>
#include <string>
#include "Employee.cpp"

using namespace std;
```

```
class SalariedEmployee : public Employee
{
  private:
    float annualSalary;


  public: SalariedEmployee()        //Constructor Method
  {
     cout << "Salaried Employee's Constructor" << endl;
  }

  public: float GetGrossPay()
  {
     grossPay = annualSalary / 26;
     return grossPay;
  }


  public: void Display()
  {
     cout << "*** SALARIED EMPLOYEE RECORD ***" << endl << endl;
     cout << "Employee ID: " << empID << endl;
     cout << "Name: " << name << endl;
     cout << "Annual Salary: $" << annualSalary << endl;
     cout << "Gross Pay: $" << GetGrossPay() << endl;
  }


  public: void SetAnnualSalary(float temp)
  {
     annualSalary = temp;
  }

  public: float GetAnnualSalary()
  {
     return annualSalary;
  }


};                              //end of class
```

"Any guesses as to what will happen when I reexecute Example9_2?" I asked, after recompiling the SalariedEmployee class. "How many constructor methods will execute? And which ones?"

My students seemed evenly divided—half of the class felt that both constructors would execute. The other half felt that only the constructor for SalariedEmployee would execute.

I then recompiled and executed Example9_2. The following screenshot was displayed on the classroom projector:

"There's our answer," I said, "both constructors were executed. With the base class and the derived class each having its own constructor methods, both constructors were executed. This is something to bear in mind when you derive a class from a base class—you need to be aware that any code contained within the constructor method of the base class will be executed, and executed prior to code in the constructor method of the derived class being executed. In general, because constructor methods are used to perform the initialization of member variables, you'll find that base class constructor methods are performing initialization of the member variables of the base class. If you code a constructor method for your derived class, you should use it to perform initialization of the member variables unique to the derived class."

Planning Your Object Hierarchy in Advance

I paused for a few moments before continuing.

"Not all base classes and derived classes are built using the scenario we've just seen here," I said.

"What do you mean?" Kate asked. "Is this what you were getting at earlier when you were talking about the structured approach versus the evolutionary approach?"

"Exactly, Kate," I said. "In the current scenario, we started out with a class—Employee—that was originally intended to stand on its own. At the time we designed the Employee class, we didn't envision that any classes would be derived from it—although as we saw, when it became evident a

```
public: float GetGrossPay()
{
   grossPay = hourlyRate * hoursWorked;
   return grossPay;
}

public: void Display()
{
    cout << endl << "*** EMPLOYEE RECORD ***" << endl << endl;
    cout << "Employee ID: " << EmployeeBase::empID << endl;
    cout << "Name: " << name << endl;
    cout << "Hourly Rate: $" << hourlyRate << endl;
    cout << "Hours Worked: " << hoursWorked << endl;
    cout << "Gross Pay: $" << GetGrossPay() << endl;
}

};                              //end of class
```

"Notice," I said, "how the HourlyEmployee derived class has implemented two member variables unique to an hourly employee—hourlyRate and hoursWorked. In addition, accessor and mutator methods for each have been coded. We've also coded a **GetGrossPay**() function and a **Display**() function—and before I forget to mention it, take note of the fact that we also used the include statement to reference the EmployeeBase class."

"That's what you meant earlier when you said we might have a duplicate definition, is that right?" Kate asked.

"Exactly, Kate," I said. "In a minute you'll see that the SalariedEmployee class will also include a reference to the EmployeeBase class."

I then saved the program as HourlyEmployee.cpp and compiled it. Once again, except for a message from the linker complaining that there was no **main**() function, the class compiled fine.

"Now," I said "before we write code to use the HourlyEmployee class in a client program, let's modify the derived class SalariedEmployee that we created earlier so that it's derived from EmployeeBase instead of Employee. All we need to do, really, is change two line of codes: the include statement and the line of code that specifies the base class."

I then displayed this code on the classroom projector:

```
//SalariedEmployee.cpp

#include <iostream>
#include <string>
#include "EmployeeBase.cpp"
```

```cpp
using namespace std;

class SalariedEmployee : public EmployeeBase
{
  private:
    float annualSalary;


  public: SalariedEmployee()       //Constructor Method
  {
     cout << "Salaried Employee's Constructor" << endl;
  }

  public: void SetAnnualSalary(float temp)
  {
     annualSalary = temp;
  }

  public: float GetAnnualSalary()
  {
     return annualSalary;
  }

  public: float GetGrossPay()
  {
     grossPay = annualSalary / 26;
     return grossPay;
  }

  public: void Display()
  {
     cout << endl<< "*** SALARIED EMPLOYEE RECORD ***" << endl << endl;
     cout << "Employee ID: " << empID << endl;
     cout << "Name: " << name << endl;
     cout << "Annual Salary: $" << annualSalary << endl;
     cout << "Gross Pay: $" << GetGrossPay() << endl;
  }

};                              //end of class
```

I then saved the program as SalariedEmployee.cpp and compiled it. Once again, except for a message from the linker complaining that there was no **main()** function, the class compiled fine.

"Notice," I said, "that this version of the SalariedEmployee derived class has implemented one member variable unique to a salaried employee: annualSalary. In addition, accessor and mutator methods for the annualSalary attribute have been coded. Finally, the SalariedEmployee derived class also contains code for the **GetGrossPay()** and **Display()** methods."

"Overall, then," Dave said, "it looks like the EmployeeBase base class has three member variables and seven methods. The HourlyEmployee derived class has two member variables and seven methods, and SalariedEmployee has one member variable and five methods."

"Excellent analysis," I said. "Using inheritance and giving some thought to the base class can result in much less code in the classes derived from it."

"I'm starting to get a feel for the class hierarchy you're talking about," Linda said. "Now I see that if the need arose to create a new type of employee class—a member of the board of directors, for instance, who receives a one-time stipend payment each year—we can create a class called EmployeeBoardOfDirectors and derive it from the EmployeeBase class, adding just the member variables necessary to describe that kind of employee and adding code to implement its own version of the **GetGrossPay()** and **Display()** methods."

"Excellently stated, Linda," I said.

"This may not be a good time to ask this," Dave said, "but suppose the designer of the EmployeeBoardOfDirectors class 'forgets' to code a **GetGrossPay()** and **Display()** method. Or codes them but gives them a different name."

"What do you mean?" Rhonda asked, turning to Dave.

"In some other object-oriented languages I've worked with," Dave replied, "there's a way for the designer to ensure some consistency in the classes derived from a base class—for instance, to ensure that each derive class code have methods called **GetGrossPay()** and **Display()**."

"There is a way to do that in C++," I said, "and we'll be examining it shortly."

I then paused a moment before continuing.

"Now let's write a client program that creates an instance of each of these derived class objects, HourlyEmployee and SalariedEmployee."

I then displayed this code on the classroom projector:

```
//Example9_3.cpp

#include "HourlyEmployee.cpp"
#include "SalariedEmployee.cpp"

int main()
{
```

```
HourlyEmployee x;
x.SetEmpID("086");
x.SetName("John Smith");
x.SetHourlyRate(12.50);
x.SetHoursWorked(40);
x.Display();

SalariedEmployee y;
y.SetEmpID("337");
y.SetName("Mary Jones");
y.SetAnnualSalary(52000);
y.Display();

return 0;
}
```

I saved the program as Example9_3.cpp and then compiled and executed it. The following screenshot was displayed on the classroom projector:

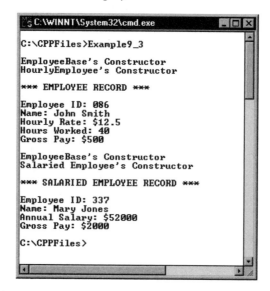

"As you can see," I said, "our client program has created an instance of both the HourlyEmployee and SalariedEmployee objects, set some attributes, and displayed the calculated gross pay for each type of object. Notice that the constructor for the EmployeeBase class was executed prior to the constructor for the HourlyEmployee and SalariedEmployee classes. Again, constructor methods are where you should place code that initializes the state—or member variables—of an object."

Abstract Classes and Pure Virtual Functions

"Can we get back to what Dave asked about earlier?" Peter asked. "A way the designer of the base class can 'force' classes deriving from the base class to code methods with a certain name."

"I still don't quite 'get' why you would want to do this if you were the designer of the base class." Rhonda said.

"There are two reasons," I replied. "First, consistency. As Dave mentioned, it makes sense that each class derived from EmployeeBase have methods called **GetGrossPay()** and **Display()**. From a functional point of view, it's necessary, and having identical names for these methods in each derived class will help maintain the 'sanity levels' of the programmers using their objects. You can force this consistency by creating what C++ calls a *pure virtual function*, also known as a *virtual method*, which is essentially a method containing only a header with no code. When a derived class uses a base class containing a pure virtual function, the derived class must supply the implementation code for it."

"Okay, that makes sense," Linda said. "What's the second reason?"

"As the designer of the base class," I said, "you may realize that the class isn't really suitable to having objects directly instantiated from it—in other words, you only want the class to be used as a base class in derived classes. This is done by creating an *abstract* class, which is a class that is meant to be a 'blueprint' for derived classes. In other words, objects cannot be directly instantiated from an abstract class. In C++, you create an abstract class by including in the class at least one pure virtual function."

"So a class containing at least one pure virtual function is automatically an abstract class, and no objects can be created from it, correct?" Peter asked.

"Exactly right, Peter," I said, "although other classes can be derived from an abstract class. Let's 'convert' our EmployeeBase class to an abstract class by including in it two pure virtual functions—**GetGrossPay()** and **Display()**."

I then displayed this code on the classroom projector (the modified code is shown in bold):

```cpp
//EmployeeBase.cpp
#include <iostream>
#include <string>
#ifndef EmployeeBase_cpp
#define EmployeeBase_cpp

using namespace std;

class EmployeeBase
{
   protected:
```

```
        string empID;
        string name;
        float grossPay;


   public: EmployeeBase()      //Constructor Method
   {
       cout << endl<< "EmployeeBase's Constructor" << endl;
   }

   public: void SetEmpID(string temp)
   {
       empID = temp;
   }

   public: string GetEmpID()
   {
       return empID;
   }

   public: void SetName(string temp)
   {
       name = temp;
   }

   public: string GetName()
   {
       return name;
   }

public: virtual float GetGrossPay() = 0;

  public: virtual void Display() = 0;

};                                  //end of class

#endif
```

"As before," I said, "the base class EmployeeBase implements the member variables—empID, name, and grossPay—that are common to any type of employee, whether hourly or salaried, along with the corresponding accessor and mutator methods for empID and name. However, this time we also included a reference to the **GetGrossPay**() and **Display**() methods that we want our derived classes to actually implement. We do that with these two lines of code:"

```
public: virtual float GetGrossPay() = 0;

public: virtual void Display() = 0;
```

"Including the Virtual keyword in the signature of the method, along with assigning it a value of 0, is what tells C++ that this method is a pure virtual function, and it also designates this class as an abstract class. As you can see, pure virtual functions are really nothing more than method signatures without code."

"Can you explain again what the purpose is of a pure virtual function?" Kate asked. "Why would the designer of a base class use one?"

"The designer of the class," I continued, "may decide that it makes perfect sense to include a **Display**() method in the EmployeeBase base class, but isn't exactly sure how derived classes 'inheriting' from it will choose to implement the details of the **Display**() method. As we saw with our previous example of hourly and salaried employees, the display for each type is slightly different."

"Does the presence of a pure virtual function in the base class force the designer of a class derived from it to provide the detailed code?" Dave asked.

"Yes, Dave, that's exactly what it means," I replied. "When you derive a class from a base class containing pure virtual functions, you are forced by the compiler to provide actual implementations for them in the derived class. Of course, how you choose to do that is entirely up to you."

"Are you saying," Linda asked, "that if a class derived from the EmployeeBase class does not contain its own methods called **Display**() and **GetGrossPay**(), the derived class won't compile?"

"Exactly right, Linda," I said. "Any class derived from the EmployeeBase base class must implement both the **GetGrossPay**() and **Display**() methods."

"This is all pretty interesting," Rhonda said. "In some ways, a pure virtual function reminds me of when I worked as a secretary in a law firm. If a client came in to have a will drawn up, one of the staff attorneys would take some notes, hand them to me, and I would then incorporate their notes into boilerplate sections in a will template we had created in WordPerfect."

"Boilerplate sections?" Mary asked, looking at Rhonda.

"Boilerplate is standard legal language," Rhonda answered. "And much of a standard will is standard legal jargon. In the templates I worked with, there were many boilerplate section headers that had nothing in them. In essence, they were just there to serve as reminders to us to ensure that we didn't forget to include the necessary verbiage to make the will valid."

"Kind of like a pure virtual function!" I said. "Rhonda, that's a brilliant analogy. That's exactly the idea behind pure virtual functions in a base class. Pure virtual functions ensure that the designer's vision for the base class, and the classes to be derived from it, are adhered to. Through the use of pure virtual functions in a base class, the designer knows that each and every class derived from the base class will implement those methods—even though the implementation details are up to the programmer who codes the derived class. And remember, any class that contains a pure virtual function is also an abstract class—and no objects can be directly instantiated from it."

"That means we can't create an EmployeeBase object?" Blaine asked.

"Right on the mark, Blaine," I said. "A class containing pure virtual functions is automatically an abstract class—and that means it's really nothing more than the 'boilerplate' for derived classes to be derived from it. Unlike this class, which contains a mixture of regular methods and pure virtual functions, there are also some abstract classes that contain *only* pure virtual functions."

"Are you going to show us how to derive a class from an abstract base class?" Ward asked. "What changes need to be made to the HourlyEmployee and SalariedEmployee classes?"

"None at all, Ward," I said. "The fact that we are now deriving from an abstract version of EmployeeBase simply means that we must have code in both HourlyEmployee and SalariedEmployee that implements the **GetGrossPay()** and **Display()** methods. Because we already have that code in those classes, no changes are required to them. If we failed to implement those methods in a class derived from the EmployeeBase base class, we would have generated a compiler error when we compiled the derived class."

"Can we see the compiler error that would generate?" Kate asked.

"Sure thing, Kate," I said.

I then temporarily deleted the implementation of the **GetGrossPay()** method from HourlyEmployee and compiled it. The following screenshot was displayed on the classroom projector:

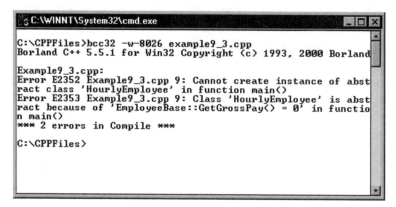

```
C:\CPPFiles>bcc32 -w-8026 example9_3.cpp
Borland C++ 5.5.1 for Win32 Copyright (c) 1993, 2000 Borland

Example9_3.cpp:
Error E2352 Example9_3.cpp 9: Cannot create instance of abst
ract class 'HourlyEmployee' in function main()
Error E2353 Example9_3.cpp 9: Class 'HourlyEmployee' is abst
ract because of 'EmployeeBase::GetGrossPay() = 0' in functio
n main()
*** 2 errors in Compile ***

C:\CPPFiles>
```

"Do you see what happened?" I said. "The compiler error message is a bit cryptic, but it is telling us that we failed to define a **GetGrossPay()** method."

I then reinserted the **GetGrossPay**() method into the HourlyEmployee derived class and recompiled Example9_3 with no problem.

"Just out of curiosity, as it's not directly related to abstract classes," Dave said, "but is there a way to keep a derived class from overriding a method in a base class? For instance, right now, there's nothing stopping the designer of SalariedEmployee from including their own version of the **SetEmpID**() method, is there?"

"Good question, Dave," I said. "You're right. The designer of the derived class can choose to implement their own version of each one of the methods defined in the base class—something that the designer of the base class may not want to happen. In some other languages, it is possible to prevent this from happening, but unfortunately there is no way to prevent this from happening in C++. Once again, this is an illustration of the great power of C++. It can do a lot, but it also lacks some of the 'protection features' that other languages have built in to prevent programmers from stepping on their own toes."

I noticed several students were starting to fidget. I realized that we had been working pretty intensely for some time without coming up for air, and so I asked everyone to take a short break.

Creating a Base Class and Derived Classes in the Grades Calculation Project

Fifteen minutes later I resumed class by explaining that it was now time to examine the Grades Calculation Project to see if we had a candidate for a base class.

"Normally," I said, "we would do this kind of analysis prior to this point, but because you're learning C++ while we're writing the Grades Calculation Project, it can't really be helped. Does anyone have any thoughts on base classes and derived classes?"

"I think one obvious base class would be a Student class," Dave said. "Right now the EnglishStudent, MathStudent, and ScienceStudent classes have a lot of duplicated code. If we create a Student base class, we'll be able to cut down significantly on the size of those three classes."

"Dave's right," I said. "The member variables midterm, finalExamGrade, finalNumericGrade, and finalLetterGrade are used in all three of those classes—plus the research and presentation member variables are used in the EnglishStudent class, and the research member variable is used in the ScienceStudent class."

"We also have duplication of the mutator and accessor methods for each of those member variables," Linda said "These are all candidates for inclusion in a base class."

"Each one of the three student classes also have a **Calculate**() method," Mary said, "although the code details are different in each one. Might the **Calculate**() method be a good candidate for a pure virtual function in a Student base class?"

"That's a great idea, Mary" I said. "That way, any class that inherits from the base class would be required to implement its own version of the **Calculate()** method."

I then distributed this exercise for the class to complete.

Exercise 9-1   **Create the Student Base Class for the Grade Calculation Project**

In this exercise, you'll create the base class Student for the Grades Calculation Project.

1. Use Notepad (if you are using Windows) to enter the following code:

```
//Student.cpp
#ifndef Student_cpp
#define Student_cpp

#include <iostream>
#include <string>

using namespace std;

class Student
{
   protected:
       int midterm;
       int finalExamGrade;
       int research;
       int presentation;
       float finalNumericGrade;
       char finalLetterGrade;

   public: Student()
   {
      cout << "Student's Constructor" << endl;
      midterm = 0;
      finalExamGrade = 0;
      research = 0;
      presentation = 0;
      finalNumericGrade = 0;
   }

   protected: void SetMidterm(int temp)
   {
```

```
   if (temp < 0 || temp > 100)
   {
      cout << "Invalid Midterm Grade (" <<
        temp << ") " << "Program Terminating" << endl;
      exit(1);
   }
   else
      midterm = temp;
}

public: int GetMidterm()
{
   return midterm;
}

protected: void SetFinalExamGrade(int temp)
{
   if (temp < 0 || temp > 100)
   {
      cout << "Invalid Final Exam Grade (" <<
         temp << ") " << "Program Terminating" << endl;
      exit(1);
   }
   else
      finalExamGrade = temp;
}

public: int GetFinalExamGrade()
{
   return finalExamGrade;
}

protected: void SetResearch(int temp)
{
   if (temp < 0 || temp > 100)
   {
      cout << "Invalid Research Grade (" <<
         temp << ") " << "Program Terminating" << endl;
      exit(1);
   }
   else
```

```cpp
            research = temp;
   }

   public: int GetResearch()
   {
      return research;
   }

   protected: void SetPresentation(int temp)
   {
      if (temp < 0 || temp > 100)
      {
         cout << "Invalid Presentation Grade (" <<
            temp << ") " << "Program Terminating" << endl;
         exit(1);
      }
      else
         presentation = temp;
   }

   public: int GetPresentation()
   {
      return presentation;
   }

   public: float GetFinalNumericGrade()
   {
      return finalNumericGrade;
   }

   public: char GetFinalLetterGrade()
   {
      return finalLetterGrade;
   }

   public: virtual void Calculate() = 0;
};

#endif
```

2. Save your source file as Student.cpp in the \CPPFiles\Grades folder (select File | Save As from Notepad's menu bar). Be sure to save your source file with the filename extension .cpp.

3. Compile your source file. Look for any compiler error messages. If you receive one, correct the problem so that the compiler runs cleanly. Because your source file contains a class, once the class compiles cleanly, you will still receive an error from the linker program indicating that you don't have a **main()** function. If that's the only error you receive, don't worry. You won't be testing the behavior of your base Student class until we have completed the work on the other classes in the project.

Discussion   No one had any major problems completing the exercise (of course, we had our share of typos and minor problems). One student forgot to code the inclusion guards, which didn't impact the cability to compile the class but would have caused problems further down the line.

"All we've really done then," Rhonda said, "is take the member variables common to all three classes—EnglishStudent, MathStudent, and ScienceStudent—and incorporate them into the Student class. Is that right?"

"That's basically correct, Rhonda" I said. "But remember, research and presentation are not common to all three classes."

"That's right," Peter said, obviously troubled. "Research and presentation don't appear in the MathStudent class, and the presentation member variable doesn't appear in the ScienceStudent class. Is it okay to place these in the Student base class anyway?"

"It's not a problem, Peter," I said. "We could have chosen to declare only the two 'common' member variables in the Student base class, but we really should design the Student base class not only for the three student types that currently exist but for those that may be required in the future as well."

"Other student types?" Mary asked. "Such as?"

"Well," I suggested, "there's always the possibility that other departments in the university—such as the Business department and the Computer Science department—after hearing about the fine work we've done for Frank Olley, may ask us to modify the Grades Calculation program for their use as well. These departments, I suspect, may compute their final grades based on combinations of the midterm, finalExamGrade, research, and presentation components, so that's why we should include all these in the Student base class."

There were no more questions, so I distributed this exercise for the class to complete.

Exercise 9-2	**Modify the EnglishStudent Class to Inherit from the Student Base Class**

In this exercise, you'll modify the EnglishStudent Derived Class for the Grade Calculation Project.

1. Using Notepad (if you are using Windows), locate and open the EnglishStudent.cpp source file you worked on last week. (It should be in the \CPPFiles\Grades folder.)

2. Modify your code so that it looks like this.

```
//EnglishStudent.cpp
#include <iostream>
#include <string>
#include "Student.cpp"

using namespace std;

class EnglishStudent: public Student
{
    private:
        float ENGLISH_FINALEXAM_PERCENTAGE;
        float ENGLISH_RESEARCH_PERCENTAGE;
        float ENGLISH_PRESENTATION_PERCENTAGE;
        float ENGLISH_MIDTERM_PERCENTAGE;

    public: EnglishStudent()
    {
        cout << "English Student's Constructor" << endl;
        ENGLISH_FINALEXAM_PERCENTAGE = .25;
        ENGLISH_RESEARCH_PERCENTAGE = .30;
        ENGLISH_PRESENTATION_PERCENTAGE = .20;
        ENGLISH_MIDTERM_PERCENTAGE = .25;
    }

    public: void Calculate()
    {
        char response[256];
        string moreGradesToCalculate;

        cout << "Enter the Midterm Grade: " ;
        cin.getline(response,256);
        SetMidterm(atoi(response));
```

```
            cout << "Enter the Final Examination Grade: " ;
            cin.getline(response,256);
            SetFinalExamGrade(atoi(response));
            cout << "Enter the Research Grade: " ;
            cin.getline(response,256);
            SetResearch(atoi(response));
            cout << "Enter the Presentation Grade: " ;
            cin.getline(response,256);
            SetPresentation(atoi(response));
                finalNumericGrade =
                  (midterm *
                      ENGLISH_MIDTERM_PERCENTAGE) +
                  (finalExamGrade * ENGLISH_FINALEXAM_PERCENTAGE) +
                  (research * ENGLISH_RESEARCH_PERCENTAGE) +
                  (presentation * ENGLISH_PRESENTATION_PERCENTAGE);
            if (finalNumericGrade >= 93)
                finalLetterGrade = 'A';
            else
            if ((finalNumericGrade >= 85) &&
                (finalNumericGrade < 93))
                finalLetterGrade = 'B';
            else
            if ((finalNumericGrade >= 78) &&
                (finalNumericGrade < 85))
                finalLetterGrade = 'C';
            else
            if ((finalNumericGrade >= 70) &&
                (finalNumericGrade < 78))
                finalLetterGrade = 'D';
            else
            if (finalNumericGrade < 70)
                finalLetterGrade = 'F';
    }
    };
```

3. Save your source file as EnglishStudent.cpp in the \CPPFiles\Grades folder
   (select File | Save As from Notepad's menu bar). Be sure to save your source
   file with the filename extension .cpp.

4. Compile your source file. Look for any compiler error messages. If you
   receive one, correct the problem so that the compiler runs cleanly. Because

your source file contains a class, once the class compiles cleanly, you will still receive an error from the linker program indicating that you don't have a **main()** function. If that's the only error you receive, don't worry. You won't be testing your modified EnglishStudent class until we have completed the work on the other classes in the project.

Discussion "So EnglishStudent is now a derived class, is that right?" Joe asked.

"That's right, Joe," I said. "It's this line of code that tells C++ that the EnglishStudent class is deriving the member variables and methods of the Student class. Don't forget to code the Public keyword."

```
class EnglishStudent: public Student
```

"In addition to the EnglishStudent class inheriting from the Student base class," I continued, "we 'removed' from the EnglishStudent class the member variables and methods that are now contained in the Student base class. The EnglishStudent class contains the member variables necessary for its unique **Calculate()** method to function properly."

```
private:
        float ENGLISH_FINALEXAM_PERCENTAGE;
        float ENGLISH_RESEARCH_PERCENTAGE;
        float ENGLISH_PRESENTATION_PERCENTAGE;
        float ENGLISH_MIDTERM_PERCENTAGE;
```

"It also contains its own constructor method, **EnglishStudent()**, which, in addition to displaying a message to the C++ console, initializes the values of its member variables

```
public: EnglishStudent()
    {
        cout << "English Student's Constructor" << endl;
        ENGLISH_FINALEXAM_PERCENTAGE = .25;
        ENGLISH_RESEARCH_PERCENTAGE = .30;
        ENGLISH_PRESENTATION_PERCENTAGE = .20;
        ENGLISH_MIDTERM_PERCENTAGE = .25;
    }
```

as well as its own unique **Calculate()** method, which overrides the pure virtual function **Calculate()** method in the Student base class."

```
public: void Calculate()
    {
        char response[256];
        string moreGradesToCalculate;

        cout << "Enter the Midterm Grade: " ;
```

```
cin.getline(response,256);
SetMidterm(atoi(response));
cout << "Enter the Final Examination Grade: " ;
cin.getline(response,256);
SetFinalExamGrade(atoi(response));
cout << "Enter the Research Grade: " ;
cin.getline(response,256);
SetResearch(atoi(response));
cout << "Enter the Presentation Grade: " ;
cin.getline(response,256);
SetPresentation(atoi(response));
    finalNumericGrade =
        (midterm *
            ENGLISH_MIDTERM_PERCENTAGE) +
        (finalExamGrade * ENGLISH_FINALEXAM_PERCENTAGE) +
        (research * ENGLISH_RESEARCH_PERCENTAGE) +
        (presentation * ENGLISH_PRESENTATION_PERCENTAGE);
if (finalNumericGrade >= 93)
    finalLetterGrade = 'A';
else
if ((finalNumericGrade >= 85) &&
    (finalNumericGrade < 93))
    finalLetterGrade = 'B';
else
if ((finalNumericGrade >= 78) &&
    (finalNumericGrade < 85))
    finalLetterGrade = 'C';
else
if ((finalNumericGrade >= 70) &&
    (finalNumericGrade < 78))
    finalLetterGrade = 'D';
else
if (finalNumericGrade < 70)
    finalLetterGrade = 'F';
}
```

"So none of the code in the EnglishStudent class has really changed, has it?" Linda asked. "We've really just removed code from it."

"That's right, Linda," I replied. "Because we're deriving member variables and methods from the Student base class, we've been able to significantly reduce the amount of code in the EnglishStudent class."

"Where are the variables that are in the EnglishStudent's **Calculate()** method located?" Rhonda asked. "Are those the member variables found in the Student class?"

"That's exactly right, Rhonda," I said. "EnglishStudent derives these member variables from the Student class, so the **Calculate()** method can refer to them as if they were declared in EnglishStudent—that's the whole idea behind inheritance."

There were no more questions, so I distributed this exercise for the class to complete.

Exercise 9-3	**Modify the MathStudent Class to Inherit from the Student Base Class**

In this exercise, you'll modify the MathStudent derived class for the Grade Calculation Project.

1. Using Notepad (if you are using Windows), locate and open the MathStudent.cpp source file you worked on last week. (It should be in the \CPPFiles\Grades folder.)

2. Modify your code so that it looks like this:

```cpp
//MathStudent.cpp
#include <iostream>
#include <string>
#include "Student.cpp"

using namespace std;

class MathStudent: public Student
{
   private:
     float MATH_MIDTERM_PERCENTAGE;
     float MATH_FINALEXAM_PERCENTAGE;

  public: MathStudent()
  {
    cout << "Math Student's Constructor" << endl;
    MATH_MIDTERM_PERCENTAGE = .50;
    MATH_FINALEXAM_PERCENTAGE = .50;
  }
```

n this chapter, you'll learn about one of the most fundamental data structures in the world of programming: arrays. *Arrays* are collections of variables, each having the same name but possessing a unique number called a *subscript*. Arrays permit a programmer to easily solve certain types of problems that would otherwise be extremely tedious to code.

Why Arrays?

I began our tenth class by telling my students that the entirety of this day's class would be devoted to the topic of arrays.

"Is an array similar to a regular variable?" Dave asked.

"Yes it is, Dave," I said. "You've learned that a variable is a single piece of data stored in the computer's memory and given a name. An array is a collection of variables—I sometimes call arrays *families of variables*—of the same data type, such as int or string, stored in the computer's memory. Each member of the collection has the same name but possesses a unique number called a *subscript*, which is used to identify it. Individual members of an array are called elements of the array."

 NOTE
You sometimes see the terms subscript and index used interchangeably.

"In the world of programming," I continued, "certain kinds of programming problems can more easily be solved using arrays. In fact, it's probably safe to say that there are certain types of programming problems that could *not* be solved without the use of arrays."

"What kinds of problems?" Chuck asked, his curiosity aroused.

"In general, Chuck," I said, "arrays are useful for problems where there is a requirement to manipulate large amounts of data and where the data isn't really unique but there are huge volumes of it."

"Could you give us an example of something like that?" Kate asked.

I thought for a moment and then said, "Let's suppose, Kate, that you are a weather meteorologist and, armed with the knowledge of C++ that you have picked up in this class, you decide to write a C++ program to keep track of 365 days worth of daily high temperature readings."

"That sounds interesting," Ward said. "That's an awful lot of data—at least more than we're used to."

"Furthermore," I continued, "let's presume that Kate would also like to calculate the yearly high average for her temperature readings. From what you've learned so far in the class, you know that she could declare and store these temperature readings in 365 separate variables called highTemperature1 through highTemperature365."

"I agree, that would do the trick," Dave said, "but who really wants to code 365 variable declaration statements, plus the 365 assignment statements to store the value of the variables? Plus, the calculation for the yearly average would require that Kate sum each and every one of those variables and then divide by 365—what a tedious exercise that would be! Is this where an array can help?"

"That's exactly the case, Dave," I answered. "Let's think about this for a moment. Each one of the 365 recorded high-temperature readings isn't really unique. It represents the same kind of thing: a temperature reading. What's different about each one? Only the day that the temperature is recorded, and the value of the temperature measurement. You'll see in a few minutes that an array is a much better choice than an ordinary variable in which to store those 365 temperature readings. Arrays are so common in programming that they are generally very easy to declare. In fact, an array declaration to store 365 high-temperature readings is just a single line of code."

"Amazing," I heard Valerie say.

"Not only does an array eliminate the need to declare 365 separate variables," I continued, "but once the values for the year's temperature readings are stored in the array, it's a simple process to use a For loop to access each individual element of the array and then retrieve the value, add it to an accumulator variable, and then calculate an average temperature. Believe it or not, this all can be done in about five lines of code."

"I can't wait to see this in action," Steve said.

"Let me give you another example," I said. "On Wednesday evenings, I teach a database administration class here at the university. Last Wednesday, I gave a quiz to each one of the six students in the class. What would you say if I asked you to write a C++ program to calculate the overall class average for that quiz? Based on what you've learned in the first nine weeks of the course but excluding what we've discussed so far about arrays, do you have any idea as to how we could calculate the class average?"

"I guess," Rhonda suggested, "that one way would be to borrow the functionality that we are currently using with the Grade Calculation program."

"How's that, Rhonda?" I asked.

"Well, we could prompt the user of the program to enter quiz grades for each one of the six students," she replied. "You told us to discount today's discussion of arrays, so the best I can suggest is to declare six variables, one to represent the quiz grades for each one of the students, and assign the user's input to one of those variables. Once the user has entered all six student grades, we can then sum the values of the variables and divide by six to calculate an overall class average."

"Based on what you've learned so far during the course, Rhonda, that's an excellent approach," I said. "However, once you learn more about arrays, I bet you'll come to the conclusion that this method, as effective as it is, is really a 'brute-force' method, as I like to call it."

I gave everyone a chance to ponder that statement.

"Now, suppose I told you that my database management class doesn't have just six students; it really has 150 students. Would that change your approach to solving the problem?"

"I would think we need to find a better approach to solving the problem than this," Rhonda replied. "I really don't want to have to declare 150 variables! There must be a better way."

"Absolutely, Rhonda," I said, "and you'll see shortly that the 'better approach' you sense must exist is to use an array instead of individual variables. But before we start to discuss arrays in detail, I think it's a good idea if we code the solution to the problem using the 'brute-force' method. That will allow you to see how tedious programming would be without arrays."

I then distributed this exercise for the class to complete.

Exercise 10-1   The Brute-force Method—Life Without Arrays

In this exercise, you'll write a program that prompts the user for six quiz grades and then calculates and displays the grades plus the overall class average to the C++ console.

1. Use Notepad (if you are using Windows) to enter the following code:

```
//Practice10_1.cpp

#include <iostream>
#include <string>
using namespace std;

int main()
{
    int grade1,grade2,grade3,grade4,grade5,grade6;

    int accumulator = 0;
    int counter = 6;
    float average = 0;
    char response[256];

    cout << "What is the first grade? ";
    cin.getline(response,256);
```

```
    grade1 = atoi(response);

    cout << "What is the second grade? ";
    cin.getline(response,256);
    grade2 = atoi(response);

    cout << "What is the third grade? ";
    cin.getline(response,256);
    grade3 = atoi(response);

    cout << "What is the fourth grade? ";
    cin.getline(response,256);
    grade4 = atoi(response);

    cout << "What is the fifth grade? ";
    cin.getline(response,256);
    grade5 = atoi(response);

    cout << "What is the sixth grade? ";
    cin.getline(response,256);
    grade6 = atoi(response);

    accumulator  = grade1 + grade2 + grade3 +
                   grade4 + grade5 + grade6;

    average = accumulator / counter;

    cout << endl << "The class average is " << average << endl;

    return 0;
}
```

2. Save your source file as Practice10_1 in the \CPPFiles\Practice folder (select File | Save As from Notepad's menu bar). Be sure to save your source file with the filename extension .cpp.

3. Compile your source file into an executable file.

4. Execute your program. The program will prompt you for six grades. Enter **82** for the first grade, **90** for the second, **64** for the third, **80** for the fourth, **95** for the fifth, and **75** for the sixth.

5. The program will then display the calculated overall class average, which is 81.

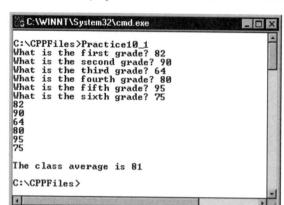

```
C:\CPPFiles>Practice10_1
What is the first grade? 82
What is the second grade? 90
What is the third grade? 64
What is the fourth grade? 80
What is the fifth grade? 95
What is the sixth grade? 75
82
90
64
80
95
75

The class average is 81

C:\CPPFiles>
```

Discussion Everyone agreed that the code in this exercise did what every good program must do: It worked. Beyond that, it had been an extremely tedious exercise to code.

"Brute force is right," Peter said. "What a boring program to write! I can't wait to see how an array can improve upon this."

"You'll see that in a minute, Peter," I said, "but first, let's take a look at the code. Much of it will be pretty familiar to you, because we're using the same technique we used in the Grade Calculation Project. As usual, the first thing we do is to declare the variables that we need to use in our program. We have six local variables in the **main()** method."

```
int grade1,grade2,grade3,grade4,grade5,grade6;
```

"Notice that we've declared an integer variable for each one of the six quiz grades," I continued. "In addition, I've introduced two special types of variables in this code. The first variable, appropriately named *accumulator*, is called an 'accumulator' variable. It's really just an ordinary variable that is used to sum values. In this case, we'll use *accumulator* to sum the values of the six grade variables."

```
int accumulator = 0;
```

"The second special type of variable is called a 'counter' variable, which we've named *counter*, and like an accumulator variable, a counter variable is just an ordinary variable that is used to count something—in this case, we're using it to count the number of students in the class. We could get fancier than this, but for now, because we'll eventually divide the value of *counter* into *accumulator* to arrive at a class average, we assign the number 6 to the counter variable, which is the total number of grades that will be entered."

```
int counter = 6;
```

"We also declare a float variable type called *average*, into which we will store the class average."

```
float average = 0;
```

"Float, that's a data type with a fractional part, isn't it?" Blaine asked.

"That's right, Blaine," I answered. "Because we want to calculate the class average as precisely as possible, we need to declare a variable that can handle fractions. Our final variable declaration is for the *response* variable—actually an array—which is used to hold the user's response to our prompts for grades."

```
char response[256];
```

I went on to explain that in the next section of code, we used a combination of cin and cout objects to prompt the user for each of the six quiz grades for the class.

"Notice that the return value of the user's response is assigned to the *response* variable," I said, "which is then, in turn, assigned to one of the six grade variables. This is where the problem arises: If all of a sudden we have 150 students in the class, not the six that we have here, this code can really balloon in size."

```
cout << "What is the first grade? ";
cin.getline(response,256);
grade1 = atoi(response);

cout << "What is the second grade? ";
cin.getline(response,256);
grade2 = atoi(response);

cout << "What is the third grade? ";
cin.getline(response,256);
grade3 = atoi(response);

cout << "What is the fourth grade? ";
cin.getline(response,256);
grade4 = atoi(response);

cout << "What is the fifth grade? ";
cin.getline(response,256);
grade5 = atoi(response);

cout << "What is the sixth grade? ";
cin.getline(response,256);
grade6 = atoi(response);
```

"Here's the code that assigns a value to the *accumulator* variable. As we progress through today's class, the code to work with the *accumulator* variable will become a little more elegant. For now, we assign it the values of each one of the six grade variables."

```
accumulator  = grade1 + grade2 + grade3 +
                grade4 + grade5 + grade6;
```

"This line of code is probably the most important one in the program," I continued, "in that it assigns the class average to the *average* variable. Notice that we take the value of the *accumulator* variable and divide it by the value of the *counter* variable."

```
average = accumulator / counter;
```

"Is there anything magical about the names of those two variables, the *accumulator* and *counter* variables?" Joe asked.

"Not at all, Joe," I answered. "We can name them anything we want."

I paused before continuing.

"This next section of code displays the values of the individual grades," I said. "This is another problematic section of code if the number of students in the class increases, because we would need to add additional lines of code."

```
cout << grade1 << endl;
cout << grade2 << endl;
cout << grade3 << endl;
cout << grade4 << endl;
cout << grade5 << endl;
cout << grade6 << endl;
```

"Finally," I said, "this line of code displays the class average."

```
cout << endl << "The class average is " << average << endl;
```

I checked the room for signs of confusion, but no one seemed to be having any trouble understanding what we had just done.

"I think you're all pretty comfortable with this code," I said. "There's really nothing in this code that you haven't seen before."

I then made this suggestion.

"Now I'd like you all to modify this code to calculate the class average for a class with 500 students," I said.

"I hope you're kidding," Joe said smiling.

"Well, I am...but suppose we really needed to calculate the average for a class with 500 students. Could we do it?" I asked.

Everyone agreed that modifying the code to calculate the class average for 500 students would be a real nightmare.

"We would need 500 prompts to the user and 500 variables in which to store their responses," Kate said. "Plus, we would need multiple lines of code to sum the values of the 500 variables and assign them to the *accumulator* variable."

What's an Array?

"All your points are excellent ones, Kate," I said. "Examining the brute-force method gives us a chance to see the types of problems that can be more easily solved using array processing."

"Is an array a separate data type, like an integer or a single?" Peter asked.

"Many beginners make the mistake of thinking of an array as a separate data type," I said, "but arrays are just a special implementation of one of the other C++ data types. In C++, you can have arrays of any data type, such as integer arrays, double arrays, string arrays, and as you'll see later, even object arrays."

"I'm still a little confused as to exactly what an array is," Rhonda said. "Do you have any analogies up your sleeve that might make this a little clearer?"

"In the past when I've taught arrays," I said, "many of my students have found my analogy of a hotel to be pretty useful."

"A hotel?" Rhonda asked.

"That's right, Rhonda," I said. "Just about everyone at one time or another has stayed in a hotel or motel. As you know, a variable is just a storage location in your computer's memory. Getting back to the hotel analogy, think of an ordinary variable as a storage location consisting of just a single floor. An array, on the other hand, is a storage location having more than just one floor, with each floor having its own unique floor number."

"Just like a hotel," Joe said. "I see what you mean."

"I'm not much of an artist," I said, "but here's a graphic depiction of what I mean."

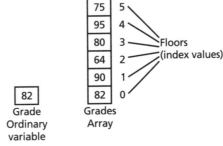

"This drawing is an attempt to illustrate the difference between an ordinary variable and an array," I said. "On the left side of the drawing, we have an ordinary integer variable called *grade* with an assigned value of 82. On the right side of the drawing, we have an array of integer variables called *grades*, the array containing six elements and each element having its own value. As you can see, the ordinary variable *grade* can hold only one value at a time. The integer array, however, can hold all six quiz grades at one time."

"What are those numbers to the right of the grades in the array?" Barbara asked.

"In keeping with our hotel analogy," I said, "those are the floor numbers of the hotel or, in computer terms, the array subscript or index values. A subscript uniquely identifies the element within the array. Each element has a subscript, and subscripts cannot be duplicated. This ensures that once a value is entered into an element of the array, you'll later be able to retrieve that value by using its subscript."

"Why does the first element of the array begin with zero?" Ward asked. "Why doesn't it begin with one?"

"Let me guess, that's the basement!" Rhonda said, obviously joking.

"In a way, Rhonda, you're right," I replied. "In the computer world, many things begin with the number zero instead of one, and array element numbers are one of them. In C++, the first element of an array begins with the number zero—it's just something that you'll need to get used to."

Declaring an Array

"How do you declare an array?" Steve asked. "Is declaring an array different from declaring an ordinary variable?"

"Declaring an array isn't much different from declaring an ordinary variable," I continued. "C++ knows you are declaring an array if you follow the name of a variable with a pair of brackets in which you include a number, like this:"

```
int grades[5];
```

"That looks familiar," Dave said. "That's similar to the declaration of the *response* variable in the practice exercise we just completed."

"Good observation, Dave," I replied. "That's because the *response* variable in Practice10_1 was actually a string array containing 257 elements. In this example, what we've done is tell C++ that we are declaring an integer array called *grades* containing six elements. Just like with an ordinary variable declaration, an array declaration must begin with a data type—in this case, int for integer."

"And it's the brackets containing a number that follow the variable name—I mean the *array* name—that tells C++ that?" Chuck asked.

"That's right, Chuck," I said. "C++ knows we are declaring an array because of the brackets and the number contained within them. To carry our analogy forward, we are telling C++ that we are declaring an integer array called *grades* and that it will have a total of six elements or floors."

"I want to be certain I'm clear about this," Kate said. "Is the number six the number of elements in the array or the top floor of the hotel?"

"That's a key distinction, Kate" I said. "In C++, the number within brackets represents the total number of elements in the array, which is not the same as the top floor. This array has six elements, with its subscripts numbered from 0 through 5. In C++, all array elements begin with the number 0, which is why they are said to be 'zero based'. Many beginners have difficulty remembering this, believing that the first element of an array is 1. This also means that the highest index value in the array is one less than the number of elements, so the highest index value in a six element array is 5."

Adding Data to the Elements of an Array

"How do we assign a value to an individual element of an array?" Steve asked. "And once we have values in the array elements, how can we retrieve the value from one of those elements?"

"Working with array elements isn't much different from working with an ordinary variable," I said. "The difference is that we need to reference the element number within the array by using its subscript within brackets. For example, if we had an array called *grades*, this code would be used to assign the value of 64 to element number 2:"

```
grades[2] = 82;
```

"By the way," I cautioned, "the array element with a subscript equal to 2 is actually the third element in the array. Remember, element numbers start with 0, not 1. Therefore, the first element in the array has a subscript of 0, the second element has a subscript of 1, and so forth."

"Are array values referred to in the same way?" Steve asked. "Using the subscript number within brackets?"

"That's right, Steve," I replied. "Again, as was the case with the assignment statement, just reference the subscript of the array element within brackets. For instance, you can use this syntax to display the value of element number 0 of the grades array in the C++ console:"

```
cout << grades[0];
```

"This isn't too bad at all," Kathy said. "I must confess, when I first heard the term 'array,' I thought it would be a lot more complicated than this."

"I just noticed something," Dave said. "I've been experimenting with an array of my own, and I accidentally assigned a value to an array element that is beyond the range I specified with my array declaration. No other language I've ever worked with would permit me to do such a thing—I would have expected an error message of some kind."

"You're right, Dave," I said, "most other programming languages would prevent you from making a mistake like this—but C++ is different. C++ permits programmers to manipulate computer memory in a way other languages don't, even when it can mean causing you problems."

I took a walk to Dave's PC, flipped a switch, and displayed Dave's code for the rest of the class to view:

```
int dave[10];

dave[10] = 44;

cout << "dave[10] is " << dave[10] << endl;
```

"As Dave indicated," I said, "he declared an integer array called *Dave* with ten elements, but then he assigned a value to subscript number 10."

```
dave[10] = 44;
```

"The array element with subscript 10 is actually the eleventh element of the array. Because you told C++, via the declaration statement, that it would have only ten elements, you expected to receive an error message of some kind. Not only didn't Dave receive an error message, but the assignment statement 'worked,' in that the value 44 was assigned to the computer's memory. Not only that, but the value of that memory location was then accessed and printed via the cout object."

"That is confusing, isn't it?" Peter said, as Rhonda nodded her head knowingly.

"I agree, Peter," I said. "The fact that elements of an array are numbered starting with zero can be confusing. Just remember that the last element number in the array—the top floor of our hotel—is always one less than its size. Therefore, if an array is declared with ten elements, the last element number is 9."

"Perhaps even more confusing is the fact that assignments to memory locations can be made outside the scope of the array bounds," Linda said. "Where exactly did C++ place the number 44?"

"A good question, Linda," I replied. "Most computer languages prevent this kind of assignment—but not C++. In this case, C++ placed the number 44 right 'next' to the memory location it had allocated for the final element of the array. That area in memory could actually be holding the value of another variable declared in our program—it could also be holding some of the actual program instructions for our program. Even worse, it could be an area in the computer's memory that has nothing to do with our program, and that when executed, causes a memory error on our PC, with the result that we have to reboot our computer."

"Wow," Kate said, "I had no idea a simple mistake like that could cause so much trouble. Can we hurt the PC?"

"No, we can't damage the PC this way," I said, "because the memory error is temporary, but if we are doing other work on it when this memory error occurs, the PC can 'freeze' and we can lose all our work."

"Can we use something other than a numeric literal to refer to the array's subscript?" Dave asked.

"You can use any expression within the brackets, as long as the expression evaluates to a valid subscript." I answered.

"I'm not sure I'm following this," Chuck said.

"For instance," I explained, "if we have a variable called *counter* containing an integer value, and that value represents a valid subscript in the *grades* array, this is a valid assignment statement that uses the value of the variable, not an actual number to represent the subscript."

```
grades[counter] = 80
```

"The ability to do this," I said, "will come in very handy in the exercise we're about to complete, because it will enable us to use loop processing to quickly access all the elements of an array."

I waited for questions, but there were none. I think everyone, for the moment anyway, felt comfortable declaring and working with arrays.

"I have an exercise for you to complete that will give you a chance to use an array to perform the same average calculation we did in the last exercise using the brute-force method—but I think you'll enjoy this one a whole lot more."

I then distributed this exercise for the class to complete.

Exercise 10-2   **Our First Look at Arrays**

In this exercise, you'll create your first array.

1. Use Notepad (if you are using Windows) to enter the following code:

```cpp
//Practice10_2.cpp

#include <iostream>
#include <string>
using namespace std;

int main()
{
    int grades[6];
    int accumulator = 0;
    int counter = 6;
    float average = 0;
```

```
          grades[0] = 82;
          grades[1] = 90;
          grades[2] = 64;
          grades[3] = 80;
          grades[4] = 95;
          grades[5] = 75;

          accumulator = grades[0] + grades[1] + grades[2] +
                          grades[3] + grades[4] + grades[5];
          average = accumulator / counter;


          cout << grades[0] << endl;
          cout << grades[1] << endl;
          cout << grades[2] << endl;
          cout << grades[3] << endl;
          cout << grades[4] << endl;
          cout << grades[5] << endl;


          cout << endl << "The class average is " << average << endl;

          return 0;
    }
```

2. Save your source file as Practice10_2 in the \CPPFiles\Practice folder (select File | Save As from Notepad's menu bar). Be sure to save your source file with the filename extension .cpp.

3. Compile your source file into an executable file.

4. Execute the program. The program will then display each of the six grades, plus the calculated overall class average, which is 81.

Discussion   Except for a student or two who confused the parentheses with square brackets, no one had any trouble completing this exercise.

"As you can see," I said, "the results of this program are identical to those in the first exercise: the display of six grades, plus the calculated overall class average. Of course, this version uses an array. Let's take a closer look at the code now. It's this line of code that declares a six-element array called grades:"

```
    int grades[6];
```

"As you know by now, this means the first element in the array has a subscript of 0 and the last element has a subscript of 5. By the way, I didn't mention this before, but it's a good idea to name arrays using the plural form of a noun—that enables programmers reading your code to recognize immediately that the variable is actually an array.

"Using an array here, we've reduced the number of lines of code necessary to declare the variables to store our six grades from six to one. As was the case with the first exercise, these next three lines of code declare our *accumulator* variable, our *counter* variable and our *average* variable. Once again, we initialize the value of our *accumulator* variable to 6, although shortly you'll see there's a more elegant way to keep track of the number of grades to use in our average calculation. For now, we'll initialize it to 6."

```
int accumulator = 0;
int counter = 6;
float average = 0;
```

"You probably remember that the previous version of this program assigned values to variables named *grade1* through *grade6*. This version does the same, but this time we assign values to individual elements of the *grades* array. In the next exercise, you'll learn that there's a more compact method for assigning values to array elements."

```
grades[0] = 82;
grades[1] = 90;
grades[2] = 64;
grades[3] = 80;
grades[4] = 95;
grades[5] = 75;
```

"As in our first exercise, we then sum the values of all six grades and assign the result to the *accumulator* variable. This time we refer to the individual elements of the *grades* array using the subscript."

```
accumulator   =   grades[0] + grades[1] + grades[2] +
                  grades[3] + grades[4] + grades[5];
```

"And with this line of code we calculate the overall class average:"

```
average = accumulator / counter;
```

"This next section of code is similar to the first exercise—it displays the values of the individual grades to the C++ console, referring to the individual elements in the *grades* array to do so."

```
cout << grades[0] << endl;
cout << grades[1] << endl;
cout << grades[2] << endl;
cout << grades[3] << endl;
```

```
cout << grades[4] << endl;
cout << grades[5] << endl;
```

"Finally, this line of code displays the calculated class average in the C++ console."

```
cout << endl << "The class average is " << average << endl;
```

The Wonders of Array Processing

"So far," Ward said, "I can see that array processing reduces the number of variables we need to declare in our program, but quite honestly, I don't see what the big deal is all about. Everything we did in this exercise was very similar to what we did in the first exercise, but instead of referencing individual variable names, we referenced elements of an array. There was still quite a bit of tedious typing referring to individual elements of the array."

"I agree with Ward," Lou said. "Surely there's got to be an easier way to assign values to an array. And once we have the values in the array, what then? Suppose we have an array with 365 elements like the daily high-temperature readings you mentioned earlier. Would we need to code up 365 separate assignment statements?"

"Glad you asked that, Lou," I said. "There is a shorter form of assigning values to an array, and its one to which I alluded earlier when I said there's a method to declare and initialize an array just by assigning values to it. Check out this code:"

```
int grades[6] = {82,90,64,80,95,75};
```

"Notice that the values for the array elements are contained within the braces," I said. "Now, with a single line of code, we have declared an array called *grades* as well as initialized it with values. How does C++ know how large to size the array? There are two ways: First, we declare the array to have six elements. Also, the six values within the braces tell C++ that the *grades* array should have six elements.

"I should also mention here that you will see this syntax, which, although acceptable, is not nearly as readable, especially to a beginner programmer."

```
int grades[] = {82,90,64,80,95,75};
```

"There's no number in the bracket," Rhonda said. "Is that correct?"

"That's correct Rhonda," I said. "The compiler doesn't really care if you specify the array size since you are providing it with a list of initial values. C++ determines the size of the array by counting the number of elements that have been initialized. As I said, although it's acceptable, it's not ideal for readability, and my preference is to always place a number within the brackets."

"Combining the declaration and initialization of the array is an improvement," Ward persisted, "but I still say big deal. I can see that this method will reduce the number of lines of code required to assign values to the elements of an array, but what else can arrays do for me? Why is it that the programmers at work always tell me they couldn't live without arrays? If I still need to refer to each and every element within the array individually, I still have quite a bit of work ahead of me."

"Arrays allow you to use loop processing to quickly refer to each element in the array," I said, "and that can be a big timesaver. This exercise, I believe, will illustrate why the programmers at your work love arrays so much."

I then handed out this exercise for the class to complete.

Exercise 10-3 **The Wonders of Array Processing**

In this exercise, you'll modify the code from Exercise 10-2, using a C++ For loop to quickly and easily access the elements of the array.

1. Use Notepad (if you are using Windows) to enter the following code:

```cpp
//Practice10_3.cpp

#include <iostream>
#include <string>
using namespace std;

int main()
{
   int grades[6] = {82,90,64,80,95,75};
   int accumulator = 0;
   int counter = 0;
   float average = 0;

   for (int row = 0;
      row < sizeof grades/sizeof grades[0]; row++)
   {
      cout << grades[row] << endl;
      accumulator = accumulator + grades[row];
      counter++;
   }

   average = accumulator / counter;

   cout << endl << "The class average is " << average << endl;

   return 0;
}
```

2. Save your source file as Practice10_3 in the \CPPFiles\Practice folder (select File | Save As from Notepad's menu bar). Be sure to save your source file with the filename extension .cpp.

3. Compile your source file into an executable file.

4. Execute the program. The program will then display each of the six grades, plus the calculated overall class average, which is 81.

<table>
<tr><td>**Discussion**</td><td>"Okay, I'm beginning to see the light," Ward said. "This version of the program is certainly a lot more streamlined than the other code, and I'm happy to see we never directly referred to an individual element of the array."</td></tr>
</table>

"I'm not quite sure I understand what's happening," Rhonda said. "Can you explain the code to us?"

"Sure thing, Rhonda," I said. "This time, instead of declaring and initializing the *grades* array using the new statement, we declare and initialize the array in a single statement by assigning values to each one of the six elements of the *grades* array."

```
int grades[] = { 82, 90, 64, 80, 95, 75};
```

"As before, we declare the variables *accumulator*, *counter*, and *average*. But notice that this time, the *counter* variable is assigned a value of 0, not 6. We'll be arriving at a value for the *counter* variable a little later on in the code, and it will make our program much more flexible in being able to deal with different numbers of quiz grades to calculate."

```
int accumulator = 0;
int counter = 0;
float average = 0;
```

"At this point in our program," I continued, "the *grades* array now has six elements, with values assigned to each. In the previous version of this program, we used the cout object to display the values for each element of the array, using six separate lines to do so. The problem with that version—and it's one that bothered the heck out of Ward—is that if the number of students in the class increases, we'll have to change the number of elements in the array and write another line of code to display that additional student's grade. That's why this next section of code is so powerful: It uses a C++ For loop to access every element in the *grades* array, displaying its value in the C++ console, adding its value to the *accumulator* variable, and incrementing the value of the *counter* variable by one."

```
for (int row = 0; row < sizeof grades/sizeof grades[0]; row++)
{
    cout << grades[row] << endl;
    accumulator = accumulator + grades[row];
    counter++;
}
```

"The wonderful thing about this code is that it works without modification, regardless of the number of elements in the array."

"Are you saying," Linda asked, "that if we changed the declaration of the *grades* array to have 250 student grades, this code wouldn't need to be changed? Is that what the sizeof keyword is doing for us?"

"That's exactly right, Linda," I said.

"I'm a little confused," Rhonda said. "How are we specifying the subscript for the array elements?"

"Do you remember a little earlier I said that we could refer to an array's subscript using a variable?" I asked. "That's what we're doing here by using the *row* variable, which is the 'loop control' variable for the For loop. As you can see, *row* is initialized to 0, which is the value for the first element of the array. We then increment *row* by one each time the For loop executes. The For loop continues to execute while the value of the *row* variable is less than the length attribute of the *grades* array."

```
for (int row = 0; row < sizeof grades/sizeof grades[0]; row++)
```

"Sizeof?" Rhonda asked. "What's that? Sizeof what?"

"Sizeof is a C++ operator," I said, "that enables us to determine the number of memory bytes that a variable is using. When dealing with an array, we can use the sizeof operator in two ways: First, to determine the total number of bytes in the array, which is what this code does:"

```
sizeof grades
```

"Second, to determine the number of bytes for an individual array element—in this case element 0—which is what this code does."

```
sizeof grades[0]
```

"I see," Ward said excitedly. "Dividing these two values gives us the number of elements in the array—regardless of how large the array is declared to be."

"Exactly right," I said. "By specifying that the For loop should continue to execute while the value of the *row* loop control variable is less than the expression

```
sizeof grades/sizeof grades[0]
```

"...we ensure that we access each and every element of the array."

"Powerful," Ward said.

"I'm afraid I still don't see how we specify the subscript for the individual array elements," Rhonda said. "Is it because we are using the loop control variable *row* within the brackets?"

"Absolutely, Rhonda," I said. "The loop control variable is used, within brackets, to specify the subscript of the array element we wish to display in the C++ console. Each time the body of the For loop is executed, an incrementing value of *row* is used as the subscript for the array element."

```
cout << grades[row] << endl;
```

"After we have displayed the value of the array element in the C++ console, we then add it to the current value of the variable *accumulator*," I continued. "In this way, the *accumulator* variable maintains a running total of the value of the array elements we have displayed in the C++ console."

```
accumulator = accumulator + grades[row];
```

"To make things easier to understand," I said, "visualize that the first time the body of the For loop is executed, the value of the *row* variable is 0. That means this statement is interpreted by C++ like this:"

```
accumulator = accumulator + grades[0]
```

"This statement, in turn, is then interpreted by C++ like this:"

```
accumulator = 0 + 90
```

"The second time through the loop," I continued, "the value of *row* in incremented, making it 1, and the statement is then interpreted by C++ like this:"

```
accumulator = accumulator + grades[1]
```

"Or like this:"

```
accumulator = 90 + 91
```

I explained that this process is repeated until the For loop terminates and all the elements of the array have been processed.

"We can't forget the role of the *counter* variable in the process," I said. "It's this line of code that increments the value of the *counter* variable, each time the For loop is executed. When the For loop terminates, the value of the *counter* variable is equal to the number of elements in the array."

```
counter++;
```

"Finally, this section of code is identical to the previous versions, displaying a blank line in the C++ console, calculating the average, and displaying that average in the C++ console as well. The big difference here is that the value of the *counter* variable is assigned within the For loop, not at the time the *counter* variable is declared."

```
average = accumulator / counter;
cout << endl << "The class average is " << average << endl;
```

Using an Array for Averaging

"I would really love to see arrays used with the code we wrote in the first exercise," Mary said. "Is it possible to use arrays there, even when the user is being prompted for grades to calculate?"

"Yes, it is possible," I said.

I hadn't really considered having the class do this, but it sounded like a great idea, and so, after a few minutes of thought, I distributed this exercise for the class to complete.

Exercise 10-4   Use Arrays with Interactive Processing

In this exercise, you'll modify the program you wrote in Exercise 10-1 to use arrays to make the process of calculating the average of six grades much easier.

1. Use Notepad (if you are using Windows) to enter the following code:

```cpp
//Practice10_4.cpp

#include <iostream>
#include <string>
using namespace std;

int main()
{
    int grades[6];
    int accumulator = 0;
    int counter = 0;
    float average = 0;
    char response[256];
    string moreGradesToCalculate;

    cout << "Do you want to enter a grade? ";
    cin >> moreGradesToCalculate;
    for (int i = 0;
       i < moreGradesToCalculate.length(); i++) {
        moreGradesToCalculate[i] =
            toupper(moreGradesToCalculate[i]);
    }

    if (moreGradesToCalculate != "YES") {
        exit(1);
    }

    for (int i = 0;
       i < moreGradesToCalculate.length(); i++) {
        moreGradesToCalculate[i] =
            toupper(moreGradesToCalculate[i]);
    }
```

```
        while (moreGradesToCalculate == "YES") {
           cout << endl << "What is the grade? ";
           cin.getline(response,256);
           grades[counter] = atoi(response);

           cout << endl << endl
              << "Do you have another grade to enter? ";
           cin >> moreGradesToCalculate;
           for (int i = 0;
              i < moreGradesToCalculate.length(); i++) {
              moreGradesToCalculate[i] =
                 toupper(moreGradesToCalculate[i]);
           }                              // end of for
           counter++;
        }                 // end of while

        for (int row = 0; row < counter; row++)
        {
           cout << grades[row] << endl;
           accumulator = accumulator + grades[row];
        }

        average = accumulator / counter;

        cout << endl << "The class average is " << average << endl;

        return 0;
     }
```

2. Save your source file as Practice10_4 in the \CPPFiles\Practice folder (select File | Save As from Notepad's menu bar). Be sure to save your source file with the filename extension .cpp.

3. Compile your source file into an executable file.

4. Execute your program. The program will prompt you for six grades. Enter **82** for the first grade, **90** for the second, **64** for the third, **80** for the fourth, **95** for the fifth, and **75** for the sixth.

5. Execute the program. The program will then display each of the six grades, plus the calculated overall class average, which is 81.

"As you can see," I said, "the changes between this version of the program and the one from the first exercise are pretty dramatic. Using arrays to prompt for and process a series of grades like this is a great deal easier than using six variables."

"I see that," Steve said, "and I can also see that we married the methodologies from the first three exercise to write a program that allows the user to load values into the elements of the array themselves, instead of the program doing so within code."

"That's right, Steve," I said. "Much of the code in this program is found in the first exercise. The main difference is that the user's input of a quiz grade is assigned to an element of an array instead of to a dedicated variable. Let's take a look at the code now. The first thing we did was declare an integer array called *grades* containing six elements, plus the variables *accumulator*, *counter*, and *average*."

```
int grades[6];
int accumulator = 0;
int counter = 0;
float average = 0;
```

"Because this program will be accepting responses from the user, we also declared a 256-element character array to hold their response."

```
char response[256];
```

"You should recognize the string variable *moreGradesToCalculate*," I said, "from the Grade Calculation Project as a variable we use in a While loop test expression to determine whether we should continue processing the loop to prompt the user for more grades."

```
string moreGradesToCalculate;
```

"This section of code asks the user whether they have a grade to enter, takes their response, and, using the **toupper** function, converts the response to uppercase."

```
cout << "Do you want to enter a grade? ";
cin >> moreGradesToCalculate;

for (int i = 0; i < moreGradesToCalculate.length(); i++) {
    moreGradesToCalculate[i] =
        toupper (moreGradesToCalculate[i]);
}
```

"If for some reason, the user immediately indicates a response other than 'YES,' these three lines of code will detect that and immediately end the program. Notice that we check for a response of other than 'YES' using the C++ inequality operator, !=."

```
if (moreGradesToCalculate != "YES") {
   exit(1);
}
```

"Provided the user answers 'YES' to the initial question, this section of code establishes a While loop, in which the user is prompted for a grade and then asked whether they have any others to input. Notice that the body of the loop will only execute if the value of *moreGradesToCalculate* is equal to an uppercase 'YES.' Any other value, and the loop will immediately terminate."

```
while (moreGradesToCalculate == "YES") {
```

"Provided the value of *moreGradesToCalculate* is 'YES,' we prompt the user for a grade and assign its value to the *response* variable."

```
cout << endl << "What is the grade? ";
cin.getline(response,256);
```

"This next line of code is crucial, in that it uses the value of the *counter* variable to establish the subscript number as the user's value for a grade and is then added as an element to the array."

```
grades[counter] = atoi(response);
```

"With the user's response now stored as an element in the *grades* array, it's time to ask the user whether they have more grades to enter."

```
cout << endl<< endl<< "Do you have another grade to enter? ";
cin >> moreGradesToCalculate;
```

"Their response is then converted to uppercase using the For loop we've been using the last few weeks."

```
for (int i = 0; i < moreGradesToCalculate.length(); i++) {
   moreGradesToCalculate[i] =
      toupper(moreGradesToCalculate[i]);
}                                    // end of for
```

I paused to give my next statement some added weight.

"This line of code is absolutely crucial—it's at this point that we increment the value of the *counter* variable so that if the user does have another grade to input, we load that value into the next element in the *grades* array. As you'll see, we also use the value of the *counter* variable later to calculate the class average."

```
counter++;
```

"The While loop continues to execute until the user indicates they have no more grades to input. At that point, we have an array loaded with grade values, and it's time to read the values in the *grades* array and calculate an overall average, just as we did in the third exercise. However, you'll note there's a slight difference here in how we do that. In the third exercise, we used the sizeof operator to determine the number of elements in the array. In this program, it's ultimately the user who determines the number of elements in the array. In fact, the total number of elements in the array is equal to the value of the *counter* variable, and that's the value we use to determine the number of elements in our array."

```
for (int row = 0; row < counter; row++)
{
    cout << grades[row] << endl;
    accumulator = accumulator + grades[row];
}

average = accumulator / counter;
cout << endl << "The class average is " << average << endl;
```

Problems with Arrays

"I'm really pleased with what I've seen here," Ward said, "but I just noticed a problem. I tried to enter a seventh grade, and the program let me, even though I only declared the array to have six elements."

"That's what I alluded to earlier, Ward," I said. "C++ has no built-in error checking for this. If you assign a value beyond the bounds of your array declaration, C++ will just place the value at the storage location adjacent to the last element of the array—which can result in a host of problems, such as other variables in your program being overwritten, program instructions in your own program being corrupted, and even your PC 'hanging' because you're overwriting part of the loaded operating system with an array value."

"Wow, I guess it really didn't hit home until I did it myself," Ward replied. "I guess I better be more careful."

"I just did the same thing," Rhonda said. "I entered ten values—and nothing bad seemed to happen."

"*Seemed* is the key word, Rhonda," I answered with a smile. "Believe me, something was overwritten in your computer's memory—just remember to be careful. C++ programming gives you enormous power to manipulate computer memory in ways that other programming languages don't—and along with that power comes a certain sense of danger, which adds to the adventure and lore of being a C++ programmer."

"Wow, this opens up a whole can of worms," Dave said. "I would think there would be times when you don't know ahead of time how many elements you need to have in your array, such as when you use an array to store values you read from a file. What should we do, declare the array with a large number?"

"You raise a good point, Dave," I said. "There will be times when, as is the case here, you can't be certain of the size of your array prior to writing the program. In that case, one approach is to declare the array with an overly large size. For instance, we could declare the *grades* array with 10,000 elements—that would certainly take care of our needs."

```
int grades[10000];
```

"Isn't that a waste of the computer's memory?" Bob asked. "Isn't there a way, while the program is running, to make the array larger if it needs to be?"

"Good question, Bob," I said. "And you're right, allocating an array with a larger-than-necessary size is a big waste of the computer's memory. Depending on your compiler, there will be a limitation on the size you can allocate an array—for the compiler we're using here in the classroom, it's the positive limit for an integer data type. Additionally, even if your compiler permits the size you have chosen, it's possible to declare an array with so many elements that it exceeds the available memory in your PC. If you do, you'll receive an error message when you run the program."

"So what's the answer?" Linda said. "Is there a way, while the program is running, to make the array larger?"

"The answer is yes," I replied. "That's called *dynamic memory allocation,* and doing so requires that you first learn about C++ pointers, which is a topic we'll be taking up next week."

Multidimensional Arrays

We were making great progress on what can be a difficult topic, so I began my discussion of multidimensional arrays.

"All the arrays we've seen so far have been one-dimensional arrays," I explained. "Now it's time to discuss multidimensional arrays."

"Dare I ask the difference?" said Kathy tentatively.

"They say a picture is worth a thousand words," I said. "Let's use Notepad to see the difference. In Notepad, one-dimensional arrays appear as a single column of data. Two-dimensional arrays appear as rows and columns of data, much like a worksheet." I said, as I displayed this file on the classroom projector:

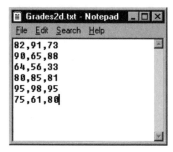

"This is a two-dimensional text file," I explained. "This file contains not only the original quiz grades we worked with in our exercises so far today, but also two other quiz grades."

"So the first column of numbers are scores from the first quiz, the second column are scores from the second quiz, and the third column are scores from the third quiz?" Ward asked.

"That's right," I replied. "Each row represents a record of three quiz scores for one student, and each column represents a different quiz."

"You mentioned the word 'multidimensional' a minute ago," Joe said, "and you just said this is the depiction for a two-dimensional array. Does that mean you can have an array with more than two dimensions?"

"Yes you can, Joe," I answered. "Creating an array with more than two dimensions is easy in C++. Visualizing one is something else and requires a little imagination, but C++ doesn't limit you to a two-dimensional array. In fact, C++ allows you to declare an array with any number of dimensions."

NOTE
Although array dimensions are not limited, the total size of an array is limited and will vary based on the PC and the operating system in use. Bear in mind that arrays tend to grow geometrically in size as dimensions are added to it.

"So far," Kathy said, "both types of arrays you've shown us, the one-dimensional and two-dimensional varieties, have represented some real-world object. What kind of real-world object would you represent with a three-dimensional array?"

"One classic example," I said, "is a farm. We can use a three-dimensional array to represent a farmer's crops. A farmer plants crops in fields (the first dimension), and within a field, he plants crops in rows (the second dimension) and columns (the third dimension). Try to imagine a farm that has ten fields, each field made up of 100 rows and columns. A three-dimensional array is a perfect way to represent the crop plants in a particular row and column of a field on the farm."

I gave everyone a chance to visualize this.

"Is there any limitation to how large an array can be?" Steve asked.

"There's no limitation per se on the number of dimensions," I said, "however, the size of an array is limited by the PC and the operating system. Multidimensional arrays, in particular, can use up the available memory in your computer very quickly. Each dimension that you add to an array geometrically increases the storage requirements for the array."

I sensed that my students were becoming tense with this discussion of multidimensional arrays, so I sought to comfort them a bit.

"Don't worry," I told everyone, "in the real-world of programming, most of your work will be with one- and two-dimensional arrays. Just remember that everything you learn today about two-dimensional arrays can be applied to an array with three or more dimensions."

"How are two-dimensional arrays declared?" Joe asked.

"The declaration for a multidimensional array is slightly different from that of a one-dimensional array," I said. "With a multidimensional array, you need to declare a size for each dimension of the array. For instance, here's the declaration for the file we just viewed in Notepad that contains scores for three quizzes for six different students:"

```
int grades[] [] = new int[6] [3];
```

"Notice that there are two sets of brackets," I said, "one for each dimension of the array. The two sets of brackets tell C++ that we wish to declare a two-dimensional array. For a three-dimensional array, we would have three sets of brackets. By convention, for a two-dimensional array, the declaration for the rows appears first, followed by the declaration for the columns, although there's no requirement to do it that way."

"So the number 6 refers to the number of rows in the array, and the number 3 refers to the number of columns?" Barbara asked.

"That's right," I said. "C++ knows that the number of bracket pairs it sees in the declaration equates to the number of dimensions in the array. With this declaration, C++ initializes a two-dimensional array, the first dimension having six elements, with the lowest subscript being 0, and the highest subscript being 5. The second dimension has three elements, with the lowest subscript being 0 and the highest being 2. Let me ask you a question: If this array were actually a worksheet, how many cells would it contain?"

"Eighteen," Dave said. "Just multiply the two size figures—six by three is eighteen."

"That's right, Dave," I said. "A two-dimensional array containing six rows and three columns contains a total of 18 elements, each element holding a quiz score. You can see why I said earlier that each dimension you add to an array increases its storage requirements geometrically."

"How do we refer to individual elements within a multidimensional array?" Peter asked. "Is it similar to referring to the elements of a one-dimensional array?"

"It is similar," I answered. "As you've seen, one-dimensional arrays are referenced by using a single subscript within brackets. Two-dimensional array elements are referenced by using two subscripts, one for each dimension. For example, to refer to the third quiz grade for the second student, we would use this notation:"

```
grades[1] [2] = 88;
```

"The number within the first pair of brackets," I said, "refers to the first dimension, or row, of the array, and that's the dimension that represents students. Don't forget, subscript 1 is actually the second row, or student, in the array. The number within the second set of brackets refers to the second dimension, or column, of the array, and that's the dimension that represents quizzes. Subscript 2 is the third quiz score."

"It looks strange how you put spaces between the subscripts," Kathy remarked, "but I guess the compiler doesn't really care about that, does it?"

"Not at all," I agreed.

I looked for signs of confusion in the faces of my students, but happily, I didn't see any. I suggested that now would be a great time for them to get their feet wet completing an exercise with a two-dimensional array.

Exercise 10-5   A Two-dimensional Array

In this exercise, you'll create your first two-dimensional array.

1. Use Notepad (if you are using Windows) to enter the following code:

```cpp
//Practice10_5.cpp

#include <iostream>
#include <string>
using namespace std;

int main()
{
    int grades[6][3];
    grades[0] [0] = 82;
    grades[0] [1] = 91;
    grades[0] [2] = 73;

    grades[1] [0] = 90;
    grades[1] [1] = 65;
    grades[1] [2] = 88;

    grades[2] [0] = 64;
    grades[2] [1] = 56;
    grades[2] [2] = 33;

    grades[3] [0] = 80;
    grades[3] [1] = 85;
    grades[3] [2] = 81;

    grades[4] [0] = 95;
    grades[4] [1] = 98;
    grades[4] [2] = 95;
```

```
        grades[5] [0] = 75;
        grades[5] [1] = 61;
        grades[5] [2] = 80;

    for (int row = 0; row < 6; row++)
    {
        for (int col = 0; col < 3; col++)
        {
            cout << grades[row][col] << " ";
        }
        cout << endl;
    }
    return 0;
}
```

2. Save your source file as Practice10_5 in the \CPPFiles\Practice folder (select File | Save As from Notepad's menu bar). Be sure to save your source file with the filename extension .cpp.

3. Compile your source file into an executable file.

4. Execute your program. The program will display the three quiz grades for the six students in row and column format.

Discussion   I immediately ran the program myself and the following screenshot was displayed on the classroom projector:

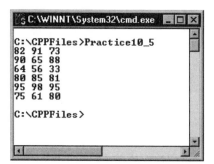

"As you can see," I said, "what we've done is write code to load the three quiz grades for six students into a two-dimensional array and then display them in the C++ console."

"This is pretty impressive," Rhonda said. "Although I must confess, I'm not real clear with how you did this."

"Don't worry, Rhonda," I said, "I'll be glad to explain it."

"That first line of code in the **main()** function, is that the declaration for the two-dimensional array?" Peter asked.

"Yes it is, Peter," I replied. "The two sets of brackets tell C++ that we are declaring a two-dimensional array, and the numbers within the brackets indicate the size of each dimension. Remember, by convention, in a two-dimensional array, the row is specified first, followed by the column."

```
int grades[6][3];
```

"Once we've declared the array," I said, "this next section of code initializes each element of the array, here, one line of code at a time:"

```
grades[0] [0] = 82;
grades[0] [1] = 91;
grades[0] [2] = 73;

grades[1] [0] = 90;
grades[1] [1] = 65;
grades[1] [2] = 88;

grades[2] [0] = 64;
grades[2] [1] = 56;
grades[2] [2] = 33;

grades[3] [0] = 80;
grades[3] [1] = 85;
grades[3] [2] = 81;

grades[4] [0] = 95;
grades[4] [1] = 98;
grades[4] [2] = 95;

grades[5] [0] = 75;
grades[5] [1] = 61;
grades[5] [2] = 80;
```

"It's possible to initialize the elements of a two-dimensional array the same way we initialized the elements of the one-dimensional array in the third exercise, like this:"

```
int grades[6] [3] = {
              { 82, 91, 73}, // First row
              { 90, 65, 88}, // Second row
              { 64, 56, 33}, // Third row
              { 80, 85, 81}, // Fourth row
```

```
          { 95, 98, 95}, // Fifth row
          { 75, 61, 80}  // Sixth row
          };
```

"Some students find this syntax confusing, so I'll leave it up to you to determine which syntax you wish to use. Now, with our two-dimensional array loaded with values, all that remains is to navigate through the 18 elements of the array and display them on the C++ console. This next section of code is similar to the code we saw in the fourth exercise, but because we are dealing with an array that has not just one dimension but two, the technique is more complex, requiring us to use something called *nested For loops*."

```
for (int row = 0; row < 6; row++)
   {
       for (int col = 0; col < 3; col++)
       {
         cout << grades[row][col] << " ";
       }
     cout << endl;
   }
```

"This is where I got totally lost when I did the exercise," Kate said. "You say this is a nested For loop? I think I've heard some programmers at work use that term. It sounds very complicated."

"Nested For loops can be intimidating, Kate," I said, "but if you just remember that a nested For loop is nothing more than a loop whose body itself contains a For loop, I think you'll be okay."

I paused a moment to give everyone in the class a second to take in what I had just said.

"A nested For loop is a For loop that contains another For loop in its body," I repeated. "The first For loop structure is called the *outer loop*, and the For loop that appears in its body is called the *inner loop*. If you check the code, you'll see that each For loop has its own unique loop control variable. I've named the loop control variable of the outer loop *row*, and the loop control variable of the inner loop *column*. This is because the outer loop is intended to process the rows in the two-dimensional array, and the inner loop is intended to process the columns. Think of these For loops almost like a mouse pointer that is directing a screen cursor to various positions within the array."

"This is confusing," Rhonda chimed in. "I keep trying to visualize what's going on with the code but...."

"I think if you take it a step at a time, you'll be fine," I said. "And that's exactly what we're going to be doing in a minute. Notice that the outer loop has a body consisting of another For loop and a redirection of a linefeed to the cout object. The inner loop has a body consisting of just one line of code: the redirection of an array value to the cout object."

"Isn't the redirection of the linefeed to the cout object part of the body of the inner loop?" Barbara asked.

"No, it's not," I said. "The inner loop—the one that uses *col* as the loop control variable—has just one line of code in it."

```
cout << grades[row][col] << " ";
```

"Okay," Barbara said, "I see what you mean now."

I paused for a moment before continuing.

"You'll see in a minute," I said, "as we step through this code, that the body of the inner loop will be executed a total of 18 times, whereas the body of the outer loop will be executed just six times."

"Is that because there are six rows of data in the array?" Dave asked.

"Exactly, Dave," I said.

"But there are only three columns in the array," Blaine said. "Why would the inner loop be executed 18 times? Shouldn't it be executed just three times?"

"That's a good question, Blaine," I responded. "The inner loop is executed three times, but each time the outer loop is executed, which is six times, the inner loop is once again executed three times. Six multiplied by three is eighteen—that's the total number of times the inner loop is executed."

"It also happens to be the number of elements in the array," Dave said.

I saw a great deal of confusion on the faces of my students.

"Don't worry if you feel a little overwhelmed by this right now," I said. "I think this will all make a lot more sense to you in a few moments. Let's get back to the body of the inner loop now. Amazingly, it consists of just this single line of code."

```
cout << grades[row][col] << " ";
```

"All in all, this line of code will be executed a total 18 times," I explained, "which, as Dave pointed out, is the total number of elements, or quiz grades, in our two-dimensional array. Using nested For loops, the values of the two loop control variables, *row* and *col*, are varied to point to each element in the array and displayed in the C++ console."

```
for (int row = 0; row < 6; row++)
{
    for (int col = 0; col < 3; col++)
```

"Again, the first loop is known as the *outer loop*," I continued, "and we use it to move through the rows in the array. We initialize its loop control variable, *row*, to 0, and for its termination point, we use the number of elements in the first dimension of the array, which is 6."

```cpp
for (int row = 0; row < 6; row++) {
```

"That means the outer loop is executed six times, is that right?" Chuck asked.

"Exactly right, Chuck," I said. "Now let's take a look at the inner loop, which is used to process the columns in the array."

```cpp
for (int col = 0; col < 3; col++)
```

"Notice that for the termination point of this loop we use the number of elements in the second dimension of our array, which is 3."

"Isn't there any way to use the sizeof operator the way we did in the previous exercise?" Linda asked.

"Yes there is, Linda," I said. "I hesitated to ask you to code it that way because of the nested For loops and because the usage of the sizeof operator for a multidimensional array is a bit confusing, but here goes."

```cpp
for (int row = 0; row < sizeof grades/sizeof grades[0]; row++)
{
    for (int col = 0;
        col < sizeof grades[0]/sizeof grades[0][0]; col++)
```

"The sizeof syntax for the outer loop looks familiar," Linda said, "but the syntax for the inner loop looks foreign."

"You're right, Linda," I said. "The sizeof syntax for the outer loop is identical to what you saw earlier. This tells C++ to divide the total number of bytes in the array by the 'width' of the first row of the array, which will give a result equal to the number of rows in the array. Ultimately, C++ interprets this code to look like this:"

```cpp
for (int row = 0; row < 6; row++)
```

"This syntax is a bit more confusing:"

```cpp
for (int col = 0;
    col < sizeof grades[0]/sizeof grades[0][0]; col++)
```

"This tells C++ to divide the total number of bytes in the column dimension of the array by the width of an array column element, which gives us the total number of columns. Ultimately, C++ interprets this code to look like this:"

```cpp
for (int col = 0; col < 3; col++)
```

"And that's why the inner loop is executed three times?" Chuck asked.

"That's right, Chuck," I said. "Maybe this will help to give you an appreciation for the sequence of code execution."

I then displayed this table on the classroom projector:

Statement	Row	Col	Grades	Value of Grades	Comment
For (int row...)	0				First execution of the outer loop.
For (int col...)	0	0	0,0	82	First execution of the inner loop.
cout << grades[row][col]	0	0	0,0	82	Displays 82 in the C++ console.
For (int col...)	0	1	0,1	91	Second execution of the inner loop. The value of *col* is incremented by 1.
cout << grades[row][col]	0	1	0,1	91	Displays 91 in the C++ console.
For (int col...)	0	2	0,2	73	Third execution of the inner loop. The value of *col* is incremented by 1.
cout << grades[row][col]	0	2	0,2	73	Displays 73 in the C++ console.
cout << endl	0	2	0,2	73	A new line is generated in the C++ console.
For (int row...)	1				Second execution of the outer loop. The value of *row* is incremented by 1.
For (int col...)	1	0	1,0	90	First execution of the inner loop.
cout << grades[row][col]	1	0	1,0	90	Displays 90 in the C++ console.
For (int col...)	1	1	1,1	65	Second execution of the inner loop. The value of *col* is incremented by 1.
cout << grades[row][col]	1	1	1,1	65	Displays 65 in the C++ console.
For (int col...)	1	2	1,2	88	Third execution of the inner loop. The value of *col* is incremented by 1.
cout << grades[row][col]	1	2	1,2	88	Displays 88 in the C++ console.
cout << endl	1	2	1,2	88	A new line is generated in the C++ console.

Statement	Row	Col	Grades	Value of Grades	Comment
For (int row...)	2				Third execution of the outer loop. The value of *row* is incremented by 1.
For (int col...)	2	0	2,0	64	First execution of the inner loop.
cout << grades[row][col]	2	0	2,0	64	Displays 64 in the C++ console.
For (int col...)	2	1	2,1	56	Second execution of the inner loop. The value of *col* is incremented by 1.
cout << grades[row][col]	2	1	2,1	56	Displays 56 in the C++ console.
For (int col...)	2	2	2,2	33	Third execution of the inner loop. The value of *col* is incremented by 1.
cout << grades[row][col]	2	2	2,2	33	Displays 33 in the C++ console.
cout << endl	2	2	2,2	33	A new line is generated in the C++ console.
For (int row...)	3				Fourth execution of the outer loop. The value of *row* is incremented by 1.
For (int col...)	3	0	3,0	80	First execution of the inner loop.
cout << grades[row][col]	3	0	3,0	80	Displays 80 in the C++ console.
For (int col...)	3	1	3,1	85	Second execution of the inner loop. The value of *col* is incremented by 1.
cout << grades[row][col]	3	1	3,1	85	Displays 85 in the C++ console.
For (int col...)	3	2	3,2	81	Third execution of the inner loop. The value of *col* is incremented by 1.
cout << grades[row][col]	3	2	3,2	81	Displays 81 in the C++ console.
cout << endl	3	2	3,2	81	A new line is generated in the C++ console.

Statement	Row	Col	Grades	Value of Grades	Comment
For (int row...)	4				Fifth execution of the outer loop. The value of *row* is incremented by 1.
For (int col...)	4	0	4,0	95	First execution of the inner loop.
cout << grades[row][col]	4	0	4,0	95	Displays 95 in the C++ console.
For (int col...)	4	1	4,1	98	Second execution of the inner loop. The value of *col* is incremented by 1.
cout << grades[row][col]	4	1	4,1	98	Displays 98 in the C++ console.
For (int col...)	4	2	4,2	95	Third execution of the inner loop. The value of *col* is incremented by 1.
cout << grades[row][col]	4	2	4,2	95	Displays 95 in the C++ console.
cout << endl	4	2	4,2	95	A new line is generated in the C++ console.
For (int row...)	5				Sixth execution of the outer loop. The value of *row* is incremented by 1.
For (int col...)	5	0	5,0	75	First execution of the inner loop.
cout << grades[row][col]	5	0	5,0	75	Displays 75 in the C++ console.
For (int col...)	5	1	5,1	61	Second execution of the inner loop. The value of *col* is incremented by 1.
cout << grades[row][col]	5	1	5,1	61	Displays 61 in the C++ console.
For (int col...)	5	2	5,2	80	Third execution of the inner loop. The value of *col* is incremented by 1.
cout << grades[row][col]	5	2	5,2	80	Displays 80 in the C++ console.
cout << endl	5	2	5,2	80	A new line is generated in the C++ console.

"This table shows the statements that are being executed," I said, "as well as the values of the *row* and *col* loop control variables, the array element that is being pointed to by the value of *row* and *col*, the value of that array element, and the result of the execution of the statement."

We spent the next few minutes going over the table.

"I hope that helped," I said, as I scanned the faces of my students for signs of confusion.

"Yes, it did," Ward said.

That explanation satisfied Ward and the other students, so before continuing onto the next topic of creating arrays of objects, I asked everyone to take a 15-minute break.

Creating Arrays of Objects

"Something that's asked of me all the time," I said, after resuming from break, "is whether it's possible to create an array of objects in C++."

"You mean like the Student objects we've been working with throughout the class?" Mary asked.

"That's right, Mary," I said, "that kind of object. In fact, creating an array of objects is easy to do. Do you remember the Banner object we worked with several weeks ago? Let's create an array of Banner objects."

I displayed this code on the classroom projector:

```
//Example10_1.cpp

#include "Banner.cpp"

int Banner::numberOfBannerObjects;

int main()
{
    Banner x[2];
    x[0].favoriteProgram = "C++";
    x[0].Display();

    x[1].favoriteProgram = "Visual Basic";
    x[1].Display();

    for (int row = 0; row < 2; row++)
        {
            cout << x[row].favoriteProgram << endl;
```

```
        }

    return 0;
}
```

I saved the program as Example10_1.cpp and then compiled and executed it. The following screenshot was displayed on the classroom projector:

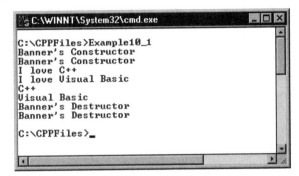

"Working with an array of objects is very similar to working with an array of C++ primitive data types, such as int or string," I said. "First, we need to declare the array of objects, and then we need to go about the business of actually working with the objects, just as we would normally—assigning values to member variables, if they are public, and executing object functions. But because we're dealing with an array of objects, we need to use subscript values when we refer to the object variable. Let's start with the array declaration. This line of code declares a two-element array of Banner objects called *x*. This is the same as an array declaration for an array of integers:"

```
Banner x[2];
```

"With two Banner objects created and referenced as elements 0 and 1 of the *x* array, we can now work with the object just as we normally would—we just need to remember to reference the element number any time we refer to the object. With this line of code, we set the favoriteProgram attribute of the Banner object to 'C++':"

```
x[0].favoriteProgram = "C++";
```

"And then we execute its **Display()** method:"

```
x[0].Display();
```

"Just to prove that we can have multiple Banner objects alive at the same time, this code sets the favoriteProgram attribute of element 1 to 'Visual Basic' and then executes its **Display()** method."

```
x[1].favoriteProgram = "Visual Basic";
x[1].Display();
```

"So we have two Banner objects loaded in our array?" Mary asked.

"You can think of it that way, Mary," I said. "In reality, the array contains a reference—a memory address, really—pointing to both objects. The important thing is that when we refer to an element in the array, C++ can find the Banner object we intend to work with in the computer's memory, along with any attributes that belong to that particular object. That's why we can use the For loop logic we've been employing in today's class to display the favoriteProgram attribute of every Banner object referenced by our array."

```
for (int row = 0; row < 2; row++)
{
    cout << x[row].favoriteProgram << endl;
}
```

"That is really neat," Blaine said. "I'm beginning to like arrays more and more—too bad we can't include one in the Grade Calculation Project."

"I don't see why we can't," I said. "Frank Olley never requested it, but I don't think he would mind if we calculated an overall average for every student's grade entered into the program. I think an array would be a perfect way to do that."

I then distributed this exercise for the class to complete.

Exercise 10-6   **Modify the Grade Calculation Project to Use an Array**

In this exercise, you'll modify the grades class to include array processing to calculate an overall class average.

1. Using Notepad (if you are using Windows), locate and open the Grades.cpp source file. (It should be in the \CPPFiles\Grades folder.)

2. Modify your code so that it looks like this (changed code appears in bold):

```
//Grades.cpp

#include <iostream>
#include <string>
#include "EnglishStudent.cpp"
#include "MathStudent.cpp"
#include "ScienceStudent.cpp"
```

```cpp
#include "DisplayGrade.cpp"

using namespace std;

int WhatKindOfStudent();
char response[256];
string moreGradesToCalculate;
float grades[1000];
float accumulator;
int counter;
float average;

int main ()
{
   int lresponse;

   cout << "Do you want to calculate a grade? ";
   cin >> moreGradesToCalculate;

   for (int i = 0;
      i < moreGradesToCalculate.length(); i++) {
      moreGradesToCalculate[i] =
         toupper (moreGradesToCalculate[i]);
   }

   while (moreGradesToCalculate == "YES") {
      lresponse = WhatKindOfStudent();

      switch(lresponse)
      {
         case 1:
           {
            EnglishStudent eStudent;
            eStudent.Calculate();
            grades[counter] =
               eStudent.GetFinalNumericGrade();
            counter++;
            DisplayGrade x(eStudent.GetMidterm(),
                       eStudent.GetFinalExamGrade(),
                       eStudent.GetResearch(),
                       eStudent.GetPresentation(),
```

```
                               eStudent.GetFinalNumericGrade(),
                               eStudent.GetFinalLetterGrade());
            }
          break;
        case 2:
          {
          MathStudent mStudent;
          mStudent.Calculate();
          grades[counter] =
             mStudent.GetFinalNumericGrade();
          counter++;
          DisplayGrade y(mStudent.GetMidterm(),
                        mStudent.GetFinalExamGrade(),
                        mStudent.GetFinalNumericGrade(),
                        mStudent.GetFinalLetterGrade());
          }
          break;
        case 3:
          {
          ScienceStudent sStudent;
          sStudent.Calculate();
          grades[counter] =
             sStudent.GetFinalNumericGrade();
          counter++;
          DisplayGrade z(sStudent.GetMidterm(),
                        sStudent.GetFinalExamGrade(),
                        sStudent.GetResearch(),
                        sStudent.GetFinalNumericGrade(),
                        sStudent.GetFinalLetterGrade());
          }
          break;
        }        // end of switch

cout << endl << endl <<
    "Do you have another grade to calculate? ";
cin >> moreGradesToCalculate;
for (int i = 0; i < moreGradesToCalculate.length(); i++) {
   moreGradesToCalculate[i] =
      toupper (moreGradesToCalculate[i]);
}                                   // end of for
```

```
    }                    // end of while

    for (int row = 0; row < counter; row++)
    {
        cout << grades[row] << endl;
        accumulator = accumulator + grades[row];
    }
    average = accumulator / counter;
    cout << "The class average is " << average << endl;

    cout <<
        "Thanks for using the Grades Calculation program!";
    return 0;
}


int WhatKindOfStudent()
{
    cout << "Enter student type " <<
        "(1=English, 2=Math, 3=Science): ";

    cin.getline(response,256);

    if (strlen(response) == 0) {
        cout << "You must select a Student Type";
        exit(1);
    }

    if ((atoi(response) < 1) || (atoi(response) > 3)) {
        cout << response <<
            " - is not a valid student type";
        exit(2);
    }

    return atoi(response);
}
```

3. Save your source file as Grades.cpp in the \CPPFiles\Grades folder (select File | Save As from Notepad's menu bar). Be sure to save your source file with the filename extension .cpp.

4. Compile your source file into an executable file.

5. After you start up your program, it should ask whether you have a grade to calculate.

6. Answer **Yes** and calculate the grade for an English student. Enter **70** for the midterm, **80** for the final examination, **90** for the research grade, and **100** for the presentation. A final numeric grade of 84.5 should be displayed with a letter grade of C.

7. After the grade is displayed, the program should ask whether you have more grades to calculate.

8. Answer **Yes** and calculate the grade for a math student. Enter **70** for the midterm and **80** for the final examination. A final numeric grade of 75 should be displayed with a letter grade of D.

9. After the grade is displayed, the program should ask whether you have more grades to calculate.

10. Answer **Yes** and calculate the grade for a science student. Enter **70** for the midterm, **80** for the final examination, and **90** for the research grade. A final numeric grade of 78 should be displayed with a letter grade of C. After the message is displayed with the calculated grade, the program should ask whether you have more grades to calculate.

11. Answer **No**. All three final numeric grades will be displayed in the C++ console, along with an overall average of 79.1667. You should be thanked for using the program, and the program should end.

Discussion

"I'm not sure that the changes we've just made to the Grade Calculation Project are something Frank Olley requires," I said, "but I think they will add greatly to your learning experience—and it didn't require all that much additional code. Our first step was to declare a *grades* array to store the values of the individual calculated final grades. We declared *grades* as an array of the double data type, having 1,000 elements, which should be more than large enough to hold the grades a user will calculate in this program."

```
float grades[1000];
float accumulator;
int counter;
float average;
```

"We needed to modify our existing code to add the student's calculated grade as an element of the *grades* array. To do that, all we needed to do was add a line of code to each of the individual Case statements and add the finalNumericGrade attribute of the various Student objects to the array, using the current value of the *counter* variable to specify the subscript. Here's the code to do that for the EnglishStudent object:"

```
case 1:
    {
        EnglishStudent eStudent;
```

```
eStudent.Calculate();
grades[counter] = eStudent.GetFinalNumericGrade();
```

"Once we have the student's grade in the *grades* array, we need to increment the value of the *counter* variable so that the next student's grade is assigned to the next available location in the array."

```
counter++;
```

"This process of adding an element to the *grades* array continues for each student calculated. Finally, when the user indicates there are no more grades to calculate, it's time to move through the elements of the array, calculate the average, and display it."

```
for (int row = 0; row < counter; row++)
   {
      cout << grades[row] << endl;
      accumulator = accumulator + grades[row];
   }
average = accumulator / counter;
cout << "The class average is " << average << endl;
```

"Seeing the array used in the Grade Calculation program really helped me," Rhonda said. "This doesn't seem so bad after all."

I waited to see if there were any questions, but there were none. I then dismissed class for the day.

Summary

In this chapter, you learned about the basics of array processing. In particular, you learned about the various types of arrays and about array dimensions. Arrays are a frequent source of confusion for new programmers, and I hope our coverage of them will make your future work with them easier.

Specifically, you learned the following:

- ■ Why arrays are useful in making your code easier to write and use
- ■ How to use one-, two-, and multidimensional arrays
- ■ How arrays can reduce the amount of hard-coding you write in your projects.

In the next chapter, you'll learn about C++ pointers and references—and how C++ works with your computer's memory. Then we'll finish the course by examining some of the common errors that can occur in C++ programming and examine ways to make allowances for problems that might occur when your programs run.

Chapter

11

Pointers

I n this chapter, we'll cover a topic that almost every beginning C or C++ student dreads—pointers. But never fear, pointers give C and C++ their great power, by enabling you to do something you can't do with most other programming languages—manipulate your computer's memory.

Why Pointers?

I began class by telling my students that the entirety of this day's lesson would be devoted to the topic of pointers.

"The topic of pointers is one that just about every C or C++ student dreads," I said, "but I think you're going to enjoy it. Using pointers, you can do something you can't do with other programming languages—access and manipulate your PC's memory."

"I've heard of pointers," Rhonda said, "and they scare me to death. I actually thought about cutting class today to avoid the trauma. All I know is that whenever the C and C++ programmers at work want to go off into their own little world, they start up a discussion of pointers, and everyone vacates the area."

"Never fear, Rhonda," I said, "pointers can be a bit intimidating, but I think that by the end of today's class, you'll be fine with them. Pointers were built in to the C language to handle a problem with function calls. C++ also provides for something called a *reference*, which is an advance over pointers. In fact, a few weeks ago we used a reference to call a function and have that function change the value of a variable back in the **main**() function."

NOTE
We used a reference in Example6_9 in Chapter 6.

The Classic Example: The Swap Program

"Rather than use that example from several weeks ago over again," I said, "I thought I would show you what has become the classic illustration of a program that calls for the use of a pointer. This is the same program that my C instructor used in my first programming class. It's a program that's intended to take the values found in two variables and exchange or 'swap' them. For example, if a variable called *x* contains the number 13, and a variable called *y* contains the number 22, ultimately we want the variable *x* to contain the value 22 and the variable *y* to contain the value 13."

"That shouldn't be a big problem," Dave said. "I believe if we use a third variable, that's a piece of cake."

I invited Dave to code the program for us, and in no time, he was finished and had displayed it on the classroom projector.

```cpp
//Example11_1.cpp

#include <iostream>

using namespace std;

int main()
{
   int x = 13;
   int y = 22;
   int temp;

   cout << "The value of x is " << x << endl;
   cout << "The value of y is " << y << endl;

   temp = x;
   x = y;
   y = temp;

   cout << "The value of x is now " << x << endl;
   cout << "The value of y is now " << y << endl;

return 0;
}
```

"Dave's idea," I said, admiring his code and watching the rest of the class study it, "is to use a third variable to accomplish the swapping of the values. In other words, the value of the variable *x* is placed in a variable called *temp*. The value of the variable *y* is then assigned to the variable *x*, and the value of the variable *temp* is assigned to the variable *y*. Here's a schematic of what is going on."

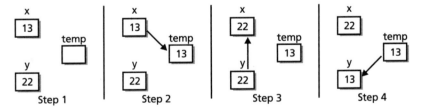

"Seems like a lot of trouble to exchange two values," Rhonda said. "Can't we just set *x* to *y* and *y* to *x*?"

"Unfortunately not," I said. "If you do that, after you copy the value of *x* to *y*, you'll have two variables with the same value, and you'll lose your ability to exchange the values. Doing a swap of values like this always requires a third variable. Let's compile and execute Dave's program and see it in action."

I saved Dave's program as Example11_1.cpp and then compiled and executed it. The following screenshot was displayed on the classroom projector:

"Does everyone see what's going on here?" I asked. "The values in the variables *x* and *y* have been swapped: *x* started out with a value of 13, but now it has a value of 22, and *y* started out with a value of 22, but now it has a value of 13."

"I see," Ward said, "that the values of the variables *x* and *y* have been swapped. This worked fine. Now why do we need pointers?"

"We need pointers," I said, "because of what happens if we take the code to do the exchange of the variables and place it in a function of its own—the program no longer works properly."

I then modified Dave's code to look like this, taking the code to perform the exchange of the variables and placing it in a function called **Swap()**.

```
//Example11_2.cpp

#include <iostream>

using namespace std;

void Swap(int number1, int number2);          // Function Prototype

int main()
{
    int x = 13;
```

```
    int y = 22;

    cout << "The value of x is " << x << endl;
    cout << "The value of y is " << y << endl;

    Swap(x,y);

    cout << "The value of x is now " << x << endl;
    cout << "The value of y is now " << y << endl;

    return 0;
}

void Swap(int number1,int number2)
{
    int temp;

    temp = number1;
    number1 = number2;
    number2 = temp;
}
```

"As you can see," I said, "what we've done is to create a custom function named **Swap()**, designed to accept two integer arguments called number1 and number2, and we placed the code to do the exchange of the variable values in there."

```
void Swap(int number1,int number2)
{
    int temp;

    temp = number1;
    number1 = number2;
    number2 = temp;
}
```

"We then 'call' the function **Swap()** from within **main()**," I continued, "passing it the names of the variables *x* and *y* as the two arguments."

```
Swap(x,y);
```

"I would think," Kate said, "that the **Swap()** function will take the values of the two variables and exchange them, just as the program did when this code was contained within the **main()** function."

"Let's see, Kate," I said.

I saved the program as Example11_2.cpp and then compiled and executed it. The following screenshot was displayed on the classroom projector:

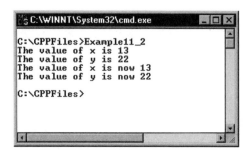

"Looks fine to me," I heard Rhonda start to say, but then she immediately realized that the values of *x* and *y* hadn't been swapped at all.

"Hey, what happened?" asked Rhonda. "The values haven't been switched—they're still the same. Did we make a mistake somewhere in coding the **Swap()** function. The code in the **Swap()** function looks the same as it did when it was contained in the **main()** function. Should we have named the arguments in the **Swap()** function *x* and *y*?"

"You're right, Rhonda," I said, "this program does have a problem. Unfortunately, it's not a problem that can be fixed simply by renaming the arguments in the **Swap()** function to *x* and *y*. It goes much deeper than that."

"What is the problem, then?" Blaine asked. "Is the problem with the code in the **Swap()** function?"

"No, the code in the **Swap()** function is fine," I said. "The real issue here is how we 'passed' our arguments to the **Swap()** function."

"What do you mean *how* we passed the arguments?" Steve asked.

"By passing our variables as arguments," I continued, "we were hoping that the **Swap()** function would change the values of our variables back in the **main()** function. However, C++ passes arguments to functions by value, not by reference."

"I'm afraid I'm totally confused," Kate said. "What does that mean? By value? By reference?"

"By value," I said, "means that the **Swap()** function was passed the actual value of the variables *x* and *y* as arguments, not the variables themselves. As a result, after the **Swap()** function executed, the values of the variables *x* and *y*, declared in the **main()** function, were still the same. They hadn't been changed at all."

"I guess I hadn't realized the nuance of passing arguments to functions," Linda said. "This *is* starting to ring a bell. Didn't we address this issue in a program we coded a few weeks ago? I thought we wound up using an ampersand (&) to make it work."

"You have a great memory, Linda," I said, "and you're right. When I first introduced you to passing arguments to functions, we had the same problem. We 'got around' it by using something called a C++ reference, and we can solve our problem in this program in the same way. Let me show you."

I then modified the code to look like this, changing the argument declaration within both the function prototype and function header to include the ampersand character.

```cpp
//Example11_3.cpp

#include <iostream>

using namespace std;

void Swap(int &number1, int &number2);            // Function Prototype

int main()
{
    int x = 13;
    int y = 22;

    cout << "The value of x is " << x << endl;
    cout << "The value of y is " << y << endl;

    Swap(x,y);

    cout << "The value of x is now " << x << endl;
    cout << "The value of y is now " << y << endl;

    return 0;
}

void Swap(int &number1,int &number2)
{
    int temp;

    temp = number1;
    number1 = number2;
    number2 = temp;
}
```

"Using an ampersand in the function header," I said, "tells C++ we wish to pass the argument by reference, not by value. In effect, this gives the function the 'address' of the variable in memory, giving the function full access to the variable itself—not just a copy of the value of the variable."

```
void Swap(int &number1,int &number2)
```

"As a result, when this program is executed, we should see the correct results of our variable exchange displayed in the C++ console."

"What do you mean by *address?*" Bob asked.

"Each variable that we declare," I said. "In fact, everything in our program is stored in the computer's memory and is given a unique address so that our program can find it. A reference—and as we'll see shortly, a pointer—is just the actual address by which the variable is known to the computer."

I saved the program as Example11_3.cpp and then compiled and executed it. The following screenshot was displayed on the classroom projector:

"Now we're back on track." Linda said. "The **Swap()** function successfully exchanged the values of the variables *x* and *y.*"

"That's right, Linda," I said. "Using a C++ reference—the ampersand—did the trick."

I paused a moment to see if there were any questions.

"I know the theme of today's class is pointers," Ward said, "but if a C++ reference gives us the results we need, why do we need to use pointers? I hear pointers are very difficult to work with. In fact, I've heard they're a nightmare."

"You're right, Ward," I said. "In this particular program, a C++ reference can give us the same functionality as a pointer—and references are easier to work with than pointers. But there are things that pointers can do for us that references simply cannot—more on that later in the class. Besides, I think by the end of today's class you'll be pretty comfortable with the concept of pointers, and the topic is simply too important to skip. Pointers are engrained in the C and C++ world. It's difficult to imagine any of you finding employment without a working knowledge of pointers—and I would dare say that if you get a job as a C++ programmer, it won't be very long before you're asked to modify a program that uses pointers. For that reason, it makes good sense to learn about them—and the best place to do so is in the friendly confines of our classroom."

"Are you going to modify this program to use pointers instead of references?" Joe asked.

"Eventually," I said, "but before we rush into that, let's slow things down just a bit and take up the subject of pointers in a more leisurely fashion. I think it will make it easier on everyone that way."

What Is a Pointer?

"So exactly what is a pointer?" Chuck asked.

"In a single word, an *address*," I replied. "Think of a pointer as a type of variable that contains a memory address."

"Isn't that basically what a reference is?" Barbara asked hesitantly.

"Yes and no, Barbara," I said. "When you place an ampersand in front of a variable name, as we did in the program we just wrote, we tell C++ to work with a variable's address, and not its actual value. In that way a reference is like a pointer. The difference with a pointer, however, is that the pointer is a variable that actually contains the address to another variable or object. There's more work involved in using a pointer. The programmer must explicitly declare a pointer and then assign the memory address of a variable or object to it. As you'll see, the process of using pointers is much more complicated than merely using a reference—although the end results will be the same."

"So a pointer is just a variable that contains a memory address?" Barbara asked.

"Exactly, Barbara," I said. "Using pointers, it's possible to work directly with a variable or object by using its address—not its name. In fact, it's also possible to call a function by using its address instead of its function name."

"Why would you ever want to do something like that?" Kathy asked. "I have enough trouble already."

"Experienced C++ programmers love the flexibility working with pointers gives them," I said. "Also, working with pointers is sometimes faster than working with variables and objects themselves. C++ programmers are always looking to optimize the speed of their programs. And perhaps most importantly, by using pointers it's possible to dynamically create variables and objects at runtime. You may recall that last week we discussed having to declare an array 'large' enough to hold the largest number of elements we could envision. Using pointers, as you'll see later on today, we don't need to do that. We can create the array and the exact number of elements we need, at runtime."

"Can you explain a little bit more about this memory address that a pointer contains?" Bob asked. "What does a memory address look like?"

"An address is nothing more than a number," I said. "The exact look and feel depends on the computer and operating system you're using. What's important to remember is that when you declare a variable in your program, the operating system takes care of finding an available piece of computer memory, noting the physical memory address, and then associating the name of your variable with the address. We'll be writing some programs later on that will allow you to see what the addresses of the PCs located here in our computer lab look like."

Declaring and Naming a Pointer

"You said a pointer is a variable that contains an address," Lou said. "Is a pointer declared in the same way that we declare a variable?"

"It's similar, Lou," I said. "However, because a pointer is a special type of variable, we need to alert C++ to the fact that we are declaring a pointer, and we do that by declaring a pointer with an asterisk, like this."

```
int* pNumber1
```

"What we're telling C++ to do here," I said, "is to allocate, in the computer's memory, a variable called *pNumber1* that itself will contain a memory address. It's the asterisk that tells C++ this variable is a pointer. By the way, notice how I have named the pointer beginning with a lowercase *p*. This makes identifying pointer variables in your program much easier."

NOTE
All pointers are 4 bytes long.

"I know that the first time you see this notation it can be very confusing. Even more confusing is the fact that you will often see three different styles of pointer declarations. For example, all three of these pointer declarations styles are valid—notice that the position of the asterisk in each is slightly different."

```
int* pNumber1
int * pNumber1
int *pNumber1
```

"Is one of these styles more correct than the others?" Kate asked.

"All three are perfectly fine," I said, "although my preference is to use the first one. Please be careful when declaring more than one pointer. For example, this syntax results in one pointer variable called pNumber1 being declared, and two regular variables called *pNumber2* and *pNumber3* being declared."

```
int* pNumber1, pNumber2, pNumber3;
```

"To declare more than one pointer variable, either declare them on separate lines or use this syntax."

```
int *pNumber1, *pNumber2, *pNumber3;
```

"By the way," I added, "it's always a good idea to initialize pointers with a value of zero—also called a *null* value. A pointer initialized in this way really points to no address. Assigning no initial value means that the pointer value contains a random value, and if you accidentally perform an operation using that address, your program can have some very unpredictable results. You can declare and initialize a pointer variable using this syntax."

```
int* pNumber1 = 0;
```

NOTE
A pointer initialized with a value of zero is called a null pointer.

"Why is there a type of int designated with the pointer?" Dave asked. "It appears here that you are saying that *pNumber1* is an integer variable. I presume C++ understands this to mean that *pNumber1* is a pointer to a variable of the integer data type. Does it really matter?"

"Specifying the type is required," I said, "because some pointer operations we'll be performing will need to know the type of data they will find at a particular address. In addition, because different data types have different storage requirements, C++ needs to know the data type your pointer is referring to so that in addition to knowing where the variable 'starts' it also knows its length, and therefore where the variable 'ends.'"

The AddressOf Operator (&)

"Okay," Mary said, "now that we have a pointer declared, what do we do with it? A pointer initialized to zero doesn't seem very useful to me. I presume there's a way to assign a valid memory address to a pointer. How do I know the address to assign to the pointer?"

"A good point, Mary," I said, "and a good question. Assigning a memory address to a pointer variable can be done in one of two ways. First, you can directly assign the memory address to the pointer variable—in much the same way that we initialize a pointer to zero—but doing so requires that we know the actual physical memory address that we wish to assign to the pointer. In most cases, we won't know that. Instead we'll know the name of the variable, object, or function whose address we wish to store in the pointer."

"How do we get the address, then?" Peter asked.

"We can use the C++ AddressOf operator," I said, "to either determine the memory address or assign it to the pointer variable. Here's some code in which we declare two integer variables called *number1* and *number2* and then display both their addresses to the C++ console."

```cpp
//Example11_4.cpp

#include <iostream>

using namespace std;

int main()
{
    int number1 = 12;
    int number2 = 22;

    cout << "The value of number1 is " << number1 << endl;
    cout << "The address of number1 is " << &number1 << endl;

    cout << "The value of number1 is " << number2 << endl;
    cout << "The address of number1 is " << &number2 << endl;

    return 0;
}
```

I saved the program as Example11_4 and then compiled and executed it. The following screenshot was displayed on the classroom projector:

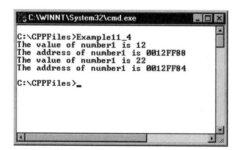

NOTE
The addresses displayed on your PC will most likely be different from these.

"Does everyone see what happened here?" I asked. "We displayed the values of the variables *number1* and *number2* as well as their memory addresses. Here's a schematic."

"I'm a little confused," Rhonda said. "I understand that we displayed the values of *number1* and *number2*, but what's up with those addresses? Shouldn't they be numbers? Why is there a letter *F* in the address?"

"Addresses in a computer are usually represented in something called hexadecimal notation," I said. "The hexadecimal number system contains the digits 0 through 9, just like the decimal number system we're more familiar with. In addition, the letters *A, B, C, D, E,* and *F* are also used as digits."

"So the letter *F* in the addresses that we see is like a number?" Linda asked.

"Exactly, Linda," I said, "but don't worry about this—or try to read too much into the actual address itself. Most times you won't even know the actual address contained in your pointer variable—your program will take care of that. The key point here is that each variable we declare in our program has a unique address in the computer's memory, and that address can be retrieved using the C++ AddressOf operator, which is the ampersand (&)."

```
cout << "The address of number1 is " << &number1 << endl;
```

"So all we're doing here is using the AddressOf operator to display the address of the variable *number1* to the C++ console?" Rhonda asked.

"Exactly, Rhonda," I said.

"I knew that ampersand looked familiar," Blaine said. "Isn't that the way we passed a reference to the **Swap()** function in Example11_3?"

"Great observation, Blaine," I said. "You're right—by using the AddressOf operator in the **Swap()** function's header and function prototype, we told C++ to work directly with the address of the arguments—not the values themselves."

"I may be missing something here," Kate said, "but did we work with pointers at all in this example?"

"Not yet, Kate," I said, "We'll be doing that shortly. At this point, I simply wanted to show you how easy it is to retrieve the address of a variable—or for that matter an object or function—by using the AddressOf operator."

"Did you say we can use the AddressOf operator to determine the address of a function?" Dave asked.

"That's right, Dave," I said. "Let's write a program that contains a custom function and use the AddressOf operator to display the memory of the function."

```cpp
//Example11_5.cpp

#include <iostream>

using namespace std;

void Dummy();    //Function Prototype

int main()
{
    Dummy();
    cout << "The address of Dummy() is " << &Dummy << endl;

    return 0;
}

void Dummy()
{
    cout << "Dummy() has been executed" << endl;
}
```

I saved the program as Example11_5 and then compiled and executed it. The following screenshot was displayed on the classroom projector:

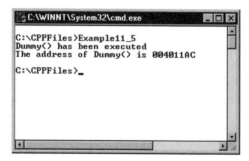

"As you can see," I said, "by using the AddressOf operator, we were able to display the address in memory of the **Dummy()** function. Take note to be careful to specify only the name of the function. Don't include the parentheses after the function name."

```
cout << "The address of Dummy() is " << &Dummy << endl;
```

"Again, working with function addresses is something that an experienced C++ programmer would love to do, but it's a bit beyond the scope of this class."

I waited a moment before continuing. So far, so good.

"Why don't we experiment with our first pointer now," I suggested. "Let's declare a pointer and then use the AddressOf operator to assign the address of an ordinary variable to it. Then we'll display both the value of the variable and the address we stored in the pointer to the C++ console."

```cpp
//Example11_6.cpp

#include <iostream>

using namespace std;

int main()
{
    int number1 = 12;
    int* pNumber1 = 0;

    cout << "The value of number1 is " << number1 << endl;
    cout << "The address of number1 is " << &number1 << endl;

    cout << "The initial value of pNumber1 is " << pNumber1 << endl;

    pNumber1 = &number1;
    cout << "The value of pNumber1 is now " << pNumber1 << endl;

    return 0;
}
```

I saved the program as Example11_6 and then compiled and executed it. The following screenshot was displayed on the classroom projector:

```
C:\WINNT\System32\cmd.exe

C:\CPPFiles>Example11_6
The value of number1 is 12
The address of number1 is 0012FF88
The initial value of pNumber1 is 00000000
The value of pNumber1 is now 0012FF88

C:\CPPFiles>
```

"Can anyone explain what's going on here?" I asked.

"I think I can," Linda volunteered. "We first displayed the value of the variable *number1*, 12, to the C++ console. Then we used the AddressOf operator to display the memory address of the variable *number1*, which is 0012FF88. Then we displayed the initial value of the pointer *pNumber1*, which is zero. Finally, after we assigned the address of the variable *number1* to the pointer *pNumber1*, we displayed its value to the C++ console."

"That's excellent, Linda," I said. "Notice that the result of displaying the value of the pointer variable *pNumber1* and the result of the AddressOf operation against the variable *number1* are identical. Let's take a good look at the code now. The first thing we did was to declare an ordinary integer variable called *number1*, followed by the declaration of our pointer variable, *pNumber1*."

```
int number1 = 12;
int* pNumber1 = 0;
```

"Remember," I said, "when C++ sees the asterisk following the word int, it knows that *pNumber1* is not an ordinary variable but rather is a pointer variable meant to store a memory address. This distinction is very important, because C++ will not permit us to assign the return value of the AddressOf operator to an ordinary variable—only to a pointer variable. Also notice that we initialized our pointer variable to zero, which is always recommended."

The week I discuss pointers in class is always a challenge, and from experience, I expected a bit of confusion. However, I was pleasantly surprised to find that no one seemed to be having any great difficulties so far.

"This next line of code," I continued, "displays the value of the variable *number1* to the C++ console."

```
cout << "The value of number1 is " << number1 << endl;
```

"This is followed by the line of code that uses the AddressOf operator to display the memory address of the variable *number1*."

```
cout << "The address of number1 is " << &number1 << endl;
```

 NOTE
Remember, don't read too much into the value of the memory address itself. The address that you see on your monitor will be affected by the PC upon which your program is running and the operating system. Most likely, the address you see will not match the one in this example.

"With this next line of code, we display the value of the initialized pointer. I wanted to show you that it is indeed equal to zero. Notice that nothing 'special' needs to be done to display the value of a pointer variable."

```
cout << "The initial value of pNumber1 is " << pNumber1 << endl;
```

"Next we execute the AddressOf operation against the variable *number1*. The return value is an address that we then assign to the pointer variable *pNumber1*. As I mentioned earlier, this is the method normally used to assign an address to a pointer variable, although you could assign the address directly if you knew it."

```
pNumber1 = &number1;
```

"Finally, this line of code displays the value of *pNumber1*—an address—to the C++ console. Notice again that nothing 'special' needs to be done to display the address."

```
cout << "The value of pNumber1 is now " << pNumber1 << endl;
```

No one seemed to be having any problems so far.

The Indirection Operator (*)

"If you have a pointer variable containing an address," Chuck said, "is there any way to determine the value of the variable to which that address belongs. By that I don't mean the address of the variable—we already know that, it's in the pointer—but rather the value of the variable that the pointer 'points to.'"

"That's quite a tongue twister, Chuck," I said, "and it's an excellent question. Yes, it is possible by using the C++ indirection operator, which is the asterisk."

"Did you say *indirection* operator?" Rhonda asked.

"You heard me right, Rhonda," I said. "The indirection operator, the asterisk, is also called the *dereference operator*. Using it, we can obtain the value of a variable whose address is stored in a pointer. You can think of the indirection operator as the opposition of the AddressOf operator. The AddressOf operator returns the address of an ordinary variable. Given an address, the indirection operator returns the value stored at that address."

"Could you elaborate on that?" Ward asked.

"Sure thing, Ward," I said. "Suppose we have a variable called *number1*, containing the value 22, and we have a pointer variable called *pNumber1*, containing the address of the variable *number1*. By using the indirection operator, we can determine that the value of *number1* is 22."

"Sounds like a roundabout way of obtaining a value," Linda said. "Of course, if we know the name of the variable, we can simply use that to obtain the value, right?"

"Absolutely right, Linda," I said. "But as you'll see later on today, it's possible to create a variable with no name, just a pointer, in which case using the indirection operator is the only way to obtain its value. Let's take a look at the indirection operator now."

I then displayed this code on the classroom projector:

```cpp
//Example11_7.cpp

#include <iostream>

using namespace std;

int main()
{
    int number1 = 12;
    int* pNumber1 = 0;

    pNumber1 = &number1;

    cout << "The value of number1 is " << *pNumber1 << endl;

    return 0;
}
```

I saved the program as Example11_7.cpp and then compiled and executed it. The following screenshot was displayed on the classroom projector:

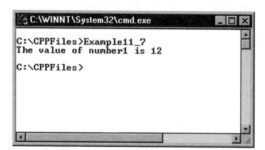

"Let's review the code now to make sure you're all with me," I said. "Here are the declarations for both the variable *number1* and the pointer variable *pNumber1*."

```
int number1 = 12;
int* pNumber1 = 0;
```

"This line of code uses the C++ AddressOf operator to assign the address of the variable *number1* to the pointer variable *pNumber1*."

```
pNumber1 = &number1;
```

"As we know," I continued, "ordinarily, to display the value of a variable, we simply reference the name of the variable, but using the C++ indirection operator we tell C++ to 'look up' the value associated with an address, like this. Notice the asterisk in front of the pointer name."

```
cout << "The value of number1 is " << *pNumber1 << endl;
```

The Swap() Function Using Pointers

"I feel pretty confident in the mechanics of what you've shown us so far this morning," Rhonda said. "Can we have a chance to put it all together—perhaps with a practice exercise?"

"You read my mind, Rhonda," I said. "Do you remember the Swap program we wrote a little earlier? Our last version of that program used a C++ reference to get the job done. Let's complete this exercise so that we use pointers to perform the exchange of values between two variables. You'll see that the program is more complicated than the version we have now, but it will be a great learning experience."

I then distributed this exercise for the class to complete.

Exercise 11-1   Using Pointers with the Swap() Function

In this exercise, you'll write a program that uses pointers to swap variable values.

1. Use Notepad (if you are using Windows) to enter the following code:

```
//Practice11_1.cpp

#include <iostream>

using namespace std;

void Swap(int* pNumber1, int* pNumber2);

int main()
{
    int x = 13;
    int y = 22;
```

```
        int* pX = 0;
        int* pY = 0;

        cout << "The value of x is " << x << endl;
        cout << "The value of y is " << y << endl;

        pX = &x;
        pY = &y;

        Swap(pX,pY);

        cout << "The value of x is now " << x << endl;
        cout << "The value of y is now " << y << endl;

        return 0;
    }

    void Swap(int* pNumber1,int* pNumber2)
    {
        int temp;

        temp = *pNumber1;
        *pNumber1 = *pNumber2;
        *pNumber2 = temp;
    }
```

2. Save your source file as Practice11_1 in the \CPPFiles\Practice folder (select File | Save As from Notepad's menu bar). Be sure to save your source file with the filename extension .cpp.

3. Compile your source file into an executable file.

4. Execute your program. The program will display the initial values of the variables *x* and *y*, along with their new values after the **Swap()** function has executed.

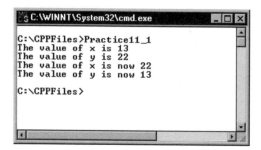

Discussion Only one student, Blaine, had a problem completing the exercise—and it was a minor one. While coding the exercise, although he properly initialized his pointer variables to zero, he forgot to later assign valid addresses to them using the AddressOf operator. His program compiled and linked fine, but when he ran it, when the **Swap()** function executed, the two addresses passed to the **Swap()** function as arguments were null, and his program 'bombed' with a memory read error. It didn't take Blaine too long to correct the problem, and soon he was happily on his way. It was a great learning experience for the whole class.

"This exercise gave us a chance to practice everything we learned this morning about pointers," I said, after returning from Blaine's workstation, "although I suspect declaring a pointer as an argument to a function may have confused some of you. Let's take a detailed look at the code now, beginning with the function prototype for **Swap()**. Something you hadn't seen before now is the use of a pointer as an argument to a function. Not surprisingly, if you intend to pass an argument that is a pointer to a function, you need to let C++ know that in both the function prototype and the function header. Here's the prototype for the **Swap()** function."

```
void Swap(int* pNumber1, int* pNumber2);        // Function Prototype
```

"That syntax did confuse me a bit when I first saw it," Rhonda said. "I must say I was pretty proud of myself when I eventually recognized what was going on. One thing that really confuses me is the multiple use of asterisks in C++. We use the asterisk to declare a pointer and for the indirection operator—not to mention the use of the asterisk for multiplication."

"Your confusion is absolutely understandable," I said. "I've participated in many discussions with C++ programmers lamenting the use of the asterisk for both pointer declaration and for the indirection operator. You would have thought that the developers of the C and C++ languages would have come up with another way to designate these—but that's all water under the bridge now. This is the syntax we have to work with. Let's take a look at the code in the **main()** function now. We start out by declaring two ordinary integer variables called *x* and *y*."

```
int x = 13;
int y = 22;
```

"Then we declare two pointer variables called *pX* and *pY*, which we initialize to zero."

```
int* pX = 0;
int* pY = 0;
```

"Now we display the current values of *x* and *y*."

```
cout << "The value of x is " << x << endl;
cout << "The value of y is " << y << endl;
```

"Blaine, it was at this point where you had the problem with your program, forgetting to assign the addresses of the variables *x* and *y* to the pointers *pX* and *pY*. We do that by using the AddressOf operator."

```
pX = &x;
pY = &y;
```

"In Blaine's case, when his program called the **Swap()** function, instead of passing it two pointers with valid addresses as arguments, it actually passed two null pointers. Because a null pointer contains an invalid memory address, Blaine's program bombed with an address error. In our case, both pointers now contain valid addresses, which are then passed to the **Swap()** function with this code."

```
Swap(pX,pY);
```

"You're going to see in a few minutes," I said, "that there's a way to streamline this code quite a bit by *not* explicitly declaring pointers at all. What we'll do in the next exercise is to pass references to the **Swap()** function, not pointers. But let's not look ahead too far. Instead, let's take a look at the **Swap()** function. As you can see, both the function header and the function prototypes are identical—including two arguments declared as integer type pointers."

```
void Swap(int* pNumber1,int* pNumber2)
{
```

"Within the **Swap()** function, we declare a variable called *temp*, which will be used to exchange the values of the variables *x* and *y*."

```
int temp;
```

"Here's the difference between this version of the program and the one we wrote in Example11_3. In this one, we use the indirection operator against the first passed argument—which is really the address of the variable *x* in the **main()** function—and assign it to the *temp* variable."

```
temp = *pNumber1;
```

"This next line of code you may find a bit confusing at first," I said. "Here we are using the indirection operator on the second passed argument, and we assign its return value to the variable 'pointed to' by the pointer *pNumber1*—in essence, exchanging the value *x* with the value of *y*."

```
*pNumber1 = *pNumber2;
```

"Because of this, for the moment anyway, both the variables *x* and *y* in the **main()** function have the same value."

"If both variables have the same value," Rhonda said, "we're in trouble. Where's the old value of the variable *x*?"

"The value of *x* is in the *temp* variable," I said, "and we'll then assign it to the variable 'pointed to' by the pointer *pNumber2*."

```
*pNumber2 = temp;
```

"Oh, I see," Rhonda replied. "The value of *temp* is being assigned to the variable pointed to by *pNumber2*—that's what the asterisk means."

"Exactly, Rhonda," I said.

"All this pointer notation can be tough to follow," Kathy said, "but I think if you take your time as you read the code, remembering that a pointer is an address, that an ampersand in front of a variable name returns its address, and that an asterisk in front of a pointer points to the variable whose address is stored in the pointer, you'll be okay."

"That's a pretty good summation of the operation of pointers, Kathy," I said.

"Did you say there's a simpler way to code this program?" Linda asked.

"Slightly," I replied. "Experienced C++ programmers are always looking to streamline code—so saving a few lines of code here and there can be significant. In the modified code that follows, we can save some lines by *not* declaring the two pointer variables in the **main()** function of our program. Instead, we can pass, as arguments, the address of the variables *x* and *y* using the AddressOf operator. As practice, why don't you code this yourself."

I then distributed this exercise for the class to complete.

Exercise 11-2 More on Pointers with the Swap() Function

In this exercise, you'll modify the program you wrote in Exercise 11-1, streamlining it just a bit to achieve the same results.

1. Use Notepad (if you are using Windows) to either modify the code in Practice11_1.cpp or enter the following code from scratch (four lines of code have been deleted, and the one line of modified code is in bold):

```
//Practice11_2.cpp

#include <iostream>

using namespace std;

void Swap(int* pNumber1, int* pNumber2);

int main()
{
    int x = 13;
```

```
    int y = 22;

    cout << "The value of x is " << x << endl;
    cout << "The value of y is " << y << endl;

    Swap(&x,&y);

    cout << "The value of x is now " << x << endl;
    cout << "The value of y is now " << y << endl;

    return 0;
}

void Swap(int* pNumber1,int* pNumber2)
{
    int temp;

    temp = *pNumber1;
    *pNumber1 = *pNumber2;
    *pNumber2 = temp;
}
```

2. Save your source file as Practice11_2 in the \CPPFiles\Practice folder (select File | Save As from Notepad's menu bar). Be sure to save your source file with the filename extension .cpp.

3. Compile your source file into an executable file.

4. Execute your program. As was the case with Practice11_1, the program will display the initial values of the variables *x* and *y*, along with their new values after the **Swap()** function has executed.

Discussion

"Not much changed in this version of the program," Ward said, "Most importantly, it appears that the program still works in the same way."

"Absolutely, Ward," I said. "We dropped four lines of code, the code within the **main()** function in which we declared two pointers, and two lines of code to assign the addresses of the variables *x* and *y* to our pointers. In addition, we modified one line of code, the call to the **Swap()** function, to pass the address of the variables *x* and *y* via the AddressOf operator instead of explicitly passing the pointers."

```
    Swap(&x,&y);
```

"I know saving four lines of code like this would make the programmers back at work very happy," Dave said, with a smile on his face. "It seems to me their goal is to write their programs with as few lines as possible."

Pointers and Arrays

"I'd like to address the issue of pointers and arrays now," I said.

"Do you mean we can create a pointer to an array?" Ward asked.

"Yes we can, Ward," I said.

"I'm trying to conceptualize exactly what that means," Linda said. "Because an array is a collection of data, what does the pointer contain? The address of the first element?"

"That's exactly right, Linda," I said. "In fact, every pointer—whether a pointer to a variable or a pointer to an array—really contains the address of the starting point of that piece of data. Take a look at this code, which declares a six-element array called *grades* and then uses pointer notation to display the address of the array and the value of its first element."

```cpp
//Example11_8.cpp

#include <iostream>
using namespace std;

int main()
{
    int grades[6] = {82,90,64,80,95,75};
    int* pGrades = grades;

    cout << "The value of pGrades is " << pGrades << endl;
    cout << "The value of the first element of grades is "
        << *pGrades << endl;

    return 0;
}
```

I saved the program as Example11_8.cpp and then compiled and executed it. The following screenshot was displayed on the classroom projector:

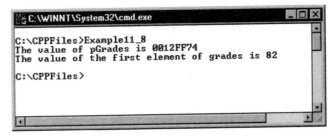

"As you can see," I said, "both the address of our array—in hexadecimal notation—and the value of the first element of the array have been displayed in the C++ console. Using pointers to arrays is much the same as working with pointers to ordinary variables, but there are some differences you need to be aware of and careful with. Here's the declaration of a six-element integer array called *grades*."

```
int grades[6] = {82,90,64,80,95,75};
```

"This is followed by the assignment of the address of the array to the pointer called *pGrades*."

```
int* pGrades = grades;
```

Notice how in this program, we combine the declaration of the pointer and the assignment of the address to the pointer with one line of code rather than declare the pointer, initialize it to zero, and then assign the address. We've saved two lines of code by using this syntax. By the way, notice that the data type of the pointer is identical to that of the array."

"Hmmm," I heard Valerie say, "where's the AddressOf operator?"

"That's right," Joe said. "In our other programs, when assigning the address of an ordinary variable to a pointer, we've been using the AddressOf operator, haven't we? We didn't do that here."

"Great observations," I said, "This is one of the differences in working with an array pointer. When you assign the address of an array to a pointer variable, you don't use the AddressOf operator—in fact, if you use it, the compiler will flag that line of code as an error."

 NOTE

When assigning the address of an array to a pointer variable, do not use the AddressOf operator.

I paused a moment before continuing.

"These next two lines of code display both the address of our array and the value of the first element in our array to the C++ console."

```
cout << "The value of pGrades is " << pGrades << endl;
cout << "The value of the first element of grades is " << *pGrades << endl;
```

"One interesting feature of an array is that we can display the memory address of an array without using a pointer at all, just by using the name of the array itself, like this."

```
cout << "The value of pGrades is " << pGrades << endl;
```

"When you say 'address of the array,'" Kate said, "you really mean the starting point of the array, don't you?"

"That's right, Kate," I said. "To C++, an array, no matter how many elements it contains, is really just a continuous piece of data storage, so when we display the address of the array, what we are seeing is the address of the starting point of the array. Addresses for all data storage are expressed the same way. For instance, when we display the address of an integer variable, we display its starting point as well."

"Displaying the first element of an array is great," Ward said, "but what about the other elements in the array? Isn't there a way to display the other elements of the array by using the pointer to the array?"

"Great question, Ward," I said. "The answer is yes. Using what is known as *pointer arithmetic*, we can display the values in all the elements of the array."

Pointer Arithmetic

"Did you say *pointer arithmetic*?" Peter asked. "Not more math to learn!"

"You heard me right, Peter," I said, "but don't worry, it's basic addition and subtraction. Using pointer arithmetic, you can increment (add to) or decrement (subtract from) the value of a pointer. Pointer arithmetic makes the most sense if the pointer contains the address of an array. For instance, if you add 1 to the value of a pointer that 'points to' an array, the pointer address is updated with the address of the second element of the array. Add 1 again, and now the pointer contains the address of the third element of the array, and so forth. Subtracting 1 from the value of a pointer that 'points to' an array works in reverse."

"So adding 1 to a pointer doesn't simply add 1 to the physical address stored there," Dave said. "I presume this is why it's important to designate a data type along with the pointer declaration so that C++ knows how much data storage each array element consumes and can properly increment the address."

"Exactly, Dave," I said. "C++ is smart enough to know, for instance, that an integer array element uses four bytes of storage. Therefore, when you increment the value of its pointer by 1, it actually 'adds' 4 to the address stored in the pointer."

I could see some confused looks on the faces of my students, so I displayed this code on the classroom projector:

```
//Example11_9.cpp

#include <iostream>
using namespace std;
```

```
int main()
{
   int grades[6] = {82,90,64,80,95,75};
   int* pGrades = grades;

   cout << "The value of pGrades is " << pGrades << endl;
   cout << "The value of the first element of grades is " << *pGrades
        << endl << endl;

   pGrades++;
   cout << "The value of pGrades is now " << pGrades << endl;
   cout << "The value of the second element in grades is " << *pGrades
        << endl << endl;

   pGrades+=4;
   cout << "The value of pGrades is now " << pGrades << endl;
   cout << "The value of the sixth element in grades is " << *pGrades
        << endl << endl;

   pGrades-=3;
   cout << "The value of pGrades is now " << pGrades << endl;
   cout << "The value of the third element in grades is " << *pGrades
        << endl << endl;

   return 0;
}
```

I saved the program as Example11_9.cpp and then compiled and executed it. The following screenshot was displayed on the classroom projector.

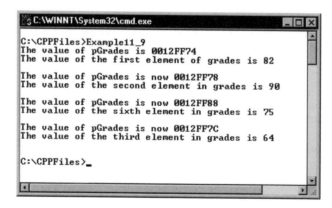

"As you can see," I said, "this program started out by displaying the initial value of both the pointer *pGrades* and the first element in our array. Then by using pointer arithmetic, we were able to change and display the address contained in the pointer and also display the elements of the array pertaining to that updated address. We first incremented the value of the pointer variable *pGrades* by using the C++ increment operator."

```
pGrades++;
```

"Then we used this code to display the value of its pointer and second element. Notice by adding 1 to the value of the pointer that the address really 'jumped' by 4—that's the number of bytes in an integer data type."

```
cout << "The value of pGrades is now " << pGrades << endl;
cout << "The value of the second element in grades is " << *pGrades
     << endl << endl;
```

"With the pointer now containing the address of the second element of the array, this line of code, which increments the pointer by 4, results in the address of the sixth element of the array being stored in the pointer."

```
pGrades+=4;
```

"Just to prove that we can also work our way 'backward' in an array using pointer arithmetic, this code, which subtracts 3 from the pointer, results in the address of the third element of the array being stored in the pointer."

```
pGrades-=3;
```

"I can see some potential danger here," Dave said. "Suppose you increment past the end of the array—or decrement past the beginning."

"What does Dave mean?" Kate asked.

"What Dave means," I said, "is that C++ gives the programmer a lot of freedom. If you have a three-element array and add 10 to the value of its pointer, the pointer will contain an address that is well 'beyond' the last element of the array. If you try to read the value there, or worse yet, update it in some way, your program can bomb—and you can even cause your PC to 'freeze.' Be very careful when performing pointer arithmetic."

"Is it possible to use pointers with multidimensional arrays?" Dave asked.

"Yes it is," I said, "but that's a topic that is well beyond the scope of this class. In general, particular for beginners, it's recommended that when working with arrays, particularly multidimensional arrays, that you use the standard type of array processing that we discussed last week."

"Can you perform pointer arithmetic on a pointer that refers to an ordinary variable?" Steve asked.

"In theory, you can," I said, "although pointer arithmetic is most useful on pointers referring to an array. Let's put it this way: C++ won't prevent you from incrementing or decrementing the value of a pointer that refers to an ordinary variable, although you may not obtain the results you are looking for. For instance, suppose you declare two variables, called *x* and *y*, and declare a pointer called *pX* containing the address of *x*. You might think that incrementing the pointer *pX* by 1 would result in the address of the variable *y* being stored in the pointer, but that's not necessarily the case. On our computers here in the computer lab, the address location of the variable *y* is actually *before* the address of the variable *x*. The bottom line: When it comes to pointer arithmetic, only arrays can be guaranteed to behave the way we've seen today."

"Can you create a pointer that refers to an object?" Dave asked.

"Good question, Dave," I said. "Let's tackle that one after our break."

We had been working for quite some time, so I suggested that we take a 15-minute break before tackling our last topics of the day—pointers to objects, the free store, and dynamic memory.

Pointers to Objects

"So is it possible to create a pointer to an object," Linda asked, as we resumed after our break, "and are there any advantages to doing so? Why would you want to?"

"Yes, Linda," I said, "it is possible to create a pointer to an object. Using a pointer to an object, you can work with the object's attributes and execute its functions just as you ordinarily would, although the syntax is a bit unruly. As far as advantages? Not really."

"Then why do it?" Ward asked.

"The primary reason for creating a pointer to an object," I replied, "is because that's the only way to dynamically create an object at runtime, which is something that can come in very handy. Dynamic memory allocation is the last topic we'll cover in today's class, so let's hold off until then to discuss it. For now, let's see how we can create a pointer to an object by writing a program to create an instance of a Banner object from the Banner class we created several weeks back. Once we have the object created and its address in a pointer, you'll see that it's possible to update the object's member attributes and even execute its functions via the pointer. Take a look at this code."

```
//Example11_10.cpp

#include "Banner.cpp"

int Banner::numberOfBannerObjects;

int main()
{
```

```
    Banner x;
    Banner* pX = &x;

    pX->favoriteProgram = "C++";
    pX->Display();

    return 0;
}
```

I saved the program as Example11_10.cpp and then compiled and executed it. The following screenshot was displayed on the classroom projector:

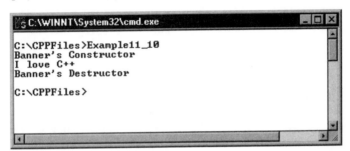

"The C++ console," I said, "indicates that a Banner object has been created, its **Display()** function has been executed, and finally the object has been destroyed. The code itself is very similar to the code we first wrote several weeks ago, except this first uses a pointer instead. We start by executing this line of code, which declares an instance of a Banner object called *x*."

```
Banner x;
```

"This code creates a pointer called *pX*."

```
Banner* pX = &x;
```

"Notice how we specify a pointer type of Banner, which tells C++ the type of pointer we are establishing. As is the case with the other pointers we've created today, we use the AddressOf operator to assign the address of our Banner object to the pointer.

"These next two lines of code update the favoriteProgram attribute of the Banner object and execute its **Display()** function."

```
pX->favoriteProgram = "C++";
pX->Display();
```

"Now we could have chosen to use standard object dot notation to do this, but both can be done using the pointer, although as you can see, the syntax is something you haven't encountered before. Notice the hyphen and the greater than sign following the pointer name."

"I was wondering what that was," Rhonda said.

"The use of the hyphen, followed by the greater than sign," I said, "is required when you refer to an attribute or function of an object by using its pointer."

"This still seems like a lot of trouble to me," Rhonda said. "Why not just use object notation to 'get at' the attributes and functions of the objects? This must have something to do with the dynamic memory allocation you mentioned earlier."

"That's right, Rhonda," I said. "Accessing the attribute of an object or executing its function via a pointer is a bit more trouble. Unfortunately, if you create an object on the free store, it's the only way you can 'get at' the object's attributes or functions."

The Free Store

"What in the world is a *free store*?" Mary asked.

"Sorry, Mary," I said, "that term just slipped out. When you create variables, arrays, and objects at runtime—in other words, *dynamically*—they are created on something known as the *free store*, sometimes also called the *heap*."

"How is that different from the variables, arrays, and objects we've been creating so far?" Kate asked.

"Up until now," I said, "the variables and objects we've declared—with the exception of global variables that we examined very briefly early in the course—have been created and maintained in something called the *stack*."

"I think I've heard of that term before," Dave said, "Is the stack another term for *local memory*?"

"That's right, Dave," I said. "Most of the variables and objects we've created during the course have been local. For instance, whenever a variable or object is declared within a function, such as the **main**() function, the storage allocation for that variable or object is made within the stack. The stack is a relatively small area of computer memory that is allocated to an individual program—each program that runs on a PC gets its own stack. The stack 'holds' both programming instructions and data. As your program executes, data is constantly placed on and removed from the stack. There are several key points to bear in mind about the stack.

"First, the amount of stack space available to your program can be limited—in other words, it's possible to write a program that simply runs out of stack space. The storage allocated for the free store, or the *heap*, is much larger.

"Second, when you compile your program, the C++ compiler analyzes your program code for storage requirements, based on the declaration statements for the variables, arrays, and objects it finds. Without the use of pointers, it's impossible for your program to get more storage at runtime for variables, arrays, and objects.

"Finally, when a function is executed, variables and objects declared within that function are placed on the stack. Variables and objects declared in a function can only be 'seen' within that function, and when the function ends, they are removed from the stack. As a result, the life span of data that is placed on the stack is relatively short—it's not the full duration of your program."

"Suppose you need to have data 'last' for the duration of your program?" Steve asked. "Or be 'seen' by code in another function?"

"That's why you use global variables and objects," I said. "Global variables and objects are declared outside of any of the functions in our program—usually just under the compiler directives—and are actually stored in something called the *global namespace*. They 'last' for as long as the program is running. In addition, they can also be 'seen' by every part of our program."

"So where does the free store you mentioned fit in?" Joe asked, "So far, we have local variables, which are stored on the stack, and global variables, which are stored in the global namespace. It would seem to me that between stack memory and global memory we have pretty much all we need."

"You're right, Joe," I said. "Between stack and global memory, it would appear we have all the functionality we require. Stack memory allows us to create local variables and objects whose lifespan and scope—where they can be seen—begins and ends with the function in which they're declared. And global variables allow us to create variables whose lifespan is for the duration of the program and whose scope is program wide. However, there's a potential problem with global variables."

"What is it?" Mary asked.

"The rule of thumb in programming," I said, "is to restrict the scope of a variable or object as narrowly as possible. C and C++ programmers have traditionally objected to declaring variables or objects as global just to give them a longer life span. Declaring a variable or object on the free store can give it a lifespan equal to the duration of the program, yet still give it local scope."

"I'm afraid I don't understand," Rhonda said, obviously perplexed.

"Declaring a variable or object on the free store," I continued, "gives the variable or object local scope but still allows it to 'live' for as long as the program is running."

"So a variable or object declared on the free store can only be 'seen' by the function that creates it?" Kathy asked.

"That's exactly right, Kathy," I said.

Declaring Variables and Objects on the Free Store

"How do we declare variables or objects on the free store?" Steve asked. "Is it like declaring an ordinary variable?"

"Not quite," I said. "Variables and objects to be created on the free store require that we use a pointer and that we assign an address to it that is obtained by executing the C++ 'new' statement. Once variables and objects are created on the free store, thereafter they can only be referenced by using the address, which of course is stored in the pointer."

"And that's why they have local scope," Dave said. "There's no way for another function to *accidentally* access or modify the value of a free store variable or object, the way there is with a global variable or object, because only the function has access to the address via the pointer."

"That's right, Dave," I said. "And one other valuable feature of declaring variables and objects on the free store, which I've hinted strongly at earlier, is that it gives us the ability to allocate memory dynamically—that is, at runtime."

"And why would we want to do that again?" Mary asked.

"With ordinary variables, arrays, and objects," I said, "the C++ compiler determines space requirements at compile time. There may be instances in your programs where you just don't know, when you write your program, exactly how many variables or array elements you'll need within your program. For instance, you may write a program in which you read a file or a database, and for each record you find there, you create an array element. You may have ten records in the file today, and 10,000 records in the file tomorrow. The point is that ideally, the array declaration should reflect only the amount of data storage actually needed, but this can't be done using an ordinary variable. However, with variables and objects declared on the free store, memory isn't allocated until the program actually executes—which means you can write a program whose array declaration is based on some condition it finds at runtime, such as the number of records in a file or a database table."

"Array size was an issue last week, wasn't it?" Linda volunteered. "Someone in the class asked how large to declare an array if you weren't sure what the size should be. So it's possible to decide on the 'size' of an array when the program is running?"

"That's right, Linda," I said. "Dynamic memory allocation is one of the big advantages in declaring variables on the free store."

"I'm afraid I'm going to have to see how this free store variable declaration works in order to clear this all up for me," Chuck said. "Can you show us an example?"

"I'd be glad to, Chuck," I said, as I displayed this code on the classroom projector:

```cpp
//Example11_11.cpp

#include <iostream>
using namespace std;

int main()
{
    int* pY = new int;       //Create variable on the Free Store
    *pY = 22;

    cout << "The value of pY is " << *pY << endl;
```

```
delete pY;              //Delete variable from the Free Store
pY=0;                   //Assign a Null value to the pointer

    return 0;
}
```

I saved the program as Example11_11.cpp and then compiled and executed it. The following screenshot was displayed on the classroom projector:

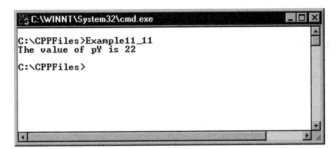

"As you can see," I said, "what we've done here is to declare a variable on the free store and then display its value in the C++ console. Although its functionality is pretty simple, working with the free store is different than anything you've seen before, and it does require some explanation. First, in order to declare a variable on the free store, we must declare a pointer variable, which will contain the address of the free store variable. It's important to note that there is no name declared for the free store variable—it can only be accessed via its address, which is returned by executing the C++ 'new' statement. In this program, we combined the declaration of the pointer and the assignment of the address of the free store variable into a single statement. You can read this line of code as asking C++ to create a new integer variable and to assign its address to the integer pointer variable *pY*."

```
int* pY = new int;      //Create variable on the Free Store
```

"So there's no way *not* to use a pointer here?" Rhonda asked. "For instance, by assigning the return value of the new keyword to an ordinary variable?"

"No there's not, Rhonda," I said. "The return value of the new keyword is an address, and you now know that only a pointer variable can store an address. Once we have our free store variable's address stored in our pointer variable, we can use the indirection operator to assign a value to the variable via its pointer, like this."

```
*pY = 22;
```

"Oh, I see now," Rhonda said. "I was a little confused with this syntax when I first saw it. So everything having to do with the free store variable is now done via the address stored in the pointer variable."

"Exactly, Rhonda," I said, "which is why we then use the indirection operator to display its value on the C++ console."

```
cout << "The value of pY is " << *pY << endl;
```

"Is there any way to initialize a free store variable when you declare it?" Steve asked.

"Great question, Steve," I replied. "You can combine the declaration and initialization by specifying its initial value within parentheses, like this."

```
int* pY = new int(22);
```

"What's going on with that next line of code?" Chuck asked. "What does 'delete' do?"

"Being able to declare variables on the free store gives us as C++ programmers enormous power," I said, "because the variable exists for the duration of our program. It also requires more responsibility on the part of the programmer for that reason. Therefore, when we are done using the variable, it is extremely important that we delete it from the free store—and that's done using the C++ delete statement."

```
delete pY;              //Delete variable from the Free Store
```

"It's also a good idea to assign a null address to the pointer as well so that we don't accidentally refer to the address in it again. Even though the data associated with free store variable has been deleted, the address contained in the pointer is still there, and we don't want to accidentally use it in our code."

```
pY=0;                   //Assign a Null value to the pointer
```

"How important is it to execute the delete statement?" Kate asked. "I mean, what will happen if the program ends without us deleting the variable?"

"Failure to delete the variable from the free store using the delete statement," I said, "can result in a variety of minor, and sometimes not-so-minor, problems. The primary problem occurs when a program—usually one intended to run for a long period of time—continues to use more and more memory. Specifically, it continues to write data in the form of free store variables and arrays to the free store, without 'remembering' to free the data. Eventually, the PC or server will run out of available memory and the program—or even worse, the entire PC—will come to a grinding halt. This problem is called a *memory leak* and invariably is caused by the programmer forgetting to delete free store memory after using it. Sometimes the programmer gets it 'half right' by remembering to assign a null value to the pointer containing the free store variable's address—but by itself, this doesn't free up any of the storage that variable is using on the free store. The bottom line: Free up the space using the delete statement, then assign a null value to the pointer containing the address of the free store variable."

"What happens when the program ends and you've forgotten to delete the free store variables?" Ward asked. "Will this storage be returned to the operating system?"

"Yes, it will," I said. "There's a misconception among beginners that this space is never returned to the operating system, but it is, and it will be made available to other programs. The misconception probably comes about because many C++ programs are intended to run indefinitely—that is, they never end. Therefore, a program with a small memory leak problem can cause the PC or server to run out of memory eventually."

"How do you declare an object on the free store?" Bob asked.

"The basic steps are the same," I said. "Declare a pointer of the object's type, assign it the address of the return value of the new statement, use the notation you saw in Example11_1 to work with the object's attributes and functions, and when you're done with it, delete it using the delete statement. In fact, why don't you take a shot at creating an object on the free store by completing this exercise?"

I then distributed this exercise for the class to complete.

Exercise 11-3   **More on Pointers with the Swap() Function**

In this exercise, you'll write a program that creates an instance of a Banner object on the free store.

1. Use Notepad (if you are using Windows) to enter the following code:

```
//Practice11_3.cpp

#include "Banner.cpp"

int Banner::numberOfBannerObjects;

int main()
{
  Banner* pX = new Banner;

  pX->favoriteProgram = "C++";
  pX->Display();

  delete pX;  //Delete variable from the Free Store
```

```
        pX = 0;      //Assign Null value to pointer

        return 0;
}
```

2. Save your source file as Practice11_3 in the \CPPFiles\Practice folder (select File | Save As from Notepad's menu bar). Be sure to save your source file with the filename extension .cpp.

3. Compile your source file into an executable file.

4. Execute your program. You should see the following screenshot:

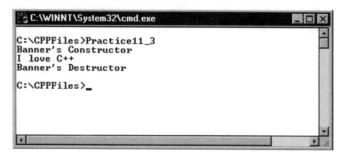

Discussion

"This program looks much like Example11_10," I said, "in which we created an instance of the Banner object and assigned its address to a pointer variable. The difference here is that we've declared our Banner object on the free store by using the new keyword."

```
Banner* pX = new Banner;
```

"The pointer *pX* now contains the address of the newly created Banner object. Using this pointer, we can then update the favoriteProgram attribute of the Banner object using this syntax."

```
pX->favoriteProgram = "C++";
```

"And we can execute its **Display()** function as well."

```
pX->Display();
```

"Finally, because we're all done with the Banner object, we should delete the object on the free store by using the delete statement."

```
delete pX;
```

"And we should also assign a null value to its pointer."

```
pX = 0;
```

"I'm still having a hard time conceptualizing what happens when you execute the delete statement," Mary said. "Is it the value in the pointer *pX* that is being erased, or is it the data stored in the address that *pX* contains that is being erased?"

"It's the data stored at that address that's erased," I said. "Executing the delete statement has no impact on the address stored in the pointer. After the delete statement is executed, the pointer *pX* still has the address that the new statement returned to it. However, there's no valid data there any longer. That's why, after executing the delete statement, we then assign a null address to the pointer."

Creating and Destroying Arrays on the Free Store—Dynamic Memory

I waited a moment before continuing. There was only one topic left to discuss—declaring a dynamically-sized array on the free store.

"I want to show you how to create an array on the free store now," I said, "but before we do that, let's first create a program using an ordinary array that asks the user for the names of their family members and then displays them in the C++ console."

I then displayed this code on the classroom projector:

```
//Example11_12.cpp

#include <iostream>
#include <string>

using namespace std;

int main()
{
    string names[3];

    int counter = 3;
    char response[256];

    cout << "What is the first name? ";
    cin.getline(response,256);
    names[0] = response;

    cout << "What is the second name? ";
    cin.getline(response,256);
    names[1] = response;
```

```
cout << "What is the third name? ";
cin.getline(response,256);
names[2] = response;

cout << endl << "The 3 names you entered are " << endl << endl;

for (int row = 0; row < counter; row++)
{
    cout << names[row] << endl;
}

return 0;
}
```

I saved the program as Example11_12.cpp and then compiled and executed it. Entering three names at the prompts, the following screenshot was displayed on the classroom projector:

"As you can see," I said, "this program asks the user for the names of three family members and then displays them in the C++ console. We use an array to store the user's family members and to later display them in the C++ console. The first thing we did was to declare a three-element string array called *names*."

```
string names[3];
```

"As you know, an array declared in this way is fixed in size, and storage for the array is determined at compile time by the compiler—there's no way to change it at runtime. As you'll see in a few minutes, declaring an array on the free store will overcome this limitation.

"Next, we declare an integer variable called *counter*, which will assist us in displaying the values of each element of our array in the C++ console."

```
int counter = 3;
```

"You've seen this declaration time and time again throughout the course—it's a 256-element character array to hold the user's response to the questions we ask."

```
char response[256];
```

"Next, we have a series of code that prompts the user for the name of the first family member."

```
cout << "What is the first name? ";
```

"Their answer is then stored in the *response* variable via the **getline()** function of the cin object."

```
cin.getline(response,256);
```

"Then the value of the *response* variable is stored in the first element—element 0—of the *names* array."

```
names[0] = response;
```

"This process is repeated for the second and third family member names."

```
cout << "What is the second name? ";
cin.getline(response,256);
names[1] = response;
cout << "What is the third name? ";
cin.getline(response,256);
names[2] = response;
```

"With all three family member names entered by the user, and each stored as an element of the *names* array, we then use a For loop to display the value of each of the three elements in the C++ console. Notice how the value of the variable *counter*—which we initialized to 3—is used to determine how many times to execute the body of the For loop."

```
for (int row = 0; row < counter; row++)
{
    cout << names[row] << endl;
}
```

"Not very elegant, is it?" Dave asked.

"And not very flexible either," Linda added. "The program only asks for three family members. Suppose the user has five family members—or two. We would have to modify the program, changing the declaration of the *names* array, and then the value of the *counter* variable, to get the program to function properly."

"Both Dave and Linda are right," I said. "This program isn't flexible at all, and it's not very elegant either. There's already a lot of code here—and that's just for three names. If we had to accept ten names, we'd have to modify the program, and then we would have three times as much code. Ordinary arrays declared in this way are allocated on the stack, and their size is determined at compile time—there's simply no way to change it at runtime. Before I show you how to declare a free store array, let me show you what some beginner programmers attempt to do to make this program more flexible. In fact, it's not far from the ultimate solution to the problem. Unfortunately, this program won't compile—and you'll see why in a minute."

```cpp
//Example11_13.cpp

#include <iostream>
#include <string>

using namespace std;

int main()
{
    int HOWMANY = 0;
    char response[256];

    cout << "How many people in your family? ";
    cin.getline(response,256);
    HOWMANY = atoi(response);

    string names[HOWMANY];

    for (int row = 0; row < HOWMANY; row++)
    {
        cout << "Enter name #" << row+1 << " ";
        cin.getline(response,256);
        names[row] = response;
    }

    cout << endl << "The names you entered are " << endl << endl;

    for (int row = 0; row < HOWMANY; row++)
    {
```

```
        cout << names[row] << endl;
    }

    return 0;
}
```

"I think I see what you are trying to do," Kate said. "You're asking the user to tell you how many family members they have and then assigning that value to the variable *HOWMANY*. Then you're using *HOWMANY* in your variable declaration. Sounds like a great idea to me—but will it work?"

"Let's see," I replied.

I then saved the program as Example11_13.cpp and tried to compile it. Unfortunately, the following error message from the compiler was displayed on the classroom projector:

"It sounded like a great idea," I said, "but the compiler didn't agree. Here's the problem line of code."

```
string names[HOWMANY];
```

"What's the problem?" Rhonda asked.

"Because storage for local variables and arrays are determined at compile time," I said, "the C++ compiler needs a size for the number of elements in the *names* array that it knows cannot change. The compiler recognizes that *HOWMANY* is a variable, whose value, although initially set to zero, will be changed when the program runs, and so it flags this line of code as an error. The compiler would have been perfectly fine with it if *HOWMANY* had been defined as a C++ constant. In fact, that's what the error message is telling us: *HOWMANY* needs to be a constant."

"So what can we do?" Rhonda said. "How can we make the program flexible enough to deal with different numbers of family members? You said it was a good idea to have the user be able to determine the number of elements in the *names* array, but now it seems like we can't do it."

"It can be done," I said, "but only if we declare the *names* array on the free store."

"Are you going to show us how to do that now?" Kate asked.

"Even better," I said. "You're going to code it up yourself by completing our final exercise of the day."

I then distributed this exercise for the class to complete.

Exercise 11-4 **Using Pointers to Create an Array on the Free Store**

In this exercise, you'll write a program that creates a dynamic array on the free store.

1. Use Notepad (if you are using Windows) to enter the following code:

```cpp
//Practice11_4.cpp

#include <iostream>
#include <string>

using namespace std;

int main()
{
    int HOWMANY = 0;
    char response[256];

    cout << "How many people in your family? ";
    cin.getline(response,256);
    HOWMANY = atoi(response);

    string* pNames = new string[HOWMANY];

    for (int row = 0; row < HOWMANY; row++)
    {
        cout << "Enter name #" << row+1 << " ";
        cin.getline(response,256);
        pNames[row] = response;
    }

    cout << endl << "The " << HOWMANY
         << " names you entered are " << endl << endl;

    for (int row = 0; row < HOWMANY; row++)
    {
        cout << pNames[row] << endl;
    }
```

```
        delete [] pNames;    //Delete array from the Free Store
        pNames = 0;          //Assign Null value to pointer

        return 0;
    }
```

2. Save your source file as Practice11_4 in the \CPPFiles\Practice folder (select File | Save As from Notepad's menu bar). Be sure to save your source file with the filename extension .cpp.

3. Compile your source file into an executable file.

4. Execute your program. Enter the number of members in your family and then enter their names. You should see a screenshot similar to the following:

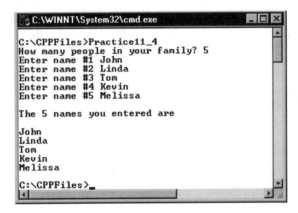

```
C:\WINNT\System32\cmd.exe

C:\CPPFiles>Practice11_4
How many people in your family? 5
Enter name #1 John
Enter name #2 Linda
Enter name #3 Tom
Enter name #4 Kevin
Enter name #5 Melissa

The 5 names you entered are

John
Linda
Tom
Kevin
Melissa

C:\CPPFiles>
```

Discussion

No one had any major problems completing the exercise. In fact, I detected quite a bit of satisfaction in the faces of my students. I think they're really beginning to catch on to the notion of pointers.

"Creating an array on the free store," I said, "follows the same pattern as creating a variable or object on the free store. Once again, you declare a pointer, use the new statement to declare the array, and assign its return value to the pointer variable. When we are done with the array, we execute the delete statement and set the pointer variable equal to null. I must warn you, however, that the delete statement for an array declared on the free store is a bit quirky—but we'll discuss that in a minute. Let's take a look at the code now and see how this results in a program that's extremely compact and flexible enough to handle any number of family members. The first thing we did was to declare and initialize a variable called *HOWMANY*, designed to store the number of members in the user's family."

```
int HOWMANY = 0;
```

"This code prompts for, and then receives, the user's answer, which is then converted to an integer via the **atoi()** function and stored in the variable *HOWMANY*."

```
cout << "How many people in your family? ";
cin.getline(response,256);
HOWMANY = atoi(response);
```

"It was at this point in Example11_13 that we attempted to declare an array with a size equal to the value of the *HOWMANY* variable. As you learned when we tried to compile that program, with an ordinary variable, that's something we may not do. However, with an array on the free store, whose size can be dynamically determined at runtime, it's perfectly legal, and that's what this code does by instructing C++ to allocate a free store string array containing a number of elements equal to the value of the *HOWMANY* variable. The return value of the new statement is the address of the starting point of the array, which is then assigned to the pointer variable called *pNames*."

```
string* pNames = new string[HOWMANY];
```

"With the array declared on the free store, we then ask the user to enter the names of their family members. Using a For loop, determined by the value of *HOWMANY* variable, which contains the number of family members, this code prompts the user for a name and then assigns it to an element of the *pNames* array. The user continues to be prompted for family member names based on the value they entered earlier."

```
for (int row = 0; row < HOWMANY; row++)
{
    cout << "Enter name #" << row+1 << " ";
    cin.getline(response,256);
    pNames[row] = response;
}
```

"That's incredibly compact," Ward said. "I really love this code."

"When the loop to load the elements of the array finally ends," I said, "this code is then used to display each element of the array to the C++ console."

```
cout << endl << "The " << HOWMANY
    << " names you entered are " << endl << endl;

for (int row = 0; row < HOWMANY; row++)
{
    cout << pNames[row] << endl;
}
```

"Finally," I said, "we can't forget to delete the array from the free store using the delete statement and to set the value of our pointer variable to a null value. By the way, notice the syntax for deleting the array from the free store—you must include an empty set of brackets *before* the array name in order to delete the array from the free store."

```
delete [] pNames;          //Delete array from the Free Store
pNames = 0;                //Assign Null value to pointer
```

"I've got to say, I'm pretty impressed with this code," Ward said. "Better yet, I think I understand what's going on. I'm beginning to feel like one of those experienced C++ programmers you're always talking about."

"Will we be using pointers in the Grades Calculation Project?" Kathy asked.

"We could probably come up with an excuse to use one or two," I said, "but there's no sense modifying the project if we don't need to. If we had the need to create a dynamic array, that would be a great reason to use a pointer, but offhand, I can't think of an urgent need for pointers in our project. Perhaps that's something we can do in our intermediate C++ class next semester."

I then dismissed class for the day, reminding my students that our next class would be our final one.

"Next week should be pretty exciting around here," I said. "We'll be completing the Grades Calculation Project and delivering it to Frank Olley."

Summary

In this chapter, you learned about a topic that many C++ beginners find very difficult—pointers. I hope you found my treatment of pointers easy to understand and nonthreatening. If you keep your wits about you, pointers aren't all that difficult to work with and understand.

Specifically, you learned the following:

- A pointer is a variable that contains the memory address of a variable, array, or object.

- Each variable, array, and object—and even each function—has a memory address that can be returned using the AddressOf operator, which is the ampersand character (&).

- If you have a memory address stored in a pointer variable, you can determine the value stored there by using the indirection operator, which is the asterisk character (*).

- Local variables are stored on something called the *stack*. It's possible to declare variables on the free store, and these variables are allocated at runtime.

■ Use the "new" statement to declare a variable, array, or object on the free store.

■ Use the "delete" statement to "free up" the storage consumed by your free store variable, array, or object.

In the next chapter, we'll finish the book by exploring some of the common errors that can occur in C++ programming. We'll also examine ways to make allowances for problems that might occur when our programs run.

Chapter

12

Errors and Error Handling

n this chapter, you'll follow my university class as we learn how to avoid some of the common mistakes that beginner C++ programmers make. You'll also learn how to detect and handle the errors that slip through your fingers. Finally, we'll wrap up the course by delivering and installing our program in the English department.

Errors and Error Handling

I began the final class of my Introduction to C++ course by saying that in our final meeting together, we would cover error handling in a C++ program as well as deliver and install our program on a PC in the English department.

"So we'll actually be delivering the program today?" Ward asked.

"That's right, Ward," I said. "We'll be doing that at the end of today's class. Frank Olley called me earlier in the week to find out if we were on target to complete the project today, and when I told him we were, he asked if it would be possible to deliver and install the program as part of today's class. I told him that would be fine with me, and he was elated. He told me that he would arrange to have his two work study students come in today to get acquainted with the program. This might mean that today's class goes a little bit longer than usual. I do hope you can all hang in there and help me deliver and install our program in the English department."

"I wouldn't miss it for anything," Linda said.

"Me either," Steve said. "I think it will be exciting to see how the work study students like the program."

From the looks on the rest of my students' faces, I had a feeling they all felt the same way and would be paying a visit to the English department as well.

"It's a shame," Mary said suddenly, "but it doesn't look like Rose and Jack will make it to our final class. Has anyone heard from them? Are they still in Liverpool?"

"I've heard from them," I said. "I spoke with both of them on Thursday night, and at the time, they were aboard their ship somewhere in the North Atlantic. They said the weather was unusually frigid for April, and when asked whether they would be making it back on time for today's class, they told me they had spoken to the ship's captain, who assured them they'd be arriving in New York harbor early this morning—a few hours ahead of schedule. I expect both of them to be here before the end of class."

"That's great news," Rhonda said. "It will be good to see them again."

"Will our delivery and installation of the Grades Calculation program on a PC in the English department wrap up the SDLC?" Valerie asked.

"Just about," I replied. "Phase 5 of the SDLC, which is the Implementation phase, will begin today with the delivery and installation of the program, and it will conclude over the course of the next week as I and hopefully some student volunteers train work study students in the English, math, and science departments in the use of the program. Phase 6 of the SDLC, which is the Audit and Maintenance phase, will begin today as well, as we observe and study how well the program performs."

"So besides delivering the program to Frank Olley," Ward said, "what's on the agenda today? Error handling?"

"That's right, Ward," I said. "Error handling involves writing code to handle errors that can creep into our programs even after we do our best to ensure that they are free of errors."

I then went on to explain that as a teacher of computer programming, it's frequently tempting to show my students examples of bad code early on in a class in an effort to show them what 'not' to do. However, after many years of teaching, I have learned that there's a huge danger in illustrating bad code or code that contains errors too early in the class.

"For that reason," I said, "I try to wait until we've established a strong foundation in good coding techniques before discussing the types of errors you can make, which can quickly ruin your programming reputation. In today's class, we'll examine the types of common errors that beginners make and then you'll learn how to implement error-handling techniques in our C++ programs to detect and handle the errors that can occur anyway, even in the best of programs."

Common Beginner Errors

"What kinds of errors are you talking about detecting?" Dave asked. "I assume you mean runtime errors—you're not talking about compiler errors."

"That's a good point, Dave," I said. "There are actually three kinds of errors that we'll be discussing today. The first kind are compiler errors, and those are the errors detected by the C++ compiler, most of which we've already seen in the class. Compiler errors prevent us from ever getting to the point where we can run our program. The second kind are runtime errors. These are the kinds of errors that the C++ compiler can't detect, and which unfortunately occur when we run our compiled program. Runtime errors display nasty error messages to the user of our program, and in the case of pointers, they can cause the PC running our program to 'freeze.' The third kind of errors are the most dangerous. These are logic errors, and they are not detected by the compiler, nor, for the most part, do they cause your program to 'bomb' or abnormally terminate at runtime. Logic errors are programming mistakes that can cause horrific results—such as generating a paycheck for an employee for one million dollars instead of one thousand dollars, or ordering a dosage of medicine for a patient that is incorrect, or opening a valve or an engine of the space shuttle prematurely. Logic errors can be very difficult to track down—in fact, some programs have run for years with subtle logic errors that went unnoticed."

Compiler Errors

"Let's start by examining the common types of compiler errors that you are likely to make," I said. "Remember, compiler errors are those errors detected by the C++ compiler."

C++ Is Case Sensitive

"Probably the most common types of compiler errors," I said, "are caused by the case sensitivity of C++. In C++, just about everything is case sensitive. The names of classes, the names of functions, and the names of variables are all case sensitive. This can give programmers, especially those who have experience in other languages that are not case sensitive, a lot of trouble. Improperly referencing the name of a class, a function, or a variable in your program will generate a 'cannot resolve symbol' compiler error. Remember, any reference to a class name, a function, or a variable that you declare in your program must match its case exactly. For instance, if we declare a variable called *counter* (in lowercase) and then attempt to increment its value like this…"

```cpp
//Example12_1.cpp

#include <iostream>

using namespace std;

int main()
{
   int counter = 0;
   Counter++;

   cout << "The value of counter is " << counter;

   return 0;
}
```

"…we'll generate a compiler error indicating that there is an 'undefined symbol.'"

The following screenshot was displayed on the classroom projector:

```
C:\CPPFiles>bcc32 Example12_1.cpp
Borland C++ 5.5.1 for Win32 Copyright (c) 1993, 2000 Borland

Example12_1.cpp:
Error E2451 Example12_1.cpp 10: Undefined symbol 'Counter' i
n function main()
*** 1 errors in Compile ***

C:\CPPFiles>
```

"What's a symbol?" Lou asked.

"C++ keeps track of class, function, variable, and constant names in something called a *symbol table*," I said. "So you see, C++ is just telling us that we're referencing a name for which it doesn't have a record—and that's because, in this case, we declared the variable *counter* in all lowercase but later referenced it with a capital *C*."

"I think I've seen this error a million times," Rhonda said laughing.

"I would say this is probably the most common error message a beginner will see," I said. "Until you get used to the case sensitivity of C++, this may be an error that you generate every time you compile your program. Just remember, whenever you see the 'undefined symbol' error, check the spelling of your class, function, and variable names."

Spelling main as Main

"I sometimes get a compile error when I'm not careful with the spelling of the word 'main,'" Peter said. "I think it took me about three weeks before I got it into my head to spell the name of the **main**() function with a lowercase *m* instead of a capital *M*."

"That's a good point, Peter," I said. "You've learned that every C++ program that is executed from a command prompt must contain a **main**() function—and C++ is very picky about the spelling of **main**(). It must begin with a lowercase *m*. Let's take a look at the compiler error we receive if we spell the name of the **main**() function with a capital *M*."

```cpp
//Example12_2.cpp

#include <iostream>

using namespace std;

int Main()
{
    int counter = 0;
    counter++;

    cout << "The value of counter is " << counter;

    return 0;
}
```

I saved the program as Example12_2 and then compiled it. The following screenshot was displayed on the classroom projector:

```
C:\WINNT\System32\cmd.exe                               _ □ ×

C:\CPPFiles>bcc32 Example12_2.cpp
Borland C++ 5.5.1 for Win32 Copyright (c) 1993, 2000 Borland

Example12_2.cpp:
Turbo Incremental Link 5.00 Copyright (c) 1997, 2000 Borland

Error: Unresolved external '_main' referenced from C:\BORLAN
D\BCC55\LIB\C0X32.OBJ

C:\CPPFiles>_
```

"Notice," I said, "this error message is pretty descriptive. It says it can't find '_main.' This either means there's no function named **main()** or the letter *m* is capitalized."

Forgetting to Reference the std Namespace

"I was just following along with you," Valerie said, "and everything was going fine. However, when I corrected the spelling of **main()** by changing my capital *M* to a lowercase *m*, I still received a missing symbol error for cout."

"I think I know what that is Valerie," Rhonda volunteered. "It happens to me all the time. You must have either omitted the reference for the iostream header file or for the std namespace."

Valerie looked puzzled, and before saying anything, I displayed her code on the classroom projector:

```
//Example12_3.cpp

#include <iostream>

int main()
{
   int counter = 0;
   counter++;

   cout << "The value of counter is " << counter;

   return 0;
}
```

I then saved the program as Example12_3 and attempted to compile it. The following screenshot was displayed on the classroom projector:

```
C:\WINNT\System32\cmd.exe                              _ □ ×

C:\CPPFiles>bcc32 Example12_3.cpp
Borland C++ 5.5.1 for Win32 Copyright (c) 1993, 2000 Borland

Example12_3.cpp:
Error E2451 Example12_3.cpp 10: Undefined symbol 'cout' in f
unction main()
*** 1 errors in Compile ***

C:\CPPFiles>_
```

"Rhonda's, right," I said. "You did properly include a reference to the iostream library, which contains the 'definition' for the cout object. However, you didn't include a namespace statement for the std namespace. Namespaces are 'subdivisions' within libraries, and by default C++ needs to know the particular namespace within the iostream library to find the 'definition' for the cout object. There are two ways of doing this. The first is to specify the name of the namespace when referencing the cout object, like this."

```
std::cout << "The value of counter is " << counter;
```

"Notice how we precede the name of the cout object with the name of the std namespace, and then two colons. That's how we tell C++ to look for the cout object in the std namespace of one of the included libraries. As I mentioned earlier in the course, preceding every object reference with its appropriate namespace can get pretty tedious, which is why C++ permits us to simply include the entire namespace as a reference in our program using this statement."

```
using namespace std;
```

Valerie now seemed to fully understand what was going on.

Forgetting to Include the iostream Library

"Will we get the same compiler error message if we forget to include the iostream library in our program?" Blaine asked.

"Good question, Blaine," I said. "That's something beginners frequently forget to do that results in a failure of their programs to compile. The error message will be different however, and it's pretty misleading. For instance, here's some code that fails to include the iostream library."

```
//Example12_4.cpp

using namespace std;

int main()
```

```
{
    int counter = 0;
    counter++;

    cout << "The value of counter is " << counter;

    return 0;
}
```

"Let's save this as Example12_4.cpp, compile it, and then take a look at the error message the compiler generates."

I did just that, and the following screenshot was displayed on the classroom projector:

"It doesn't say anything about a missing library," Blaine said. "It's telling us that it's expecting a namespace name, but we included one for the std namespace."

"The compiler is confused, Blaine," I said, "and doesn't recognize the name of the namespace that we are telling it to use in our program."

"Why is that?" Barbara asked.

"The reason," I answered, "is that the std namespace is located in the iostream library—and because we forgot to include a reference to iostream in our program, the compiler can't find the std namespace."

Forgetting the Semicolon at the End of a Statement Is a Syntax Error

"The next error I'd like to discuss may seem pretty obvious to you," I said, "but I've seen many students ponder over this one for minutes on end without realizing what they had done."

"What's that one?" Rhonda asked. "I bet it's one I've seen!"

"Forgetting to end a statement with a semicolon," I said, "like this."

```
//Example12_5.cpp

#include <iostream>

using namespace std;

int main()
{
    int counter = 0;
    counter++

    cout << "The value of counter is " << counter;

    return 0;
}
```

"I see the problem," Lou said. "There should be a semicolon on the line of code incrementing the *counter* variable."

"Exactly, Lou," I agreed.

"What kind of error message will this generate?" Kate asked.

"It's a pretty explicit error message," I said, as I compiled Example12_5.

The following screenshot was displayed on the classroom projector:

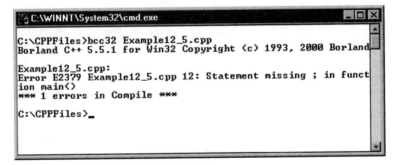

A Semicolon Must End a Class Definition

"Speaking of semicolons," I said, "something else that drives C++ programmers crazy—and not just beginners—is the fact that a C++ class definition must end with a semicolon."

"What do you mean?" Rhonda asked. "I don't remember doing that."

"You may not have realized it," I said. "Take a look at this version of the Banner class, which I introduced way back in the early part of our course. Notice the semicolon that follows the ending brace in the class definition."

```
//Banner.cpp
#include <iostream>
#include <string>

using namespace std;

class Banner
{
  public: string favoriteProgram;
  public: void Display()
  {
    cout << "I love " << favoriteProgram << endl;
  }
};                    //Class definition must end with a semicolon
```

"I honestly never noticed that either," Chuck said. "What happens if we erase the semicolon and then try to compile the class without it?"

"Let's see," I said, as I erased the semicolon and compiled the Banner.cpp file.

The following screenshot was displayed on the classroom projector:

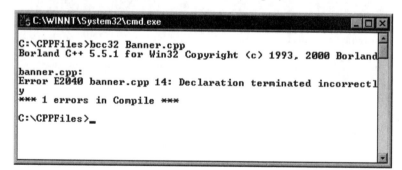

Braces (and Parentheses) Must Occur in Matching Pairs

"Another common error that beginner programmers make," I said, "is dealing with braces in their code. In a C++ class, everything following the class name must be 'sandwiched' between braces. In addition, functions—such as the **main()** function in a C++ startup program and custom functions in a class—must also be sandwiched between braces. The same applies to blocks, such as If statement blocks. As your programs get more complex, it can be pretty easy to become confused—particularly if your program has a number of custom functions. Here's an example of correct code we wrote earlier in the course—notice that we have the same amount of left curly braces as we do right curly braces—two of each. The same applies for parentheses—we have the same number of left and right parentheses and square brackets."

```
//Example12_6.cpp

#include <iostream>

void DisplayMessage();    // Function Prototype

int main()
{
  using namespace std;

  DisplayMessage();    // Call to Custom Function
  return 0;
}

void DisplayMessage()    // Custom Function
{
  using namespace std;

  cout << "I Love C++";
}
```

"I have to admit," Linda said, "I did find the whole issue of braces and parentheses confusing at first—all those curly braces can really be confusing."

"I don't blame you," I said. "By the way, that's a good reason to indent your code. Another way to eliminate this error altogether is to double-check your code to ensure that you have the same number of right and left curly braces and parentheses."

"What kind of error message will you get if you make this kind of mistake?" Rhonda asked.

"Let's see, Rhonda," I said. "Let's modify the code from Example11_4 by intentionally eliminating the right closing curly brace of the **main()** function."

```
//Example12_7.cpp

#include <iostream>

using namespace std;

void DisplayMessage();    // Function Prototype
```

```
int main()
{
  DisplayMessage();    // Call to Custom Function
  return 0;
}


void DisplayMessage()    // Custom Function
{
  cout << "I Love C++";
}
```

"Now let's compile the program and see what kind of error message we get," I said. I did so, and the following error message was displayed on the classroom projector:

```
C:\CPPFiles>bcc32 Example12_7.cpp
Borland C++ 5.5.1 for Win32 Copyright (c) 1993, 2000 Borland

Example12_7.cpp:
Error E2141 Example12_7.cpp 16: Declaration syntax error in
function main()
Error E2139 Example12_7.cpp 18: Declaration missing ; in fun
ction main()
Error E2134 Example12_7.cpp 18: Compound statement missing }
 in function main()
*** 3 errors in Compile ***

C:\CPPFiles>_
```

"Unfortunately, " I said, "this error message can be confusing. But the last statement by the compiler—'Compound statement missing }'—is a good tip off that a right curly brace is missing. Unfortunately, it does a terrible job of telling us where in our source file the missing right curly brace should be. It isn't line 18 of our source file that is missing the right curly brace; it's actually line 14. Recognizing this error can be a difficult task."

Forgetting the Left and Right Parentheses in an If Structure

"An error that is closely related to the one we just examined," I said, "is one that I see a lot of beginners make, and it concerns the If statement. Beginners tend to forget that the test expression for an If statement must be enclosed within parentheses."

"Ah, yes," I heard Joe say.

"What's that?" Rhonda asked. "Test expression?"

"That's right, Rhonda," I said. "Let me show you an example."

I then displayed this code on the classroom projector.

"This code," I said, "uses an If statement to determine if the value of the counter variable is 0."

```
//Example12_8.cpp

#include <iostream>

using namespace std;

int main()
{
    int counter = 0;

    if (counter == 0)
    {
        cout << "The value of counter is " << counter;
    }

    return 0;
}
```

"Notice," I said, "how the test expression 'counter == 0' is enclosed within parentheses."

```
if (counter == 0)
```

"Oh my gosh," Rhonda said, "you're right. I totally forgot about having to enclose the test expression within parentheses—what kind of compiler error will that generate if we don't do it?"

"Let me show you," I said, as I changed the code in Example12_8 to look like this:

```
//Example12_9.cpp

#include <iostream>

using namespace std;

int main()
{
    int counter = 0;

    if counter == 0
```

```
    {
        cout << "The value of counter is " << counter;
    }

    return 0;
}
```

"Notice how the test expression is no longer enclosed within parentheses," I said. "Now let's compile the program and see what error message it generates."

I did so, and the following error message was displayed on the classroom projector:

```
C:\WINNT\System32\cmd.exe                              _ □ ×

C:\CPPFiles>bcc32 Example12_9.cpp
Borland C++ 5.5.1 for Win32 Copyright (c) 1993, 2000 Borland

Example12_9.cpp:
Error E2376 Example12_9.cpp 11: If statement missing ( in fu
nction main()
Warning W8004 Example12_9.cpp 17: 'counter' is assigned a va
lue that is never used in function main()
*** 1 errors in Compile ***

C:\CPPFiles>
```

"This error message is not quite as clear as some of the other compiler messages we've seen," I said, "but it does point us in the right direction by listing the line of code in error, and by telling us that C++ is expecting a left parenthesis."

Confusing the Equality Operator (==) with the Assignment Operator (=)

"This next error is one I see all the time from beginners," I said, "and occurs when they confuse the equality operator (==) with the assignment operator (=), generally in the test expression of an If statement. Here's the code we just examined with a properly formatted test expression checking to see if the value of the counter variable is 0."

```
//Example12_10.cpp

#include <iostream>

using namespace std;

int main()
{
    int counter = 0;
```

```
    if (counter == 0)
    {
        cout << "The value of counter is " << counter;
    }

    return 0;
}
```

"Notice how we check the value of counter against the numeric literal 0 by using the equality operator (==)."

```
if (counter == 0)
```

"It's relatively easy," I said, "especially for those you have programmed in other languages, to confuse the equality operator (==) with the assignment operator (=) and code the test expression like this instead."

```
if (counter = 0)
```

"If we compile a program that includes a test expression formatted like this…"

```
//Example12_11.cpp

#include <iostream>

using namespace std;

int main()
{
    int counter = 0;

    if (counter = 0)
    {
        cout << "The value of counter is " << counter;
    }

    return 0;
}
```

"…we will get this error message."

```
C:\WINNT\System32\cmd.exe                          _ □ ×

C:\CPPFiles>bcc32 Example12_11.cpp
Borland C++ 5.5.1 for Win32 Copyright (c) 1993, 2000 Borland

Example12_11.cpp:
Warning W8060 Example12_11.cpp 11: Possibly incorrect assign
ment in function main()
Warning W8004 Example12_11.cpp 9: 'counter' is assigned a va
lue that is never used in function main()
Turbo Incremental Link 5.00 Copyright (c) 1997, 2000 Borland

C:\CPPFiles>_
```

"The C++ compiler has properly identified the line of code with the error," I said, "and is telling us that some kind of incorrect assignment is occurring—that's the clue to the error."

"I understand," Blaine said. "That's something that I've been guilty of on more than one occasion."

Forgetting to Code a Function Prototype

"It's time to turn our attention," I said, "to a series of compiler errors that are related to the custom functions we write. The first type of error that occurs is when we code a custom function but forget to code a function prototype. Here's a program that calls a custom function called **test()** from within **main()**. Notice how we declare the function prototype before the **main()** function."

```cpp
//Example12_12.cpp

#include <iostream>

using namespace std;

void test();    //Function Prototype

int main()
{
   test();

   return 0;
}

void test()
{
   cout << "I love C++" << endl;
}
```

"When you first start writing C++ programs," I said, "it's pretty easy to forget to declare the function prototype—and if you do, you'll wind up with a compiler error that looks like this."

I then deleted the function prototype from the program, saved it as Example12_12.cpp, and tried to compile it. The following screenshot was displayed on the classroom projector:

```
C:\WINNT\System32\cmd.exe                                    _ □ ×

C:\CPPFiles>bcc32 Example12_12.cpp
Borland C++ 5.5.1 for Win32 Copyright (c) 1993, 2000 Borland

Example12_12.cpp:
Error E2268 Example12_12.cpp 9: Call to undefined function '
test' in function main()
*** 1 errors in Compile ***

C:\CPPFiles>
```

"It's important to realize," I continued, "that when the compiler examines our code, it needs to see a definition of any custom function prior to the call to the function. Because the call to the **test()** function occurs in **main()**, the compiler needs to see the function prototype before that point in our code."

"Isn't it also possible to place the **test()** function above the **main()** function and have our code compile?" Dave asked.

"That's a good point, Dave," I replied. "You're right. Rather than code a function prototype, we could place the **test()** function 'above' the line of code that calls it. In this case, the **main()** function, like this."

```
//Example12_13.cpp

#include <iostream>

using namespace std;

void test()
{
   cout << "I love C++" << endl;
}

int main()
{
   test();

   return 0;
}
```

"I didn't realize we could do this," Kate said. "Do you have a preference as to which style we use?"

"I prefer to use function prototypes for a number of reasons," I said. "First, stylistically, I like to have the **main**() function appear first in my code. Second, by declaring function prototypes in the beginning of a program, you and other programmers who read your code know immediately the names and signatures of all the functions in the program."

Forgetting to Specify a Return Type for a Function You Write

"Another type of compiler error related to custom functions," I said, "is when we forget to specify a return type in the function header. Remember, every function—except for a constructor function—requires that we specify a return type. That includes functions that are written not to return a value. Those kind of functions must be defined with a function return type of void. Here's the function header for the **test**() function from Example12_12. Notice how we specify a return type of void."

```
void test()
```

"Now let's accidentally omit the void return type in both the function prototype and the header."

```
//Example12_14.cpp

#include <iostream>

using namespace std;

test();      //Function Prototype

int main()
{
    test();

    return 0;
}

test()
{
    cout << "I love C++" << endl;
}
```

"And now let's see what happens when we compile the program."

I did so, and the following screenshot was displayed on the classroom projector:

Chapter 12:   Errors and Error Handling   **551**

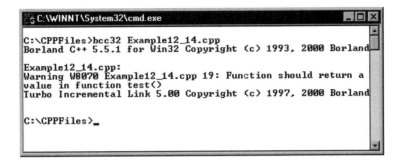

```
C:\CPPFiles>bcc32 Example12_14.cpp
Borland C++ 5.5.1 for Win32 Copyright (c) 1993, 2000 Borland

Example12_14.cpp:
Warning W8070 Example12_14.cpp 19: Function should return a
value in function test()
Turbo Incremental Link 5.00 Copyright (c) 1997, 2000 Borland

C:\CPPFiles>_
```

"Again," I said, "this is a pretty informative compiler message, telling us that the **test()** function must return a value."

Forgetting to Return a Value from a Function You Write

"Another error related to a custom function," I continued, "occurs when we declare a function with a return type—such as int or String—but then forget to return a value from within the function. This will also generate a compiler error. Take a look at this code. Once again, we've created a function called test, but this time with a declaration and prototype specifying a return value of an integer data type. From what you've learned in the course, you know that we need to return an integer value from within the **test()** function, and we do that in the last line of the function using the return statement."

```
//Example12_15.cpp

#include <iostream>

using namespace std;

int test();     //Function Prototype

int main()
{
    int retval = 0;

    retval = test();
    cout << "The return value of test() is " << retval << endl;

    return 0;
}

int test()
```

```
{
    cout << "I love C++" << endl;

    return 1;
}
```

"However, if we forget to code a return statement, like this…"

```
//Example12_16.cpp

#include <iostream>

using namespace std;

int test();     //Function Prototype

int main()
{
    int retval = 0;

    retval = test();
    cout << "The return value of test() is " << retval << endl;

    return 0;
}

int test()
{
    cout << "I love C++" << endl;

}
```

"…when we compile the program, we'll receive this compiler error."

"By the way," I added, "forgetting to return a value from a function applies not only to custom functions you write but also to the **main**() function itself. If you declare the **main**() function with a integer return type—as we have during this course—you must, somewhere within the **main**() function, execute the return statement with an integer argument."

Returning the Wrong 'Type' of Return Value for a Function You Write

"Suppose you return the wrong type of return value?" Kathy asked.

"Kathy, you must have read my mind," I said. "That's exactly the next type of compiler error I intended to cover."

"What does Kathy mean?" Rhonda asked.

"In Example12_15, Rhonda," I said, "we declared our **test**() function with a return type of int and returned the integer 1 within the body of the function. Suppose, instead of returning the number 1, we return a string instead."

```cpp
//Example12_17.cpp

#include <iostream>

using namespace std;

int test();      //Function Prototype

int main()
{
   int retval = 0;

   retval = test();
   cout << "The return value of test() is " << retval << endl;

   return 0;
}

int test()
{
   cout << "I love C++" << endl;

   return "Kathy";

}
```

"I see what you mean," Rhonda said. "Here we're returning the string 'Kathy', not an integer. That should confuse the compiler."

"Exactly, Rhonda" I replied, as I compiled the program.

The following screenshot was displayed on the classroom projector:

```
C:\WINNT\System32\cmd.exe                          _ □ ×

C:\CPPFiles>bcc32 Example12_17.cpp
Borland C++ 5.5.1 for Win32 Copyright (c) 1993, 2000 Borland

Example12_17.cpp:
Warning W8004 Example12_17.cpp 11: 'retval' is assigned a va
lue that is never used in function main()
Error E2034 Example12_17.cpp 23: Cannot convert 'char *' to
'int' in function test()
*** 1 errors in Compile ***

C:\CPPFiles>_
```

"The warning that we see here," I said, "is a result of the error that the compiler has flagged in the **test**() function. The compiler is telling us that it can't convert a string—which it designates as a character array—to an int. In other words, we can't return a string from a function that has been declared to return an integer data type."

Returning a Value from a Function Whose Return Type Is Void

"I didn't realize there were so many ways to foul up a function!" Rhonda said laughing, "I would think we've covered just about all the possibilities—are there any others?"

"There are at least two other types of errors that you can make with functions," I said. "For one, you can generate a compiler error by trying to return a value when you've declared the function to have a void return type. Let me show you."

```
//Example12_18.cpp

#include <iostream>

using namespace std;

void test();       //Function Prototype

int main()
{
   int retval = 0;

   retval = test();
   cout << "The return value of test() is " << retval << endl;
```

```
    return 0;
}

void test()
{
    cout << "I love C++" << endl;

    return 1;

}
```

"Notice that the declaration for the **test()** function specifies a return type of void," I said, "yet, within the body of the function, we execute the return statement. Let's see what happens when we compile this program."

The following screenshot was displayed on the classroom projector:

```
C:\WINNT\System32\cmd.exe                                    _ □ ✕

C:\CPPFiles>bcc32 Example12_18.cpp
Borland C++ 5.5.1 for Win32 Copyright (c) 1993, 2000 Borland

Example12_18.cpp:
Error E2109 Example12_18.cpp 13: Not an allowed type in func
tion main()
Error E2467 Example12_18.cpp 23: 'test()' cannot return a va
lue in function test()
*** 2 errors in Compile ***

C:\CPPFiles>
```

"The compiler message," I said, "is telling us that we cannot return a value from within the **test()** function—again, this is a pretty informative error message."

Creating an Overloaded Function with What You Believe to Be a Different Signature

"Here's the last of the error messages pertaining to functions that we'll examine today," I said, "and it deals with overloaded functions. Does everyone remember what an overloaded function is?"

"Overloaded functions are functions that have the same name but a different *signature*—that is, number and type of arguments," Dave said.

"Exactly right, Dave," I said. "Beginners tend to misunderstand what comprises a function signature."

"How so?" Kate asked.

"For instance," I said, "I've seen a number of beginner C++ programmers code two functions with the same name, having the same number and type of arguments, but with different argument names, believing that the signatures are different and therefore they've created overloaded functions."

"Haven't they?" Blaine asked.

"No," I replied. "Despite the fact that the argument names are different, if the name of the functions are identical and the number and type of arguments in the function header are identical, you haven't created overloaded functions. For instance, in this code, I've created two functions called **test**(), the signature of each specifying a single integer parameter. The parameter name in the first **test**() function is called 'a,' and in the second **test**() function it's called 'b.'"

```cpp
//Example12_19.cpp

#include <iostream>

using namespace std;

void test(int a);     //Function Prototype
void test(int b);     //Function Prototype

int main()
{
    int retval = 0;

    test(44);
    test(33);

    return 0;
}

void test(int a)
{
    cout << "The value of the passed argument is " << a << endl;
}

void test(int b)
{
    cout << "The value of the passed argument is " << b << endl;
}
```

"What do you think?" I asked. "Does C++ consider the two signatures to be different?"

"I'm not really sure," Valerie said.

"I'm guessing it doesn't," Dave said.

"The answer," I said, "is that to C++, both function signatures are identical, and compiling this code will result in a compiler error message."

The following screenshot was displayed on the classroom projector:

```
C:\WINNT\System32\cmd.exe                                    _□×

C:\CPPFiles>bcc32 Example12_19.cpp
Borland C++ 5.5.1 for Win32 Copyright (c) 1993, 2000 Borland

Example12_19.cpp:
Warning W8004 Example12_19.cpp 18: 'retval' is assigned a va
lue that is never used in function main()
Error E2171 Example12_19.cpp 26: Body has already been defin
ed for function 'test(int)'
Error E2451 Example12_19.cpp 27: Undefined symbol 'b' in fun
ction test(int)
Warning W8057 Example12_19.cpp 28: Parameter 'a' is never us
ed in function test(int)
*** 2 errors in Compile ***

C:\CPPFiles>_
```

"The first error message," I said, "E2171, is the significant one. It tells us that the body of our second **test**() function has already been defined with a single integer argument. As far as C++ is concerned, this program already has a function called **test**(), having a single integer argument."

"So argument names really do nothing to differentiate a function's signature?" Kate asked.

"That's right, Kate," I said. "Argument names themselves mean nothing—it's the number and type of arguments in the signature that differentiates the function signatures."

NOTE
A function signature can also be differentiated by varying the position of the arguments. For instance, two functions, one having a function signature calling for one integer argument followed by a string argument, and a second function signature calling for one string argument followed by an integer argument, would be considered different.

"I hesitate to ask this," Rhonda said, "but are there any other mistakes you can make when creating functions?"

"Just one, Rhonda," I said. "Some beginners also believe that creating two functions with identical signatures but with different return types will differentiate the two functions—but that isn't the case either. Identical function signatures, with different return types, like this..."

```cpp
//Example12_20.cpp

#include <iostream>

using namespace std;

void test(int a);    //Function Prototype
int test(int b);     //Function Prototype

int main()
{
```

```
   int retval = 0;

   test(44);
   test(33);

   return 0;
}

void test(int a)
{
   cout << "The value of the passed argument is " << a << endl;
}

int test(int b)
{
   cout << "The value of the passed argument is " << b << endl;
   return 1;
}
```

"…will also generate a compiler error similar to the one we saw a moment ago."

Runtime Errors and Logic Errors

"The types of errors that we've examined so far this morning," I said, "have been exclusively compiler errors. Compiler errors, though sometimes a real nuisance to correct, do little to tarnish the image of your program in the eyes of the user. Because a program with compiler errors can't generate an executable, the user never sees compiler errors. Unfortunately, there are some types of errors that escape the watchful eye of the C++ compiler and don't show up until runtime when an unsuspecting user is interacting with your program. These types of errors are called *runtime errors*, and they usually result in your program abnormally terminating, or 'bombing' as we sometimes call it. Runtime errors are often serious, sometimes resulting in the user of your program losing hours of work. Another type of error that we'll examine today is called a *logic error*, and it can be even more serious. Logic errors usually do not result in your program abnormally terminating. Worse yet, the program seems to be working just fine, when in reality it's producing incorrect results. Sometimes, if you are lucky, the user will quickly detect a programming logic error, thus minimizing its damage. However, some logic errors may not be discovered by the user for a long period of time, in which case the damage is multiplied. As you can imagine, both runtime and logic errors can drastically affect your programming reputation and even your career."

Not Initializing a Variable Is a Logic Error

"One question that I'm asked quite often," I said, "is whether or not, in a C++ program, we have to initialize our variables. I believe for the most part in this class, we've followed the good practice of initializing all the variables we've used in our programs. It's a good practice to get into."

"I thought we *had* to initialize our variables," Bob said.

"Actually," I said, "C++ doesn't require us to initialize any of the variables we declare, but there's a danger in not initializing our variables."

"What's that?" Steve asked.

"As you saw last week when we discussed pointers," I said, "when a variable is declared, an area of computer memory is assigned to the variable, and the address of that memory is then associated with the variable name. The problem in *not* initializing the variable is that the address location assigned to your variable already has data in it."

"It does?" Barbara asked.

"That's right," I said. "There's already data stored in the variable, and it can be just about anything."

"That's dangerous," Dave said.

"Absolutely," I agreed. "I've seen programmers declare a variable, fail to initialize it, expecting that valid data would be stored in the variable sometime during the running of the program, and then use the value of that variable somewhere else within the program—either in a calculation or as output to the user. The problem is that the program is working with invalid data, and the results of this erroneous operation can be anything from a nuisance to a disaster."

"I'm afraid I don't quite understand what you're getting at," Rhonda said.

"Let me show you," I said, as I displayed this code for the class to examine. "Here's a program in which we declare a variable called *counter* within the **main**() function and initialize its value to zero."

```
//Example12_21.cpp

#include <iostream>

using namespace std;

int main()
{
   int counter = 0;
   cout << "The value of counter is " << counter << endl;

   counter++;
```

```
    cout << "The value of counter is now " << counter << endl;

    return 0;
}
```

I saved the program as Example12_21.cpp and then compiled and executed it. The following screenshot was displayed on the classroom projector:

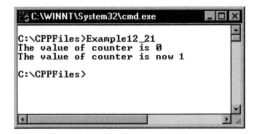

"Nothing surprising there," I said. "We initialized the variable to zero, displayed its value in the C++ console, then incremented it by 1 and displayed its new value. Now let's see what happens if we fail to initialize the value of the variable."

```
//Example12_22.cpp

#include <iostream>

using namespace std;

int main()
{
    int counter;
    cout << "The value of counter is " << counter << endl;

    counter++;
    cout << "The value of counter is now " << counter << endl;

    return 0;
}
```

I saved the program as Example12_22.cpp and then compiled and executed it. The following screenshot was displayed on the classroom projector:

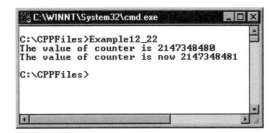

"Because we failed to initialize the value of the *counter* variable," I said, "our program was left to work with the value that happened to be stored at the address location of that variable—which in this case turned out to be 2147348480. Many an unsuspecting programmer believes that C++ automatically initializes variables and therefore might assume that the value of the counter variable is 0—an assumption that could have a devastating impact on their program. The bottom line: It's a good idea to initialize all variables."

"So this is a logic error, is that right?" Peter asked.

"That's right, Peter," I said. "The program ran to completion, without an error code, yet it produced erroneous results. This is a logic error."

Referring to an Element Outside the Array Bounds Is a Logic Error

"Let's continue," I said, " by examining one of the more frequent logic errors that occurs when working with arrays—and that's when we erroneously work with an array element that is outside of the array's defined boundaries. Let's take a look at this code in which we have declared an array called *grades* that has six elements."

```
//Example12_23.cpp

#include <iostream>

using namespace std;

int main()
{
    int grades[6];

    grades[0] = 82;
    grades[1] = 90;
    grades[2] = 64;
    grades[3] = 80;
```

```
grades[4] = 95;
grades[5] = 75;
grades[6] = 100;

cout << grades[0] << endl;
cout << grades[1] << endl;
cout << grades[2] << endl;
cout << grades[3] << endl;
cout << grades[4] << endl;
cout << grades[5] << endl;
cout << grades[6] << endl;

return 0;
}
```

"I don't see anything wrong with this code," Rhonda said. "Is there a problem with it?"

"Yes there is," I said. "It's a very subtle error—our array is declared with six elements."

```
int grades[6];
```

"But because element numbers in an array begin with the number zero, the 'upper floor' of the array is always one less than its size. In other words, with a size of 6, the highest element number that we can legally reference is 5. Therefore, this line of code…"

```
grades[6] = 100;
```

"…is referencing an element of the array that does not exist, because the upper floor of the array is actually 5."

"I understand now," Rhonda said. "And you say if we compile this program, the C++ compiler won't detect the problem?"

"Unfortunately it won't, Rhonda," I said.

I then compiled the program, and as I predicted, there were no error messages.

"Let's see what happens if we run the program," I said.

The following screenshot was displayed on the classroom projector:

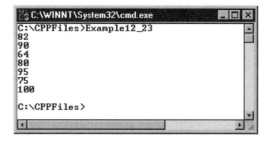

"The program looks okay to me. It didn't bomb," Ward said.

"This is most often a logic error, Ward," I said. "The program appears to have worked fine. In fact, as you can see, it actually stored a value in what it believed to be element six of the array—one beyond its declared size—and later successfully retrieved and displayed this value."

"That somehow doesn't seem 'safe,'" Linda said. "What are the repercussions?"

"The problem is that C++ allowed us to overwrite a piece of computer memory that didn't belong to the array," I said. "That can mean that we placed the value of 100 in an area of memory allocated for another variable in our program—or worse yet, in an area of memory allocated for another program on the computer our program is running. Ultimately, that can cause big problems, such as causing the computer to freeze or perform erroneous operations. The bottom line: Be very careful when working with array elements."

Forgetting to Increment a Counter Variable

"Forgetting to increment a counter variable," I said, "is one of the most common errors I see."

"Counter variable?" Steve asked.

I continued by explaining that many of the programs we had written during the course, particularly those we wrote two weeks ago when dealing with arrays, depended heavily on declaring, incrementing, and examining a counter variable somewhere within a program.

"Counter variables," I explained, "are variables that you declare to do exactly that—count something. For example, two weeks ago in Practice10_3, we wrote code that loaded the values of six quiz grades to an array. We then used a For loop to access each element of the array, add its value to an accumulator variable, increment a counter, and finally calculate an average. Here's the code from Practice10_3."

```
//Example12_24.cpp

#include <iostream>
#include <string>
using namespace std;

int main()
{
    int grades[6] = {82,90,64,80,95,75};
    int accumulator = 0;
    int counter = 0;
    float average = 0;

    for (int row = 0; row < sizeof grades/sizeof grades[0]; row++)
    {
        cout << grades[row] << endl;
```

```
      accumulator = accumulator + grades[row];
      counter++;
   }

   average = accumulator / counter;

   cout << endl << "The class average is " << average << endl;

   return 0;
}
```

I then saved the program as Example12_24.cpp, compiled and executed it, and an average of 81 was displayed on the classroom projector.

"Crucial to this program correctly calculating the class average," I said, "is knowing the number of student grades in the array. In order to keep track of that number, we declared a variable called *counter* and incremented it by 1 each time we added an element to the array."

```
counter++;
```

"Had we forgotten to increment this counter variable, a number of problems could have resulted. Most often, we get a 'division by zero' runtime error. Let me show you."

I then deleted the line of code that increments the counter so that the program looked like this:

```
//Example12_25.cpp

#include <iostream>
#include <string>
using namespace std;

int main()
{
   int grades[6] = {82,90,64,80,95,75};
   int accumulator = 0;
   int counter = 0;
   float average = 0;

   for (int row = 0; row < sizeof grades/sizeof grades[0]; row++)
   {
      cout << grades[row] << endl;
      accumulator = accumulator + grades[row];
   }

   average = accumulator / counter;
```

```
    cout << endl << "The class average is " << average << endl;

    return 0;
}
```

I saved the program as Example12_25 and then compiled and executed it. The program began to execute, values were displayed in the C++ console, but then this message box was displayed on the classroom projector:

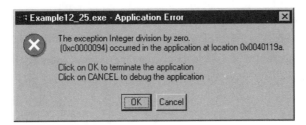

NOTE
Depending on the operating system you are running, and other installed products on your PC (such as Microsoft Visual Studio), you may receive a slightly different error message. Regardless, division by zero is not permitted, and it causes your program to bomb.

"This is the 'division by zero' error I said might occur," I continued. "Division by zero is a big no-no in most computer languages. Because we never incremented the counter variable, we divided the value of our accumulator variable by the initial value of the counter variable, which is zero. Division by zero is something we'll discuss later in a little more detail. For now, just remember that it's vitally important to increment the value of any counter variables you declare."

Forgetting to Add to an Accumulator

"Forgetting to add values to an accumulator," I said, "is similar to forgetting to increment a counter variable—both mistakes result in runtime errors. A counter variable is used to count the instances of something—such as the number of quizzes taken or the number of employees in a company. An accumulator variable is a little different in that it is used to hold the running total of something—such as the total scores of all the quiz grades taken or the total value of all employee salaries in a company. In the same example we used to illustrate the problem with a counter variable," I said, "we also added the value of the quiz grade to an accumulator variable. If we had forgotten to add the grade to the accumulator variable, we would have displayed an incorrect average in the C++ console—most likely zero."

"And there goes our reputation!" Rhonda said.

"That's right, Rhonda," I agreed. "It only takes a few mistakes to tarnish it."

I displayed the code from Example12_24 on the classroom projector and highlighted the line of code where we added the grade to the accumulator variable:

```
accumulator = accumulator + grades[row];
```

"Forgetting to add a value to the accumulator variable is a very common type of C++ error," I explained.

"What kind of error would this generate again?" Ward asked.

"The program would run," I said, "but most likely the program would display an average of zero."

I then deleted the line of code where we add the value of the quiz grade to the accumulator variable and then added back the line of code to correctly increment the counter variable so that it looked like this:

```cpp
//Example12_26.cpp

#include <iostream>
#include <string>
using namespace std;

int main()
{
   int grades[6] = {82,90,64,80,95,75};
   int accumulator = 0;
   int counter = 0;
   float average = 0;

   for (int row = 0; row < sizeof grades/sizeof grades[0]; row++)
   {
      cout << grades[row] << endl;
      counter++;
   }

   average = accumulator / counter;

   cout << endl << "The class average is " << average << endl;

   return 0;
}
```

I saved the program as Example12_26 and then compiled and executed it. The following screenshot was displayed on the classroom projector:

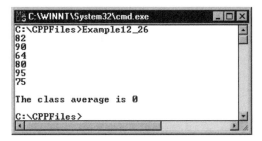

"As you can see," I said, "because we forgot to increment the value of the accumulator variable, its value is equal to its initial value of zero. Therefore, when we divided the accumulator variable by the value of the counter variable—which in this case was 6—our result was zero. The program didn't bomb, but it did result in an incorrect answer."

"So this is a logic error," Valerie said, "because the program didn't bomb."

'That's right, Valerie," I said. "And as you can all see, an error like this can be far worse than a runtime error, particularly if an unsuspecting user takes the result at face value."

Not Providing a Way for a While Structure to End

"Another type of runtime error that is common for beginners," I said, "is to code a While loop and forget to provide a way for it to ultimately end. A few weeks ago, we wrote this code, in Practice5_7, to display the floor numbers of a hotel."

```cpp
//Example12_27.cpp
#include <iostream>

using namespace std;

int main()
{
   int counter = 2;

   cout << "The floors in the hotel are..." << endl;

   while (counter < 21)    {
      cout << counter << endl;
      counter++;
   }

   return 0;
}
```

"Beginners," I continued, "frequently forget that in a While loop, it's important to include, somewhere within the body of the loop, code that enables the loop to eventually end. Otherwise, you have what is known as an *endless loop*. In the case of this code, we told C++ to continue executing the loop *while* the value of the counter variable is less than 21. Because we initialized the counter variable to 2, this means if we didn't place some code in the body of the loop to do something to cause the value of the counter variable to become 21 or greater, the loop would never end. What we did, of course, was write this line of code, which increments the value of the counter variable every time the body of the loop is executed."

```
counter++;
```

"And what happens if we were to forget this code?" Joe asked.

"Let me show you," I said, as I displayed this version of the program on the classroom projector."

```cpp
//Example12_28.cpp
#include <iostream>

using namespace std;

int main()
{
   int counter = 2;

   cout << "The floors in the hotel are..." << endl;

   while (counter < 21)    {
      cout << counter << endl;
   }

   return 0;
}
```

"We'd create a program that would display the number 2 indefinitely," I said. "In other words, an infinite loop."

I saved the program as Example12_28.cpp and then compiled and executed it. My prediction was right. The number 2 continued to display on the C++ console. Because the program wouldn't stop, I had to use the Windows Task Manager to terminate it.

"So that's an infinite loop," Rhonda said, "and all because we forgot one little line of code."

Forgetting to Code a Break Statement in a Switch Structure

"This next 'error' isn't so much an error as it is a C++ feature," I said, "but it's a feature that can trip many beginners up—that is, when coding a Switch structure, once a Case statement evaluates to true, the code in *every* succeeding Case statement is also executed."

"That's why we use the break statement, isn't it?" Dave asked.

"That's right, Dave," I said. "The break statement is normally included as the last statement of a Case statement to tell C++ to skip the remainder of the Case statements if the Case statement is found to be true. Here's a program that uses a Switch statement to evaluate the value of the variable *x*. Depending on the value of the variable, the program displays one of several alternative messages to the C++ console. Notice the break statement in each of the Case statements. This program, when run, will display the message 'x is 2' in the C++ console."

```cpp
//Example12_29.cpp
#include <iostream>

using namespace std;

int main()
{
  int x = 2;
  switch (x)
   {
      case 1:
         cout << "x is 1" << endl;
         break;
      case 2:
         cout << "x is 2" << endl;
         break;
      case 3:
         cout << "x is 3" << endl;
         break;
      default:
         cout << "x is not 1, 2 or 3" << endl;
   }
   return 0;
}
```

"If however, we remove the break statements from the program, so that it looks like this…"

```cpp
//Example12_30.cpp
#include <iostream>

using namespace std;

int main()
{
  int x = 2;
  switch (x)
   {
      case 1:
         cout << "x is 1" << endl;
      case 2:
         cout << "x is 2" << endl;
      case 3:
         cout << "x is 3" << endl;
      default:
         cout << "x is not 1, 2 or 3" << endl;
   }
    return 0;
}
```

"…we get a different result. When we compile and execute this version of the program, because of our failure to include a break statement, we get multiple messages displayed in the C++ console."

I saved the program as Example12_30.cpp and then compiled and executed it. The following screenshot was displayed on the classroom projector:

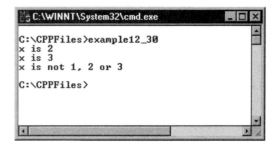

"As you can see, forgetting to code the break statements led to the execution of each one of the Case statements following the *first* Case statement that evaluated to true."

Division by Zero

"Let's revisit that issue of division by zero again," I said. "You saw earlier that in C++, like most programming languages, division by zero generates a runtime error. Now I'm going to explain why."

I continued by stating that in the computer world, division by zero is a big no-no.

"What's 12 divided by 1?" I asked.

"12," Mary replied.

"Now what about 12 divided by 1/2?" I continued.

After a moment's hesitation, Dave answered, "24."

"Correct," I said.

There were some puzzled faces.

"I know I've caught those of you with math phobia on that one," I said. "A number, divided by a number smaller than 1 always results in an answer larger than the original number."

"In math terms," Ward said, "I believe you mean to say that when we divide a number (called the *dividend*) by another number (called the *divisor*) that's smaller than 1, we take the reciprocal of that number and multiply by it. In other words, 12 divided by 1/2 becomes 12 multiplied by 2, whose result is 24."

"Well said, Ward," I stated. I then displayed the following chart on the board:

Number 1 (Dividend)	Number 2 (Divisor)	Answer
12	1	12
12	1/2	24
12	1/3	36
12	1/4	72
12	1/10	120
12	1/100	1200
12	1/1000	12000

I continued by telling my students that as the divisor approaches zero, the answer becomes larger and larger. In fact, it becomes an infinite number, which is impossible to represent in a computer.

"For that reason," I continued, "dividing a number by 0 in your computer program causes most programs to bomb, and C++ is no exception. Let's take a look at this code."

```
//Example12_31.cpp
#include <iostream>

using namespace std;
```

```
int main()
{
   int x = 4;
   int y = 0;

   float z = 0.0;

   z = x / y;

   cout << "The value of z is " << z;

   return 0;
}
```

"As you can see," I said, "this code will eventually divide the value of the variable *x*, which is 4, by the value of the variable *y*, which is 0."

I saved the program as Example12_31.cpp and then compiled and executed it. As was the case when we executed Example12_25, the program bombed and this message box was displayed on the classroom projector:

I went on to explain that most beginners aren't aware of the problems with division by zero and that their immediate response would most likely be that they would never *intentionally* divide by zero.

"That's what I was going to say," Dave said. "However, I can imagine that this kind of error can occur in many different ways—for instance, input from a user via a C++ cin object."

"That's excellent, Dave," I said. "That's exactly how it could happen. The user can enter zero at runtime. If our program then divides by that value, we have a 'division by zero' error."

"Isn't that something we could prevent with an If statement?" Barbara suggested.

"That's exactly what we'll need to do, Barbara," I said, "and we'll be doing that a little later when we examine C++ error handling when we return from our break."

Dealing with Errors in Your Program

Fifteen minutes later I was about to begin discussing error handling in a C++ program when I noticed two people approach our classroom door. It was Rose and Jack, back from their long journey.

"Rose and Jack," I said, "welcome back. It's great to see you! I was getting a little worried that you might not make it back in time for our final class."

"Professor Smiley has been keeping us apprised of the development with the Grades Calculation Project," Rose explained to the class. "And of course, we took our laptops along with us. We're right on pace—well, just about on pace—to complete the course, and the project, with all of you. I don't think we've missed a beat."

"I'm glad that you both were able to be with us today," I said. "Your attendance will help put a nice close to the project we all started together so many weeks ago."

I continued by explaining to my students that during the first part of our class, we had intentionally created errors to cause our programs to bomb. During the last half of our class, we would be examining ways of gracefully handling those errors in such a way that our programs just don't come to a grinding halt.

"As I've mentioned several times today," I said, "nothing can ruin your reputation faster than having one of your existing customers tell a prospective client that they love your programs but that they bomb once in a while. As you can imagine, this can be very bad for business!"

I explained that it isn't always possible to write a program that will never produce a runtime error. As we discussed right before break, sometimes the user can enter data into the program that causes a runtime error. You might also write a program that reads data from a disk file, asking the user for the name and location of the file at runtime.

"Suppose," I said, "the user of your program indicates that the file is located on a diskette, but then forgets to insert the diskette into the drive."

"I do that all the time," Rhonda said. "Will that cause our program to bomb?"

"It can," I said, "because our program is attempting to open a file that doesn't exist."

"That generates an error?" Ward asked. "I'm surprised. When I do that while using my word-processing software, a warning message is displayed."

"That's exactly the point, Ward" I replied. "The programmers who wrote your word processor anticipated that the user might specify a nonexistent file to be opened and therefore implemented C++ error handling in the program, substituting a user-friendly message in place of a system-generated runtime error. That's the warning message you say you receive. Most importantly, though, your word processor continues running instead of coming to a grinding halt, which is what we want our C++ programs to do in the event a runtime error occurs. Remember, when a C++ program comes to a jarring stop, it can result in the loss of hours of work on the part of the user."

"So we can do something like that in our C++ program?" Barbara asked. "I mean, intercept those nasty runtime error messages we saw earlier today and replace them with user-friendly messages of our own."

"It's not so much intercepting messages as it is anticipating these errors," I said, "and checking for them and reacting to them. For instance, in the case of a 'division by zero' error, we'll check to see whether the user has supplied our program with a denominator of zero—and if they have, we'll display a warning message. If we were to write a program that prompts the user for a filename to open, we would first check for the existence of the file prior to trying to open it. That's what I mean."

"I've programmed in Visual Basic, Java, and C#," Dave said, "and each one of those languages allows you to intercept runtime errors, such as division by zero. Can't we do that in C++?"

"That's a good point, Dave," I said. "There are certain runtime errors that can be intercepted in that way. However, the 'division by zero' error isn't one of them. We'll examine how to intercept those runtime errors in our intermediate C++ course, which begins in a few weeks. Let's begin our look at C++ error handling by completing an exercise in which we write a program that permits the user to cause a 'division by zero' error."

I then distributed this exercise to the class.

Exercise 12-1   **Intentionally Generate an Error**

In this exercise, you'll write a program that prompts the user for two numbers and then divides the first number by the second number. You'll then execute the program and intentionally generate a 'division by zero' error. But don't worry—in the next two exercises, you'll see how you can implement error handling to more gracefully deal with the error.

1. Use Notepad (if you are using Windows) to enter the following code:

```cpp
//Practice12_1.cpp
#include <iostream>

using namespace std;

int main()
{
    int number1 = 0;
    int number2 = 0;
    float answer = 0.0;

    char response[256];

    cout << "Enter Number 1: ";
    cin.getline(response,256);
    number1 = atoi(response);

    cout << "Enter Number 2: ";
    cin.getline(response,256);
    number2 = atoi(response);

    answer = (float)number1/(float)number2;
```

```
        cout << endl << number1 << " divided by " << number2
             << " is " << answer;

        return 0;
}
```

2. Save your source file as Practice12_1 in the \CPPFiles\Practice folder (select File | Save As from Notepad's menu bar). Be sure to save your source file with the filename extension .cpp.

3. Compile your source file into an executable file.

4. Execute your program. Enter **9** for the first number and **4** for second. The program will display a result of 2.25.

5. Now run the program again. Enter **4** for the first number and **0** for the second. The program will terminate with a 'division by zero' exception, as shown here:

"What we've done here," I said, "is to write some innocent-looking code that prompts the user for two numbers. Certainly, there's nothing in the code itself that would suggest the program would have a problem. It isn't until the user enters a zero for the second number, and we then divide the first number by that value, that the program bombs with a runtime error."

"I understand why the error was generated," Kate said, "but I do have a question about some code you used that I don't believe we've seen before. What's going on with that line of code that divides *number1* by *number2* and then assigns the result to the *answer* variable. Why is the word 'float' in parentheses before the variable names?"

```
        answer = (float)number1/(float)number2;
```

"This is a technique called *coercion*, also known as *casting*," I said, "and we used it here to ensure that the *answer* variable contains a fraction part. By default, in C++, if you divide an integer by an integer, the result will be an integer. Placing the word 'float' within parentheses in front of the variable tells C++ to convert, or 'coerce,' the data type of the variable to a float. As a result, we wind up dividing two floating-point data types, which generates a result that is also a float."

"Getting back to the 'division by zero' error," Kate said, "you say we will be able to prevent this type of problem?"

"There's nothing we can do to prevent the user from entering zero for the second number," I said, "but we can certainly anticipate what the user may do and react accordingly. Anticipating and reacting to problems like this leads us quite nicely into a discussion of C++ exceptions and error handling."

C++ Exceptions and Error Handling

"Is a C++ exception the same thing as a C++ error?" Steve asked. "I think you've used both terms in the last few minutes."

"Strictly speaking," I said, "a C++ exception is an object that is created when an error occurs. That's why you may hear the terms used interchangeably."

"How are Exception objects created?" Kate asked.

"Some Exception objects we create," I said, "and some are created by the system—for instance, when one of those 'interceptable' runtime errors occurs, which I mentioned earlier. I should mention that it's not absolutely necessary for us to create an Exception object in order to implement error handling in our program. In fact, we won't be doing that today—although that's the route most experienced C++ programmers take."

Basic Error Handling

"So what should we do when we realize that the code we've written could result in an error?" Ward asked.

"The first step," I said, "is to write code that detects the error condition. In the case of Practice12_1, we can check to see whether the value of the variable *number2* is zero. Then, if we detect an error condition, we need to react in some way—in the case of our exercise, we'll notify the user of the problem. Finally, you need to decide what to do next in the program. For instance, is there a way for the program to continue processing, perhaps by asking the user for a value for *number2* again, or should you simply gracefully end the program? Let's see how we can implement this methodology by modifying the program we wrote in Practice12_1 to anticipate and react to the user's entry of a zero for the denominator."

Exercise 12-2   **Basic Error Handling**

In this exercise, you'll modify the program from Exercise 12-1 to use a simple If statement to deal with the 'division by zero' error.

1. Use Notepad (if you are using Windows) to enter the following code:

```
//Practice12_2.cpp
#include <iostream>
```

```cpp
using namespace std;

int main()
{
    int number1 = 0;
    int number2 = 0;
    float answer = 0.0;

    char response[256];

    cout << "Enter Number 1: ";
    cin.getline(response,256);
    number1 = atoi(response);

    cout << "Enter Number 2: ";
    cin.getline(response,256);
    number2 = atoi(response);

    if (number2 == 0)
    {
        cout << endl <<
            "Sorry, but you may not divide by zero";
        return 1;
    }

    answer = (float)number1/(float)number2;

    cout << endl << number1 << " divided by " << number2
        << " is " << answer;

    return 0;
}
```

2. Save your source file as Practice12_2 in the \CPPFiles\Practice folder (select File | Save As from Notepad's menu bar). Be sure to save your source file with the filename extension .cpp.

3. Compile your source file into an executable file.

4. Execute your program. Enter **9** for the first number and **4** for second. The program will display a result of 2.25.

5. Now run the program again. Enter **4** for the first number and **0** for the second. This time, instead of terminating, the program will display a warning message indicating that division by zero is not permitted and then gracefully end.

Discussion I ran the program myself, entering 4 for the first number and 0 for the second. The following screenshot was displayed on the classroom projector:

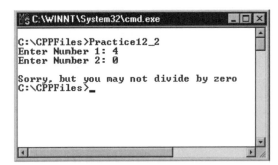

"As you can see," I said, "the additional code we wrote detected the impeding 'division by zero' error by looking for a value of zero in the variable *number2*."

```
if (number2 == 0)
```

"It then displayed a warning message to the user."

```
cout << endl << "Sorry, but you may not divide by zero";
```

"Finally, the program gracefully terminated."

```
return 1;
```

"That seemed to work out fine," Rhonda said. "Is that all there is to it?"

"What we did here, Rhonda," I answered, "was to implement some pretty basic error handling. One problem with this code is that if we give the user the opportunity to make this same error in several places in our program, we need to duplicate this error-handling code in several places as well. The C++ Try-Catch blocks give us the ability to more centrally handle errors."

Try-Catch

"Try-Catch blocks?" Kate said. "What does that mean, and do we have to discard the code we just wrote?"

"Not to worry, Kate," I replied. "The code we just wrote doesn't have to change—we just need to enclose it within a Try-Catch block. The idea behind a Try-Catch block is that we tell C++ to 'try' the code in the Try block, that it may potentially cause an exception, and to execute the code in the Catch block if an exception should occur. For certain runtime errors, the system will generate an exception, and for errors that we detect on our own, such as division by zero, we generate the exception ourselves by executing the 'throw' statement within the Try block."

"Oh, I get it," Ward said. "The exception is *thrown* from the Try block and *caught* in the Catch block."

"That's the idea, Ward," I said.

"So the code in the Try block is the code that we would execute ordinarily," Mary said, "and the code in the Catch block is the code to execute if an exception does occur."

"That's perfect, Mary," I replied.

"I'm going to need to see this in action," Rhonda said. "I think it's pretty confusing."

"Let's take the code in Practice12_2," I said, "and modify it to include a Try-Catch block. I think that will clear up some of your confusion. While you're coding the exercise, don't be too concerned if you don't understand perfectly the syntax of the throw statement and of the Catch block—I'll be explaining those after you're done."

I then distributed this exercise for the class to complete.

Exercise 12-3   Try-Catch

In this exercise, you'll modify the program from Exercise 11-2 to use Try-Catch blocks to deal with the "division by zero" error.

1. Use Notepad (if you are using Windows) to enter the following code:

```cpp
//Practice12_3.cpp
#include <iostream>

using namespace std;

int main()
{
    int number1 = 0;
    int number2 = 0;
    float answer = 0.0;

    char response[256];

    try
    {
        cout << "Enter Number 1: ";
        cin.getline(response,256);
        number1 = atoi(response);

        cout << "Enter Number 2: ";
        cin.getline(response,256);
        number2 = atoi(response);

        if (number2 == 0)  //Detect divide by zero
            throw(12345);      //Throw an exception of type int
    }
```

```
        catch(int n)              //Catch the exception
        {
           cout << endl
              << "Sorry, but you may not divide by zero";
           return 1;
        }


        answer = (float)number1/(float)number2;

        cout << endl << number1 << " divided by " << number2
           << " is " << answer;

        return 0;
     }
```

2. Save your source file as Practice12_3 in the \CPPFiles\Practice folder (select File | Save As from Notepad's menu bar). Be sure to save your source file with the filename extension .cpp.

3. Compile your source file into an executable file.

4. Execute your program. Enter **9** for the first number and **4** for second. The program will display a result of 2.25.

5. Now run the program again. Enter **4** for the first number and **0** for the second. This time, instead of terminating, the program will display a warning message indicating that division by zero is not permitted and gracefully end.

Discussion

Only one student, Blaine, had a problem completing the exercise—and a minor one at that. He accidentally inserted the code to calculate the value of the *answer* variable between the end of the Try block and the beginning of the Catch block.

"The compiler," I said, "at least the one we're using here in class, wants the Catch block to follow the Try block. Inserting just a single line of code in between confused the compiler."

After a moment, Blaine had his code fixed and we were on our way again.

"Let me explain what we've done here," I said. "We took the code that could potentially lead to a 'division by zero' error, along with the code to detect it, and placed them within a Try block. A Try block starts with the word *try* and its code is enclosed within a pair of braces."

```
     try
        {
           cout << "Enter Number 1: ";
           cin.getline(response,256);
           number1 = atoi(response);
```

```
        cout << "Enter Number 2: ";
        cin.getline(response,256);
        number2 = atoi(response);

        if (number2 == 0)      //Detect divide by zero
           throw(12345);       //Throw an exception of type int
   }
```

"Notice how the Try block contains only the code that might cause an error," I continued, "plus the throw statement. The code to react to the error is now contained in the Catch block."

"Can you go over the syntax of the throw statement?" Ward asked. "What are we doing here—it looks like we're passing an error code to the Catch block."

"That's exactly what we're doing," I said. "In this case, the number 12345 is just a number I randomly selected to be our program's error code for division by zero. We could have passed the Catch block anything—including a character, a string, or even a reference to an object."

NOTE

Many advanced C++ programmers design exception classes of their own and instantiate objects from these classes within the Try block, passing them to the Catch block as an argument.

"So we could have chosen any number we wanted to here," Barbara said.

"Absolutely," I answered. "Within our program, we might decide to pass the Catch block 12345 for a 'division by zero' error, 34567 for a 'missing file' error, and so on. The important thing to realize is that if and when the throw statement is executed, the next line of code executed will be its corresponding catch statement."

"What do you mean *corresponding*?" Peter asked. "Can you have more than one Catch block?"

"Good question, Peter," I said, "and the answer is yes. A program can contain multiple Catch blocks, each one designed to react to a different set of error conditions if you like, or alternatively, have a single Catch block and use If statements or Case statements to handle multiple error conditions."

"How does C++ know which of the multiple Catch blocks to execute?" Dave asked.

"C++ will match the data type of the throw statement with the declaration for the Catch block," I said. "Since our throw statement is passing an integer argument, C++ will look for a Catch statement defined to accept an Integer parameter, like this."

```
   catch(int n)              //Catch the exception
   {
```

```
        cout << endl << "Sorry, but you may not divide by zero";
        return 1;
    }
```

"…within the body of the catch block, we display a message to the user, then gracefully end the program by executing the return statement, using an argument of 1. Remember, we've been using non-zero return statements to indicate abnormal terminations of our program."

NOTE

Return codes from our startup program mean nothing to us—but are meaningful if our program was executed by another program.

"What's the significance of the letter *n* within the parentheses?" Rhonda asked.

"That's the parameter corresponding to the argument that is passed to the Catch block," I said, "and can be used to determine the value that has been passed by the throw statement. For instance, if we wrote code in another part of our program that throws an error of 34567, we could use either an If statement or a Case statement to determine the error code, like this."

```
catch(int n)
{
    switch (n)
    {
        case 12345:
            cout << endl << "Sorry, but you may not divide by zero";
            return 1;
            break;
        case 34567:
            cout << endl << "Sorry, but I cannot find that file";
            return 1;
            break;
    }
}
```

"By the way," I said, "if you want a single Catch block to handle any throw statement in your program, code your Catch block with an ellipsis for an argument, like this."

```
catch(…)
```

Should We Modify the Grades Calculation Project to Include Error Handling?

"Can we modify the Grades Calculation Project to provide for error handling?" Kate asked.

"Actually," I said, "we already have. Our base class Student already has logic built in to handle invalid grade entries on the part of the user—that's all coded into the various mutator methods of the Student class. Although it's true we didn't enclose that logic within Try and Catch blocks, I'm not sure what advantages we might gain from doing so now—plus, we're almost out of time for today's class, and we need to get down to Frank Olley's office. Why don't we do this: If you'd like to tackle adding Try and Catch blocks to the Student class on your own, do that on your own; otherwise, I'm ready to deliver our project to Frank Olley."

Testing the Program

"So we're done?" asked Ward.

"That's right, Ward," I said. "We're now done with the Grades Calculation Project."

"When do we deliver it?" Mary asked.

"And what version do we deliver?" Linda asked. "Will you be installing your version of the project?"

"When I spoke to Frank Olley earlier in the week," I said, "I explained to him that, excluding my version of the program, we had 18 different versions of the program—and that because this was a student project, I'd rather have him use one of yours, not mine."

I could see some excitement building among the students in the class.

"I invited Frank to visit us today to select the 'winning' project," I said, "but in Frank's mind, you're all winners—and I have to agree. It's going to be hard to select one project to install in the English department."

"So what are we going to do?" Ward asked.

"Frank had a good suggestion," I said, "and here it is. He suggested that prior to traveling over to the English department at the end of today's class, we all select one project as *the* one to install in the English department. So here's what I'm going to ask you to do. I would like everyone to take a few moments to test their own version of the program to verify that it's working properly, then walk up to the front of the classroom and pick up a voting ballot that I've prepared. Take the ballot, walk around the classroom and observe everyone's project, and then record your vote for what you consider to be the best project you see. The project that receives the most votes will be the one that we install in the English department. By the way, I'm removing my version of the project from consideration—so please don't vote for mine! This is your project and one of you deserves to have the place of honor in Frank Olley's English department."

"Can you give us some guidelines on testing our programs?" Linda asked, after a moment or two.

"That's a good question," I said. "Obviously, at a minimum, the program must work—that is, it needs to properly calculate the grade for each one of the three types of students. You should also make sure that the console interface, as far as possible, is attractive and easy to use."

"I would think that most of the bugs have been discovered by now," Valerie commented.

"I'm not sure we can say that with 100-percent certainty," I said. "There's always the possibility that something has slipped through our fingers. But I would say that I'm fairly confident our programs are bug free. Obviously, the more complicated the programs you write, the less certain you can feel, and the more thorough your testing needs to be."

"Is it possible to test each and every combination of grades and student types?" Rhonda asked.

"You're right, Rhonda," I said. "There are quite a few possible combinations of different student types and grades, and testing every one of them would be next to impossible. We've been testing our programs all along with a scenario for each type of student—and we should take this testing one step further. For instance, you should test scenarios where each component grade is zero, where one or more component grades, but not all, are zero, where all component grades are 100 percent, and where only some are 100 percent. Above all, make sure you calculate the grades manually first so that you know what the correct answer should be."

"In other words," Dave said, "test the extreme limits of each component."

"That's right, Dave," I said. "We saw today how the introduction of a zero into a program can produce errors. Try to 'break' your program now, before you give it to one of the work study students to work with."

"I've been testing my project all along using a similar methodology," Chuck said, "except that I used Microsoft Excel to develop a worksheet of possible scenarios, along with the correct answers, and then ran my program to test as many of these scenarios as I could, verifying each correct answer."

"That's a great idea, Chuck," I said.

I then gave the class 15 minutes to test their projects one last time and then asked them to review and evaluate their fellow students' projects and vote for the project they thought was "best." As I collected their ballots and tallied the results, I asked everyone to give me a diskette with a copy of their project on it as well.

"Class is officially dismissed for today," I said. "I hope to see you all in the English department in a few minutes!"

I called Dave aside. Dave had volunteered to coordinate the installation of C++ on a PC in the English department, along with the installation of the 'winning' program's executable. I handed Dave a CD-ROM containing the C++ compiler, along with a diskette containing the project that had received the most votes.

"Would you mind installing these?" I asked him. "I have a few things to wrap up here."

"Not at all," Dave said, as he glanced at the student's name on the diskette and smiled. "That project really was great—I guess it pays to ask a lot of questions! I'll take care of this."

Delivering and Implementing
the Grades Calculation Project

No sooner had I packed up my things and was preparing to make my way out the door of the classroom than a former student of mine approached me with a problem. Half an hour later, I finally arrived in the English department.

As I entered, I could hear quite a bit of excited talk and conversation. I could see an incredible amount of activity taking place. The area was packed with students—my students, plus two students whom I recognized as work study students—plus Frank Olley, David Burton, and Robin Aronstram were there.

Frank Olley caught sight of me.

"John, this program is absolutely great," he said excitedly. "I can't believe what an excellent job your students did with this. I, David, and Robin really love it—plus the two people who really count, the work study students who will be using it."

Amid all the hullabaloo, I glanced toward the middle of the open space in the English department and noticed a small table with a computer sitting on it. Seated at the table were the two work study students, and there was Rhonda, standing in front of the computer, training these students who would be using *her* version of the program to calculate grades for the English, math, and science departments!

"Rhonda's been proudly demonstrating her program to our work study students for the last 15 minutes," Frank explained. "She's obviously very proud of it, and they love it also—they haven't gotten up from their chairs yet. Rhonda really did a great job with it."

I wandered over to them and caught Rhonda's eye.

"I'm flabbergasted that the class voted for my version of the project," Rhonda said. "To say that this has made my week is an understatement—more like my year! I'm just so honored that someone like me, with absolutely no programming background, could actually write a program like this. I felt like I asked so many stupid questions during the course."

"Rhonda," I interrupted, "you know what I always say—the only stupid question is the question you don't ask. Your questions were always good ones, plus I know they were questions that some of the other students in the class were dying to ask. By the way, when I put this C++ course together, I had someone just like you in mind—an inquisitive person, anxious to learn, but with no programming background. You did a great job."

"Really?" she said. "You know I enjoyed the course very much. You should consider taking those notes of yours and writing a C++ book."

"Maybe I'll do that someday," I told her.

I spent the next few minutes observing the two work study students, Rita and Gil, experiment with the program. They had no problem whatsoever with it. Rhonda's console interface was neat, easy to read, and easy to use—both of them really seemed to be enjoying working with it.

"Believe me," Rita said, "this is a lot better than the method we were using before."

"You can say that again," Gil said, "calculating these grades using a calculator was a real pain in the neck."

"From what I can see," I told the assembled class as they gathered around us, "the system works as designed. The ultimate users of the project, Rita and Gil, have been using the program for the last few minutes to calculate grades, and as you've all probably seen, they're extremely pleased with it. I want to thank Dave for installing C++ and Rhonda's version of the project on this PC. By installing the software, we have begun phase 5 of the SDLC, the Implementation phase. Installation, fine-tuning, and training are all part of this phase."

Frank Olley came over and stood right next to me, obviously pleased at the time savings and accuracy the program would achieve. I turned to him and told him that this phase of the SDLC would last for at least the next week.

"Pairs of students have volunteered to be 'on site' during the week to make observations and assist with any problems that might come up," I explained.

"It's comforting to know they'll be here," he said. "What are those notes I've seen you taking?"

"I'm making notes about Phase 6 of the SDLC," I said. "Even though we're now in the midst of phase 5 of the SDLC, we can proceed concurrently with phase 6, which is the Feedback and Maintenance phase—and observation is an important part of the Feedback and Maintenance phase."

"Feedback and maintenance?" Frank asked.

"We want to make sure the program is behaving according to the Requirements Statement you and I agreed upon before the class began to write the program for you," I explained. "A big part of this phase is just observing the system to see how it's being used."

"And how it's being admired," Frank Olley added.

"Positive feedback is a wonderful thing," I said, smiling.

"What about program maintenance?" Frank asked.

"The maintenance phase handles any changes to the program that are necessitated by governmental regulations, changes in business rules, or changes that you decide you want to make to the program," I replied.

"After seeing the great work you've done on the project," he said, "I'm sure I'll have more work for your class."

"Sadly though," I said, "this is the end of our introductory C++ course. But many, if not all of these students, will be signed up for my intermediate C++ programming course starting in five weeks. Maybe we can work on any enhancements you have then. Perhaps we'll produce a version with a graphical user interface like Windows."

Frank Olley seemed happy with that idea and left to chat with the two work study students. Linda, meanwhile, stopped by to see me and asked to see the notes I had taken.

"Interesting observations," Linda said. "I can see we still have some work to do."

"Frank," I said, as I approached him, Rhonda, and the two work study students, "on behalf of the class, I want to thank you for a wonderful learning experience. I'm sure we'll be in touch."

I shouted across the room to the rest of my students, "I've got to take off now. Everyone please be mindful of your coverage schedules, and if you have any problems at all, you know where to find me—remember, my e-mail address is johnsmiley@johnsmiley.com. I hope to see you all in five weeks."

Summary

Congratulations! You've finished the introductory C++ class and completed and implemented the Grades Calculation Project. I hope you felt the excitement of completing, delivering, and installing the Grades Calculation program as much as the students in my class did, because you were a big part of it.

What's next? At this point, you should feel confident enough to tackle a variety of C++ programs. I hope that by following my introductory computer programming class, you've seen how real-world applications are developed. The step-by-step methodology that we followed to complete the program should be one that you follow in your own programming work.

That's not to say that all projects go as smoothly as this one did. You can expect your share of mistakes, misinterpretations, and misunderstandings along the way. Nonetheless, developing a computer program is always exciting, and if you love it as I do, it's always fun.

As I close, I just want to give you a few words of advice.

First, remember that in programming there's rarely a single correct solution. Ultimately, if your program achieves the desires of the person who needs to use it, you've developed the correct solution. In the beginning of your programming experience, don't waste your time trying to achieve the best solution. Move on to other projects to broaden your experience.

Second, always be your own best friend. Inevitably, while trying to work through a solution, there will be frustrating moments. Never doubt yourself, and never get "down" on yourself.

Finally, remember that there is always more to learn. The world of programming is an endless series of free learning seminars. All you need to do is open up a manual, read a Help file, surf the Internet, or pick up a copy of a good book, and you are well on your way. You can never know it all, let alone master it all. But always move in that direction. Good luck, and I hope to see you in another C++ class some day!

INDEX

D

T

INTERNATIONAL CONTACT INFORMATION

AUSTRALIA
McGraw-Hill Book Company Australia Pty. Ltd.
TEL +61-2-9900-1800
FAX +61-2-9878-8881
http://www.mcgraw-hill.com.au
books-it_sydney@mcgraw-hill.com

CANADA
McGraw-Hill Ryerson Ltd.
TEL +905-430-5000
FAX +905-430-5020
http://www.mcgraw-hill.ca

GREECE, MIDDLE EAST, & AFRICA
(Excluding South Africa)
McGraw-Hill Hellas
TEL +30-1-656-0990-3-4
FAX +30-1-654-5525

MEXICO (Also serving Latin America)
McGraw-Hill Interamericana Editores S.A. de C.V.
TEL +525-117-1583
FAX +525-117-1589
http://www.mcgraw-hill.com.mx
fernando_castellanos@mcgraw-hill.com

SINGAPORE (Serving Asia)
McGraw-Hill Book Company
TEL +65-863-1580
FAX +65-862-3354
http://www.mcgraw-hill.com.sg
mghasia@mcgraw-hill.com

SOUTH AFRICA
McGraw-Hill South Africa
TEL +27-11-622-7512
FAX +27-11-622-9045
robyn_swanepoel@mcgraw-hill.com

SPAIN
McGraw-Hill/Interamericana de España, S.A.U.
TEL +34-91-180-3000
FAX +34-91-372-8513
http://www.mcgraw-hill.es
professional@mcgraw-hill.es

UNITED KINGDOM, NORTHERN,
EASTERN, & CENTRAL EUROPE
McGraw-Hill Education Europe
TEL +44-1-628-502500
FAX +44-1-628-770224
http://www.mcgraw-hill.co.uk
computing_neurope@mcgraw-hill.com

ALL OTHER INQUIRIES Contact:
Osborne/McGraw-Hill
TEL +1-510-549-6600
FAX +1-510-883-7600
http://www.osborne.com
omg_international@mcgraw-hill.com